Ivan Bunin
The Twilight of Emigré Russia, 1934–1953

IVAN BUNIN
THE TWILIGHT OF EMIGRÉ RUSSIA, 1934–1953

* * *

A Portrait from
Letters, Diaries, and Memoirs

*

EDITED WITH AN INTRODUCTION AND NOTES BY

Thomas Gaiton Marullo

IVAN R. DEE
Chicago • *2002*

For Marc Raeff, scholar, teacher, and friend

Grateful acknowledgment is made to Possev-Verlag for permission to use excerpts from *Ustami Buninkh*, and to *Voprosy literatury*, *Novyi zhurnal*, *Literaturnoe nasledstvo*, the *Russian Review*, and Duke University Press to use excerpts from articles and reviews.

Library of Congress Cataloging-in-Publication Data:
Ivan Bunin : the twilight of emigré Russia, 1934–1953 : a portrait from letters, diaries, and memoirs / edited with an introduction and notes by Thomas Gaiton Marullo.
    p. cm.
    Includes bibliographical references and index.
    ISBN 1-56663-433-4 (alk. paper)
    1. Bunin, Ivan Alekseevich, 1870–1953. 2. Authors, Russian—20th century—Biography. I. Marullo, Thomas Gaiton.
PG3453.B9 Z724 2002
891.78'309—dc21
[B]   2001052986

PREFACE

IN 1974 Harrison Salisbury, the well-known correspondent and observer of life in the former Soviet Union,[1] observed that "Profligate Russia has cast to us her most splendid talents, squeezing them out from the Russian soil. . . . Profligate Russia! But fortunate America. Fortunate world to possess the riches of Nabokov and others."[2]

Vladimir Putin—only the second democratically elected president in Russia's thousand-year history—most likely shared similar thoughts about Russia's departed comrades. On November 1, 2000, while on an official visit to France, Putin made a pilgrimage to the cemetery of Sainte-Geneviève-des-Bois. Some forty miles south of Paris, Sainte-Geneviève is the final resting place of more than twenty thousand Russians who fled the political and artistic persecution of the Soviet Union and died in exile abroad.

Putin had been in office only seven months. But before he could confront the skeletons of "Lenin's Tomb"[3]—the seventy-five-year legacy of failed communism—Putin sought reconciliation with a key segment of the "humiliated and injured" of his land. He wished forgiveness from *zarubezhnaya Rossiya* or "Russia Abroad," i.e., the millions of compatriots who had left their homeland after the Bolsheviks came to power in 1917.

Reverently, Putin walked past the tombs of tsarist grand dukes, White Army officers, and Soviet-era dissidents. He paused before the crypts of Russia's exiled cultural elite, such writers as Dmitri

[1]See for instance, *The 900 Days: The Siege of Leningrad* (New York, 1969), and *Black Night, White Snow: Russia's Revolution (1905–1917)* (Garden City, 1978).
[2]H. Salisbury, "The Russian Writer as Conscience," *Saturday Review/World* (July 27, 1974), 18–20.
[3]D. Remnick, *Lenin's Tomb: The Last Days of the Soviet Empire* (New York, 1993).

Merezhkovsky, Alexei Remizov, Nadezhda Teffi, and Boris Zaitsev; such dancers as Rudolph Nureyev and Olga Preobrazhenskaya; and such artists as Alexander Benois who, at Sainte-Geneviève in 1939, designed the Church of the Assumption of the Mother of God, a weathered Russian chapel modeled after the famous medieval shrines of Novgorod and Pskov.[4]

Only at one resting place, though, did Putin lay a wreath of red carnations: a small unpretentious monument topped by an Orthodox cross and bearing the name of the writer, Ivan Bunin. "It is time for us [Russians] to unite," Putin told the receptive crowd. "We must never forget that we are the children of the same mother whose name is Russia."[5]

Putin's choice was apt. Ivan Bunin, born in Russia in 1870, died in France in 1953. His literary career of almost seventy years was not only the longest in Russian literature, surpassing even that of Leo Tolstoy; but his writings, formal and informal, provided a firsthand commentary on the violent transformations wrought in his homeland and in his adopted home, Europe, during the turbulent years of the first half of the twentieth century.

Bunin was also a major formative influence in both pre-Revolutionary and Russian emigré fiction. Before the Revolution of 1917, he achieved stature in both the Golden and Silver ages of Russian Literature. After the Revolution of 1917, as a political and artistic exile in France, Bunin became the acknowledged—if unwilling—spokesman of Russian emigré writers; and in 1933, he became the first Russian writer and also the first artist in exile to receive the Nobel Prize in Literature.[6]

Bunin studies now enjoy a revival both in Russia and in the West. Researchers document a "Bunin craze" among Russian youth;[7] and, since 1985, publishing houses in the former Soviet Union have been printing Bunin's works at a feverish rate. Of particular interest are pieces that were banned from publication in the years of Soviet domination. For instance, by 1991 Russians had published no fewer than

[4]For a detailed listing of the famous Russians who are buried at Sainte-Geneviève, see B. Nosik, *Na pogoste XX veka* (Saint Petersburg, 2000).

[5]As quoted by ITAR-TASS News Agency (November 1, 2000).

[6]Although Bunin is known primarily for his short stories, his longer works, e.g., *The Village* (*Derevnia*, 1909–1910), *Dry Valley* (*Sukhodol*, 1911), *The Gentleman from San Francisco* (*Gospodin iz San-Frantsisko*, 1915), *Mitya's Love* (*Mitina liubov'*, 1924), and *The Life of Arseniev* (*Zhizn' Arsen'eva*, 1927–1933), are "classics" of Russian literature that incisively portray Russian life while they plumb the depths of universal human passion and struggles.

[7]See Mark Scott's introductory article in Ivan Bunin, *Wolves and Other Stories* (Santa Barbara, 1989), 7.

fifteen separate editions of *The Cursed Days* (*Okaiannye dni*), Bunin's scathing account of life in Bolshevik Russia during 1918 and 1919.[8]

Despite this surging interest, much of Bunin's life and art continues to be unknown. The Russian stance toward the emigré years of the writer is almost schizophrenic. On one hand, Bunin is seen by some contemporary Russians as a prophet. He was a Moses who carried the tablets of Russian literature into the exile-desert, and who, in his own work, held fast both to the memory of "patriarchal" Russia and to visions of a promised (read: ex-Soviet) land. But other countrymen regard Bunin as a pervert. As portrayed by Alexander Uchitel', in his recent film *His Wife's Diary* (*Dnevnik ego zheny*), Bunin was a sybarite-cynic, who, having turned his back on Russian soul and soil, moved from callous disregard for his loving wife to manic devotion to a mistress, forty years his junior, to decline and ruin with an alleged prostitute, and, in a Chekhovian twist,[9] to somber if bittersweet solace with a stray dog.[1] Almost a half-century after Bunin's death, his life and art remain the subject of controversy and debate.

Ivan Bunin: The Twilight of Emigré Russia, 1934–1953 is the final volume of a diary-trilogy in which I have attempted to solve the "riddle" of Ivan Bunin by integrating the colorful and contradictory pieces of his life into a coherent and comprehensive whole. Like its predecessors, *Ivan Bunin: Russian Requiem, 1885–1920,* and *Ivan Bunin: From the Other Shore, 1920–1933,* this volume is important for two reasons. First, it is a diary in the broadest sense of the word, that is, a compendium of Bunin's last twenty years that includes selections from his diaries, letters, speeches, and articles; and interpolations from the memoirs of his wife, Vera Muromtseva-Bunina, and from the writings of friends, colleagues, and critics in the same period. Second, it seeks to

---

[8]The new Russian interest in Bunin also resonates in the West. At present there are four reprints of earlier collections of Bunin's writings, four new anthologies of his short stories, and a new translation of *The Life of Arseniev.*

[9]See, for instance, Chekhov's story, "Heartache" ("*Toska*"), written in 1886.

[1]Uchitel''s *His Wife's Diary* was applauded by Russian audiences but censured by both the government and the press. Members of the State Cinema Financing Commission refused to fund the film. (Only a last-minute intervention from the film minister saved the project from oblivion.) Liberal newspapers fretted that *His Wife's Diary* would initiate a trend whereby the private lives of Russian writers and musicians would be recycled as soap operas. A critic warned: "Pushkin, Dostoevsky, and Tchaikovsky are next to go from classical artists to pop stars."

Adding to the furor about *His Wife's Diary* was the fact that the film was attracting attention outside the homeland. As is the case with many artistic works in Russia, what is condemned at home is praised abroad. Western critics saw *His Wife's Diary* as high drama, not tabloid exposé. The screenplay for the film was awarded the Hartley-Merill International Screenwriting Prize. Even more tantalizing, perhaps, *His Wife's Diary* was put forward as Russia's entry for an Oscar as the best foreign film for 2001. See Amelia Gentleman, "Ivan the Terrible," *The Guardian* (London) (November 3, 2000), 12.

capture the "twilight" of "Russia Abroad," the triumphs and tragedies, joys and sorrows of more than a million Russians who fled their homeland in the wake of the Russian Revolution and civil war, and who, in their final years, preserved their love of country even as they faced unrelenting poverty, sickness, and death, and an economic depression and a new world war which, for the second time in twenty years, transformed their existence into a Darwinian struggle for survival.

My hope for this work is similarly twofold. I want to present Bunin in a new light to the English-speaking world, so that readers will take up his works and accord him the respect and admiration he deserves. Equally important, I want to show Bunin as an exemplar of what Russians, both at home and abroad, have always seen (and demanded) in their writers. He was a *pravednik* or "righteous man" who, like Christ, was tempted by devils in the desert but who suffered and would die willingly for his people. Bunin too was a good shepherd who fought off "wolves"—Bolsheviks, fascists, dictators, and other ideologues of "secular" and "modern" thought—to protect his flock from evil, to champion beauty and truth, and to uphold the values of Russian soul and soil.

As in the first two volumes of this enterprise, almost all of the translated materials in this volume appear in English for the first time and are mine alone. Dates for all excerpts have been rendered according to the New Style calender, when this could be ascertained; dates for Bunin's fictional works and essays denote when Bunin either completed or published his work.

For their invaluable assistance at various stages in the preparation of this book, I wish to acknowledge Professors Alan Toumayan, Marie-Christin Escoda-Risto, and Odette Menyard of the Department of Romance Languages at Notre Dame for their help with French phrases and accents; and Linda Gregory, Marcia Stevenson, Linda Sharp, Linda Doversberger, Margaret Porter, Cameron Tuai, Joni Kanzler, Michael Lutes, Hector Escobar, Kay Ryan-Zeugner, Cheri Smith, Elizabeth Van Jacob, Douglas Archer, and others of the staffs of the Departments of Reference, Interlibrary Loan, and Microtexts of the Theodore M. Hesburgh Library at Notre Dame for obtaining many of the materials for this study, for researching footnotes, and for photocopying texts.

Several individuals deserve a special note of gratitude: the *troitsa* or "trinity" of Helen Sullivan, Julia Gauchman, and Angela Cannon of the Slavic Department of the Library of the University of Illinois, for unearthing sources, researching additional footnotes, and answering myriad questions about Bunin and Russian emigré life; Matthew Anderson and Zenovia Lockhart, who proved to be quick and ready research assistants; Nancy McMahon, who typed correspondence, prepared the manuscript, and organized mountains of data in readable and accessible form; and, finally, Ivan Dee, who has shepherded this project on Bunin for almost a decade, who taught me much about publishing in the scholarly world, and who, as a loyal patron and guide, called me to excellence in my work.

In assembling this volume I was haunted by Bunin's enduring fear that "some 'hard-working monk' . . . would penetrate into his creative laboratory . . . root about in his manuscripts, and arrive at conclusions . . . that he would consider absurd or infuriating."[2] So, for their patient reading of the text, I wish to thank Marc Raeff, Bakhmeteff Professor Emeritus of Russian Studies at Columbia University, and Gary Hamburg, professor of Russian history at Notre Dame.

Most important, I wish to thank my wife, Gloria, who supported me in this endeavor from the beginning, and who, with me, rode the peaks and valleys of my long sojourn with Bunin and "Russia Abroad." Indeed, I did not realize the extent to which I had exhausted her goodwill and cheer until we visited Bunin's grave in March 1998. Unlike Putin, Gloria did not beg Bunin's forgiveness. She wished precisely the opposite. Ignoring her deeply moved husband, she looked squarely at the writer's resting place and said, "Mister, you have made my life very difficult." I also salute my four cats—Margaret Mary, Bernadette Marie, Monica Anne, and Gonzaga ("Gonzo")—who, grouped on or about my desk in various stages of repose and recline, kept things in perspective for me and who, like Bunin, showed me how to live and love life.

Finally, it is with special warmth that I again cite Marc Raeff for his generous and expert help not only in the preparation of these three volumes on Bunin but also for my annotated translations of Bunin's *Cursed Days* and *The Liberation of Tolstoy.* For more than a decade he has been a vital force in my growth as a scholar, and it is to him that I dedicate this work as a token of my heartfelt affection and esteem.

T. G. M.

Notre Dame, Indiana
January 2002

2. A. Bakhrakh, "Po pamiati, po zapiskam (II) . . . ," *Mosty,* No. 12 (1966), 278.

CONTENTS

INTRODUCTION

ON December 17, 1933, Ivan Bunin was preparing to leave Stockholm for his home in Paris. Only a week before, he had been the focus of international acclaim and lavish ceremonies when he received the Nobel Prize in Literature. With gusto, Bunin had thrown himself into the whirlwind of activities celebrating his status as a Nobel laureate. He had attended testimonials and dinners, given speeches and interviews, and posed for pictures and crowds. Toward the end of the festivities, though, Bunin had had his fill of fame. In fact, he seemed almost traumatized by the sensation he had caused. Looking out onto a deserted, snow-covered embankment, he told Andrei Sedykh: "How nice it would be to get out of town, to wander a bit through the snow, and then to drop in at a Swedish tavern and drink a glass of hot punch." Bunin was even more relieved on the way home. "Well, thank God, that's over with," he again confessed to Sedykh.[1]

In his almost seventy years as a writer, peace and quiet eluded Bunin. He endured the passing of "patriarchal" Russia, surviving the repeated onslaughts of revolution and war that destroyed a centuries-old way of life. In his thirteen-year exile in France, he endured homesickness and despair, even as he sought to preserve the literary culture of his forebears against Soviet "Mongols" who were equally intent on destroying it.

Having won the Nobel Prize, the sixty-three-year-old Bunin believed that his job was done. He had received affirmation not only for himself but also for all of "Russia Abroad." Before the world, he had proclaimed vindication for what he and his countrymen had suffered at Bolshevik hands. He had also provided humankind with a singular in-

---

[1] A, Sedykh, "Ot"ezd Bunina iz Stokgol'ma," *Poslednie novosti* (December 20, 1933), 3.

tegrity and courage: he and his fellow exiles had risen, phoenixlike, from the ashes of revolution and war; together they were rebuilding their lives and contributing to the lands and peoples that had given them refuge.

More important, perhaps, with his award Bunin had invested the collective tragedy-turned-triumph with a profoundly cultural cast. As the self-proclaimed "last Mohican" of a literary era that had its roots and flowering in pre-Revolutionary Russia, Bunin saw that his new status as a Nobel laureate had sent a compelling message to the world. It had extolled the "superiority" of "gentry" fiction over "proletarian" models. It had legitimated the creative and ethical voice of an exiled writer working far from his homeland. It had also hallowed the freedom of the artist in defiance of incipient "socialist realism" and of politically inspired coercion and force. With such works as *Mitya's Love, The Elagin Affair,* and the *Life of Arseniev,* Bunin showed that he had followed in the footsteps of Pushkin and Turgenev, Chekhov and Tolstoy, and that, singlehandedly and against all odds, he had safeguarded and extended a language and literature that had given rise to *Eugene Onegin,* passed through *Fathers and Sons,* and reached near perfection with *War and Peace* and *Anna Karenina.*

Content if not thrilled by all he had accomplished, Bunin wished now only to divide his time between Paris and Grasse, and to resume his monastic existence, thinking and writing in undisturbed peace. Or so he thought.

To his chagrin, Bunin would find that the tumult and chaos that had marked the first sixty or so years of his life would continue and even intensify in his last twenty. Trouble was Bunin's constant companion and guide, tormenting him with life pressures that challenged him from both without and within.

From without, Bunin the laureate first had to contend with reviewers and readers in the community of "Russia Abroad." Before he had been honored with the award, emigrés throughout the world had been among Bunin's most ardent supporters and devotees. He was for them a prophet, a saint, even a man-god who had penetrated the mysteries of existence and who now radiated peace, light, and love. Galina Kuznetsova, in her memoirs, wrote: "Like people who embark on a spiritual journey, Bunin lived his life, 'purifying' himself. . . . Looking at him, I thought about hermits, mystics, and yogis—those who live in the world they summon forth."[2]

---

[2]See A. Baboreko, *I. A. Bunin. Materialy dlia biografii s 1870 po 1917* (Moscow, 1983), 241; and Kuznetsova's diary entry of February 11, 1933, in G. Kuznetsova, *Grasskii dnevnik* (Washington, D.C., 1967), 279.

Of the near-hagiographical features that "Russia Abroad" had imparted to the writer, Kuznetsova later recalled: "Bunin was all in white . . . [and] the sharp line of his profile was framed by light surrounding his head and hair. . . . When he read aloud, I found it somewhat painful to listen to him, as if he had become a shrine and not the person . . . who could be . . . just like all simple mortals." Almost twenty years later, Irina Odoevtseva agreed, writing that "Bunin's face, [when] illuminated by the sunset . . . seemed surrounded by a halo, like the faces of saints in icons. . . ."[3]

The emigré consensus changed radically, though, once Bunin entered the literary pantheon. In a manner not unlike Stavrogin and his disciples in Dostoevsky's *The Possessed*, Bunin was now seen by Russian exiles as a myth-idol of their own making. He was to be the spokesman for "Russia Abroad," a plenipotentiary and even a media star who would breathe life into their dying hopes and dreams. Specifically, Bunin was to advance the emigré cause, denigrate the Soviet state, and continue the work of the gentry masters. He also was to conform to emigré notions of behavior and bearing. With a persistence that was both irksome and poignant, Russian exiles counseled Bunin on what to say, how to dress, where to live, even on how to furnish his home!

The demanded style was indeed "otherworldly": regal and urbane. Emigré elites demanded that Bunin and his wife, Vera Muromtseva-Bunina, exemplify what they saw as the best of "patriarchal" Russia. To the denizens of "Russia Abroad," the couple should emphasize past wealth and elegance to offset present disorientation and despair. To the citizens of the world, they should project the resurrected aura of a post-Bolshevik homeland. An irritated Mark Aldanov wrote to Bunin on May 5, 1934: "What is the point of your being awarded the Nobel Prize if you are going to rot in that hole, Grasse! You should travel around France and Europe!"[4] Less than a year later, Aldanov continued to Muromtseva-Bunina: "I have not been to your apartment, but just as well; for I am sure it would annoy me greatly. . . . In my opinion, you should rent an apartment that is somewhat nicer . . . and buy some furniture that is more fashionable so that you can receive French people and foreigners. . . . After all, Ivan Alexeevich is the only person whom we can call our cultural 'ambassador' to Europe. . . . You should be more visible."[5]

---

[3]See Kuznetsova's diary entries of July 2, 1927, and January 14, 1929, in Kuznetsova, 16 and 95; and I. Odoevtsva, *Na beregakh Seny* (Paris, 1983), 347.

[4]M. Grin, "Pis'ma M. A. Aldanova k I. A. i V. I. Buninym," *Novyi zhurnal*, vol. 81 (1965), 115.

[5]See Aldanov's letter to Bunin, written on January 5, 1935, in Grin, 115, 116.

Russian emigrés were keeping a strict eye not only on Bunin's personal deportment but also on his fictional activities, chiding him whenever the quantity or quality of his work did not meet their expectations. Fifteen months after Bunin was honored with the Nobel Prize, Aldanov wrote to him: "The rumor is that you have not written a line since your award. . . . Your friends are angry with you, not to mention the public at large."[6]

This formidable pressure from members of "Russia Abroad" is understandable for several reasons. By 1933, whatever hopes the Russian exiles had had for a speedy collapse of Bolshevik power (and an equally swift return to the homeland) were quickly fading. Despite years of unprecedented upheaval, the Soviet regime was stable and strong. "We gave them two weeks, then two months, then two years," an emigré journalist lamented on November 7, 1937, the twentieth anniversary of the October Revolution;[7] but every prediction proved wrong. Indeed, the bolshevized homeland had become a leper only to its vanquished Russian foes abroad, since most countries had recognized the Kremlin leadership as the de facto, if not de jure, legitimate authority in Russia. Everyone, it seemed, had been seduced by the sirenlike calls wafting from the land of the Soviets. Western leaders and public figures were intrigued by the successes of the "planned economy" in a tranquil East as compared with the failures of "runaway capitalism" (read: the Great Depression) in a restless West. French workers, with unshakable passion, venerated Lenin and Soviet Russia.[8] European and American intellectuals and writers—H. G. Wells, George Bernard Shaw, Lincoln Steffens, Romain Rolland, and André Gide[9]—extolled the new Soviet state. In so doing they censured fascism but sanctioned utopia by grabbing a leg, tail, or ear of the Soviet elephant and insisting that it stood for the whole. Indeed, nothing infuriated Russian expatriates more than the profuse blessings with which Western intellectuals and writers hallowed the revolutionary homeland, particularly the grandeur of Stalin's rule. The Western consensus was that the Russian people, having submitted to the iron necessity of Progress, were forging a new, just, and noble society; but that their backward-

---

[6]See Aldanov's missive to Bunin, dated February 14, 1935, in Grin, 116.
[7]As quoted in R. Johnston, *"New Mecca, New Babylon": Paris and the Russian Exiles, 1920–1945* (Montreal, 1988), 140.
[8]*Ibid.*, 80.
[9]For Bunin's quarrel with Wells and Rolland over their sanction of the new Soviet state, see Marullo, *Ivan Bunin: From the Other Shore, 1920–1933* (Chicago, 1955), 48–49, 194–198.

ness, penchant for autocracy, and infinitely suffering Russian soul left them unsuited for Western "bourgeois" liberty.[1] In such a schema, some Western observers of the Soviet scene even justified Stalin's Terror as the "means" toward the "end" of a great Russian state!

The diaspora, of course, dismissed such theories as more hypocritical than naive. European and American intellectuals and writers were lashing out at the shortcomings of their own countries while drawing glowing pictures of Soviet life, however brief their visit to the homeland or however the reality there.[2] "Why does world public opinion," one emigré journalist wondered, "so hotly outraged by Fascist and Hitlerite regimes, remain indifferent when confronted with the unheard-of, unprecedented crimes of the Soviet government? Why do public circles of the left in Europe and America, parading their devotion to the ideas of freedom and justice, remain so blind and deaf to the sufferings of the Russian people, even as they so often ingratiate themselves with its executioners?"[3]

Increasingly, the members of "Russia Abroad" realized that their exile would be not only painful but prolonged. For the first fifteen or so years of their time abroad, they had sat proudly on closed suitcases and trunks, waiting to return to the land of their birth. Now, sorrowful and resigned, they began to unpack their belongings, hoping vainly that the Soviet state would "wither away," not according to Marxist ideology but from the emptiness of its own brutality and decay.

Russian emigrés also appealed to Bunin as a man-god because, by the time he was named a Nobel laureate, no one else in the diaspora could provide the political leadership that "Russia Abroad" so desperately needed. The diaspora was wracked by ongoing (and often pointless) political wrangling and by the decline and death of key leaders and statesmen. Pavel Miliukov, Anton Denikin, and Vasily Maklakov, now all in their early sixties, had failed to capture the popular imagination. Alexander Kerensky incited only emigré anger and scorn. Indeed, such statesmen were seen as loser-"liberals" who, in the homeland, had failed to stave off Bolshevik barbarians in 1917 and who, in truth, had

---

[1]See, for instance, such works as W. Duranty's *I Write as I Please* (New York, 1935); and A. L. Strong's *I Change Worlds* (New York, 1937).

[2]See, for instance, both Georgy Adamovich's and Alexander Kerensky's heated responses to Gide who, in his celebrated 1936 "return" to Russia, expressed his continued faith in the revolution, even as he deplored the philistinism, arrogance, and political repression that he found there. See *Poslednie novosti* (November 26, 1936); and A. Kerensky, "André Gide. Retour de l'U.R.S.S.," *Sovremennye zapiski*, vol. 62 (1936), 454–457.

[3]V. Rudnev, "Out of the Deep. Letters from Soviet Timber Camps," *Sovremennye zapiski*, vol. 50 (1934), 448–449.

never offered Russia anything then or since. Disorder and chaos bedeviled all factions, parties, and groups; helplessness and nostalgia fanned smoldering frustration and despair. No one could hear a clear or consistent voice on the future of Russia on either side of the border in the din raised by anarchists, Mensheviks, and Social Revolutionaries on the left, and by monarchists, reactionaries, and fascist-oriented groups on the right.

Complicating matters was that the fact that the politicians of "Russia Abroad" had become isolated both at home and abroad. By 1934, contacts with the homeland had become almost impossible, courtesy of the Soviet police who had terrorized native citizens and sealed off the borders with the outside world. Emigré political leaders also failed to influence the governments of their host countries. Their calls for democratic socialism, constitutional monarchy, and the rights of man and his property fell on deaf ears, as did their warnings of the "danger" of Soviet Russia; the growing specter of fascism; xenophobic and nationalist backlashes; and the discrimination, disfranchisement, and despair that affected Russian exile workers.[4]

To their further dismay, the civic leaders of "Russia Abroad" had found that the peoples of their host countries were taking an even harsher view of their exile-charges than they had earlier. Western pacifists, socialists, and Communists continued to look favorably upon the Revolution. In their pro-Soviet mood, they showed little interest in "patriarchal" Russia other than the reasons for its collapse. The ignorance could be appalling. A 1941 French novel à la russe featured heroines named Annushka ("Annie"), Babushka ("Granny"), and Petrushka ("little Peter"). A French textbook insisted that Ivan the Terrible was called "Vasilievich" for his cruelty.[5] With anger and contempt, Western liberals often dismissed exiles as spoiled princes and generals, as ex-

---

[4]France was a notable exception to this rule. For instance, in 1936 the "Front Populaire" of Léon Blum did much to improve the legal and economic security of Russian emigrés. Among other things, it ended practices which expelled Russian exiles who did not have a work permit, or who had violated even simple traffic regulations. Also under Blum, Russian emigrés gained access to French trade unions with the same rights and privileges as native workers. In fact, the *Confédération Générale du Travail*, the largest national labor union in France at that time, had a Russian section whose members enjoyed the same benefits and protections as other individuals in the group.

Still, emigré life in France was not easy. A 1937 report on the Russian colony at Lyons noted that only one percent of the emigrés there believed they were leading a normal life. Eighty percent of the group declared they were barely subsisting, while roughly one hundred Russians were living as vagrants under bridges on the Rhone.

See M. Raeff, *Russia Abroad: A Cultural History of the Russian Emigration, 1919–1939* (New York, 1990), 38; Johnston, 147.

[5]M. Osorgin, *Pis'ma o neznachitel'nom, 1940–1942 gg.* (New York, 1952), 249.

emplars of Russian "barbarism" and the incomprehensible "Slavic soul," and as folk oppressors who richly deserved their disfranchised fate. If Russian exiles gained anything in their time abroad, it was in their status as an enigma to the West. To their host peoples, they were little more than caricatures of "nostalgia, fatalism, and balalaikas" who dressed in "crimson shirts," performed "frenzied dances," and sang "lugubrious songs of the Volga."[6]

Even the ultimate rallying cry of "Russia Abroad"—the absolute rejection of both the Revolution and the Bolshevik regime—was being reevaluated and rejected. No longer did expatriates believe blindly in the collapse of communism. Émigré rancor at the new Soviet state now alternated with balance and even begrudging admiration for all that the new regime had accomplished. Some emigrés, taking heart in the "great Russian nationalism" promoted by Stalin in the late 1930s, sanctioned the "imperial" rebirth of their homeland, particularly its technological and scientific achievements. Even as the editors of *Latest News* (*Poslednie Novosti*), the most respected and widely circulated newspaper of "Russia Abroad," denounced the brutal terrorism and dictatorship of the Bolsheviks—what the émigré writer Roman Gul' called the "The Union of Sons of Bitches of the Revolution"[7]—they applauded Soviet reforms in education, social services, and military power.

In a more scholarly vein, other Russian exiles dared to think, say, and write "heresy": the Revolution was not an historical accident or an aberrant departure from some "normal" path. Nor was it a cosmic upheaval, an alien, anti-national coup, or a grievous, ephemeral episode that no one could have foreseen or prevented. Rather, for these émigré scholars, the events of 1917 were a period in Russian history that was logical, legitimate, and located deeply within national history and culture. "Patriarchal" Russia, this pro-Soviet group reasoned, had reached an impasse, unable to solve the difficulties of its time and place. With the Revolution, national soil and soul had undergone a profound and irrevocable change. The homeland and its citizens no longer related to the West as contributor or beneficiary. Rather, having abandoned their Petrine veneer, they were unearthing organic images and ideals to fashion a new and better life for all. The "new" Russia, these scholars concluded, was worth studying—and serving. Collectivization and five-year plans were ending centuries-old darkness and initiating a

[6]J. Delage, *La Russie en exil* (Paris, 1930), 28.
[7]In his robust epithet, Gul' kept the Russian equivalent for "USSR," i.e., *Soiuz sukinykh synov revoliutstii*. See R. Gul', *Ia unes Rossiiu*, vol. 2 (New York, 1984), 72.

"golden age." These same scholars hoped that the new Russia would be an inspiration for the West. As they saw it, Bolshevik pragmatism and Orthodox faith would fashion a Christian socialism that would legitimate national messianism and bring about "heaven on earth."

Meanwhile, Russian emigrés looked to Bunin to halt "denationalization"—the surrender of body and soul to their country of refuge, and with it the loss of Russianness for both their children and themselves. As hopes of return to the homeland faded, many Russian exiles damned "denationalization" as a betrayal of their identity in the West and of their stance as a foil to the "whore" Russia in the East. To their credit, members of "Russia Abroad" had fought off assimilation for as long as they could. They had acted, worked, and created as an extension of Russia, convinced that they represented the best of their native land, spiritually and culturally. They had sought to school their children in the Russian "faith," instilling a knowledge and love of the national language, literature, and history, and, more important, perhaps, a sense of loyalty and even of identification with Russia itself. "High" Russian culture was the focus of churches, theatres, and schools; the scientific, literary, and artistic achievements of the pre-Soviet nation were the grist for books, journals, and plays; for readings, lectures, and debates; for concerts, circles, and clubs; for unions, societies, and associations.

The emigré struggle against "denationalization," though, was destined to fail. It had been the fate of the sons and daughters of "Russia Abroad" either to have been born in a foreign land or to have been too young or too traumatized to remember life in their native one. Even as their parents vaunted Russia at every turn, the new generation in exile had no direct or experiential knowledge of the homeland. At best, the land of their forefathers was for them an abstraction or myth.[8] Further, systems of solace and support for Russian exile youth were declining precipitously. A low birthrate, a high mortality rate, and chronic financial difficulties and sociopolitical upheavals had deci-

---

[8]The older generation agreed. "The years pass," a group of exiled academics wrote in a 1930 appeal, "and our physical isolation from our motherland . . . is having a special impact upon the next generation [of exiles abroad]. Indeed, the very idea [of Russia] is becoming ever more abstract [to them]. Feeling for the homeland is weakening, and there is reason to fear that it will fade more each year. People of the older generation, having lived a good part of their lives in Russia, and having had the good fortune to experience the country directly, are disappearing gradually. . . .

"Thus, those [of us] who still can, must immediately transmit everything they have been preserving [about Russia]; [they must pass on] all the information they have about our country, and, in general, about everything Russian to the young persons who are coming forward to replace them." As cited in T. Aleksinskaia, "Emigratsiia i ee molodoe pokolenie," *Vozrozhdenie*, vol. 65 (May 1957), 27.

mated the number of emigré schools. On the eve of World War II, Paris was home to only one Russian lycée. As a result, emigré children found it increasingly difficult to evade French life, its language and culture. French schools were powerful agents of denationalization. A 1938 report concluded that most Russian emigré youth thought and acted like the "average European" of their age.[9] At every stage of the social ladder, the use of French tended to supplant that of Russian. An investigator of Russian scout camps found that by 1937, emigré children were encountering significant problems with their native language. Although, in theory, the participants of such groups were to speak Russian only, the reality of the situation was quite different. Of the 379 emigré children in scout camps that year, 10 percent spoke it poorly and 50 percent not well. Five percent spoke no Russian at all. Nine years later, researchers found that Russian children were more at ease with French than with Russian, and that only under close supervision did they use their native tongue.[1]

Given such pressures, it is not surprising that the children of Russian emigrés lacked a commitment to Russia on any level. When they looked to the past, they had no interest in deepening their knowledge of Russian history and culture. When they looked to the future, they did not wish to continue the struggle against the Bolsheviks or to consider their role in a free and future homeland. The new generation in the diaspora were akin to modern-day nihilists who, like Bazarov in Turgenev's *Fathers and Sons*, saw as both obsolete and arcane the "faith" of their fathers. With jaundiced eyes and bored looks, they endured the endless personal, political, and philosophical quarrels; the frenzied finger-pointing as to "who lost Russia"; and the heated discussions over a post-Bolshevik patrimony. Even the fiery debates between Westernizers and Slavophiles—a keystone of Russian intellectual thought—were for them as "distant and incomprehensible as the Wars of the Roses."[2]

Thus with scorn and contempt the children of "Russia Abroad" endured the breast-beating of the intelligentsia, the anathema of the clergy, and the nostalgia of their parents, as all three groups bemoaned the loss of the Russian "paradise." Zinaida Shakovskaya and her youthful friends were so weary of the older generation and their nostrums that they disrupted political gatherings with stink-bombs.[3] Bitter and impoverished, the "prodigal" sons and daughters of the Russian dias-

[9]Johnston, 88.
[1]*Ibid.*, 90.
[2]See J. Glad, *Russia Abroad: Writers, History, Politics* (Tenafly, N.J., 1999), 253.
[3]Z. Shakovskaia, *Une manière de vivre* (Paris, 1965), 119; and *Otrazheniia* (Paris, 1975), 11–12.

pora were both embarrassed by their foreignness and futility, and un-happy with their elders, their prospects, and the ghettolike nature of their world. Many, resenting the fact that their parents had left the homeland, revolted against their shadowy images and ideals. For them the Russia of their parents was dead.

Not surprisingly, many Russian emigrés saw Bunin as their savior because they believed that, in the deepening twilight of their lives, their formerly radiant mission had become clouded and dark. The rise of Soviet power, the dearth of political leadership, and the surge of "denationalization" had eroded a confidence and a consensus that had transcended time and space as well as political, social, and economic differences. As the second decade of the European peace neared its end, the members of "Russia Abroad" found that Russian expatriates were no longer united by opposition to the Soviet state or by dreams of a return to the homeland. "Why are we here?" and "What have we achieved?" became the new *prokliatye voprosy* or "damned questions" that not only obsessed their minds and hearts but haunted them with their lack of action or answers. "Only we Russians walk among other peoples in a trance of universal missions," Ekaterina Kuskova wrote in 1931. "Only we go about with the proud intention of saving the world from sinful realists . . . only we know the secret of salvation . . . we who were unable to save our own country."[4]

Such pangs of self-doubt turned into an epidemic of self-pity. "The more time has passed," the editors of *Contemporary Notes* (*Sovre-menye zapiski*), the leading "thick" journal of the emigration, lamented in 1934, "the more often have our ordeals encountered the jeers of our enemies, the indifference of our European fellow writers, the doubts of the weary, and the bitterness of those who have lost faith."[5] Devoid of meaning and purpose, the members of "Russia Abroad" saw their time abroad as increasingly alien, sterile, and pointless. If earlier they had regarded themselves as Davids tackling Bolshevik Goliaths, they now believed themselves to be prisoners of a Babylonian captivity: weak, fragmented, and at the mercy of idol worshipers who tormented them in both East and West. The ways in which Russian exiles now opposed the Soviet regime were both poignant and pathetic. As one of their group recalled in 1939, "they refused to look at a Soviet film or sprat," even as they knew that such abstention "would not blow up the walls of the enemy fortress."[6]

<hr/>

[4]E. Kuskova, "Chto imenno utverzhdaetsia?" *Utverzhdeniia*, vol. 2 (August 1931), 127.
   [5]"Ot redaktsii," *Sovremennye zapiski,* vol. 54 (1934), 195–196.
   [6]Iu. Rapoport, "Konets zarubezhiia," *Sovremennye zapiski*, vol. 69 (1939), 376.

Thus, as their years in exile dragged on, the members of latter-day "Russia Abroad" had little choice but to focus their attention on the one remaining hallmark of their raison d'être: they sought to preserve and continue the values of Russian culture for both the homeland and the world.

When in 1935 Georgy Fedotov insisted that native arts deserved every sacrifice from its practitioners,[7] he was only articulating a long-held truism among exile artists and audiences. From the very beginning of their exile, Russian expatriates had striven for an intense and meaningful creative life. Scholars, scientists, artists, and thinkers had pursued their work, furthered national culture, and acquainted their haven societies with Russia's contributions to the world. Exile publics heard, read, and saw whatever their writers, musicians, and artists had produced for them and the cultural community at large. Stories, songs, and paintings moved both groups from joy and pride over the noble Russian heritage, through melancholy and pensiveness over the quixotic Russian soul, to shock and sadness over the lost Russian home. Marc Chagall spoke for both the artists and audiences of "Russia Abroad" when he wrote: "Not a single centimeter of my paintings is free of nostalgia for my native land."[8]

To their horror, though, Russian expatriates saw their cultural largesse as facing increasing threat and attack. Like the political leaders of the diaspora, the aesthetic heroes of "Russia Abroad" were leaving the exile stage. Some had died—Pavlova in 1931, Zamyatin in 1937, Chaliapin in 1938, Khodasevich in 1939, Balmont in 1942, Rachmaninoff in 1943, Gippius in 1945. Others had returned to Russia—Prokofiev in 1932, Kuprin in 1939, Tsvetaeva in 1942.[9] Because of World War II, still others had moved to America—Aldanov and Nabokov in 1940, Sedykh in 1942. And the Western world was becoming less interested in the traditions of emigré culture and more intrigued with the innovations of both the Revolution and the new Soviet state. Russian exiles were becoming real-life composites of Akaky Akakievich, the forlorn scribbler in Gogol's 1841 "The Overcoat,"[1] and of Uncle Vanya, the doleful hero of Chekhov's famed 1899 play.

From the late 1930s on, the untrammeled creative freedom that

[7]See G. Fedotov, "Zachem my zdes'?," *Sovremennye zapiski*, vol. 58 (1935), 433–444.

[8]As cited in J. Russell, "Farewell to Chagall, The Great Survivor," *New York Times* (April 7, 1985), section 2, 31.

[9]None of the three, though, found the happiness and acceptance they had been looking for. Tsvetaeva committed suicide in 1942. Prokofiev died the same day as Stalin, but his funeral was ignored in the Soviet press.

[1]See N. Berberova, *The Italics Are Mine* (New York, 1969), 235, 354.

Russian intellectuals, writers, and artists had enjoyed in the first twenty years or so of their exile was coming to an end. Ultranationalist and authoritarian policies stopped the pulse of Russian cultural life in Poland, Romania, Latvia, and Lithuania.[2] The Japanese invasion of China ended the aesthetic activities of Russian exiles in Kharbin and the Far East. Hitler's rise to power in Germany and his later occupation of Czechoslovakia cut short the scholarly, literary, and cultural vitality of Russian emigré centers in both countries. Finally, the outbreak of the war caused many expatriate intellectuals, writers, and artists either to fall silent or to suffer and die for their beliefs.

Among latter-day emigrés, the focus of the renewed cultural concern was, of course, language and literature, and for a simple reason. Throughout Russian history the word, both oral and written, had been not only the mainstay of cultural and collective identity; from the early nineteenth century on, it had also been the sword with which Russian writers and *intelligenty* had engaged both the autocracy and the "damned questions" of life.

The respect if not worship of Russian linguistic and literary values only intensified in emigration. For lack of any other cohesive unit—except, perhaps, the rite and ritual of the Orthodox church—it was Russian language and literature that bound latter-day emigrés as a "society in exile." Together the written and spoken words served as spiritual and psychological guideposts, assuaging wounds opened by war, revolution, persecution, and displacement. Together Russian language and literature evoked visions of the homeland and provided sanctuaries through which homesick emigrés could, psychically, return to the land of their birth and relive their childhood, adolescence, and youth. Together native tongue and pen upheld the fabric of Russian cultural life and convinced exile writers that they, more than anyone else, were defending the many and diverse values of its legacy. The written and oral culture of the diaspora still served as a viable weapon by which its members fought what they saw as the brutal "anti-culture" of the Soviets, particularly the products of "socialist realism."

Like everything else with "Russia Abroad," though, the renewed focus on Russian language and literature was often subject to fervid dialogue, debate—and distress. Most Russian emigré writers lived an al-

---

[2]For instance, in 1932 the Latvian government declared Latvian alone to be the official state language; and two years later the minister of education there insisted that his country free itself from alien cultures that "threatened Latvianism." As a result, many Russian periodicals in Latvia were either closed or censored. Also, families with a Latvian father and a Russian mother could no longer send their children to Russian schools. See Glad, 197–198.

most Darwinian existence, worrying about food, shelter, and clothing more than they did about their art. Many of them had succumbed to the difficulties of their existence. Kuprin had taken to drink, Balmont had gone insane. Both the quantity and quality of Russian literature in exile was declining precipitously. In 1929 the critic Marc Slonim lamented that Russian exiles had not produced either theories or works to renew national literature. Rather, they were merely "living out their days,"[3] rehashing previous images and ideas.

Russian emigré writers also fretted that, with the exception of the novels of Tolstoy and Dostoevsky, the world was losing interest in classical and contemporary Russian works. Whereas modern Russian musicians, artists, and dancers scored great success with Westerners, their counterparts in literature seemed destined for oblivion. Audiences could hear Stravinsky; they could see Chagall, Kandinsky, and Burlyuk. Few Westerners, though, could read exile practitioners of poetry and prose in the original; and translations of their works were faulty and few. Only when a new generation of emigré writers—Henri Troyat, Joseph Kessel, Nina Berberova, Elsa Triolet, Romain Gary, and Vladimir Nabokov—adopted the resident foreign language as their own did they attract attention to their works.[4]

The new group of Russian writers-in-exile also seemed little inclined to carry on the tradition of their forefathers. While they embodied the *Angst* of their generation, they lacked a firsthand familiarity with their homeland and heritage. As one elder emigré lamented, "Russian literature is not Russian because it describes birch trees, samovars, and sarafans. It is Russian because it expresses specific peculiarities of the Russian moral and artistic consciousness. The tragedy is not that young Russians have never seen a sarafan, but that they have not absorbed the basic elements of Russian life and Russian culture."[5] Even more painful to the older emigrés, the new generation of Russian writers had no interest whatsoever in the political and social questions that so preoccupied their forefathers. They preferred mirages and feelings, hallucinations and dreams. By temperament and talent, they were akin to the narrators and characters of Nabokov who, as one of their

[3]Berberova agreed. "The 'older' writers," she recalled, "admitted frankly that they did not need to renew style; rather, they had ready-made forms which they continued to use and whose obsolete qualities they continued to ignore." See Glad, 249–250, 265.

[4]For instance, in 1938, the twenty-seven-year-old Troyat was awarded the Prix Goncourt, France's highest literary honor. Twenty-one years later he was elected to the French Academy, the youngest "Immortal" in the group and the only Russian to date to have attained this honor.

[5]Glad, 253.

own group, saw people as alienated and deranged, struggling between reality and worlds of their own making.[6]

Russian expatriates were more dismayed to see that even readers in their own ranks were turning their backs on native fiction. By the end of the 1930s, many emigré books and journals had only limited reach and even more remote chances for survival. Exacerbating the decline was the fact that emigrés disagreed violently over precisely what should constitute the "canon" of their oral and written tradition. The rancor over linguistic and aesthetic matters often superseded the wrangling over political affairs. Even as purist pedagogues waged war against faulty grammar, newly minted acronyms, and foreign vocabulary and expressions—the language of "Sovdepia" or "De-Pe," the pejorative term for the homeland that evoked particular sarcasm and scorn[7]—emigré writers penned idiosyncratic variations of the mother tongue. They created personal lexicons, borrowed freely from other languages, and discarded what they saw as obsolete words and turns of phrase.

In classic Russian style, exiles also fought over the "purity" of writers, works, even orthography. Although many exile intellectuals applauded the new trends in religion and philosophy, they tended to be conservative aesthetically. Skeptical of Russian avant-garde experi-

---

[6]The second-generation Russian exile writer Boris Poplavsky captured the malaise of his generation when he wrote: "Having just separated from my family, I arrived [in Paris] alone. I was stoop-shouldered, and my entire being exuded . . . a transcendental humiliation, one which clung to me like a skin infection. Regretting immediately that I had come, I nonetheless stayed on, wandering the city, from one acquaintance to another. . . .

"With degrading politeness, I kept up my end of the emigré conversation. From time to time the boring, halfhearted talk was interrupted by sighs and tea, drunk from badly washed china. . . .

"Dragging my feet, I had left my family; dragging my thoughts, I had left God, dignity, and freedom; dragging my days, I had reached the age of twenty-four. In those years my clothing was shapeless, wrinkled, and sprinkled with ashes and shreds of tobacco. I washed rarely and slept without undressing. I lived in a twilight . . . in a strange, unmade bed. I drank water from a glass that smelled of soap. For long periods of time, I stared out of the window, inhaling the smoke of a butt discarded by the apartment's owner. . . .

"But, if one thought about it, what had happened actually, other than the fact that a million people had lost some tasteless Viennese couches, paintings by unknown artists of the Dutch school (undoubtedly forged), and featherbeds and meat-pies that lull a person hopefully into a heavy, degrading after-dinner sleep similar to death? . . .

"Proudly I often stepped out into the street, my shirt unbuttoned on my narrow hairless chest, and I stared at passersby with a patronizing, absent, and sleepy gaze." Poplavsky was thirty-three years old when he died in 1935, possibly either of a drug overdose or by suicide. See Glad, 255.

[7]"Sovdepia" draws from the abbreviation, "SOVDEP" or "*Sovet rabochikh, krest'ianskikh i krasnoarmeiskikh deputatov*" ("Soviet of Workers', Peasants', and Red Army Deputies"). The Soviets were founded first in 1905 and again in 1917 as institutions of popular government in Russia.

ments in the years before and during the Revolution, they wished to continue the "gentry" creativity of the Golden Age. They hailed Pushkin for his staunch individuality, his spiritual liberalism, and the formal excellence of his poetry and prose. By contrast, aesthetic liberals in the diaspora wished to sustain the "modern" exuberance of the Silver Age. In reply to arguments that the Symbolists and others had hailed revolution, apocalypse, and lust, they countered with the dramatic experiments of Blok in poetry and of Bely in prose. Progressives enraged conservatives even further in their belief that, in the early years of Soviet power, such poets as Mayakovsky and Esenin had actually forged a "modern" culture rooted in folk energy and talent. Still other expatriate *intelligenty* argued for the unity not only of the "golden" and "silver" pasts but also of the "emigré" and "Soviet" present. In their view, Russian literature compared favorably to an oak with weighty branches or a river with raging streams. Thus no matter the time, space, or worldview, Pushkin and Tolstoy, Babel and Pasternak, Aldanov and Bunin shared membership in the same "union" of Russian writers.

Doubtless Bunin empathized with the dangers and hazards that threatened the later years of "Russia Abroad." He too had decried the stamina of Soviet power and the seemingly endless sentence of his exile. He too had fretted over the lack of political unity as well as the increasing isolation, if irrelevance, of the Russian diaspora to the world. He too had decried "denationalization" and the indifference of emigré youth to their ancestral land. Loss of group identity and purpose had led Bunin likewise to worry not only about the "canon" of Russian language and literature but also about the ability of himself and others to continue both in a viable and meaningful way. Indeed, Bunin was a master at berating both himself and his gifts. "Sometimes I am clearly horrified by how low I have fallen," he wrote in his diary on August 16, 1936. "Almost every step I take has resulted in something stupid and base! I am continually besieged by full-blown inertia, lack of will, and a monstrous lack of talent! I have to get hold of myself, I really have to."[8] Finally, there were times when Bunin too wondered where his next meal was coming from and, with his declining health, whether he would see the light of the coming day.

Repeatedly, though, Bunin declined to accept the crown that "Russia Abroad" offered him. He was scarcely a shrinking violet, but, like everything else in his life, he wanted admiration and applause on his own highly whimsical terms. Too many bravos embarrassed him,

[8]M. Grin, *Ustami Buninykh. Dnevniki*, vol. 3 (Frankfurt-Main: 1983), 20.

too few depressed him. Although he could see himself as immortal and godlike, he refused to let others gift him with divinity. He cared little for the limelight or the fetters and chains with which emigrés, seeing him as a man-god, wished to bind him.

"We have yet to have a moment's peace," Muromtseva-Bunina wrote exactly a year after Bunin was awarded the Nobel Prize. "We are still living as if in a dream. . . . Fame, money, and congratulations; envy, requests, insults; disenchantment, powerlessness, flattery; screams of joy and happiness that we could help others. . . . Everything has gotten confused, tangled, intertwined. . . . [Everything] has kept us from concentrating and working, not to mention bringing us to endless grief."[9]

Bunin rebelled against the dictates and demands that fellow exiles made on him. He delighted in small gatherings and groups, but he avoided crowds whenever he could. When he gave public readings and the like, he seemed like a man facing execution, not a man-god seeking glory. His face was tired and pale; his voice cracked; his hands shook uncontrollably.

Russian exiles, of course, were greatly dismayed by Bunin's reticence. "I find it very painful that Ivan Alexeevich does not use his [Nobel] prize in the interest of Russian affairs, or to advance his own personal goals," Aldanov complained to Muromtseva-Bunina on January 20, 1935. "No, he cannot be our 'ambassador' and this is a great, great pity."[1] Expatriates were even more distressed by fears that the Soviet state would co-opt their "idol." "Rumors are flying around Moscow that you have decided to return [to Russia]!!" a disconsolate Aldanov wrote to Bunin on June 22, 1935. "What the hell have you been up to?!"[2]

Neither "Russia Abroad" nor the world at large would leave Bunin in peace. They engulfed the writer in new and more menacing social and political maelstroms. The darkening clouds of a new world war were casting long shadows not only on his personal welfare and security but on the well-being of the entire diaspora. In a horror born of déjà-vu, Bunin and his fellow expatriates watched as the citizens in their host countries cheered totalitarianism, brandished swastikas or hammers-and-sickles, and sang the *Marseillaise* and the *International*. Together they wondered if Western democracies would survive fascist

[9]*Ibid.*, 12.
[1]Grin, "Pis'ma M. A. Aldanova," 116.
[2]M. Grin, "Pis'ma M. A. Aldanova k I. A. i V. I. Buninym," *Novyi zhurnal*, vol. 80 (1965), 285.

assaults. Equally poignant, they pondered their response to a Nazi invasion of the homeland. To themselves and others, they asked: Should the members of "Russia Abroad" support Soviets or Germans? Must they choose between Hitler's *Lebensraum* and racism or Stalin's terror, purges, and famines? Could they, or anyone else, trust the Bolsheviks to enter into a Western coalition against the aggressors? Would they join hands with the Red Army and the Russian people if they fought for—or against—Soviet power? The questions continued unabated.

In the immediate prewar years, though, Bunin was certain about one thing: his hatred for both the Nazis and the Soviets. As he saw it, Germany under Hitler had suffered the same moral collapse as Russia under Lenin and Stalin. Both countries were governed by "insane monkeys"[3] who mocked the images and ideals of civilization. Although some in the diaspora had been taken by fascist anti-Bolshevism, Bunin agreed with Mark Vishnyak who believed that for expatriates to choose between Stalin and Hitler was like being asked if they preferred cholera over plague, or to jump out a window from the fifth floor or the sixth.[4]

In his hatred of the Nazis, Bunin spoke from experience. For the world at large, the rehearsal for universal conflict was the Spanish Civil War; but for Bunin it was a 1936 confrontation with German officials on the Swiss border. What he endured at the hands of Nazi interlocutors outdid any indignity he had suffered in both the Russian Revolution and the civil war. Without the slightest provocation, Bunin was stripped and spent three hours in a cold room; his books and belongings were tossed and pillaged. Such aggression not only shocked the world but brought Bunin to consider new threats to his survival.

Bunin also continued to oppose the Soviets. Unlike Pavel Milyukov, he did not believe that his native land was on an upward, evolutionary path. Nor did he succumb to stories of his popularity in Russia or of the allure of his homeland as a "paradise" for writers. Rather, he declared, Bolshevik Russia was the "snout of a pig,"[5] and Stalin was destroying the homeland, politically and aesthetically. The burgeoning strictures of "socialist realism" aroused Bunin's indignation and ire. Ongoing terror against peasants, the urban middle class, the army high command, and the Communist party itself convinced him that bolshevism was not only a political wrong but a spiritual evil

[3]N. Roshchin, "Vospominaniia o Bunine i Kuprine," *Voprosy literatury*, No. 6 (1981), 160.

[4]M. Vishniak, "Protiv techenii," *Sovremennye zapiski*, vol. 52 (1933), 402.

[5]A. Kaun, "Ivan Bunin," *Books Abroad* (April 1934), 145.

which denied both God and humankind. "In all of human history, even in the basest and most bloodiest of times," Bunin told an interviewer in 1934, "there has been nothing more vile, false, evil, and despotic than bolshevism."[6] Anyone in "Russia Abroad" who urged accommodation with the Soviets was met with Bunin's obdurate hostility.

For Bunin and his fellow exiles, the first years of the war in Europe were heartless if intensified replays of the chaos and suffering they had experienced in Russia only a generation earlier. In early 1941 no one in the diaspora saw light on the horizon. America was neutral; France was prostrate; Britain was struggling for its very existence. Even worse, perhaps, Stalin was Hitler's partner in crime, with both the 1939 Nazi-Soviet Nonaggression Pact and the Soviet attack on Poland and later Finland as particularly grievous blows. Emigrés in Paris were taunted as "dirty Russians."[7] Exile laborers were denied work permits, shop assistants were dismissed, and Russian taxi drivers were boycotted by the public.[8]

For Nina Berberova, the only wartime certainty for "Russia Abroad" was that the "shabby, unhappy provincial emigration was ending . . . [that their] generation would be killed in the conflict, [and that] the old would die off in quick order."[9] Whether Russian emigrés lived under bombs in Paris or braved existence in the provinces, they lived on the very edge of survival. Scrounging for every ounce of food, every scrap of news, they looked in anguish at Russians on both sides of the conflict. With the Nazi attack on the Soviet Union in June 1941, what was happening in the homeland was as unnerving as what they

[6]As quoted in S. Voitsekhovskii, "Pod russkim stiagom," *Novoe russkoe slovo* (March 27, 1973), 3.
[7]Such name-calling was particularly unfair when one considers that Russian emigrés in Paris were model citizens who were making vital contributions to the city. Although the numbers of Russian exiles in Paris is uncertain—estimates range from 72,000 to 400,000—they were so much in evidence that, as one French observer noted in 1937, one could live a completely Russian life there. The evidence is convincing. For instance, in the years before World War II, Russian expatriates supported more than thirty Orthodox churches, seven Russian institutions of higher learning, and fourteen bookstores, along with Russian schools, shops, lotteries, orchestras, pharmacies, banks, hotels, butchers, mechanics, tailors, typesetters, and printers.

Russian exiles in Paris were also active in the arts there, including a Russian Repertory Theatre, and artists such as Marc Chagall, Alexander Benois, Natalya Goncharova, and Mikhail Larionov, who were seminal in the artistic life of Montparnasse. Further, Russian exiles in Paris had the lowest crime rate of any foreign groups in that city. See Glad, 167, 168.
[8]It was not difficult to blackball the 250 or so Russian taxi drivers who worked in Paris, since they often emblazoned the doors of their cabs with the emblem of the Russian bear. See "Russkie v Parizhe," *Vozrozhdenie* (September 1, 1939), 2. See also Johnston, 157; Glad, 167.
[9]Berberova, 389.

were experiencing in their own backyards. As Russian expatriates read between the lines of the collaborationist press, or strained to catch a neutral station through the buzz of jamming on ancient radios, they were shocked both by the devastating success of Hitler's blitzkrieg in their country and by the equally stiff resistance that its citizens came to show the invaders. A key assumption of emigré conjecture and calculation had proven false: after all, the diaspora had reasoned smugly, how could a corrupt tyranny withstand the twin assaults of German might and of Russian popular fury?

To their chagrin, Russian expatriates found that the Bolshevik regime had not only remained intact but that, under the banner of communism, it was directing the Russian people to fight for itself and the homeland. In this the members of "Russia Abroad" were poor students of history. They had forgotten that the values of native soul and soil that had sustained them in exile were also crucial to their counterparts in the homeland. However wretched their lives, however cruel their leaders, Russians had always united to throw off foreign oppressors, whether they were Teutonic knights in the twelfth century, Mongols in the sixteenth, or French in the nineteenth. Now, in the twentieth, they saw that the German bombs that exploded over Moscow threatened not Stalin but Russia's very heart. Their response was both spiritual and instinctive: against all odds, and at an ultimate cost of more than twenty million Russian lives, they sought to expel the enemy from their soil.

Initially Bunin, along with everyone else in the diaspora, was deeply conflicted about the struggle in the homeland. In the early days of the Nazi assault, he agreed with Ksenia Denikina, General Denikin's wife, who wrote: "O Russia, the cup has not passed you by! The two Antichrists have come to blows. Of course, this means the end of communism in Russia, but what a cruel ordeal for your country!"[1] Bunin, though, did not accept Harry Truman's 1941 dictum that the more Slavs and Teutons killed each other, the better the world would be.[2] He continued to hate the Soviet regime and hoped for an end of Stalin's rule. But the thought of Nazi invaders ravaging Russia was too much for him to bear. In no way, Bunin believed, could he and the members

---

[1]M. Grey, ed., *Mimizan-sur-guerre. Le journal de ma mère sous l'Occupation* (Paris, 1976), 118.

[2]Specifically, Truman told an interviewer from the *New York Times* on June 24, 1941: "If we see that Germany is winning, we ought to help Russia; and if Russia is winning, we ought to help Germany. Let them kill as many as possible. . . . Neither of them think anything of their pledged word." See T. Catledge, "Our Policy Stated," *New York Times* (June 24, 1941), 1, 7.

of "Russia Abroad" cooperate with the foreign aggressors who were seizing Russian territory;[3] in no way, he insisted, could they look to fascists either to liberate Russian people from communism or to determine their postwar fate. He thus joined with Milyukov, Nikolai Berdyaev, and others who saw the struggle in the homeland as "our front, our army, our troops."[4]

Bunin was not alone in his views. Russian exiles offered as much resistance to the enemy in France as their counterparts were doing in the homeland. Many had enlisted in the French armed forces or were serving in the Resistance.[5] For these men and women, it was a way to combat the common enemy of both France and Russia; it also allowed them to believe that for the first time in their lives they were living a useful and purposeful existence. Bunin too performed great acts of heroism. To the horror of family and friends, he believed that, like Leo Tolstoy, he could "not be silent" about world evil. He publicly proclaimed Mussolini and Hitler to be "lackeys."[6] He resisted German at-

---

[3]Although officials of the Russian Orthodox church abroad supported the German invasion of the homeland (Metropolitan Serafim of Paris urged that all the "faithful sons of Russia" assist the Nazis in purging the earth of "the masonic star and the hammer and sickle," and Ioann Shakovskoy, the future archbishop of San Francisco, rejoiced that in Hitler "a skilled, seasoned surgeon [had undertaken] to overthrow the Third International"), prominent political and cultural leaders rejected the idea of a German "crusade" in the homeland.

In fact, emigré collaborators in France and elsewhere were few in number, and, as even Soviet spokesmen came to admit, not typical of the emigration as whole. The Nazis, though, did find support among ultra-right restorationists in Germany, the Balkans, and the Far East who welcomed the anti-Soviet sentiments of the Führer.

Pro-German Russian exiles believed that a Nazi victory would destroy a Jewish-Bolshevik conspiracy, not Russia and its people. It would also mean an influx of German doctors, engineers, architects, and agronomists who would revitalize the homeland and would gradually be assimilated into the population. Such was the price, these pro-German exiles concluded, that Russia would have to pay for having allowed the Bolsheviks to assume power. Not for nothing, therefore, did such groups as the All-Russian Fascist party, based in Harbin, China, circulate a manifesto through Russian Paris, proclaiming: "Heil Hitler, Viva Mussolini, Banzai Mikado, Hurrah Rodzaevsky!"

It should be noted, though, that pro-German Russian groups were regarded with suspicion by the Nazis, and that after the war, key collaborators in "Russia Abroad" were tried and punished. For instance, N. Piatnitsky, editor of the Nazi-funded *Parizhskii vestnik* (*Russian Herald*, published in Paris between 1942 and 1944), drew a ten-year sentence, even as he appeared before his accusers as sleek, prosperous, unchastened, and dressed in an expensive fur coat. For more about Nazi sympathizers in "Russia Abroad," see J. Stephan, *The Russian Fascists: Tragedy and Farce in Exile* (New York, 1978). Also see Johnston, 166, 179; Glad, 315.

[4]Johnston, 169.

[5]Sources differ as to the number of Russians in the French army during World War II. Scholars speculate that, aside from those of "Russia Abroad" who had been recruited into the French Foreign Legion in Turkey and the Balkans, between 3,700 and 10,000 Russians fought in the regular French army, mostly as volunteers. Others in the diaspora in France perished in the Resistance. See Glad, 313; Johnston, 169.

[6]G. Adamovich, "Bunin. Vospominaniia," *Novyi zhurnal*, No. 105 (1971), 130.

tempts to draft his name to the anti-Soviet cause or to have it appear in pro-German Russian publications.[7] He hid Jews from the Nazis; one, Alexander Bakhrakh, lived "underground" with the writer for almost the entire course of the war. Like Russians on both sides of the continent, Bunin suffered debilitating hunger, darkness, and cold. Like them, too, he followed the course of the war feverishly, first outraged that the Nazis had ravaged his ancestral haunts, then cheering the rout of the invaders in the homeland. The battle of Stalingrad consumed him for months on end. Speeches by Hitler and Mussolini evoked rebuke and scorn; from Churchill and Roosevelt, applause and hope.

Particularly moving to Bunin and others in the diaspora were their chance but intimate encounters with Soviet prisoners-of-war enrolled in the Wehrmacht. Soviet boys gazed upon Bunin with as much awe and bewilderment as they regarded General Denikin and others.[8] Initial awkwardness and suspicion, though, soon gave way to friendship and warmth. The Soviet youths who visited Bunin in Grasse became surrogate sons who tied him to Russia's past—and future. In a crucial and poignant way, therefore, the war years were for Bunin the worst—and best of his times.

The Allied victory may have ended war with the fascists, but it only triggered new conflicts for Bunin and "Russia Abroad." Russian exiles were quick to denounce one another as Nazi collaborators and the like.[9] They were also divided in their stance toward the homeland. To many exiles, the fact that Soviet Russia had not only been victorious in the conflict but that it had emerged as a superpower was proof that the country had undergone a fundamental change. More and more, old inflexibilities about the homeland bent and broke. Exile conservatives affirmed that when, during the war, Stalin had both reconciled with the Orthodox church and invoked the names of pre-Revolutionary warrior heroes, he was resurrecting the glorious past of the homeland. In

---

[7]Bunin also refused to publish his own works until after the Occupation.

[8]For instance, Ksenia Denikina, recalling the Soviet prisoners-of-war who gaped at her famous husband, wrote that all of the Russian motherland passed through her cottage. See Grey, 316.

[9]The wartime loyalties of Russians in France also came under increasing attack from the native population. Between April 1945 and October 1946 at least four thousand expatriates suffered reprisals as suspected collaborators of the Nazi regime. In the orgy, so-called White Russians were a convenient target for French Communists or anyone else who wished to establish healthy anti-Nazi credentials. Placards and signs in post-Liberation Paris proclaimed: "Frenchmen! Do not forget that your enemies are Germans, White Russians, and collaborators!" Berberova was tied up briefly and even threatened with hanging by a zealous Communist neighbor. Others suffered grimmer fates if only because they had been with the wrong nationality, in the wrong place, at the wrong time. See Berberova, 431–432; Johnston, 178, 225.

their view the Soviet Union was National Russia reborn: stronger, more beautiful, more united than ever. Exile liberals insisted that Russia would move from "nightmare" to "dream," that earlier mistakes and crimes would be compensated for or corrected, that native democracy would be fact, not fiction. Emigré Mensheviks asserted that the Soviet Union would capitalize on its socioeconomic system as well as its wartime experience to become the freest country in Europe. Either way, many exiles, believing that a new Russian dawn lay just beyond the Soviet horizon, looked eastward; they set aside decades-old anger and hurt to revere "our flag," "our national anthem," "our November 7th holiday," and "our Lenin as Russian patriot."

Even more stunning, perhaps, was the June 1944 appeal of Maklakov and other members of a "Russian Emigré Action Group," bidding expatriates to accept that "after all that has happened, the Russian emigration must recognize the Soviet government as a Russian government."[1] The group even ventured the unthinkable—that expatriates could someday return to the homeland! The emigré press in Paris applauded Maklakov and company, if only because, in the immediate postwar era, the pro-Soviet *Russian Patriot* (*Russkii patriot*) and *Russian News* (*Russkie novosti*) were the only Russian-language newspapers that were published in that city.[2] The author of an October 1944 editorial in *Russian Patriot* demanded that Russian emigrés hope for "maternal mercy from the homeland" and "submit to the Soviet collective." He added: "We must prepare ourselves to return to our ancestral home, to study and accept its customs and norms with every fiber of our being. We will also have to do everything in our power to reconstruct ourselves to become the new men and women created by the revolution. Otherwise we will merely trade the title of stateless exile for the fate of an 'inner emigré.' "[3]

Admiration and nostalgia for the Russia of the East, coupled with renewed poverty, loneliness, and despair in the Russia of the West, led many expatriates to see the grass as greener on the Soviet side. When exiles in France looked at their surroundings, they saw not only scorched earth but also the ground disappearing under their feet. Their numbers continued to decline: 66,000 in 1939, 55,000 in 1946, 35,000 in 1951.[4] And the center of gravity for "Russia Abroad" had

---

[1] Johnston, 172.
[2] In fact, it was not until April 1947 that the more openly anti-Soviet *Russian Thought* (*Russkaia mysl'*) began to appear.
[3] As quoted in Glad, 335.
[4] J. Vernant, *The Refugee in the Post-War World* (London, 1953), 257.

shifted westward. By the 1950s New York had replaced Paris as the political and cultural capital of the diaspora. More troublesome, perhaps, rumors that French leaders would help Soviet officials in repatriating Russians from East to West caused many exiles to consider applying for Soviet passports (read: loyalty tests to the Bolshevik regime) before they were removed forcibly from their homes. For whatever reason, everyone sensed that the emigration in Paris would soon belong to history.

To be sure, most of "Russia Abroad" remained unconvinced of a renaissance in the homeland. Stalin's renewed oppression at home and his brutal highhandedness in Eastern Europe cooled both patriotic fervor and yearnings for native haunts. "Second-wave" Russian emigrés, those who had escaped the homeland during the war, looked at these calls for reconciliation and return in shock and disbelief. And emigrés in America remained utterly defiant of any truce and relayed their anti-Soviet enmity to new audiences. Still, in the welter of mixed messages and emotions concerning the homeland, no one in the diaspora was sure as to where the "best" or "real" Russia lay.

Bunin also hoped that postwar Russia would experience a renewal; and he too was bitterly disappointed when his homeland continued on its Bolshevik path. To his greater chagrin, though, Bunin found himself embroiled in two controversies which tore apart what was left of "Russia Abroad." One was the 1946 opportunity for Russian emigrés to elect Soviet citizenship and/or return to the homeland. Although Bunin was surprisingly tolerant of expatriates who considered—and even chose—both options, he found that his (unwanted) status as a "man-god" among Russian exiles prevented him from even *speculating* about either possibility. Indeed, in the final years of his life, Bunin was hounded by rumors that were both unfounded and base, but that people who should have known better were all too willing to believe. Emigrés delighted to gossip that Bunin had "crossed over" to the Bolsheviks; that he had drunk to Stalin's health; that he had joined with "Red-loving" emigré writers and artists; that he had visited the Soviet embassy in Paris to request a passport from the ambassador there; that he had already visited the Soviet Union; that he was planning to spend his remaining years there.

It is true that Bunin considered, however briefly, a return to the country of his birth. Crushing poverty, coupled with daily struggles for food and medicine, had eroded his resolve both to stand firm against the Bolsheviks and to confront the vicissitudes of life. Calls from Russians on both sides of the border to return home cast him as a modern-day Christ, who, having spent twenty-five years in an exile "desert," was now tempted by visions of power, fame, and "mountains of gold."[5]

Bunin, however, watched closely both the *Zhdanovshchina* (a new wave of attacks on writers and artists in the homeland) as well as "official" attempts to "pirate" his works. He soon realized that if he returned to Russia he would not have the personal and creative freedom he demanded so vociferously, and that he would be merely exchanging one idol-like pedestal for another. He would be, variously, a man-god "in a mousetrap,"[6] a poster-boy "hero of the Soviet Union," and a gold-fettered ward-stooge of the state. More poignant, perhaps, Bunin realized that, even after twenty-five years of exile in the West, he could not forget the horrors of the past or cross the great gulf between him and the land of his birth. No matter how intimate his meetings with Soviet writers, reporters, and visitors, he knew he was "talking as though . . . everyone was trying to forget that a corpse lay in the neighboring room."[7] Sooner or later, like members of a dysfunctional family, Bunin and his Soviet confreres would drop all pretense to politeness and argue the merits of their sociopolitical worlds. The debate moved from issues of philosophy and freedom to the quality of wine, sausage, and vodka; but invariably it ended in rancor, not resolution. Whatever victories Bunin counted over his adversary were, at best, Pyrrhic. Even in the twilight of his life, he remained a "man without a country."

In addition to his burdensome position as a "man-god" and the political and social storms that whirled about him, Bunin was also overwhelmed by pressures from within. For one thing, he feared that he and his works would be consigned to oblivion. Although he constantly reminded family and friends of his laureate status, he also burdened them with premonitions that, after his death, he would soon be forgotten by the public.

In his own mind at least, he had sufficient evidence for such views. Only a year after being awarded the Nobel Prize, Bunin was shocked to see that his days had degenerated into "sadness, trifles, petty concerns, and frivolous correspondence," into a "life that was strange and idiotic beyond words."[8] Publishers showed little interest in his works or paid him pennies (or nothing) for what they accepted from

    [5]See Bunin's letter to Mark Aldanov, written on May 28, 1945, in A. Zweers, "Perepiska I. A. Bunina s M. A. Aldanovym," *Novyi zhurnal,* No. 150 (1983), 173.
    [6]See Bunin's missive to Yakov Polonsky, written on March 9, 1945, in V. Lavrov, *Kholodnaia osen'. Ivan Bunin v emigratsii (1920–1953). Roman-khronika* (Moscow, 1989), 330.
    [7]Um-El'-Banin, "V Parizhe posle voiny," *Slovo,* No. 10 (1990), 74.
    [8]A. Zweers, "Pis'ma I. A. Bunina k B. K. i V. A B. Zaitsevym, "*Novyi zhurnal,* No. 134 (1979), 180, 185.

him, often grudgingly. Writers and critics continued to misread his writings. The Soviets censured him, emigrés extolled him, and Westerners moved fitfully between the two extremes. There were several points of unanimity, though. Writers and critics cited Bunin's influence on native authors, for example Sholokhov at home, Nabokov abroad. They continued to applaud Bunin as a classicist and a Parnassian, and to acclaim his stylistic "filigrees,"[9] his word and mood paintings, and his memory of his youth and the homeland. Bunin, they said, was the "last representative of gentry-Russia"; his world was "so palpable . . . so 'at home' that one feels as if he were walking with Leo Tolstoy through the galleries of flesh-and-blood ancestors."[1] The critics also reiterated their love for Bunin's pagan sensuousness, the loving tenderness with which his eyes, ears, and hands caressed nature as well as the abject cruelty by which they tore into and dissected his characters.

Reviewers and readers, though, also continued to point out what they saw as Bunin's many faults. In their view, Bunin compared unfavorably to his predecessors. He was a literary lightweight—a "pigmy,"[2] Prince Mirsky called him—who accomplished only what others had already done. Soviet, emigré, and Western critics tended to stress what Bunin did *not* do in his fiction, rather than what he did. The "negatives" they ascribed to the writer and his art were overwhelming. Bunin, they said, had little imagination and lust for life. He wrote with his head, not his heart. He dwelled on top of mountains, not in the streets below. He cried, not laughed; he looked backward, not forward; he described and reflected, not challenged. He proclaimed "vanity of vanities," saw disaster in every horizon, and deemed the world and its people as dying or dead. In Bunin's poetry and prose, the critics continued, cold took precedence over warmth, peace over politics, and calm over storm. Burials eclipsed baptisms, and whimpers muted bangs.

For many readers and reviewers, Bunin had only two strong emotions. One was sex, his lovers thrashing about wildly before they killed themselves or each other. The other was his dire hatred of Bolshevik

---

[9] *Bol'shaia sovetskaia entsiklopedia*, vol. 6 (Moscow, 1951), 289.

[1] A. Lavren'tev, "O tvorchestve I. A. Bunina," *Vrata*, No. 1 (1934), 181; Kaun, 145. Given such sentiments, it is not surprising that emigré critics such as Gleb Struve saw Bunin's death in 1953 as signaling an end to "first wave" Russian literature, even though such writer-exiles as Zaitsev, Remizov, Stepun, Adamovich, Ivanov, Berberova, and others continued to write well into the 1950s, 1960s and, in some cases, beyond. See G. Struve, *Russkaia literatura v izgnanii* (New York, 1956), 5.

[2] N. Strelsky, "Bunin: Eclectic of the Future," *South Atlantic Quarterly*, No. 3 (1936), 276.

Russia. Whenever he spoke of the land of the Soviets, "his baritone broke into a falsetto; his grey eyes . . . shot ire; his noble nose twisted and wrinkled; and his delectable sense of humor forsook him utterly."[3] Simply put, Bunin and his art personified a land and a tradition that had been relegated to the dustbin of history, that were interesting only as museum artifacts of how Russians had once lived, thought, and wrote.

Akin to his dread of oblivion, Bunin also had to deal with threats to his well-being. Age-old enemies—poverty, isolation, boredom, sickness, old age, and death—pursued him doggedly, banishing happiness and peace. "A dog should not have to live the way I do," he complained bitterly on April 21, 1940.[4] The considerable sum that he had received for his Nobel Prize disappeared within less than a year, the result of previous debt, indiscriminate charity, and faulty investment. He complained bitterly of loneliness, of his "wasted" youth and life, of his few and fleeting joys, and of his early writings which, he never tired of saying, he wrote in haste or from need. He was also consumed by fears that enemies would destroy him; that biographers and scholars would misrepresent his life and art; that death would take his wife from him. It was no exaggeration when he told family and friends that a "terrible and repulsive life"[5] had turned him into a "dried-up fig tree," a Biblical Job, and Tolstoy's Ivan Ilyich and Kholostomer: an "old gelding wearing laurels."[6]

As for his health, Bunin was not unlike the hypochondriac who, on his gravestone, insisted that he had been ill. Every sneeze and sniffle filled him with mortal fear. Bouts of insomnia, anemia, and asthma hammered new nails into his coffin. Even worse were episodes of weakness, fainting, and chest pain when he sensed both his nothingness and his entry into the existential void. There was also death. Daily Bunin raged against his ultimate end. He panicked over arms that were spotted, flabby, or cold. He lamented the places he would never visit as well as the little time he believed he had left on earth. To family and friends he talked of his imminent "deathly grotesqueness,"[7] of his body rotting and ravaged by worms. Visiting cemeteries, he fixated over

[3]Kaun, 146.
[4]M. Grin, "Iz dnevnikov I. A. Bunina," *Novyi zhurnal*, No. 111 (1973), 144.
[5]Grin, *Ustami*, 18.
[6]Iu. Shumakov, ed., *Poslednee svidanie. Materialy o poseshchenii I. A. Buninym Pribalti-iskikh gosudarstv v 1938 gody* (Estonia, 1992), 202; A. Bakhrakh, *Bunin v khalate. Po pamiati, po zapisiam* (Bayville, N.J., 1979), 15; V. Zenzinov, "Zapisi. Besedy s I. A. Buninym," *Novyi zhurnal*, No. 81 (1965), 271.
[7]G. Adamovich, "Bunin. Vospominaniia," *Novyi zhurnal*, No. 105 (1971), 133.

such "vile things as the coffin and the sprinkling of earth on the lid."[8] Left to his own devices, he lay on couches and beds and assumed various corpselike positions. In no way would Bunin go gently into the night. Imagining himself on a scaffold awaiting execution, he promised to spend his final moments "letting out such a howl . . . twisting and turning . . . and acting so demonically possessed that even the hangman's hair would stand up on end!"[9]

To be sure, Bunin did fight off poverty, sickness, old age, and death with gusto and verve. Memoirists, often in surprise and admiration, recall how Bunin could "reinvent" himself at will, how before their eyes he could become the man of his youth. Even at seventy years of age, he could appear as a "most chaste little boy."[1] When Bunin was feeling feisty and spry, he refused to look, act, or feel his age. "Radiating endless youth,"[2] he lost his wrinkles, stood erect, and walked with a lively gait. He vaunted his x-ray vision and cameralike eyes, teaching family and friends how "to see" and constructing entire "biographies" from the style of a woman's hat or the veins on her legs.

Bunin also checked his physical and spiritual decline by reveling in his surroundings and proclaiming his love of life. Even when starving he could delight in a blooming tree, a fiery skyline, a beckoning moon. Even when he saw himself as life's prisoner, he could transcend his very being. Small pleasures—an ample meal, unexpected arrivals of money, and gift packages from friends—sent him into near ecstasy. Self-proclaimed ties to nature, the seasons, and the universe mingled with self-extolled bonds to his homeland, ancestors, even wild beasts. Memories of writers and artists, of trips around the world, and of life in Russia and in early exile allowed him to deny time and space, to assuage the harshness of his present, to bless and laugh at existence, and to beg God for more time on earth. Bunin had no trouble mixing generations. With paternal tenderness he exhorted young writers to excellence in their craft. Often with his wife in view, he flirted with young women, insisting on rendezvous in Venice and Paris.

Bunin also extended his happiness and his life by embarking on a singular course of action. Sensitive to the cares and concerns of latter-day "Russia Abroad," he championed the memory of Russian culture,

[8]A. Baboreko, "Pis'ma k M. V. Karamzinoi, 1937–1940," in V. Shcherbina *et al.*, eds., *Literaturnoe nasledstvo. Kniga pervaia* (Moscow, 1973), 687.
[9]A. Zweers, "Perepiska I. A. Bunina s M. A. Aldanovym," *Novyi zhurnal*, No. 154 (1984), 100.
[1]Umm-El-Banine Assadoulaeff, 75.
[2]S. Pregel', "Iz vospominanii o Bunine," in Shcherbina, *Kniga vtoraia*, 353.

particularly its language and literature. He believed that beyond his status as a Nobel laureate, he had impressive credentials for such a task. To one and all, he proclaimed his liberties as a gentry aristocrat, his observations as a student of life, his adventures as a world traveler, even his experiences as a Don Juan with a singular knowledge of women and love. With moral righteousness, if not indignation, Bunin declared that he had been one of the few writers to have been right about pre-Revolutionary Russia, its "masters," and its "men," as well as the terrible fate that awaited all three. Finally, Bunin assumed the mantle of Russian cultural memory by claiming kinship not only with the "classical" tradition of Pushkin, Turgenev, and Tolstoy but with the more restless writings of Lermontov, Tyutchev, and Gogol. Such writers, he insisted, tied him to Russia, to its people, and, most important, to the worlds of his fathers and forefathers.

Bunin sought to safeguard the memory of Russian culture in three ways. He continued to write in the idiom, tone, and orthography of gentry Russian. If the voices of Bunin's literary colleagues grew fainter, his continued strong and clear. Even in his twilight years, Bunin boasted that he "had been seized by something divine,"[3] and that he "always had something in [his] head, i.e., [he] still had to finish writing something, or to say something that [he] had written in a better way, or describe something that [he] had experienced or witnessed sometime in [his] life."[4]

In his later years Bunin reworked earlier stories and poems. He published new works: *The Liberation of Tolstoy* (*Osvobozhenie Tolstogo*, 1937), *Dark Alleys* (*Temnye allei*, 1946), and *Memories* (*Vospominaniia*, 1950)[5] being among his most important creations. Memories of the homeland continued to be dear to him, but other images and ideas entered into his purview. In his twilight years he now pursued a theme long dear to his heart, the tangled if deadly web of sex, love, and death. In *Dark Alleys* Bunin pursued what Boris Zaitsev called "all that between-the-legs stuff"[6] with such boldness and daring that critics called him a "dirty old man" and publishers feared printing his works. But he composed with his customary precision and care. He wrote multiple

---

[3]See Bunin's diary excerpt of February 24, 1943, in M. Grin, "Iz dnevnikov I. A. Bunina," *Novyi zhurnal*, No. 116 (1971), 168.

[4]A. Bakhrakh, "Bunin i 'Okhota na Kavkaze'," *Po pamiati, po zapisiam. Literaturnye portrety* (Paris, 1980), 17.

[5]Bunin was not alone in writing his memories for posterity. At various times, Nabokov, Adamovich, Stepun, Zaitsev, and Berberova also recorded their experiences of "times gone by."

[6]M. Grin, "Pis'ma B. K. Zaitseva I. i V. Buninym," *Novyi zhurnal*, No. 146 (1982), 123.

drafts and agonized over every word. Even punctuation marks caused him tribulation and torment.

Bunin also sought to preserve the memory of Russian culture by constructing a highly personal canon of writers and works which he hoped that posterity would consider and accept. Into his hallowed halls were welcomed almost all the major writers of the nineteenth century, with Pushkin, Lermontov, and Tolstoy at their head. Excluded from Bunin's roster, though, was a notable and long-standing enemy: Dostoevsky. As far as Bunin was concerned, the writer of *Crime and Punishment* "should be thrown overboard . . . to the sharks." His novels were "third-rate" and filled with "rain, slush, fog, and staircases that smell of cats." "Three-quarters" of *The Brothers Karamazov* was "the most absolute pulp fiction and farce."[7] Bunin's hatred of Dostoevsky was so intense that two years before he died he told Bakhrakh: "If I live and God gives me the strength, I will hurl Dostoevsky from his pedestal!"[8]

From his personal canon, Bunin also excluded what he saw as Dostoevsky's bastard progeny: the Symbolists, Futurists, and others of the Russian avant-garde. To many exiles in the final days of "Russia Abroad," Bunin's enmity toward the Modernists bordered on the pathological. Much of what he said about these writers was exaggerated, mean-spirited, and wrong. For instance, Bely was insane, Babel was blasphemous, and Remizov was "ludicrous and unbearable."[9] Nabokov and Blok were "clowns," Esenin was a "hack," and Berberova was a "sea-slug."[1] Collectively the Modernists were for Bunin "moral monsters" who, like Dostoevsky's villains, believed that "all was permitted" in both literature and life. Without the slightest twinge of conscience, they had applauded the Revolution and its savagery; without similar standards or scruples, they had carried their hooliganism, profanity, and arrogance directly into their art.

Bunin's hatred of the Russian avant-gardists is mitigated, though, when one considers the motives for his stance. Doubtless he was not

---

[7]See Bunin's diary entry of July 1, 1942, in M. Grin, "Iz dnevnikov I. A. Bunina," *Novyi zhurnal*, No. 115 (1971), 154; Odoevsteva, 348.

[8]A. Bakhrakh, "Po pamiati, po zapiskam (II) . . . ," *Mosty*, No. 12 (1966), 273. Bunin was not alone in his dislike of Dostoevsky. Many emigré readers and reviewers saw the writer as a "sick genius" whom they condemned for his morbid introspection, his political conservatism, his "unhealthy" probing into human psychology, and his long and short works which, in their opinion, were difficult, turgid, and artless. Many exiles also feared that since Dostoevsky personified for the West the somber and inscrutable Russian "soul," they too would be seen as irrational and deranged.

[9]A. Meshcherskii, "Neizvestnye pis'ma I. Bunina," *Russkaia literatura*, No. 4 (1961), 154.

[1]See A. Sedykh, *Dalekie, blizkie* (New York, 1962), 230; Bakhrakh, *Bunin v khalate*, 92, 110; Odoevtseva, 349.

only jealous of the success of Blok, Bely, and others in fiction but also angry that, because of their collective triumph, he "had not found a genuine place [in the national written expression] in his time."[2] More admirably, Bunin resisted the Modernists because he wished to sustain what he saw as the "purity" of Russian language and literature. He wrote to the critic Pyotr Bitsilli, on May 16, 1936: "Remizov is creating dictionaries of the most abominable Russian, of a language that has never existed nor can exist. He keeps making up the most vile and stupid words to boot. For this alone, one should hate him."[3] Eight years later Bunin confided to his diary: "I have been reading Zoshchenko's 1937 stories. They are monotonous and poor. . . . Not for nothing does he use such a wretched, half-savage language, for this is the tongue of . . . what Russia has become."[4] Even the new orthography was seen by Bunin as corrupting oral and written speech. "How should one write in the new orthography?" Bunin wrote to Georgy Adamovich on July 10, 1951. "How should one pronounce it? . . . Whom is this Russian writing destined to please? Stalin? The De-Pe—those motherfuckers who see themselves as belonging to a most talented people? . . . *Not a single* people has allowed such baseness in its language!"[5] Like many of his generation, Bunin believed that Russian language and literature were the time-honored repository of national consciousness and values. In his view, therefore, any attempt to tamper with them, even in artful or playful ways, would constrain or perhaps even suffocate the very spirit of *l'âme russe* and all that it represented to Russia and the world.

Finally, Bunin preserved the memory of Russian language and literature by correcting what he saw as the many misconceptions surrounding national writers and their works. In so doing, he echoed his own experience as a Nobel laureate. That is, he strove to portray his fellow artists not as man-gods but as simple mortals with everyday sorrows, weaknesses, and joys. He dismissed as hype and verbiage the monumentality and "personality cults" that reviewers and readers had built around such writers as Gorky and Alexei Tolstoy at home, and abroad Merezhkovsky, Gippius, and others.

In depicting Russian writers as mortals, Bunin was also quick to point out what he saw as the weaknesses of their writing. For instance, he considered Kuprin's writing often trite. Although he admired

[2]N. Berberova, *Kursiv moi*, vol. 1 (New York, 1983), 298.
[3]Meshcherskii, 155.
[4]Grin, "Iz dnevnikov I. A. Bunina," No. 116, 174.
[5]July 10, 1951, A. Zweers, "Pis'ma I. A. Bunina k G. V. Adamovichu, *Novyi zhurnal*, No. 110 (1973), 173–174.

Chekhov for his short stories, he took the writer to task for his plays, particularly for what he saw as the "errors" of situation and type in *The Cherry Orchard*. And even on his deathbed he criticized Tolstoy for the "many unnecessary and unartistic pages" in *Resurrection*.[6]

The deepest tragedy of Bunin's life was that he did not live to see the collapse of communism in the half-century or so after his death. If he had, he would have taken righteous satisfaction that, as the cultural spokesman for "Russia Abroad," he had survived revolution, war, and exile to see the land of his birth throw off a seventy-five-year legacy of misery and oppression, and experiment with democracy and its many-faceted promises for the individual and society. Bunin knew that socialism would not survive in his homeland. In the remaining moments of his life, though, all he could do was come to grips with the meaning of his existence and reflect upon why fate had dealt him so many wonderful and terrible hands. Feeling "his soul separating from his body,"[7] Bunin wondered if he, his works, and the memory of "patriarchal" Russia would be enshrined or forgotten. Always hoping against hope, Bunin chose the former, content that, like his character Bernard, he had been a "good sailor"[8] in the many swells and storms of his life. He had reason to do so. Three days before his death, Bunin lay in bed, listening to his wife reading aloud a glowing article about him in a student journal. A new generation, it seemed, was "going into raptures over his works."[9] But, like everything else in Bunin's life, the delight in such accolades was short-lived, if only because the focus of the piece was "Temir-Aksak-Khan," a story which Bunin had written more than thirty years earlier. In it a poor Tatar sings about an old prince:

"Never in the universe was there a mightier and more famous prince than Temir-Aksak-Khan. . . . Maidens died to be his slave. . . .

"But, Temir-Aksak-Khan! Where are your days and deeds now? Where are your battles and victories? Where are they, the young, tender, jealous ones who loved you? Where are the eyes that shone like black suns from your bed? . . .

"Ah, Temir-Aksak-Khan, where is your bitter wisdom now? Where are the torments of your soul . . . the honey of your earthly delusions? . . .

"And, right before his end, Temir-Aksak-Khan sat in ashes . . .

[6]Bakhrakh, 161.
[7]Sedykh, 244.
[8]See I. Bunin, "Bernar," in I. Bunin, *Sobranie sochinenii v deviati tomakh*, vol. 7 (Moscow, 1966), 346. Bunin wrote this story in 1952.
[9]M. Aldanov, "O Bunine," *Novyi zhurnal*, No. 35 (1953), 134.

and kissed the rags of cripples and beggars. 'Tear out my soul,' he said to them, *'for I no longer have even the desire to want!'* "

Muromtseva-Bunina later reported that when she read the last sentence to Bunin, he began to cry. She did not explain her husband's tears. Was it sadness that he would never see his homeland again? Or frustration that his desire to live forever would not come to pass? Was it fear that the grave he had fought all his life now yawned before him? Or relief that his difficult journey on this earth was coming to an end? Was it happiness that he had discerned the secrets of existence and that, for almost seventy years, had imparted his knowledge and insights to the world? Or anger that life was for him still a riddle and a cruel joke? With Bunin it is safe to say that his tears reflected all these sensibilities—as they would any individual who, facing his end, had lived the life that Bunin did.

Ivan Bunin
The Twilight of Emigré Russia, 1934–1953

PART ONE

Returning to Genesis
1934–1938

BUNIN IN PARIS

In 1934 Stalin celebrated his tenth year as ruler of the Bolshevik state. In his own mind at least, he had many reasons to rejoice. He had transformed a chronically dysfunctional nation into a leading industrial power. He had completed one five-year plan and was beginning a second. He had mechanized agriculture, built railroads and dams, and increased the production of coal, steel, and oil. Advances in education, science, and health rivaled innovations in art, literature, and film. To a world in political and economic free-fall, Stalin seemed to have fashioned "paradise" on earth. Like a modern-day Christ, he had resurrected "dead" workers and peasants into "newly born" (read: Soviet) men and women; he had built a "socialist" heaven on the ruins of a "capitalist" hell.

Like many in "Russia Abroad," however, Bunin saw the Soviet Eden as sacrilege, not salvation. Where many Westerners discounted the human misery of the Soviet Union as a cost of socialist success, Bunin lamented the destruction which, he believed, modern-day Mongols were wreaking on his land. As a Nobel laureate, Bunin redoubled his opposition to the Bolshevik state. Politically he was a libertarian and a citizen of the world. Socially he was an aristocrat and a gentryman. Professionally he was an artist who also saw Russia as a "paradise" but one that recalled the innocence of Adam and Eve, not the demagoguery of Stalin and the new Bolshevik state.

However begrudgingly, critics—emigré, Western, and even Soviet—applauded Bunin's vision. Although they often censured him for his political, social, and aesthetic views, they relished his Edenic pictures not only of Russia but of the universe. Perhaps the critics were unnerved by the marriage of socialism and science that had seized humankind. Perhaps they saw the "brave new world" of the Soviets as too sterile and bleak. Perhaps they were distressed that ideology had taken precedence over intuition, and that mind had triumphed over body and soul.

Whatever the reason, the critics reveled in Bunin's pictures of primordial peace and quiet. They basked in the light of his dawns and rested in the shade of his twilights. They took heart in the stability of Bunin's world, particularly the cycles of his seasons. Modern life was for them hollow and chaotic; but Bunin's poetry and prose vaunted the timeless passage of icy winters and verdant springs, and of lush summers and fiery autumns on sparkling rivers and lakes and on boundless forests and fields.

Like many of Bunin's family and friends, the critics entered into his probing view of life and learned how to see and hear, smell and touch anew. The musical whirl of a bird in flight and the smooth skin of a horse thrilled their senses; humble forget-me-nots and the wings of a beetle made them thankful for existence; the restless whispering of the sea and the sensuous aromas of pears and acacias flooded their hearts with memories of youth and of "first love."

Bunin, the critics believed, had penetrated the mysteries of existence; by memory and myth he had traveled back through time and had found the home of Adam and Eve. There, as a new "first man," he had meditated on life before the Fall and was at one with God and nature. Let others sing hymns to progress and technology, the critics agreed; it was Bunin's destiny to worship the Creator, to portray a sound and stable world, and to sing psalms of joy, hope, and love. What a pity, they lamented, that more people did not read Bunin; for, if they did, their world—public and private—might be a better place.

✳ 1934 ✳

Circa 1934
Vladimir Zenzinov, from his memoirs

[Bunin said:] "Do you wish to know my spiritual genealogy? Well, this is something that I myself do not know or even understand. I have often heard the opinion that I have descended from Turgenev and Tolstoy.[1] But why from them? After all, there was Pushkin, there was Lermontov and Gogol. . . . How can one track the influence of one writer on another? . . . What is important is that everyone has his own note—how this note develops and grows, how it is influenced not only by literature but also by life. . . .

"Of course, no matter how independent a writer may be, one can always find similarities between him and another writer. People without kith or kin do not exist. In a child one finds resemblances to his father, mother, grandfather, and grandmother. . . . He bears an affinity to all of them . . . but he is also a unique individual. In such a way, perhaps, Tolstoy and Turgenev have influenced me. But why not Gogol? I have loved Gogol since childhood; he has always been a part of me. Even now I still recite by heart passages from 'Old World Landowners' and 'The Terrible Vengeance.'[2] Such stories have always moved me, right to the present day. . . . One can see Gogol's influence in the way I structured certain phrases . . . in *The Gentleman from San Francisco* and . . . in other of my works at that time. . . .

"Tolstoy is a greater writer than Dostoevsky. . . . I have never liked Dostoevsky. I have reread Gogol, Pushkin, Turgenev, and Tolstoy

---

[1]There are two Tolstoys in the narrative: Alexei Nikolaevich Tolstoy (1883–1945), Soviet writer, and Lev Nikolaevich Tolstoy (1828–1910), the great novelist.
[2]Gogol wrote "The Terrible Vengeance" ("*Strashnaia mest'*") in 1830–1831, and "Old World Landowners" ("*Starosvetskie pomeshchniki*") in 1835.

(without end!). I have even reread Chekhov. But I have never had an urge to reread Dostoevsky. . . . My brother, Yuly, once told me: 'When you grow up, you will read Dostoevsky. And you will be so enthralled with what you are reading that you will not be able to take your eyes away from the book!' But while still a boy, and with a sinking heart, I began reading *The Brothers Karamazov*.[3] . . . But what was this? This was Dostoevsky? The first 150 pages focused on how Fyodor Ivanovich argued without end. . . .

"People who include me in the Pushkin tradition [of Russian literature] are correct in their view. . . . Pushkin begins the healthiest and most genuine line in Russian writing. Europeans are surprised if they encounter a Russian writer who is even, clear, and bright. But does not Pushkin embrace all of these qualities? . . . He embodies simplicity, nobility, freedom, health, intelligence, tact, measure, and taste.

"Did I ever try to imitate Pushkin? Of course. But who among us has not tried to do such a thing? . . . Even as a child, I sought to copy his handwriting. . . . Many times in my life I had a passionate urge to write something in the manner of Pushkin, a piece that would be splendid, well constructed, and free, and that would arise from both my feelings of love and kinship for him as well as from the wondrous feelings that God often gives us in life. . . .

"One time, during a summer stay in the woods around Pskov,[4] I felt as though Pushkin was with me day and night. Fervidly I wrote poetry all day long, imagining that everything I was writing I would lay before Pushkin's feet with feelings of great peace as well as of fear and my unworthiness before him. . . . Another time was on a wonderful summer day at an estate in Oryol.[5] I remember it as though it were yesterday. . . . I was rereading *The Tales of Belkin*,[6] and I was so moved by their charm that I could not go on reading. Right away I wanted to write something . . . from Pushkin's time. I threw down the book, jumped out of the window, and for a long time lay in the grass. In fear and joy I waited for something to emerge from that powerful work that had filled my heart and imagination. In endless happiness I felt that my entire being was tied to this summer village day, to this garden, to the entire native world of my fathers, grandfathers, and of all those people from those far-off Pushkin days. . . .

"When did Pushkin enter into me? When did I come to know

---

[3]Dostoevsky's *The Brothers Karamazov* (*Brat'ia Karamazovy*) appeared in 1880.
[4]Pskov is a city some four hundred miles northwest of Moscow.
[5]Oryol is a city approximately two hundred miles southwest of Moscow.
[6]Pushkin wrote *The Tales of Belkin* (*Povesti Belkina*) in 1830.

and love him? But then when did Russia enter into me? When did I come to know and love its sky, its air, its sun, the members of my family, and all those who are close to me?

"From the beginning of my existence, Pushkin has been with me in a special way. I first heard his name when I was a child. I came to know him not from a teacher or in school but from the very milieu from which I had emerged. At that time Pushkin was talked about constantly; his verse was repeated without end. He was the subject of conversation . . . with my father, mother, and brothers. In fact, one of my earliest memories was the way my mother read *Ruslan and Lyudmilla*,[7] in a manner that was slow, affectionate, and old-fashioned. . . .

"Several critics see me as a cruel and gloomy writer; but such an opinion is both inaccurate and unjust. Of course, in my travels throughout the world, and in my observations of human life, I have found much honey but still more bile. When I portrayed Russia, I already had a vague premonition of its imminent fate. But am I to blame that reality validated my misgivings beyond all measure? Is it my fault that the picture of folk life which I drew [in my works] and which, at that time, seemed to Russians to be so gloomy and extreme was true even as people were denying it?

"Do these portraits, though, show that my soul is full of gloom and despair? Not at all! 'Like a deer thirsting for water, my soul thirsts for you, O Lord!' "[8]

Circa 1934 and later
Zinaida Shakovskaya, from her memoirs

I first met Bunin [at a banquet in Brussels]. . . . To my surprise, and despite my youth, I was seated next to him at the banquet table. As usual, Bunin was both charming and restrained. After several toasts to "The Great Writer of the Russian Land" . . . I learned . . . why I had been asked to sit next to him. None of the organizers of the affair had ever read Bunin . . . so they decided to seat me next to him in case he began to talk about his writings. . . .

[Several years later] I was riding with Bunin in a cab in Paris. . . . When we got out, the merry-faced Russian driver said: "How pleasant it has been for me to serve as a chauffeur for the pride of our emigration. I was truly spellbound by your conversation! How well you know our Russian language!" He refused to take a tip. . . .

[7]Pushkin's *Ruslan and Lyudmilla* was published in 1820.
[8]Bunin is citing from Psalm 42:1–2.

[Another time] at a restaurant, the waiter was unable to serve a first course. Ivan Alexeevich winced in a squeamish way and demanded that he be served something. This was not the first time I had been host to Bunin's shenanigans; so right away I said to him: "If you are going to act up, I am leaving immediately, and you will have to eat alone. You always behave like this!"

Without getting the least bit angry, Bunin replied: "My, aren't you the stern one today! How you scold a Nobel laureate!" He cheered up right away and began eating. . . .

Things, though, did not improve, because I had allowed myself to attack Bunin's idol, "Tolstoy himself."

"Tolstoy is a brilliant writer," I said, "when he does not think, he is a genius. But I am afraid that Tolstoy is not all that intelligent."

Pushing back his plate, Bunin looked at me severely.

"Do you realize that you are raising your paw . . . to the greatest writer of all time?"

[I replied:] "As soon as Tolstoy begins to philosophize, he stops writing what he sees and feels, and his artistic sense disappears. Even you are much more intelligent than Tolstoy. . . . After all, you do not pass yourself off as a teacher of life."

"Yes, that is true. I do not want to teach anyone anything. Anything else?"

"You render all your thoughts with aesthetic taste. Say, for instance, that you opposed church ritual and that did not believe in religious mysteries. Would you ever use the same blasphemous words that Tolstoy did,[9] ones that are more suited to some Demyan Bednyi than a greater writer?[1]

"I would not have written such a thing," Bunin said. . . .

---

[9]Shakovskaya is referring to Tolstoy's novel *Resurrection* (*Voskresenie*, 1899), particularly his celebration of the Mass as a monstrous farce, a scene which served as the impetus for the Russian Holy Synod to issue an edict of excommunication against the writer in February 1901.

For instance, portraying communion, Tolstoy wrote: "The priest lifted the napkin covering the plate, cut the central piece of bread into four parts, dipped it in wine, and put it in his mouth. He was supposed to be eating a piece of the body of God and drinking a mouthful of his blood. . . . [Later] he carried the goblet behind the partition where he proceeded to eat up all the little pieces of God's body and drink the remaining blood. Then he carefully sucked on his moustache, wiped his mouth, cleaned the cup, and, feeling very chipper, strode resolutely forth, the thin soles of his calfskin boots creaking smartly." See D. Leon, *Tolstoy: His Life and Work* (London, 1944), 297; and H. Troyat, *Tolstoy* (Garden City, N.Y. 1967), 544.

[1]Shakovskaya has in mind such pieces as Bednyi's 1925 caustic religious tract, "A Flawless New Testament by Demyan the Evangelist" ("*Novyi zavet bez iz'iana evangelista Dem'iana*").

Bunin once said: "Have you ever been to Venice? No? Well, you and I should go there sometime and see how charming it is . . . the lagoons, the gondolas. . . ."

I burst out laughing. "If I were to go on a romantic escapade," I replied, "I would have to be in love with the person . . . and it would be with a young man, not a Nobel laureate. . . ."

Bunin changed the topic quickly. . . .

We talked about Russian writers in Paris. Like other writers of his generation, Bunin did not like a single "young" author. Also, he was offended by the fact that the new generation of [Russian emigré] writers had no intention of becoming students . . . of the older ones. . . .

"What about Sirin-[Nabokov]?" I asked.

"He is a monster, but a genuine writer," Bunin immediately replied. . . .

"(Sirin once called Bunin 'Lekseevich Nobelevsky.')"

1934
Andrei Bely, from his book, Between Two Revolutions
I have studied Bunin's brilliant talent. He really is the enemy.

1934
Alexander Kuprin, from a letter to Ivan Bunin
You cannot imagine how, in this moment of sharp and bitter need, your wondrous five thousand francs, your brotherly help, have come to the rescue.

January 1934
An emigré reviewer, from an article
Bunin! . . . Is there a place or person that does not know his name? Who among us Russians does not turn to him . . . so that we can catch but even a small ray . . . of his acknowledged glory, so that each of us can say with pleasure: "I, too, am a Russian!" . . . Indeed, in our present time when our joys are few . . . we turn to Bunin . . . and thank him for the fact that he alone inspires and unites us.

January 19, 1934
Maxim Gorky, from an article
At a meeting of the State Institute for Artistic Literature . . . F. I. Panfyorov stated . . . that Soviet critics prefer to discuss the language of Bunin, Tolstoy, and other Russian classical writers, and to ignore the language of the revolution.

February 1934
An emigré critic, from a review

As for Bunin's being the legitimate heir to the mantle of Tolstoy, the question can be safely dismissed. Tolstoy never received the Nobel Prize.

February 8, 1934
Ivan Bunin, from a letter to Gleb Struve

I have received a letter from Hogarth Press[2]—this time signed by Leonard [Woolf] himself!—saying that he wishes to continue publishing my works in English. . . . Again I propose a small book consisting of *Dry Valley* and "On the Way" ("Two Stories").[3] . . .

February 15, 1934
Boris Zaitsev, from a letter to Ivan Bunin

I am glad that you are getting back to normal. . . .

Here in Paris we have been having all kinds of political unrest[4]. . . . Monday there were strikes . . . and the Communists set up barricades not far from here. There were clashes . . . and a lathe operator was killed. . . . [A friend] says that fascism is coming. . . .

February 25, 1934
A reviewer, from the New York Times Book Review

Like all that Ivan Alexeevich Bunin, the Russian winner of the Nobel Prize for 1933, writes, *The Well of Days*[5] will endure not only in Russian literature, but also in world fiction as an example of consummate and highly original art. . . .

In the inimitable portrayal of Arseniev's father, a full-blooded, life-loving, whimsical, and good-natured nobleman of the old school, who smilingly and thoughtlessly drifts toward ruin, one immediately

---

[2]Hogarth Press was founded by Virginia and Leonard Woolf in 1917. As regards Russian writers, it published translations of Chekhov, Dostoevsky, Gorky, Andreev, and Olesha, along with Bunin's *The Life of Arseniev: The Well of Days* in 1933 and several collections of his works, e.g., *The Gentleman from San Francisco and Other Stories* in 1922 and 1934, and *The Grammar of Love* in 1935.

[3]The proposed book never came to be.

[4]Zaitsev is referring to the vicious street riots which took place in Paris on February 6, 1934, when such anti-republican groups as *Action Française* and the *Croix de Feu* attacked the government for widespread corruption and graft. In the melee, police fired on the mobs, killing fourteen and injuring more than two hundred. Although the authorities soon had the situation under control, the unrest spurred widespread political disaffection as well as new antagonism between rightist and leftist groups.

[5]*The Well of Days* was the title of the English translation of *The Life of Arseniev*.

identifies Bunin's father; and, in the decaying estates in Central Russia, with their typical, sad, and poetical atmosphere of the last traces of ancestral glory drowning in progressive impoverishment, in which Arseniev spends his childhood and youth, are the estates in which Bunin grew up; and, in the youthful Arseniev, tortured already at the age of 16 by the insatiable thirst for literary self-expression, there is very much of Bunin, the creator. . . .

Images of the Russian countryside and the nature of the indolent, easygoing life on the Arsenievs' manor; a gallery of masterfully painted provincial Russian types, from nobles to servants and peasants; little Arseniev's infancy, his games, his horseback rides and early meditations; and finally, the awakening of sex in him and his early romances—such are some of the items in the material of which the book is contrived. The author's narrative is rich in digressions; the aging Arseniev not only tells the story of his boyhood, but also comments and philosophizes upon it, on Russia, and on life in general. . . .

Bunin is an unsurpassed artist-sensualist. . . . For instance, he tells us how, in infancy, Arseniev caught . . . his first beetle; he describes its smooth, lacquered wing-cases, its busy bustle in the boy's tiny fingers, and finally, its humming flight; and, yet, out of this accurate, simple description, the feeling of the intense joy of life and the picture of the boy's greedy, astonished mind are born in a flash. *The Well of Days* is replete with the odors of the Russian soil, with colors, fragrances, life-sap; on closing the book, one remembers it as a feast of senses.

Equally impressive are the psychological qualities of the book. When Bunin describes his hero's infancy, one has an almost physical feeling of the child's first flashes of consciousness and of the mysterious process of the emergence of the human soul from the prenatal darkness. . . . Further, the sensual joy of Bunin's descriptions contrasts with the thought, or feeling, of the vanity of all things earthly and of the insignificance of man before time and nature. Life, to Bunin, is at once "a supreme joy" and a "supreme suffering." . . .

Arseniev looks at his youth from afar—from very far, indeed. He is calm and reserved. Yet an overwhelming nostalgic effect, a sadness of years irretrievably gone by, pervades the story. *The Well of Days* is an autobiography, a book of memoirs; yet, above all, it is, like most of Bunin's works, first-class poetry, told in the form of sober realistic prose.

February 26, 1934
Mark Aldanov, from a letter to Vera Muromtseva-Bunina

Everyone is doing poorly. It seems that I am the only writer who is making a living by his craft.

March 10, 1934
Vera Muromtseva-Bunina, from a letter to a friend

The doctor has determined that because of everything I have gone through . . . not all my organs are working as they should. . . .

Major and minor distresses continue to afflict me. My only surviving brother[6] is seriously ill. . . . Anything can happen [to him]. . . .

As for minor problems—these I already foresaw when I asked the Committee[7] (to whom Ian has given money from his Nobel Prize) for a small amount of funds to be placed at my disposal. . . . Just the other day, he sent them an additional 1,700 francs. I find all this very burdensome since I . . . know what should be done [with this money]. Sometimes I have to be very calculating, something I also find difficult. It is not in my character to count pennies, but I do not have any money of my own and Ian gives me barely enough to get by. . . .

I am telling you all of this . . . because I know that you sympathize with my request that the Committee give me some money—something its members have not done. Rather, having turned their backs on me, they encourage Ian to think that money is the only thing I ever think about and that I am out to ruin him completely.

There is no court of law to deal with [such a situation].

I do, though, have one piece of news: a new radio, and a marvelous one at that. It brings wonderful entertainment into our quiet, humdrum life. . . .

Zaitsev has been visiting here. He has written a very interesting book on Ian's writing.[8] We listened to it for four evenings in a row. . . . Ian liked it very much. He is becoming his old self again, even better than he has been. He finds it hard to tear himself away from the radio,

---

[6]Dmitri Nikolaevich Muromstev remained in Russia; he died on September 23, 1937. Vera's other brother, Pavel, committed suicide on November 12, 1933.

[7]Bunin's chronic inability to handle money, together with his concern for his colleague-writers, as well as his dismay over the 2,000 or so requests for relief from Russian emigrés throughout the world, led him to donate 120,000 francs, or roughly 20 percent of the money he had received from his Nobel Prize to a special committee to consider appeals for help. It is, perhaps, one of the cruellest blows in the life of Muromtseva-Bunina that she was treated so harshly by the members of this group. See I. Baboreko, *I. A. Bunin. Materialy dlia biografii s 1870 do 1917* (Moscow, 1983), 283.

[8]The work in question is B. Zaitsev, *Ivan Bunin. Zhizn' i tvorchestvo (Ivan Bunin: His Life and Work)*, published in Berlin, 1934.

especially in the evenings when everyone is in bed, and I hear him dancing around alone, listening to some foxtrot or music-hall song. . . .

March 10, 1934
Boris Zaitsev, from a letter to Ivan Bunin
There is no "movement" on the literary scene.

March 15, 1934
Ivan Bunin, from a letter to Gleb Struve
You should write to the Woolfs and say: "You purchased . . . *Arseniev* for pennies, without giving Bunin a percentage of the sales. . . . You should be ashamed of yourselves. Give Bunin what he deserves. If you do not, he will never have anything to do with you again."

April 1934
Alexander Kaun, from an article in Books Abroad
On an October morning, Bunin met my train at Cannes. Even if he did not hold a copy of *Latest News*,[9] as had been agreed upon previously, I would have recognized his face, certainly his eyes. From my boyhood on, I had been familiar with the strong features of Bunin's face . . . youthful and bearded at the time of his companionship with such "rising" authors as Gorky and Andreev, but now clean-shaven and haggard-looking. . . . Bunin's grey eyes have always struck me with their . . . severity, haughtiness, and melancholy. . . .

For some ten years Bunin has been living in Grasse,[1] about an hour's ride from Cannes. . . . Quiet, isolated, high in the hills overlooking the verdant town and the distant Mediterranean, Bunin's home has the air of a cloister. A rough simplicity reigns in the place, along with a Provençal geniality, even to the stocky landlord who, on occasion, turns cook and butler. Before the evening meal, one takes a stroll with the host, and whether he talks or gazes about in alert silence, one's senses are sharpened. Somehow Bunin imparts to his companion his own extraordinary receptivity; and, with Bunin at one's side, one responds more keenly to land, sea, and sky. . . .

[9]*Latest News (Poslednie novosti)* was published without interruption from April 27, 1920, to June 11, 1940, the day before the Germans entered Paris. Edited by the Russian liberal, Pavel Milyukov, it was the most significant, respected, and widely read newspaper in "Russia Abroad."

[1]Grasse is a city located about ten miles northwest of Cannes in the Côte-d'Azur region of southeastern France. It is known both as a winter resort and also as the center of the French perfume industry. Since 1924 the Bunins had been spending their summers at a villa named "Belvedere" in Grasse and their winters in Paris. See Marullo, *From the Other Shore,* 115–116.

A companion encourages him to reminisce, to describe. With him, the two are synonymous; his art is extremely close to that of a painter, at times disconcertingly so. Bunin perceives and records the finest details of color and line, taxing both one's vision and memory, forgetting that literary composition differs from the one on canvas, which permits one's eyes to rove up and down, back and forth, simultaneously observing both the details and the ensemble.

If possible, Bunin is even more sensitive to odors than to colors and lines. . . . Who can forget the blossoming orchard in *Mitya's Love*, the sensuous aromas of pears and acacias as they inflame adolescent passion gone wild? Bunin's olfactory sense is a catholic one; his hypersensitive nostrils have inhaled the scents of vast stretches of land and sea, from Russia's fields and steppes, through Western Europe, to exotic Asia and Africa. . . .

A deep melancholy infuses Bunin's canvases, a brooding nostalgia . . . the pathos of the irretrievable past. Himself a member of an impoverished noble family . . . Bunin is the Last Mohican of gentry Russia.[2] . . .

To this day Bunin is one of the most irreconcilable enemies of the new [Soviet] order. For him Russia ceased to live in 1917. . . . Bolshevik Russia is to Bunin "the snout of a pig." For him, the past thus acquires a multiplied charm, a splendor seen through tears of chagrin and regret. The present he brands . . . as "a shameless and contemptible age," and he entertains no hopes for the restoration of the old order. . . .

In his bitter hatred of the new Russia, Bunin is unreasoningly blind. This is one subject on which you cannot fruitfully converse with him: his fine baritone breaks into a falsetto; his grey eyes lose their haughtiness and melancholy and shoot fire; his noble nose twists and wrinkles; and his delectable sense of humor forsakes him utterly. . . .

[Among emigré writers, though] Bunin alone has kept his talent alive and creative. Perhaps this is due to the profound religiosity which permeates his work and his being. His sense of the divinity's imbuing all nature, that all life must keep him afloat, gives him hope, and urges him to fulfill his mission as a creative artist. One can only regret that . . . Bunin can only look backward. How much more vital his work might be if his vision were not so circumscribed!

[2]Bunin also often referred himself as the "last of the Mohicans" in Russian literature.

April 23, 1934
Vera Muromtseva-Bunina, from her diary

I have been with Ian for twenty-seven years. . . . [I remember] being pleasantly excited that we were heading for the Holy Land,[3] and that although I was quite divorced from Christ at that time, it was precisely there that I began my return to Him. . . . [I also remember] that I approached where our Lord was buried . . . in great anxiety and even with religious trepidation. But what happiness would I have felt [at that time], if had I been living a genuine life and had not turned my face away from God! [In the Holy Land] Ian occasionally talked so well about Christ and His Resurrection that he truly helped me to become closer to the Son of God. . . . For some reason, though, Ian has remained static [in his spirituality], while I keep striving forward and higher to Christ. Still, I am far from finding liberation from everything.

May 5, 1934
Mark Aldanov, from a letter to Ivan Bunin

What was the point of your being awarded the Nobel Prize, if you are going to rot in that hole, Grasse! You should travel through France and Europe. You should visit us in Paris. We have few joys these days. Everyone is moaning.

May 5, 1934
Mark Aldanov, from a letter to Vera Muromtseva-Bunina

In a word, life is rolling along: funerals and jubilees, jubilees and funerals. . . .

May 6, 1934
Vera Muromtseva-Bunina, from her diary

I received a letter from [my brother] Dmitri [in Moscow]. . . . His entire nervous system is failing. [He also has] arteriosclerosis of the brain. . . .

May 7, 1934
Vera Muromtseva-Bunina, from a letter to her brother, Dmitri Muromtsev

All of us—myself less so than the others, however—are disenchanted. We thought that [after Ian was awarded the Nobel Prize],

---

[3]As an unmarried couple, the Bunins visited the Holy Land in May 1907. See Marullo, *Ivan Bunin: Russian Requiem*, 106–107.

everything would be more and more affordable; but in truth, we are living the same way as before. . . . Circumstances have improved, but they are hardly lavish. After all, there were times [before the prize] when we did not even have enough to eat.

May 29, 1934
Ivan Bunin, from a letter to Gleb Struve

Generally speaking, I am surprised by England's lack of attention toward me. No one there is publishing anything of mine. And my agents are not doing anything to get even the least little something to an editor or journal there. Do you think it worthwhile for me to put together my recollections of Chekhov?[4] Perhaps you can translate them for me?

June 8, 1934
Vera Muromtseva-Bunina, from her diary

For the past three days and two nights, I have been alone with Ian. I liked that. What a sense of freedom [I have with him]. . . .

June 11, 1934
Vera Muromtseva-Bunina, from a letter to her brother, Dmitri Muromstsev

I agree with you that old age can be very, very sad, but this is only when the individual . . . stops functioning or begins to head downward. The main thing is to go forward . . . to overcome one's passions . . . and to understand one's self and weaknesses. . . . Love is a gift which is as rare as any talent. I have gotten hold of it gratis. . . .

During the years that we have been separated, I have grown very much internally. I now understand many things more deeply. I have had a great deal of time for reflection, though not as much as I would have liked. When you try to convince me of something, you appeal to Ian's authority. But for all my admiration of him . . . I have surpassed him in a thing or two. Some things that seem important to him are childish to me.

---

[4]Bunin had previously published his recollections of Chekhov in *Pamiati Chekhova* (*In Memory of Chekhov*) in Moscow in 1906; and in *Reminiscences of Anton Chekhov by Maxim Gorky, Alexander Kuprin, and I. A. Bunin* in New York in 1921. Also, Bunin's unfinished manuscript, *O Chekhove* (*About Chekhov*), appeared in New York in 1955, two years after the writer's death.

June 12, 1934
Vera Muromtseva-Bunina, from a letter to a friend

Ian loves it when the house is full. . . . For the past two summers, all eight bedrooms have been occupied. . . .

I am a carefree housekeeper. Ian almost always lives his own life; so our guests always feel at home . . . sometimes living with us for nearly half a year.

June 14, 1934
Vera Muromtseva-Bunina, from her diary

This is the third day I have not received any letters from [my brother] Mitya. . . . His atheism is killing me. I pray that God will enlighten him. . . .

For some reason Ian has suddenly become resigned to life, at least that is the way it looks on the surface. . . .

June 22, 1934
Ivan Bunin, from a letter to Gleb Struve

No one believes me when I tell them I have no money. But I am telling the truth: *I do not have any*. . . . I paid endless debts and made several donations. I took what was left, wrapped it in paper, and put it under a fence so that I would not be without a penny three or four years from now. I kept all my money in Swedish crowns; but I lost heavily on them for they suddenly took a sudden and terrible fall [in value]. Finally, there was this (most recent) misfortune: Some gentleman made off with a (rather large) sum of my money which he held in his hands.

Summer 1934
Ivan Bunin, from his diary

For the first time in my life, I had a sudden fit of fainting. . . . I was traveling [with a friend]. . . . I had been tired for the past twenty-four hours and had eaten nothing all day. . . . As the trolley was climbing up a hill, I suddenly *disappeared*. . . . I was no more. . . . Sudden death must be just like that. . . .

July 23, 1934
Vera Muromtseva-Bunina, from her diary

[A friend] says about the Bolsheviks: "If everything in Russia continues the way it is going now, I will return there in two years." . . . Ian thinks that [this friend] is talking through his hat, and that he is not going anywhere. I do not know. There is a baseness in this individual, though, that I find intolerable.

August 5, 1934
Vera Muromtseva-Bunina, from her diary
I am very unhappy with myself. I have lost my ability to work and to read a great deal.

August 17, 1934
Boris Zaitsev, from a letter to Ivan Bunin
Yesterday we attended a requiem service. . . . "All of Moscow" was there—all old people.

August 18, 1934
Vera Muromtseva-Bunina, from a letter to her brother, Dmitri Muromtsev
Everyone thinks that [because of the Nobel Prize] we have become almost as rich as Croesus.

September 1, 1934
Stepan Skitalets, from a speech given at the First All-Union Congress of Soviet Writers
Our young literature, forged in the crucible of the revolution, is still boiling and scalding. . . . It is also still going forward, even though it has already accomplished much. It is pursuing the true path of artistic realism: full-blooded, bright, radiant, and assured of a brilliant future. . . .

By contrast, emigré Russian writers are suffering from a debasement that is purely psychological. They, along with European writers in general, have to lower themselves before their readers and to conform to their ideologies in literature. . . .

Even Bunin . . . has long stopped developing as a writer. His *Mitya's Love* is like a manuscript that was written thirty years ago but is only now being published.[5] It adds nothing to what Bunin has written before; only its elevated style saves it from literary failure. It also gives the impression that Bunin has had nothing to write about for a very long time, and that, like Kuprin, he is immersed in personal memories of the past, in recollections that have almost nothing to do with society today.

[5]This is not true. *Mitya's Love* (*Mitina liubov'*) appeared in Paris and Berlin in 1925, and in New York in 1926. It also was published in Leningrad in 1925, making it one of the few works by an emigré writer to appear in Soviet Russia at the time.

September 17, 1934
Ivan Bunin, from a letter to Boris Zaitsev

Days flash by in sadness, trifles, in petty concerns and frivolous correspondence. . . .

October 3, 1934
Vera Muromtseva-Bunina, from her diary

Ian is very disturbed. He looks terrible and sad. The problem is that he does not know what he wants. He lives for excitement, but he suffers whenever he encounters it.

October 6, 1934
Alexander Kaun, from an article in Literary World

[With Bunin] we are made to understand with equal sharpness the inner and outer life of the horse, the dog, the stable man, the jealous lover, the blossoming pear tree, the billowing sea, and other manifestations of earthly existence.

October 11, 1934
Mikhail Sholokhov, from an interview

I have often been accused of being under the influence of Tolstoy. Without a doubt, I love Tolstoy . . . but Ivan Bunin influences me even more. He is great master at what he does.

October 26, 1934
Ivan Bunin, in answer to a questionnaire from the Russian Social Committee in Poland

To your question—"Why do I oppose Bolshevism?" . . . I reply that I am personally convinced that, in all of human history, even in the basest and most bloodiest of times, there has been nothing more vile, false, evil, and despotic than this phenomenon.

October 28, 1934
Boris Zaitsev, from a letter to Ivan Bunin

I am very glad that you are returning to Paris, although it is very sad to be here now. The Russians are completely depressed. What is there to be happy about? [My wife] says: "I keep having this vision: Several years have gone by, and you and I are . . . the only ones left."

On November 10th . . . there will be a ball "to benefit writers." . . . They are all old. "Papa" Kuprin is so badly off that he cannot even sign his name. . . .

November 1, 1934
Vladimir Zenzinov, from his memoirs

[Bunin said:] "We had this telephone in Moscow. It gave off endless, crackling sounds. You could not talk or hear anything on it; you would just get drowned out. Sparks would fly out from it in all directions. It would go like this: 'Tr-r-r-r-ring! Tr-r-r-r-ring! . . . Br-r-r-r-rp! Br-r-r-r-rp!' . . . It sounded just like Andrei Bely."

November 3, 1934
Vera Muromtseva-Bunina, from a letter to her brother, Dmitri Muromtsev

I do certain things because my mind, not my heart, tells me to do so. . . . In general, I have not had many rushes of emotion; and this year I have had *absolutely* none at all. . . . I get angry, but I also restrain my heart and conquer my distress. I am on sincere terms with almost everyone; and, although anyone can enter my "salon," I let few disturb the "inner peace" of my soul. . . . I have a very precise sense for human qualities, good and bad. Many of them I can forgive, but [many of them] I cannot. No one can do anything to me if I myself do not want it. . . . But my soul has been created for the life of a couple. . . . One of us must give in . . . and it is always I who does so.

November 5, 1934
Vera Muromtseva-Bunina, from a letter to Dmitri Muromtsev

Earlier, the windows of our dining room and of Ian's study looked out onto a marvelous garden where in the spring, thrushes would sing along with a quacking duck. But now an apartment building stands in its place. . . .

November 9, 1934
Vera Muromtseva-Bunina, from her diary

It was exactly one year ago that we received a call from Stockholm and that everything was turned upside down.[6] . . . We have yet to have a moment's peace. . . . We are still living as if in a dream. . . . Fame, money, and congratulations; envy, requests, insults; disenchantment, powerlessness, flattery; screams of joy and happiness that we could help others. . . . Everything has gotten confused, tangled, intertwined. . . . [Everything] has kept us from concentrating and working, not to mention bringing us to endless grief.

[6]See Marullo, *Ivan Bunin: From the Other Shore,* 279–281.

✻ 1935 ✻

1935–1939
Tatyana Loginova-Muravieva, from her memoirs

Bunin said with an intense and seemingly mocking air: "So you think that I am a thousand years older than you? My dear woman, what I would not give to be your age, so that all my impressions would be new and fresh, so that boundless distances would open up before me . . . and so that everything would lie before me! . . . Oh, how I love the expanse of life. I love life, I love love. How I love everything! But I hate death. . . . I will not surrender to it, not for anything in the world. Death will not dare take me. It will not choke me! . . ."

[He continued:] "It seems to me that I have lived for a thousand years . . . even more. . . . I feel all my ancestors within me. They seethe and boil in me. I also feel the remote depths of the ages . . . as well as my roots in the Russian soul, down to the very last one. . . ."

I asked Bunin: "Can a Russian live and write outside of Russia?"

He replied: "Some can, some cannot. But one cannot if he does not have a profound, indestructible, and bloody tie with Rus'.[7] . . .

"Yes, I feel all my ancestors in me . . . but more than that, I feel a tie to 'wild beasts.' My sense of sight, hearing, and smell is not simply human, but internal, 'beastlike.' That is why I love to live life 'like a beast.' I am tied to all the manifestations of existence, with nature, with the earth, with everything that is in life, about it, and below it. I will not give myself over to death for anything in the world. I fear it, though. Oh, how I fear it." . . .

[Natalya Goncharova told me:] "If only you could have seen how beautiful Vera Bunina was when she was young. . . . A marblelike face, huge, perfectly formed blue eyes. No one could come in contact with her without falling in love with her. She was the most beautiful girl in high school. . . ."

At a gathering, Bunin came up to me and said:

"Let's run away from Paris somewhere!"

"How? Where?" I replied.

"To the mountains, the snows. . . ."

Laughing, I said: "All right, let's go. Then what?"

---

[7]Rus' is the generic term for pre-Petrine Russia.

"The moon will be shining, and in the evenings we will sit by the fire."

"And you will read me poetry," I added. "That will be nice. But the next day, there will be more poetry and more snow. Won't we get bored quickly?"

"There is no dealing with you. So you won't run away with me?"

"No, I won't," I said, regretting in my soul that I was incapable of such adventures, and also suddenly realizing that Vera Nikolaevna Bunina was downstairs, selling pastries. How could I have run off with him? . . .

[Bunin said:] "I love Paris very much, but not only because it is a splendid city and a monument to culture. The strength of Paris lies in the fact that the city does not tie your hands. People can live in Paris for years on end, but in no way do they ever become 'Parisians.' Rather, they remain the way they were. The strength of Paris lies in the fact that it accepts and respects everyone in it. . . ."

"Paris, though, is a home, not a homeland. 'Home' is such an important word! People settle down in Paris for a long period of time because it is a 'torch'-like city. It illuminates everyone in it. Here everyone can find the 'light' that he is looking for. That is why the elite of all nations and peoples have come through Paris. Here everything is weighed on human scales. How great it is to breathe spring in Paris . . . when the buds of the chestnut trees are in bloom, to breathe their scent from afar, wafted by winds of freedom and expanse. . . .

[Bunin said:] "I photograph everything. Instead of eyes, I have a camera. Click-click, and the picture is taken. It is imprinted in my memory forever. . . ."

Circa 1935
Nadezhda Teffi, from a letter to Vera Muromtseva-Bunina
I will tell you a secret: Ivan Alexeevich is the only person in the world whose company I enjoy. I listen to and value his every word; and I often despair that not everyone understands him as I do. I once swallowed my pride and, without an invitation, went to a person's house merely to see him.

1935
Nikolai Roshchin, from a letter to Ivan Bunin
Do you remember, dear Ivan Alexeevich, that in 1935 . . . you were watching [films] of parades in Nuremberg and Milan and said that the "Führer" and "Il Duce" were "insane monkeys"?

1935
Ekaterina Peshkova, from her memoirs

After a long interval . . . I accidentally ran into Bunin in France. Outwardly he had changed a great deal. . . . [He was] completely shaven, with an Anglicized look. He kept asking me questions about life in Russia, about the youth there. It seemed that he both believed and disbelieved everything I told him.

At the end of our conversation, I told Bunin that I had not intended to see him after all he had written about [my husband] Alexei Maximovich [Gorky]. He objected, saying that he had not published anything special about my husband.[8] He promised to send me everything that he had written [about Gorky] . . . but he never did. . . .

January 5, 1935
Mark Aldanov, from a letter to Vera Muromtseva-Bunina

I rarely see Ivan Alexeevich. . . . I have not been to your apartment, but it is just as well: It would annoy me greatly. . . . In my opinion, you should rent an apartment that is somewhat nicer . . . and buy some furniture that is more fashionable so that you can receive French people and foreigners. . . . After all, Ivan Alexeevich is the only person whom we can call our cultural "ambassador" to Europe. . . .

January 20, 1935
Mark Aldanov, from a letter to Vera Muromtseva-Bunina

I find it very painful that Ivan Alexeevich does not use his [Nobel] prize in the interest of Russian affairs, or to advance his own personal goals. . . . No, he cannot be our "ambassador," and this is a great, great pity. . . .

February 3, 1935
A reviewer, from the New York Times Book Review

Dry Valley . . . is one of Bunin's greatest achievements . . . the story of the ruin and decay of the noble Russian family of the Khrushchevs. . . . [In this work] the silent ruins of a [family estate] come back to life and are filled anew with the blood of reality which once flowed there. The reader experiences, with unexpected and overpowering strength, that feeling which he would experience if, while he were standing beside the shattered fragments of an ancient Greek tem-

---

[8]This is not true. See Bunin's 1930 article about Gorky in Marullo, *From the Other Shore*, 235–236.

ple, that temple were suddenly to resurrect itself from fragments, stand up in its former beauty and fill with a colorful crowd of worshipers dead for thousands of years. . . .

Through the medium of the nobles and peasants figuring in the one hundred short pages of his novelette, Bunin has drawn so masterful a synthetic portrait of the Russian people, with its contradictions and untamed passions, with the almost biblical brutality and primitiveness of its native culture, with its cruelty and kindliness, and with the "geological layers" of prehistoric medievalism and modernism coexisting but not mixing in it, that at moments one feels as though Russia's very essence was captured.

Bunin's narrative [in *Dry Valley*] . . . contains a powerful call of life . . . as well as . . . the measured, pitiless march of time engulfing human lives and the hopeless pathos of the human beings' struggle against this march. . . . As one finishes *Dry Valley,* one feels like agreeing with those critics who assert that the day is near when the opinion of the civilized world will agree in placing Bunin's name above that of Turgenev. . . .

The Elagin Affair is also a remarkable piece of writing. It is the story of the youthful officer of a crack regiment who has agreed with his mistress, a Polish actress, hysterical, strange, and fascinating—to kill her and then to commit suicide. He, however, only carries out the first part of his program; seeing her dead body before him, he is so seized with indifference that he merely gives himself up to the authorities. . . . What gems of psychological insight and of almost mysterious penetration into the realm of sex, Bunin uncovers. What, perhaps, is most remarkable, is that he captures human feelings in such a cross-section that the reader immediately recognizes them as part of his own experience, but he knows that no one before Bunin has expressed them in words. That is the earmark of a great writer. . . .

February 5, 1935
Vera Muromtseva-Bunina, from a letter to her brother, Dmitri Muromtsev
I am rather spoiled . . . by the attention of people, but it is a completely different story with Ian. . . . He lives as though he is the only person in the world and that everything is for him alone.

February 14, 1935
Mark Aldanov, from a letter to Ivan Bunin
The rumor is that you have not written a line since being awarded

the Nobel Prize. . . . Your friends are angry with you, not to mention the public. . . .

May 16, 1935
A publisher, from a letter to Maxim Gorky
For the series *The Library for Workers of Collective Farms*[9] . . . I want to include Bunin's "The Golden Bottom," "Prince Among Princes," "The Final Day," "Tan'ka," "The Poor Devil," "The Merry Courtyard," and "A Fairytale."[1]

June 2, 1935
Marina Tsvetaeva, from a letter to Vera Muromtseva-Bunina
People say that you are indifferent [to things], but I do not think that at all. . . . Rather, you are aloof from everything that concerns your personal "I." For you, everything else is more important than your own soul and its most vital demands. . . . You do not need guests or causes. . . . You live for the home. . . .

The roots of our—strange—friendship are found in the deep earth of time. . . . I could love you a thousand more times than I do now . . . but I thank God that I do not. . . . You, perhaps, were my first rational entry into life. . . .

June 15, 1935
Vera Muromtseva-Bunina, from a letter to her brother, Dmitri Muromtsev
People have stopped developing spiritually and are not interested in anything. Such a thing happens whenever intelligent people begin to take up physical labor. They even acquire a certain repulsion for intellectual interests and for those who live for them.

June 22, 1935
Mark Aldanov, from a letter to the Bunins
I've just heard about what went on at the [First] Congress of the Union of Writers in the Defense of Culture [in Paris]. . . . I did not go "on principle," though I very much wanted to see Alyoshka [Tolstoy]—at least from afar; he had come to defend [Soviet] culture. But Teffi was there. . . . She called over to Tolstoy—and they kissed in front

---

[9]*The Library for Workers of Collective Farms* (*Biblioteka "Kolkhoznika"*) was a series of monographs that was published irregularly from 1929 to about 1935.
[1]Bunin wrote "Tan'ka" in 1892, "The Golden Bottom" (*"Zolotoe dno"*) in 1930, "The Merry Courtyard" (*"Veselyi dvor"*) in 1911, "King of Kings" (*"Kniaz vo kniaz'iakh"*) in 1912, and "A Fairytale" (*"Skazka"*) and "The Final Day" (*"Poslednii den' "*) in 1913.

of everyone and talked for about ten minutes. Tolstoy asked Teffi about you. He said he had received a postcard from you and "was very touched" by it. He also said that you are being read in the USSR. He did not ask about anyone else.

No matter how strange it sounds, I was very excited that Tolstoy was here. . . .

Oh, yes, I forgot the main thing: Tolstoy said there are rumors flying around Moscow that you have decided to return [to Russia]!! What the hell have you been up to?!

June 26, 1935
Ivan Bunin, from a letter to Nadezhda Teffi
You are a constant joy for me. . . . How many marvelous things have poured forth from you.

July 3, 1935
Boris Zaitsev, from a letter to Ivan Bunin
The latest word on Kuprin is that his health is *very* poor, and that he gets worse with each passing day. Balmont is also not doing well. He is living in a small wing in a clinic near Paris. He has been having an affair with a 75-year-old crazy woman and also has become friends with a French poet who is laying claim to the French throne. Balmont and this poet have even founded a political group for this purpose. Balmont has been promised several good estates and will forget us all if this political group, in fact, becomes a reality. . . . Not long ago, Balmont's wife told me that he "climbed up a tree in the middle of the night so that he could better hear the nightingales, and that . . . he fell and broke his leg. . . ."[2]

July 6, 1935
Ivan Bunin, from his diary
Beethoven used to say that he achieved mastery only when he stopped shoving the content of ten sonatas into a single one. . . .

July 7, 1935
Mark Aldanov, from a letter to Vera Muromsteva-Bunina
[A reporter from the emigré newspaper] had a long, private conversation with [Alexei] Tolstoy. Tolstoy told him that the USSR is a paradise, that he has two cars, and that Stalin loves him. He said that

---

[2]Balmont had been showing signs of mental illness from about 1932 on.

he worships Stalin, that the government has printed four million copies of his books, and that they have all sold out. So, the USSR is apparently a paradise. Tolstoy also said that his wife, Natalya Vasilievna, has enrolled in college courses, because "in our country, one cannot help but study."

[The reporter added] that Tolstoy asked only about you. . . .

July 25, 1935
Vera Muromtseva-Bunina, from her diary
[A friend] came by with tablecloths from Russia, but I could not buy them. I have no money at all, and I do not know how I can help [my brother] Mitya. No one believes me, but we have no revenue coming in. "Petropolis" Press[3] is publishing only 10 volumes [of Ian's collected works].[4] . . .

August 15, 1935
Ivan Bunin, from his diary
The fact that I might die in my sleep is something that I find incomprehensible. . . .

To love is to believe.

September 1, 1935
Boris Zaitsev, from a letter to Ivan Bunin
[Our entire visit to Finland] has been one absolutely heavenly autumn Russian day. . . . I could see Kronstadt[5] [in the distance]. . . . How much Russia there is here! . . . especially the smells: the sharply bitter scents of marshes, pines, and birches. . . . The entire way of life here is also Russian, as it was before the war. . . .

Walking through the forests, I experienced a joy that I have not had for a long time. I delight in the fir trees, the moss, the woodpeckers, the mushrooms, and all the other good things that abound in Russia. I also understood that while we have grown unaccustomed to

[3]"Petropolis" Press was founded as a cooperative publishing venture in Petrograd in January 1918. It moved first to Berlin in 1923, then to Brussels in 1935 where it ceased publication three years later. During its existence, "Petropolis" published more than a thousand books on Russian literature and culture, including the works of both emigré and Soviet writers. See Glad, 157.

[4]In truth, the editors of "Petropolis" published an eleven-volume edition of Bunin's writing in 1934–1936. For this work, Bunin edited almost a half-century of his poetry and prose, making them more compact and concise.

[5]Kronstadt is on an island in the Gulf of Finland approximately fifteen miles west of Saint Petersburg. It was also the site of a Russian naval base where, on February 28, 1921, soldiers revolted unsuccessfully against Communist rule.

Russian nature . . . it is also in our blood, and no Latin country can ever take it away from us. . . .

You are also part of that world that gave us all birth—and a very rare part indeed. . . .

How great and rich was the Russia in which we lived! We are also beginning to forget that!

September 19, 1935
Vera Muromtseva-Bunina, from a letter to her brother, Dmitri Muromtsev

You ask why we need a villa. We need it for the very same reasons we needed one in Glotovo[6] and at Capri. After all, you know that Ian can work only in seclusion, when his life is peaceful and happy. Almost everything that he has written [in exile], he has done here in Grasse.

We once thought about leaving [Grasse]—it has been particularly difficult this year—but I saw that Ian would suffer, and that he would miss his huge, simple, peaceful study, with its splendid view. . . .

December 28, 1935
Marina Tsvetaeva, from a letter to a friend

Over the years, I have been friends with Vera Bunina. . . .

You, perhaps, know that for about ten years now, Bunin has this young love (an adopted daughter? an affair?—*love*). She is Galina Kuznetsova, a former student from Prague. She lives with them, goes with them to Switzerland, she is *theirs*. Vera suffers—but accepts the situation. Everyone judges her, but I admire her: without Vera, Bunin could not get along. . . . She goes about as a *mother*.

I am polite to Galina.

I am also on friendly terms with the Bunins, but we are not close. . . .

---

[6]Glotovo was a village in the region around Oryol, near the Bunins' family home.

❋ 1936 ❋

1936
Mark Aldanov, from an article

Two writers have recently been awarded the Nobel Prize in literature: one is an emigré, the other is not. The latter has received all the major European distinctions; he has been worn out with public and private celebrations in all the capitals of the world.[7] The former, though, has been feted only in the country of the Nobel Prize. He has not been able to get visas to other countries; he has not received other distinctions. A quirk of fate? Hardly. The person is an emigré.

February 2, 1936
Vladimir Nabokov, from a letter

[Dining with Bunin in a restaurant] the conversation flagged; but the fault was mine. I was tired and cross. Everything he did irritated me: his intonations, his bawdy little jokes, the way he ordered . . . and his deliberate servility to the waiter. . . . I have not been that discomforted in a long time. . . .

But toward the end of the dinner, and later when we walked out onto the street, sparks of mutual admiration and respect began to flash here and there; and [when we set out for another café] . . . where the plump Aldanov was awaiting us, things got quite merry. There I saw Khodasevich . . . looking very yellowish. Bunin hates him. . . .

Aldanov said that the way Bunin and I were talking and looking at each other, one would think that two movie cameras were rolling.

March 30, 1936
Boris Zaitsev, from a letter to Ivan Bunin

Merezhkovsky . . . intends to go to Rome. For a third time, he wishes to see Mussolini and to impart some of his wisdom to him.[8]

---

[7]The individual in question is either Luigi Pirandello, who was awarded the Nobel Prize in Literature in 1934, or Eugene O'Neill, who received the honor in 1936. (No award was made in 1935.)

[8]In truth, Merezhkovsky engaged Mussolini only once, in a fifteen-minute interview on December 5, 1935. The meeting was awkward at best. For Merezhkovsky, Mussolini exuded "a vague disquietude, an inexplicable heaviness, a terror which people feel when they approach and peer into a forbidden place . . . something like what Faust felt when the Spirit of the Earth appeared to him."

Although Merezhkovsky did not admire Mussolini's totalitarian views, he did

April 16, 1936
Ivan Bunin, from a letter to Boris Zaitsev

I have been writing twelve hours a day and have gone completely crazy. . . .

April 23, 1936
Ivan Bunin, from his diary

I do not feel my years.[9] But I really should take care of myself. Otherwise one year, two—and old age.

On this day Vera and I went to Palestine, and I joined my life with hers.

April 26, 1936
Ivan Bunin, from his diary

I have been doing a lot of stupid things . . . like attending an evening of Balmont's reading his works. . . .

Yesterday the bright green of the trees and the leaden color of the sky made a burdensome impression. . . . It is time for me to submit [to life]. . . .

Kerensky[1] came to visit this evening. . . .

Now it is raining. Sadness and hopeless *Angst.* Truly, it is time to submit. . . .

April 26, 1936
Vera Muromtseva-Bunina, from her diary

I have not opened this notebook for exactly eight months. . . . All my attempts to reconcile Ian to his situation have been in vain. . . .

---

approve of Il Duce's determination to stem the tide of bolshevism in Europe. He also looked to the Italian leader to facilitate a cherished idea: a world union of church and state.

More specifically, Merezhkovsky hoped that Mussolini would fund several stays in Italy for research on a book on Dante and a *biographie romanceé* of Saint Francis of Assisi. To this end, he filled his letters to the Italian leader with abject flattery. For him, Mussolini was the "Creative Genius of the New Italy," the "Creative Soul of the New Italian Renaissance," and even a brother of Napoleon and Dante. Not surprisingly, Merezhkovsky received financial assistance for his work. (*Francis of Assisi* appeared in 1938; *Dante*, in 1939.) See C. Bedford, *The Seeker: D. S. Merezhkovsky* (Lawrence, Kans., 1975), 152–153; Glad, 286.

[9]Bunin was sixty-six years old at this time.

[1]After leaving Russia in May 1918, Alexander Kerensky spent the rest of his life in exile, living and traveling in America and Western Europe, and working as a lecturer, author, editor, and journalist.

May 8, 1936
Ivan Bunin, from his diary

I will not be allowed to read my works in Poland, even though I have received an invitation to do so. . . . "Writers from other countries"—Russians, Soviets, obviously—"would see my presence there as a discourtesy."

Right now I have a feeling of something divine—the night, the stars . . . the garden.

May 9, 1936
Ivan Bunin, from his diary

I have spent the last two years in a monstrous sort of way. And I have come to ruin from this terrible and repulsive life.

Radio, jazz, and foxtrots. . . . I find them tormenting. . . .

May 10, 1936
Ivan Bunin, from his diary

Yes, for the past two years, I have done many stupid things. . . . Literary agents *always* take their cut . . . and my *Collected Works* were printed for free. . . . I was really crazy to allow such a thing to happen. . . . I am not getting a penny's worth of income. . . . And old age lies ahead.

May 15, 1936
Gleb Struve, from an article

It is difficult to find precedents for Nabokov in Russian literature, [but] as a stylist, he has learned a thing or two from Bunin. . . .

May 16, 1936
Ivan Bunin, from a letter to Pyotr Bitsilli

Remizov is creating dictionaries of the most abominable Russian, of a language that has never existed nor can exist. He keeps making up the most vile and stupid words to boot. For this alone, one should hate him.

[Also, in one of your articles] you say that "Blok is one of the greatest Russian poets"—for that, may God forgive you.

May 28, 1936
Vera Muromtseva-Bunina, from her diary

Today I received a letter from [my brother] Mitya, saying that "there is no hope for a cure" [for his illness]. Most likely, he is very angry that I have sent him so few packages. But I did not count on his being ill. What more can I do? How can I cut back [on expenses] any more than I do? . . . If I do not eat meat, I can save three francs a day. But we are running out of money just the same. . . .

June 6, 1936
Ivan Bunin, from an article

Not long ago I happened to be walking through Nice with a friend. He suddenly came to a halt and said:

"Here is where the car stopped when Isadora Duncan's scarf fell under the wheel and strangled her."[2]

The image of this woman and the story of her life would be a terrible theme for a novelist! . . .

When Isadora first visited Russia . . . she arrived on the dawn of a January day in Petersburg. Hiring a cabby to see the city, she came across an endless funeral procession. "What is going on?" she asked the driver. He replied: "The corpses of workers who were shot yesterday in front of the Winter Palace. Unarmed and in need, they had come to the tsar to ask for help and for bread for their wives and children." Tears poured forth from Isadora's eyes. "If I had not seen such a sight," she later recalled, "my life would have taken a different turn!" Right then and there she took a solemn vow "to devote all her energy to service the people, the downtrodden and the oppressed."[3]

---

[2]About Duncan's bizarre death, a Russian biographer wrote: "On a September evening [in 1927] . . . Isadora went down to the street where a small racing car was waiting for her. Throwing a red shawl . . . over her shoulders, she waved a farewell and, smiling, uttered her last words:

"*Adieu, mes amis! Je vais à la gloire!*"

"Isadora then got into the car, not knowing that it was there that her death lay in waiting, a death that was both frenzied and cruel. Without knowing that she had only one more minute to live, to feel. A few dozen seconds, a few dozen turns of the wheel. The red shawl . . . strewn with Chinese asters, slipped from Isadora's shoulder, floated over the side of the car, and quietly licked the dry rubber. Suddenly, it wound itself wildly around the wheel, and roughly jerked Isadora by the throat. The motor of the car was very powerful; so too was the blow. At the very first revolution of the wheel . . . Isadora's neck was broken. . . .

"The moment after the fatal accident, the driver who had sat in front, kept shouting: 'I have killed the Madonna! I have killed the Madonna!'

"To free Isadora's head, which had been drawn down against the side of the car, the shawl had to be cut. . . .

"A few days later, the car was sold at auction in Nice. Some maniac smiled happily when, after some heated bidding . . . [he purchased] the car for the unheard-of sum of two hundred thousand francs. [Earlier] a no less savage crowd of eyewitnesses had flung themselves on the torn shawl, and, in a crazy race for souvenirs, tore it to shreds." See I. Schneider, *Isadora Duncan: The Russian Years* (New York, 1968), 213–214.

[3]The story is true, the event being "Bloody Sunday." On January 22, 1905, a procession of workers, seeking to present a petition of grievances to Nicholas II, was fired upon and dispersed with considerable loss of life. See Schneider, 20.

Such a promise, though, did not prevent her from becoming completely ecstatic over the paradelike spectacle of the Russian opera, over the richness and elegance of the surroundings, over the beauty and dresses of the women, and over the wealth of furs and jewels. Moscow also brought Isadora to ecstasy.

She recalled: "Imperceptibly, the fresh, snow-filled air, along with the Russian cuisine, particularly the caviar, cured me from the weakness, brought about from my previous, extremely spiritual love. Now my entire being hungered for union with a powerful man. Such an individual I saw in Stanislavsky."

With Stanislavsky there occurred this incident. Duncan recalled: "I wound my arms around his powerful neck and kissed him on the lips. When I tried to pull him still closer to me, he straightened up and exclaimed: 'And what are we going to do with the child?' 'With what child?' I asked. 'With our child,' he said and rushed away from me."[4]

June 7, 1936
Ivan Bunin, from his diary
    I suffer from feelings of injury, of total insult—as well as of shame for the way that I have been acting. Truly, the past two years, I have been sick spiritually . . . [a condition] that I fear is permanent. . . .

    Yesterday Blum took over the reins of government. There were strikes. . . .[5]

---

[4]Again, the story is true, the relationship between Duncan and Stanislavsky remaining platonic. About Duncan, Stanislavsky later recalled: "The first appearance of Duncan on the stage did not make a very great impression [on me]. Unaccustomed to seeing an almost naked body on the stage, I could hardly notice and understand the art of the dancer. . . . But after a few additional numbers, one of which was especially persuasive, I could no longer remain indifferent to the protests of the general public and began to applaud demonstratively.

    "When the intermission came, I, as a newly baptized disciple of the great artist, ran to the footlights to applaud [her]. . . . From that time on, I never missed a single one of Duncan's appearances on stage. The necessity to see her was often dictated from within me: an artistic feeling that was closely related to her art. . . . Duncan and I understood each other almost before we had said a single word." See Schneider, 31–32.

    [5]The May 1936 victory of the "Popular Front" (*"Le Front Populaire"*)—a broad coalition of parties seeking both to oppose extreme rightist groups and to end the economic depression in France—together with the naming of the socialist Léon Blum as prime minister of the country, triggered a wave of strikes by French workers who demanded that the new government be sympathetic to their needs.

    The unrest ended on June 7–8 with the so-called Matignon Agreements which, among other things, increased wages by 12 percent and affirmed the rights of workers to join unions and to engage in collective bargaining.

June 14, 1936
Ivan Bunin, from his diary

I was in Nice for a "Day of Russian Culture."[6] It was a shameful abomination. When I left there . . . a huge crowd had formed. . . . In all honesty, it looked just like Russia did [during the revolution] . . . posters, red flags, meetings.[7] . . .

There was a "holiday" going on in Grasse also. Right below [our villa] "Belvedere," on the city square, there was a crowd of kids, whores, young hooligans, and the like, singing the "Marseillaise" and the "International"[8]—and waving red velvet flags with the hammer and sickle on them. . . .

I should seriously thinking of running away from here. . . .

I am finding it particularly difficult spiritually. It is every man for himself!

July 1936
Zinaida Shakovskaya, from her memoirs

"Young writers do not know their craft," Bunin said.

"What about Nabokov?" I asked.

---

[6]The "Days of Russian Culture" were brought into being by the Association of Emigré Teachers and other sociopolitical groups so that Russian exiles throughout the world could celebrate, reaffirm, and preserve their cultural heritage. Each year, the "Days of Russian Culture" were celebrated on June 8th, the birthday of Alexander Pushkin, the "father" of modern Russian language and literature.

On the "Days of Russian Culture," members of the diaspora read and enacted Pushkin's works. They also conducted literary readings, engaged in musical and theatrical performances, and lectured on national history and culture. In this way the younger members of Russia Abroad—the key focus of the event—became acquainted with the achievements of their literary, artistic, and historical heritage. For more on the "Days of Russian Culture," see Raeff, 93–94, 211–212.

[7]Bunin was not alone in his misgivings about the "Days of Russian Culture," the problem being that such occasions tended to minimize, if not ignore, both the religious and monarchist elements of Russia's cultural tradition. To this end, conservative emigré circles in Yugoslavia proposed alternative "Days of Russian National Consciousness" to be held on the feast day of Saint Vladimir, the prince who, in 988, brought Christianity to Russia.

Proponents of the "Days of Russian National Consciousness" denounced the Pushkin-based "Days of Russian Culture" as overtly worldly and modern, and as the work of Masons, liberals, and secularists who, they believed, had brought about the Russian Revolution and the defeat of the White Army in the ensuing civil war. Despite such attacks, the "Days of Russian National Consciousness" were never as popular or widespread as the "Days of the Russian Culture." See Raeff, 94.

[8]The words of the "Internationale" were written by the French revolutionary poet Eugene Pottier, during the period of the Paris Commune in 1871; the music for the piece was composed by a French woodcarver, Pierre Degeyter, in 1888.

Although the "Internationale" was banned in tsarist Russia, it was translated into Russian in 1902 and circulated among Russian revolutionaries both at home and abroad. It also became the official anthem of Soviet Russia in 1944.

"That one has written himself into the history of Russian literature. He is a monster, but what a writer he is."

August 16, 1936
Ivan Bunin, from his diary

Sometimes I am clearly horrified by how low I have fallen. . . . Almost every step I take has resulted in something stupid and base! I am continually besieged by full-blown inertia, lack of will, and a monstrous lack of talent!

I have got to get hold of myself! I really have to!

September 17, 1936
Vera Muromtseva-Bunina, from her diary

Love is such an incomprehensible thing!

September 21, 1936
Vera Muromtseva-Bunina, from her diary

All the families we know, are facing either separation or death. . . .

October 26, 1936
Marina Tsvetaeva, from a letter to Vera Muromtseva-Bunina

Our friendship has compelled me, gradually and imperceptibly, to find my way in the native hazes of the past in which we both live so willingly and freely. You have held onto *everything*. . . . But how much have I let go of things!

November 1, 1936
Ivan Bunin, from a letter to Latest News *and other emigré newspapers*

Three weeks ago I left Paris to do some sightseeing and to meet with German, Swiss, and Italian publishers and translators. . . . At the German customs office . . . the authorities . . . took my passport but did not return it for a half hour. When they finally came back, they ordered me:

"Follow this gentleman!"

This "gentleman" was a rather young, criminal-looking type in a shabby government uniform. He quickly seized me by the sleeve and took me to a stone shed. The icy winds of a rainy day blew through its open doors. The "gentleman" led me into a chamber and silently began taking off my coat, jacket, and waistcoat. . . . I stood before him without my clothes and shoes. He even took my socks. . . .

I was trembling from shock. "What was going on?" I thought, "What was the reason for this?" . . . Never had I experienced such insult, outrage, and anger. I was not only close to fainting but also on the verge of death itself from a heart attack.

I began to protest. As I did not know any German, I could ask questions only in Russian—"What is the meaning of this?" "Why are you doing this?" But the "gentleman" continued to undress me and to rummage through everything I had—silently, spitefully, and with the most extreme vulgarity. . . .

My teeth were chattering and my entire body was shivering from the cold, from the damp drafts that were blowing through the door. The "gentleman" put his fingers into the lining of my hat, tearing it in several places. He even tried to rip the heels off my shoes. . . .

After a quarter of an hour, he did not find anything that could label me as a "criminal"; so he let me go. The ship was leaving at that very minute, but I was told: "Do not worry; there is still an evening boat!" Then the customs agent took me under escort, along with a cart with all my things in it, to a huge building—most likely a jail, since I saw that the corridors there had many doors with numbers on them. . . .

It seemed to me that I was in an asylum, that all of what was happening to me was some kind of a nightmare. . . . For *exactly three hours*, the people there looked at every little thing in my suitcases and briefcase. They searched with such eagerness, as if they had caught a murderer. . . . They also kept screaming questions at me, even though I must have told them a hundred times that I did not speak or understand German. . . . They even rummaged through my handkerchiefs, holding each and every one of them up to the light. They searched through every sheet of paper, every letter, every calling card. Every page of my manuscripts and books came under their scrutiny. They kept asking:

"What is this?" "What is written here?" "Who wrote this?" "Who is this person?" "Is he a Bolshevik? a Bolshevik?"

Several of my letters and my notebook with addresses in it they put off to the side. These they took somewhere and returned to me only at the last minute. A packet of Czech newspapers with articles about me and . . . the literary readings that I had given there excited their curiosity. "Aha, Czech newspapers! Why do you have them?" they asked, despite the fact that they showed pictures of me with inscriptions which said "Bunin in Prague." . . . As I am writing a book on Tolstoy, my briefcase also had several books on him. When they saw his portrait in these books, they spat and stamped their feet: "Ah, Tolstoy, Tolstoy!"

Around four o'clock a woman appeared. With eyes that bore straight through me, she said . . . that I should immediately write down the name of my works so as to prove that I was really who I said I was. She also said . . . that I had spent the [previous] night with a woman and that I should give them her name. . . . I became thoroughly outraged . . . and in response, she announced that I was free.

Having arrived in Zurich to spend the night, I did not sleep until morning. . . . When I got to Geneva, I felt so sick that I canceled the remainder of my trip and returned to Paris.

November 5, 1936
The State German News Agency, from an official release
When Bunin entered German territory from Switzerland, the border guards treated him with extreme politeness. He was never subjected to abuse or arrest.

November 8, 1936
Alexei Tolstoy, from an interview with a Soviet newspaper
I happened to meet Bunin accidentally in a café in Paris. He was very excited to see me. I asked him what he intended to do [abroad]. He replied that he wanted to go to Rome, since he still did not wish to be connected with the Revolution.

I have read three of Bunin's latest books—two anthologies of his short stories and his novel, *The Life of Arseniev*; and I was dismayed by the profound and hopeless decline of his talent. . . . Bunin's fate stands as a graphic and terrible example of what happens to a writer-emigré who is torn from his homeland, from the political and social life of his country. Bunin has been so devastated [by his time in exile] that his work has become an empty shell containing nothing but misanthropy and regret for the past.

November 27, 1936
Ivan Bunin, from a letter to Latest News
Allow me *via* your newspaper . . . to express my gratitude to all those social organizations, newspapers, and individuals who came to my defense [as regards my unhappy experience in Germany]. . . . The outcry was so worldwide, so passionate and unanimous both in sympathy for me and in indignation over the base coarseness to which I, without any foundation, was subjected . . . that I felt doubly obligated

to write to you . . . since this response not only concerns me as a private citizen but also serves as a worthy answer to the official German communiqué which has denied [my unjust treatment] and which . . . has also indirectly accused me of "slander." The story I gave to your paper was completely factual, accurate . . . and had to be known by those in Berlin who disavowed it. . . .

December 1, 1936
Ivan Bunin, from his diary
   It is bright out. Once again I have decided to live in a healthier and more dignified way.

✳ 1937 ✳

January 1, 1937
Vera Muromtseva-Bunina, from her diary
   After dinner, we all set out for a "gathering of the nobility." It was a lot of fun and reminded me of [my life in] Moscow. No one acted like a snob.

January 23, 1937
Vera Muromtseva-Bunina, from her diary
   Ian almost set himself on fire. He was making vodka and had turned on the gas. The alcohol burst into flame.

January 30, 1937
Vera Muromtseva-Bunina, from her diary
   Wrangel stopped by today and read to Ian what he written about the Crimea.[9] Ian said: "Splendidly done."

February 1, 1937
Vera Muromtseva-Bunina, from her diary
   There were over 400 people at the Pushkin celebration.[1] Ian read very well.

[9]Wrangel's memoirs were published in two volumes in Berlin in 1928, and translated into English a year later.
[1]Russians on both sides of the border celebrated the one-hundredth anniversary of Pushkin's death in 1837.

February 4, 1937
Vera Muromtseva-Bunina, from her diary
   The Merezhkovskys came by to ask if I would arrange a reading for them. I refused, saying that it would be impossible to sell tickets for such an event.

February 6, 1937
Ivan Bunin, from an article
   [Celebrations for Pushkin] . . . What terrible days! What a terrible anniversary[2] . . . one of the most terrible events in all of the history of Russia, of that Russia which gave us Him. And that very Russia—where is it now?

   "Now, city of Peter, stand thou fast,
   Foursquare like Russia; vaunt they splendor!"

   "Oh, if only for a moment
   Poet and Tsar could break the gravelike bonds!"[3]

February 11, 1937
Marina Tsvetaeva, from a letter to Vera Muromtseva-Bunina
   Perhaps you have heard that on the evening of February 9th, Zamyatin died from angina pectoris.
   I was supposed to have met with him today. . . .
   His passing is a terrible shame, but I am comforted by the thought that he spent the last days of his life in the spiritual realm and in freedom.
   He and I met rarely, but when we did, it was always nice, since he and I were *neither* ours [emigrés], *nor* theirs [Soviets].[4]

March 31, 1937
Vera Muromtseva-Bunina, from her diary
   We visited the Rachmaninoffs. He has aged and is looking

---

   [2]On February 8, 1837, Pushkin was mortally wounded in a duel with George Heckeren d'Anthes, the point of contention being Pushkin's wife, Natalya.
   [3]Bunin is quoting first from Pushkin's 1825 poem, "The Bronze Horseman" ("*Mednyi vsadnik*"), and then from his own 1925 verse, "A Day to Remember Peter" ("*Den' pamiati Petra*").
   [4]Evgeny Zamyatin left the Soviet Union in 1931 and resided in Paris until his death. He was never comfortable with the emigré community there, though, since he still believed himself to be a Soviet writer. As Zamyatin wrote in his famous June 1931 letter to Stalin, he wished to return to Russia as soon as "it becomes possible to serve great ideas in our country without cringing before little men."

poorly. . . . At a competition of violinists in Brussels . . . the Soviets took first prize.

July 24, 1937
The Office of Soviet Intelligence, from a confidential report
For the past five years . . . Bunin has rained down curses on the Soviet Union, its structure, and its people. He cannot look at Soviet newspapers without shaking; he does not read anything of Soviet literature. Also, he mocks those who "waver" in their stance toward the homeland; and he exclaims that he is ready to kiss the shoes of any German or Japanese staff sergeant [who will end communism in his land]. To an observing person on close terms with Bunin, it is clear that such hostility [to Russia] is both the product of self-hypnosis and the result of personal anger and frustration. In no way does it have an "ideological basis."

If the Revolution had treated Bunin less severely, if Gorky had not trodden on his path to glory, if White generals had not welcomed him in such an offhand way, Bunin would have been our friend.

Internally, Bunin is only an artist. He is also a *bon vivant* who is irresponsible, egotistical, and ambitious. His [1936] meeting with [Alexei] Tolstoy shows how weak his social spine is. . . . When Bunin saw Tolstoy, he threw himself on the writer's neck and smothered him with kisses—an act that, to this day, Bunin's emigré friends have yet to forgive him for. . . .

Bunin's self-hypnosis, though, is so strong, and his new role as the "apostle of fascism" has consumed him so entirely, that no one or nothing could force him to reexamine his stance toward the Soviet Union. . . . He lives his life for pleasure, grabbing as much money as he can so that he can . . . eat, drink, and chase after young girls.

Bunin is very healthy and strong, though he is, from time to time, tormented by hemorrhoids—the single illness of his entire life. In the last few years he has increased his thirst for life. He eats a lot and greedily, and still possesses a taste for first-class cuisine. He also can drink a great deal and is a connoisseur of wines and vodkas. He gets drunk rarely, and even now can outdrink men younger than he.

By temperament, Bunin is nervous, witty, funny, resourceful, and high-strung. Desperate for attention, he loves to show off, dresses well, and shows a weakness for English things. He also loves French writers, especially Maupassant. Among Russian writers, he worships [Leo] Tolstoy. His last book, about Tolstoy, was written for Americans, and he was paid a great deal of money. . . . Most recently, Bunin has shown a special weakness for young ladies.[5] . . .

Late August 1937
Valentin Lavrov, from his book, Cold Autumn

Once, when Bunin was doing a reading in Venice, he came across some fellow emigrés. They were hale and hearty fellows, dressed in military uniforms, with high-calf boots and swastikas on their sleeves. They slouched down in the first row, their long legs stretching into the aisle. They barely heard what Bunin was saying, since they were loudly talking among themselves. One of them, with a sharp birdlike face and a closely cut moustache "à la Führer," was particularly obnoxious, since he kept asking Bunin the same question:

"Mr. Bunin! You still have not answered me: What kind of verse have you dedicated to us, real Russians, who have been crucified by the Bolsheviks?"

Bunin rolled his eyes, and the muscles of his face twitched:

"Crucified, you say? Yes, I will dedicate some verse to *you*. The freshest thing, hot from the oven. I will make up something right away."

The auditorium fell silent. Even those who were sitting in the first row put their feet back into their shoes.

Bunin stood silent for yet another moment. Then he lifted his face, and looking point-blank at the uninvited lovers of poetry, read the following, accenting every word:

> Golgotha is not always holy
> The crucified thieves were at a loss.
> For in no way did they hallow
> Either Golgotha or the cross.

The people in the calf boots headed for the exits. The evening went on as before.

---

[5]There are several untruths here. Bunin did read Soviet literature; he also opposed the Bolshevik regime on ideological grounds. He was never the "apostle of faciscm," nor did he seek favor with the German or Japanese military, throw himself on Alexei Tolstoy's neck, or write *The Liberation of Tolstoy* for money from Americans.

August 31, 1937
Ivan Bunin, to an interviewer

I have always been interested in places . . . where East meets West. For instance, I have visited Constantinople thirteen times. . . .

August 31, 1937
Alexander Afinogenov, from his diary

Whenever I read Bunin, my heart cries out from outrage and grief that the liberation of our people from their [national] nightmare came so late. . . . I feel like crying from happiness that we are now in another time, in a genuine and fully human life. . . .

November 28, 1937
Alexander Afinogenov, from his diary

I am reading *The Life of Arseniev*. . . . And I feel both pity and anger. Pity that Bunin's imagination is drying up . . . and that he is now tormented by chimeras, trying to resurrect his childhood as a model for the best of life in this world. . . . Compare this work with Tolstoy's *Childhood*. Bunin succeeds in evoking a series of interesting recollections, and his colors hold sway for a while; but such strengths are only a temporary success, like a dry branch that flares up in a fireplace . . . and then dies out. Bunin's reminiscences are uneven. His pictures of nature, of hunting, of trips to the city, of awakening emotions, these are very moving. But irksome are his scenes of church services, his marked preference for ancient words and . . . prayers, and his description of a city cathedral and of priests who have suddenly become kind and good. . . . One senses self-righteousness as well as deliberate anger and fury. . . .

Bunin maliciously slanders . . . students, revolutionaries, workers, and all those . . . who lived with the masses. . . . Such individuals, he believes, "destroyed Russia." What a pitiful, ridiculous notion! . . .

The end of *Arseniev* is a tearful, snot-filled mishmash depicting the funeral of a dead pretender to the Russian throne,[6] a bone that an old writer offers like a slave to an emigré son-of-a-bitch. . . . How can one not get angry here? To what swamplike levels has this wonderful writer descended? Bunin once knew life. He could write about it so graphically. How powerfully could he describe the life of the hungry, barefoot, and exhausted tsarist village whose only escape was the grave,

---

[6]The individual in question is Grand Duke Nikolai Nikolevich Romanov who, among Russian expatriates, was the oustanding favorite of the imperial family living abroad. See Marullo, *Ivan Bunin: From the Other Shore*, 205.

but which finally found a genuine way out in the Revolution, in socialism. But Bunin, having closed his eyes, staunchly affirms that he did not see, nor does he now see anything new in the country from which he fled like a thief. . . . There is nothing in this book worth noting; and, having finished it, I set it aside, sadly vexed that I had wasted the evening.

December 7, 1937
Ivan Bunin, from a letter to an American scholar
   I believe that I have influenced many writers. But how can I prove this, how can I determine what influence I have had on them? In my opinion, if it had not been for me, there would have been no Sirin-Nabokov (although, upon first glance, he seems so talented).

✳   1 9 3 8   ✳

1938
Tatyana Loginova-Muravieva, from her memoirs
   [Bunin said:] I do not understand what pleasure people get from inviting guests, working the entire day, buying things, hustling and bustling about, only to have it all disappear in an instant and to exclaim how happy they are that they did it all. . . .

1938
Vladimir Nabokov, from a letter
   Generally speaking, the eyes of Russian literature acquired a new vision from the middle of the last century on. . . . Fet showed it in poetry; Leo Tolstoy in prose. . . . A veil fell from the eyes of the Russian Muse . . . and Bunin appeared as a most powerful "connoisseur of colors." One could write an entire dissertation on his color schemes.

Circa April 25, 1938
A reporter, from an article
   Leaving a cemetery, Bunin noted: "Places of rest express the stance of a nation toward its past. Cemeteries and latrines say a great deal about things. . . .
   "I am reading . . . Schiller, but you yourselves will agree how far today's Germany is from that writer's ideals. . . ."

April 30, 1938
Ivan Bunin, from a letter to Vera Muromtseva-Bunina

There is *nothing* more difficult than to earn some money by read-ing one's works. First train rides, hotels, meetings, banquets . . . and then readings—play-acting. Behind the scenes, everything is going to the devil, and there is always a cold draft coming from somewhere. . . .

After one reading, there was a banquet. The speeches were so un-restrained, so *sincerely* enthusiastic and laudatory . . . that I am fully convinced that I am "Shakespeare at the very least." . . .

May 9, 1938
A Russian in Estonia, from her memoirs

[At one of Bunin's readings in Estonia] there was a huge crowd. We had to press our way through and stand against the wall. A great many young people were there—Russians, Estonians, and Germans. Bunin came onto the stage with a book in his hands. He answered the greetings with restraint, then sat down at a table. The first thing he read was "The Caucasus"[7] . . . [a work that is] three pages in all. Here Bunin writes about love in a direct and impassioned way; but is love the only thing he talks about? No, for here is also all of Russia, and everything that Bunin particularly loves about his homeland— Moscow, the road to the south, the steppe. . . . The audience listened in complete silence and with rapt attention. For us who had never seen Russia—here it was, with all its smells and voices, roads and villages, mountains and seas. He read splendidly. On stage he seemed much taller than he was. . . .

I saw Bunin offstage. He was sitting at a glass table, his face pale and mortally tired, leaning back against a carved chair. His closed eye-lids twitched nervously. This type of work was very difficult for him [to read]. . . .

When during the intermission we went to meet him . . . his face showed . . . that he was still living what he had just read. . . .

Circa May 9, 1938
A Russian in Estonia, from his memoirs

When reporters asked Bunin about his stance toward the Soviet Union, he replied sharply: "Russia was, is, and will be." . . .

[Later] he said with bitterness: "Yes, it is difficult to live without one's homeland. For all the years I have lived abroad, I still feel like a stranger in Paris . . . like a dried-up fig tree. . . ."

[7]Bunin wrote "The Caucasus" ("*Kavkaz*") in 1937.

July 5, 1938
Ivan Bunin, from a letter to Maria Karamzina

It is evening now . . . and I am sitting in a small, dirty but splendid restaurant that caters both to the simple folk of old Nice and to the snobs from the artistic bohemia of Paris. Someone once said that a "lonely person is like a rhinoceros." Well, I have enough loneliness and unhappiness for 100 rhinoceroses. . . .

[But in this restaurant] I smell garlic and fish being fried in olive oil. . . . Everything is simple and wonderfully free. The radio keeps blaring Spanish songs with castanets. It all suits the place very well. There is a lot of Italy and Spain here, and particularly old Nice. . . . There are also many women, almost naked, black from the sun, from swimming.

July 28, 1938
Ivan Bunin, from a letter to Boris Zaitsev

I am living such a strange and idiotic life that it is beyond words. . . .

August 25, 1938
Vera Muromtseva-Bunina, from her diary

I have not kept a diary for several years. Indeed, I have found this period of time difficult in all respects. But now I am trying to get back into the habit of writing. I have loved these years for their silence—but I have found people to be burdensome.

Tomorrow will be a major anniversary for me: It was twelve years ago that I became seriously ill for the first time. But such an experience changed my life, for it was then that I began—and continue—to search for God. . . .

Ian is in a bad mood. . . . He keeps talking about Kuprin.[8] . . .

September 17, 1938
Maria Karamzina, from a letter to Ivan Bunin

The political situation is so threatening that I keep thinking about you and about events which can happen any minute.

September 27, 1938
Boris Zaitsev, from a letter to Ivan Bunin

I have never seen Paris so mournful. The other day I heard two women crying. . . . One had her husband taken from her; another, her

---

[8]Alexander Kuprin died on August 25, 1938, of cancer of the esophagus.

son-in-law and two sons. . . . Everywhere there were groups of people talking in a quiet and gloomy way. . . .

The Jews here are in a particular panic. [A friend] is convinced that he will be killed as soon as the war begins. . . . [Another friend] believes that Hitler is already on the outskirts of the city. . . .

I myself believe there will not be a war. But yesterday my mood was poor . . . for we kept hearing Hitler's voice barking [from a radio] in a window. . . . But I still think that Hitler does *not* want a world war, that he is ready to concede some things so that he can immediately become master of the Sudetenland.[9] . . .

By the time you get this letter, things can change twenty times over. As I see it, there will be bargaining, the banging of hands like at a fair, periodic cursing . . . but God will not allow war to break out. . . .

October 18, 1938
Boris Zaitsev, from a letter to Ivan Bunin
I hear that you are writing a great deal. God grant that it be so. . . .

November 12, 1938
Boris Zaitsev, from a letter to Ivan Bunin
The other day my wife was reading Sirin-Nabokov in anger. I will not read him. I have had enough of his stories. I am a writer of taste, a Paul the Apostle if you will. Now, Paul could write extremely well. He was no Nabokov. . . .

[9]The Sudetenland is a region along the northern border of today's Czech Republic. Throughout the mid- and late 1930s, the Sudetan German Nazi party, led by Konrad Henlein, successfully capitalized on the political and economic discontent of the German population there to convince both Great Britain and France that the situation was extremely explosive, and that the leaders of what was then Czechoslovakia must be persuaded to avoid war by taking extreme action, even ceding the region to Germany.

In September 1938, Eduard Beneš, president of Czechoslovakia, acceded to almost all of Henlein's demands—he called for full autonomy for the Sudetenland as well as the complete adoption of a pro-German foreign policy by Czechoslovakia. Beneš, though, failed to reach an agreement with Hitler, who was using the unrest in the Sudetenland as a pretext eventually to take over all of the country. So, on September 29–30, Neville Chamberlain of Great Britain and Edouard Daladier of France met with Hitler and Mussolini to draft the so-called Munich Agreement which ordered Czechoslovakia to cede the Sudetenland to Germany by October 10 or to resist Germany alone. Beneš had no choice but to agree.

Both Daladier and Chamberlain returned home to jubilant crowds, but Chamberlain's claim of "peace in our time" was soon discredited when Hitler annexed the remainder of Czechoslovakia in March 1939 and six months later invaded Poland, thereby precipitating World War II.

PART TWO

Surviving a World at War
1939–1940

BUNIN, CA. 1930S

In early September 1939, what everyone had feared for more than a decade came true: the world was again at war. A year later, events moved with stunning quickness. On April 9, 1940, German forces invaded Norway and Denmark; on May 10 they overran the Low Countries. Three days later, Nazi paratroopers landed in northeast France, and on May 16, German units crossed the northwest extension of the Maginot Line. A month later, Nazi troops marched into Paris; on June 17, France sued for an armistice.

Hitler was triumphant. In just six weeks his forces had overrun the West, leaving England both alone and vulnerable to a cross-Channel invasion.

For Bunin and others in "Russia Abroad," the success of the Nazi advance was even more shocking in that it recalled the equally stunning victory of another enemy—the Bolsheviks—some twenty years earlier. Once again evil had triumphed over good; once again Bunin was at the mercy of individuals and events that threatened his survival.

But this time he was out of the line of fire. Whereas in both Moscow in 1918 and Odessa in 1919 and 1920 he had been an intimate witness to the carnage and chaos of the Russian Revolution and the civil war, he and his wife had left Paris for Grasse (in southeastern France) roughly one month before the Germans entered the French capital. Before the war they had summered in Grasse; now they lived there in the so-called free zone which, according to the Franco-German Armistice of June 22, 1940, had left the southeastern two-fifths of France under full if nominal sovereignty of the French. The Bunins felt the full effects of the war only three years later, when the Germans, who had come to the area only in November 1942, were ousted by the Allies.

Bunin, though, remained in close contact with emigré Russians who remained in and around Paris, if only because the city, under the Germans, had resumed an appearance of peacetime normalcy. Despite the Nazis' view of Paris as a corrupt "Babylon," they used the city as a place for rehabilitation and rest for their troops. German soldiers regularly paraded down the Champs Élysées; they rode the metro for free, had special tours of the city, and reserved for their exclusive use French movie houses, nightclubs, and restaurants. Although many Parisians had fled their city in the wake of the German advance, they soon returned to the French capital and resumed much of the prewar cultural activity there. Cinema, theatre, and nightclubs flourished, the plays of Jean-Paul Sartre enjoying the same popularity as performances by Maurice Chevalier. Pro-Axis literary and journalistic circles were also alive and well.

If life was good for the Germans and their allies in Paris, it was almost Darwinian for the the local populace. French and other civilians, barely surviving on drastically reduced rations, sought food from friends and relatives in the countryside. And, particularly in the later days of the Occupation, they were often the unavoidable casualties of Allied bombings of the city. Most grievously, Parisian Jews suffered the loss of their businesses and homes, and either went into hiding or were deported to extermination camps.

The Bunins returned to Paris in early May 1945, almost nine months after the liberation of the city. To their surprise and relief, they found almost everyone of their cultural circle alive and well; and, to their even greater joy, they found their apartment on rue Jacques Offenbach in southwestern Paris intact and ready for occupancy. Paris, it seemed, had been spared destruction twice: in June 1940, when it was declared an "open city" by the French and occupied by the Germans without resistance; and in August 1944, when a German garrison commander disobeyed Hitler's order to destroy the city rather than abandon it to the French.

Paris and Parisians thus survived, though it would take several years for both the city and its populace to recover from the privations of both the Occupation and the war.

Before 1939
Zinaida Shakovskaya, from her memoirs

I remember [visiting Paris and Bunin] immediately before the war. Some kind of elections were going on, and the results were being reported electronically, on the roof [of a building]. A dense crowd was milling around. Ivan Aleexevich, though, was never interested in the politics of the country in which he was fated to live; so he did not look at the election results but rather at the crowds, the fountains, and the sky glowing red from the city lights. . . .

With bitter hatred, Bunin looked at young couples clinging to each other as they passed by us. . . . So sharply did he feel regret for his lost youth, for the position that he now found himself in his declining years . . . that when he saw an athletic young man embracing a girl, he muttered: "Look at that son-of-a-bitch. He twists her around like a piece of meat so that he can do what he wants with her later tonight."

I replied: "Ivan Alexeevich, do you really envy him? After all, you are such a gifted man when compared to him. Would you want to return to your youth if it meant that you would stop being a writer?"

"Oh, that is a very stupid thing to ask," Ivan Alexeevich said with irritation. "I cannot renounce who I am." . . .

[Bunin told me:] "Take the moon. Young writers keep asking me, 'What should I write about?' After all, people have long written about everything. But these idiots know that no one has yet to write anything [genuine] about the moon . . . or for that matter, about love and death." Having said that, Bunin's sad and thoughtful face . . . took on a childlike reverence for the moon.

Before 1939
Sofya Pregel, from her memoirs

I was almost struck by how Ivan Alexeevich could transform himself. I recall . . . [one Easter before the war] when the table was set with several blue-and-red eggs, an inedible *kulich*,[1] and some nameless grey cheese. Bunin had been sitting at the table, dressed in some strange-looking clothes. . . . Suddenly he left for his room . . . and, to the surprise of everyone, reappeared in a light grey suit with a carnation in the lapel. His wrinkles were gone, and he radiated endless youth. . . . Here was the Bunin who had gone to see Chekhov in Yalta . . . here was the Bunin who had gone insane from a youthful, unrequited love.[2] . . . Bunin smiled a secret smile, and everyone became merry. But Vera Nikolaevna looked at him with a kind smile, like a mother at her good-for-nothing idler-son. . . .

[As a writer] Ivan Alexeevich . . . was very severe with himself. . . . I recall that in a story he had sent me . . . I took issue with one of his prepositions. I wrote to Ivan Alexeevich; and he responded to me immediately, saying not only that the transcriber had been unforgivably careless but that he too had been partially at fault: he had not corrected the manuscript as carefully as he should have. He also told me that if the story were printed in its original form, he would be in despair! . . . There was also Ivan Alexeevich's punctuation marks! . . . Every comma had to be checked, and not only for its syntactical function! . . .

Circa 1939
Nina Berberova, from her memoirs

When [Kuznetsova] left the Bunins' home at the end of the 1930s,[3] Bunin missed her terribly. For him she was probably his only genuine love in life. Bunin's male ego was wounded . . . he could not believe that such a thing (as her leaving) could happen to him. It seemed to him that she had left only for a short period of time, that she would return. But she did not. . . .

It was only very rarely, and especially after a bottle of wine, that

---

[1]*Kulich* is the tall, spectacular cake that Russians serve at Eastertime.

[2]Pregel is referring to Varvara Pashchenko, who was Bunin's wife (most likely common-law) from 1891 to 1894. In 1898, Varvara married Alexander Bibikov, a writer-director and, ironically, a friend of Bunin's whom the latter had often helped in his career. Varvara died of tuberculosis in 1918 at the age of forty-eight and was buried at the Novodevichy Convent in Moscow.

[3]This is not true. Galina Kuznetsova, who had been living with the Bunins since 1927, remained with them in Grasse until April 1942.

Bunin would "let his hair down." Then his handsome face came alive with feeling and thought. His massive strong hands underscored his cast of mind; his talk—about himself, of course—showed that he was not a petty, malicious, jealous, and conceited man but rather a great writer who had not found a genuine place in his time. . . .

1939
A Soviet scholar, from a book

The destruction of the patriarchal gentry estate and the breakdown of the village under the pressure of capitalism is a key theme in Bunin's works. . . . Poverty, ignorance, lack of culture, the oppression of the pre-Revolutionary village, in Bunin's words, of this "huge desert," "this kingdom of hunger and death"—are powerful and clear motifs in his writings. . . .

Bunin sees the Russian peasant as a cruel, primitive, and lazy half-savage . . . who harbors an elemental thirst for destruction. . . . In his view, the reasons for the folk's plight lie not in social, economic, or historical circumstances but in the peasant's dark, primordial, and elemental soul. He writes: "Rus' thirsts for self-torture; it is repulsed by work, life, and all sense of restraint. . . . Rus' is seized by dark criminal desires and lack of ambition; it is given to eternal anxiety, misfortune, sorrow, and poverty; and it has done so without end, and from time immemorial." . . .

Bunin's writings also sound motifs of gentry guilt and repentance before the peasants. At the same time, though, they show the gentry and the peasants as a "single clan" bound by ties of soil and blood, sharing an enemy . . . in industrial capitalism, and enduring a common fate—ruin, breakdown, and collapse. . . .

Mental depression, paralysis of the will, and yearning for death affect both the "masters" and the "men" in Bunin's stories . . . and align his writing with the literature of the decadents. . . . In Russia, Bunin sees Asia and *Tatarshchina*[4]—a mute land where nothing has changed since the time of the *Drevliane*.[5] It is a "place without history," a wasteland upon which "a long and quiet night is slowly descending." . . .

Bunin expands upon the demise of the patriarchal village and estate . . . to include the impoverishment, the "fading away" . . . and destruction of life in his world. [He relishes] . . . motifs of unrelieved

---

[4]A reference to the Tatars or Mongols who ruled Russia from the thirteenth to the fifteenth centuries.
[5]The *Drevliane* were tribal Eastern Slavs who lived from the sixth to the tenth centuries.

pessimism and fatalism, of the transience of life, and of the grief and loneliness of the individual in a perishing universe.

Bunin's settings feature autumnal decay and . . . roaring winter storms. . . . His hero is often a lonely old man who has lived out his time . . . or a pilgrim who walks through the mountains, sails the foggy seas . . . or journeys to famous graves . . . in Greece, Palestine, Egypt, and Babylon. In his essay, "Judea,"[6] Bunin . . . writes: "Life has completed an enormous circle. It has created . . . great religions and kingdoms; but having destroyed these . . . it has returned to primordial poverty and plainness." . . .

Bunin sees no genuine ways to rebuild life, nor does he actively search for such things. He finds subjective peace only in pictures of eternity and of other existences. He cannot think rationally about the world and human fate; he fears . . . the accidents and inscrutable forces that make life incomprehensible. . . .

If Gorky . . . calls for the renewal of humanity, oppressed by capitalism, Bunin's negation [of life] is like a biblical Ecclesiastes,[7] filled with fatalism, quietism, and assurance at the vanity of "human strivings." . . .

January 1, 1939
Vera Muromtseva-Bunina, from her diary

Ian is in a burdensome mood. He does not sleep nights; he has neither the time nor the energy to write or jot things down.

January 14, 1939
Vera Muromtseva-Bunina, from her diary

[A friend says] that "we should have only one Literary Union now, since there are so few of us left."

---

[6]Bunin wrote "Judea" ("*Iudeia*") in 1908.

[7]The book of Ecclesiastes, a product of the so-called Hebrew wisdom movement, is one of the most pessimistic writings in the Hebrew Bible. Traditionally associated with King Solomon, the real author of the work may have identified himself as the "son of David, king in Jerusalem" to give authority to his piece.

It is easy to see why Ecclesiastes was one of Bunin's favorite biblical works. The author of Ecclesiastes—crying "vanity of vanities!"—finds little meaning or security in wisdom, work, and wealth. Rather, he reiterates the uncertainties of life, the inscrutable ways of the Deity, and the stark and final reality of death. His only advice accords well with Bunin's own view: people should accept and be grateful for the small daily pleasures that God affords humankind.

March 5, 1939
Vera Muromtseva-Bunina, from her diary

It has been six years since papa died.[8] But what a remarkable time it has been. How many tragedies, triumphs, and impressions I have encountered. But I would like to have things be the way they used to be. I would like to work, of course, but to do a more incisive, religious type of labor. God grant that it be so!

I often think about death. How much longer do I have to live?[9] But I am not ready [for death]. I have not vanquished all my shortcomings. . . .

March 9, 1939
Vera Muromtseva-Bunina, from her diary

The other day Ian said that he does not know how he would survive if I died before him. "To deprive oneself of life?" Dear Lord, the human soul is such a strange thing!

We then talked about God. Ian believes that we have a divine beginning, but he still does not accept a God who is apart from us. But he has already repented of much in his past; he blames himself [for his actions]. This is something he did not do earlier, and it is good that he is doing so now. I talked to him guardedly. I am afraid to keep bringing up religious questions, since it is not we who do things but the Holy Spirit, God's grace.

March 15, 1939
Vera Muromtseva-Bunina, from her diary

I read the newspaper, and again I become anxious. Is war inevitable?

March 29, 1939
Ivan Bunin, from a letter to Maria Karamazina

I find Sirin-Nabokov unbearable. He is like a cab driver alongside a tavern, but nonetheless he is a remarkable writer.

June 17, 1939
Mark Aldanov, from a letter to Ivan Bunin

I am deeply disturbed by Khodasevich's passing. . . .[1]

I saw him in his coffin. His face was peaceful, and there was a

---

[8]Nikolai Andreevich Muromtsev died on March 5, 1933.
[9]Twenty-two years, to be exact.
[1]Khodasevich died on June 14, 1939.

slight smile on his lips. . . . He was a very intelligent and talented individual. . . .

June 20, 1939
Boris Zaitsev, from a letter to Ivan Bunin
Thank God, Khodasevich did not depart life in anger but had become quite peaceful. . . .

At the memorial service, everyone was there . . . [including] his wife and two former wives.[2] Nina [Berberova] was very shaken. . . . Her face had a tormented look; she has aged considerably. . . .

The cemetery [where Khodasevich was buried] can almost be seen from my window . . . and it is becoming the resting place for many of our close friends. . . . I find it difficult and threatening to think that Khodasevich is now also there. . . .

But "life goes on." . . . *Illustrated Russia*[3] has just chosen a "Miss Russia." . . . I had my picture taken with her . . . even though I had to "suck in my stomach."

P.S. You still have at least twelve more years to seduce the ladies and maidens.

July 30, 1939
Boris Zaitsev, from a letter to Ivan Bunin
About Khodasevich, people are writing nonsense and the most terrible lies. One would think he was a saint . . . or Pushkin. . . . Kerensky is also prattling on about him. . . .

August 2, 1939
Vera Muromtseva-Bunina, from her diary
Ian is heartbroken that [our former villa] "Belvedere" has been rented. But we could not have afforded it anyway. I try to comfort him, saying that everything happens for the best. Besides, how could we have heated such a place? There is not a single able man around. And I am weak. . . .

---

[2]Khodasevich was married to Marina Ryndina from 1905 to 1907, to Anna Chulkova from 1911 to 1912, to Berberova from 1922 to 1932, and to Olga Margolina from 1933 until his death. Since Chulkova never left Russia, it was Ryndina, Berberova, and Margolina who attended the writer's funeral.

[3]*Illustrated Russia* (*Illiustrirovannaia Rossiia*) appeared from 1924 to 1939 and was primarily a pictorial magazine, with serialized popular romances and mysteries, and special feature articles for women and children.

August 10, 1939
Vera Muromtseva-Bunina, from her diary

I received a heartrending letter from Teffi. She cannot reconcile herself either to sickness or old age. She wants everything to remain as before. She sees only suffering before her and does not look for another life in which she could find even a little happiness. The nature of an artist desires earthly existence so greedily that its host finds it impossible to be humble. Without humility, there is no peace or joy. . . .

August 17, 1939
Vera Muromtseva-Bunina, from her diary

We went looking for a villa in Cannes, and we found one that was very nice. I think that Ian could write there. . . .

August 31, 1939
Vera Muromtseva-Bunina, from her diary

We have spent the last few weeks in a state of extreme tension. Will there be war or peace? . . . We are packing our things.

September 3, 1939
A Soviet journalist, from an article

At eleven o'clock in the morning, the French radio reported that the British government had declared war on Germany. At five o'clock that evening the French government also issued a declaration of war.[4]

Stepping out onto the balcony in the twilight, Ivan Alexeevich hailed [a friend] strolling in the garden below:

"Come here! Take this postcard to the post office, please!" . . .

The postcard was addressed to Alexei Nikolaevich Tolstoy. . . . It read: "I want to go home." Besides these words and Bunin's signature, there was nothing else on the card. The postcard was mailed that evening. But Bunin's wish was not fated to come true.

September 3, 1939
Vera Muromtseva-Bunina, from her diary

England has declared war [on Germany]. Another period of our life has come to an end.

---

[4]Germany invaded Poland on September 1, 1939. On September 3, France and Britain issued an ultimatum to Germany, demanding the immediate withdrawal of German forces in Poland. When Hitler refused, both countries, along with India, Australia, and New Zealand, declared war on Germany.

Yesterday we made dark blue lampshades and covered all the windows [of our house] with blue or black paper. All of Grasse is dark. . . . For the third time in my life, I am seeing young people off to war. But the French soldiers do not resemble ours. They walk in a different, clumsy way, not with the bearing that our troops had. But they are good fighters. I pity them. . . .

September 4, 1939
Vera Muromtseva-Bunina, from her diary
My heart is torn with the thought that we may leave France and all our close friends and acquaintances. We talk about going to Switzerland. . . .

This evening I counted all our friends and acquaintances who are going off to war. There are 57 of them. . . .

September 6, 1939
Vera Muromtseva-Bunina, from her diary
[A friend writes that] a train station in Paris is "like a fortress made from mounds of sand. People go along the streets with gas masks strapped to their shoulders. The city is empty and eerie." . . .

The people in Paris had an anxious night. They spent more than four hours in the cellars!

September 7, 1939
Vera Muromtseva-Bunina, from her diary
[A friend writes] that "all Paris is living a difficult, nervous life. . . . I keep meeting with new recruits and we are all united. Yesterday . . . I ran into the Merezhkovskys. They had gotten hold of a detective novel from a secondhand store. Gippius said: 'In such times as these, I save myself only by reading detective novels. Come to my place on Sunday. *All the draftees will be there.*' . . .

The French are conducting themselves in an amazing way. They deserve great respect for their courage, endurance, and composure. . . . Our building is empty. Everyone has left. . . . But I am at peace."

September 8, 1939
Vera Muromtseva-Bunina, from her diary
I fear . . . for the Merezhkovskys. How are they going to run for shelter in the night? After all, Gippius cannot see or hear anything. . . .

September 12, 1939
Vera Muromtseva-Bunina, from her diary

[A friend writes]: "Our entire cultural life . . . the past twenty years of our poor emigré respite . . . has come to a halt. . . ."

September 18, 1939
Vera Muromtseva-Bunina, from her diary

Yesterday we rented a villa named "Jeanette."[5] . . . Its owners were in a hurry to conclude the transaction since they are leaving for London tomorrow. . . . They are letting it go cheaply—12,000 francs a year. . . . It is a marvelous place, full of "surprises." But it will be hard to climb up to it, especially when one is carrying packages.

Soviet armies have crossed the Polish border. They insist they are doing so only to protect Byelorussians.[6] I try not to think about Poland, for I find it too horrible to do so. . . .

September 22, 1939
Vera Muromtseva-Bunina, from her diary

We should get organized, but this is very difficult, given Ian's character. He never wants to keep track of expenses.

But he has become gentler, more solicitous. For some time now he has bought me all kinds of small things for my dressing table. We also often talk about philosophical and literary things.

September 26, 1939
Vera Muromtseva-Bunina, from her diary

This is our last evening at "Belvedere." I stood by the window . . . and bade farewell to the view which was especially charming, since the city was completely dark. Then Ian came in. He has been particularly nervous today. He has also been in a burdensome mood. How many thoughts and feelings did he have in this room.

[5]Villa "Jeanette" still stands, as a museum-monument to Bunin and his life.
[6]On September 17, forty divisions of the Red Army crossed Poland's thousand-mile eastern border. Russian soldiers confused the already overwhelmed Polish defenders by traveling in vehicles carrying white flags, and by yelling at the Poles, "Don't shoot. We have come to help you against the Germans."

Vyacheslav Molotov, Soviet Commissar of Foreign Affairs, defended Russia's action, saying: "Events arising out of the Polish-German War have revealed the internal insolvency and obvious impotence of the Polish state. . . . The population of Poland has been abandoned by their ill-starred leaders to their fate. . . . Poland has become a fertile field for any accidental and unexpected contingency that may create a menace to the Soviet Union . . . nor can it be demanded of the Soviet Government that it remain indifferent to the fate of its blood brothers, the Ukrainians and the Byelorussians inhabiting Poland."

October 1939 and later
Tatyana Loginova-Muravieva, from her memoirs

When war broke out in 1939, the Bunins were alone and perplexed. . . . They were now living at a new villa called "Jeanette" . . . which was much better and more spacious than "Belvedere." Its wonderful, lordly surroundings, together with its splendid view of Grasse, greatly pleased the Bunins. Of course, to climb to "Jeanette" was no easy thing. The villa was one of the last on the Napoleon Road, almost on the very outskirts of Grasse. . . . It took an hour and a half to get there from the city . . . along narrow paths and staircases, past cactuses and abandoned kitchen-gardens.

Bunin, though, loved these "heights" and "narrow paths." But he was afraid to be alone there; he wanted his nest to be filled with "lively" people.

On the top floor of the villa lived the "mountaineers"—G. N. Kuznetsova and M. A. Stepun. (They were called the "ladies" because they did not always condescend to be with the people below.) . . . People visited them by invitation only, along a rather steep staircase. . . . They were inseparable and always talked about themselves in the plural. . . . Galina was a very pleasant-looking, gentle, and feminine individual of medium height; Marga was a tall, thin singer who often wore glasses and slacks.

The "mountaineers" talked about literature and music. They loved to be alone, often going off by themselves, despite the unhappy and reproachful looks of a jealous Ivan Alexeevich. When such a thing happened, Bunin suddenly seemed older. He became flaccid-looking, with bags under his eyes and hanging cheeks. . . . But when he and the "mountaineers" took off together, his face shone brightly; he was all sparkle and youth.

It is very difficult to describe Bunin's face, because all his features were always in motion. The folds under Bunin's eyes, the wrinkles that ran lengthwise along his forehead, his somewhat flaccid cheeks, the double but strong-willed chin, and especially his mouth and lips that moved about in such a way that they seemed to give him a variety of faces. Even his somewhat eaglelike nose never seemed to stay the same.

Bunin's small, deeply set eyes lighted his very special face. Their expression and even their color could change like lightning. They expressed youthful gleam and passion, sparkling humor and secret sadness. Along with tenderness, they often featured anger, distress, even outrage. . . .

Bunin was always "on stage," making splendid use of his acting gifts. Vera Nikolaevna was more than correct when she said that her husband had all the qualities of a first-rate actor.

He also had an aristocratic bearing. Even when he leaned on a cane, he always held himself erect. Tanned and always wearing an English cap, he looked more like a sailor or a captain who had "sailed the world." He loved to travel, to change his scenery, to embrace the wide expanse of existence. . . .

Ivan Alexeevich, though, was a very private and reserved individual. He let loose only in his writing, something that he found as necessary as breathing.

The study where Bunin hid himself was located on the second floor of "Jeanette." It was filled with sunshine and light, with wide windows and a marvelous view on the extended expanse below—the far-off hills and mountains of the Esterel, and the light blue band of the sea. The furnishings facilitated intellectual work: a huge desk, several handsome soft chairs, soft rugs, and a couch on which Ivan Alexeevich slept.

Vera Nikolaevna had a far-off room with a large, glassed-in balcony that overlooked a garden. In it were a table and a typewriter on which, for years on end, she typed Ivan Alexeevich's manuscripts. Everywhere were masses of paper and books, icons and family mementos, but no knickknacks. In truth, Vera's room was a like a cell, without the slightest bit of comfort or anything specifically feminine in it. "I love to be alone here," she would say, "to think and talk with my memory."[7] On the balcony were flowers in pots that stood both on the walls and the windowsills. There also was a large ottoman with pillows, along with some garden furniture: a table and several chairs. This balcony was especially designated for guests. Vera Nikolaevna especially loved "to speak with kindred spirits." . . .

In those years, Vera Nikolaevna was still youngish-looking. Tall and well built, she always kept herself erect. Her face was pale and often seemed wasted-looking; she quickly became tired. Her straight, closely cropped hair framed her delicately featured face . . . and had begun to go completely white.

People said that as a young woman, Vera Nikolaevna's eyes were the most prominent feature of her face, and that from them shone blue rays of light. "Her eyes shone blue like flowers," Bunin once wrote. But now they had grown pale, though they still sparkled with kindness and

[7]In fact, in *New Review* in 1960 and 1961, Muromtseva-Bunina published a series of recollections entitled "A Conversation with Memory" ("*Beseda s pamat'iu*"). A posthumous supplement to her memories also appeared in *New Review* in 1969.

life. One could well imagine how beautiful Vera Nikolaevna had been in her youth, like a Greek profile in a cameo. She dressed very simply but tastefully. She never wore anything that made her look slovenly.

Vera Nikolaevna maintained such an unusually proper air that she often seemed even "majestic." . . . Her rare spiritual nobility invested her with a special aristocratic quality. But, despite her ability to take herself in hand, she was prone to extreme nervousness.

Ivan Alexeevich was very proud of her and loved to see her looking like a well-dressed society lady. He was also extremely jealous of her. But that is how he was—he did everything "without measure." . . .

Because "everyone was jealous of everyone else," the atmosphere at villa "Jeannette" was often rife with electricity or the menace of a brewing storm. . . .

At the end of every September, the people at villa "Jeanette" celebrated Vera Nikolaevna's name day. Once, for that occasion, everyone decided to dress up in costumes to distract themselves from the war. At that time people believed that the struggle would come to an early end.

Vera Nikolaevna, always so very young at heart, loved all kinds of stories, jokes, and nicknames. . . . She always laughed from the bottom of her heart. . . . One time she appeared as a "queen," wearing a pretty velvet dress and a paper crown on her head. . . .

Ivan Alexeevich also had a nickname: "Prince Literature" and "His Most Enlightened One." . . . But [despite his acting abilities] he refused to wear a costume. We were all quite annoyed, but we remained quiet for we knew . . . that it was dangerous to irritate him. Ivan Alexeevich, though, could not be angry or hold a grudge for long. . . . The "Prince" smiled condescendingly . . . at our merriment and dances to music from old records on the gramophone. When he left to go upstairs to his room, things suddenly became boring. The mood of the "Prince" was the barometer of the house. . . .

According to Vera Nikolaevna, the death of Kolya, Bunin's five-year-old son from his first marriage,[8] distressed him greatly. Kolya was an unusually gifted little boy, and Ivan Alexeevich was never reconciled with his son's untimely death. Ivan Alexeevich had an organic love for children. For him, they personified purity and chasteness, everything that blossomed under the sun. . . . If the Bunins had had their own

---

[8]Bunin's marriage to Anna Tsakni in 1898 failed in eighteen months; his son, Nikolai Ivanovich Bunin, died on January 16, 1905.

children and grandchildren, their lives would have been entirely different. . . . Whenever children fell his way, he was like a sorcerer or magician in the way he could capture their hearts!

Bunin was always moving and striving. . . . He was always going off somewhere. . . .

The continued succession of all living things was something that Bunin felt with all his soul. That is why he loved youth so much. In truth, despite the long years of hardship, he remained young spiritually. . . . He never lost his spiritual youth. . . .

October 2, 1939
Boris Zaitsev, from a letter to Ivan Bunin

I do not know what will happen next. . . . The first days [in Paris since war broke out] were the most nerve-racking ones. Now it is calmer. Maybe it is because we have gotten used to our new life, or are beginning to get used to it. But our mood is *not* an easy one. . . . I sleep and eat as usual. As Ostrovsky says, "The individual grows thin from thinking." . . .

Many people are attending church. . . .

This winter we will probably have to keep the oven going, as there will be no heat. . . . We will also have to stock up on patience. . . .

Berberova invited us to stay with her.[9] If things get too "loud" here, perhaps we will leave Paris. I do not know. I prefer to stay here. . . .

P.S. I am very glad that you are staying in Grasse. . . .

October 17, 1939
Vera Muromtseva-Bunina, from her diary

The Germans have sunk an English battleship, and 800 men have perished. I cannot even imagine such a thing!

October 20, 1939
Ivan Bunin, from a letter to Boris Zaitsev

Last winter was so sad and lonely, but now, by comparison, it seems happy. . . . I am reading Merezhkovsky's *Dante*. What a scholastic and phrasemonger that fucker is. . . .

The fall is sunny but empty and tormentingly quiet. I am perish-

---

[9]At this time, Berberova was living in the village of Longchêne, roughly twenty-five miles southwest of Paris.

ing. . . . The other day I reread *The Death of Ivan Ilyich* and was vastly disappointed. . . . That is not the way someone should live. . . .

October 20, 1939
Vera Muromtseva-Bunina, from her diary
[A friend] writes: "In a few days, the Red Army will occupy Latvia. The entire Baltic region has become Soviet."[1]

November 2, 1939
Ivan Bunin, from a letter to Boris Zaitsev
On our new identification papers, Jean de Bounine, Vera de Bounine, and Mme. Galina Kouznetzoff are listed as *homme de lettres et femmes de lettres*. But now we need new proof from the Union of Writers that we really have such a distinction. . . .

November 2, 1939
Boris Zaitsev, from a letter to Ivan Bunin
Whatever you write—be it in great literature or on a scrap of paper (which, in essence, is also great literature)—always calls forth a deep resonance in me. . . . Maybe this sounds stupid . . . but I am sure you understand.

Paris is quieting down little by little. The theatres and movie houses are open—true, only until 11 p.m. . . . The first blackouts really got on my nerves . . . but I am getting used to them. . . .

Nina Berberova came by yesterday—and burst into tears. I gave her something to calm her down. She said that the war depresses her. . . . But today I found out that before she visited us, she had been at Khodasevich's grave. . . . She spoke of you in a very tender sort of way. (She loves you, something I have known for a long time.)

I am very touched by your words about my writing. God keep you safe. Do not get depressed, but keep your shoulder to the wheel. Do not philosophize, do not try to embrace the unembraceable or to understand that which has not been given to us to understand. Open the Bible, read and reap. . . .

P.S. At a funeral . . . I saw our "lyrical brother, before whom all other poets are forerunners." . . . Balmont is being called a dead man. "How are you getting along, Balmont?" I asked. "Boris," he replied,

---

[1]On September 28, 1939, Russia and Estonia signed a ten-year treaty of mutual assistance, with the Soviets acquiring military rights and access to raw materials. Similar pacts with Latvia on October 5 and Lithuania on October 10 completed Soviet hegemony over the area.

"every swallow of liquid brings forth suffering." (Hydrophobia is a symptom of insanity.) He was quiet, tormented-looking, and evoked deep pity. So much for *We Will Be Like the Sun!*[2]

November 10, 1939
Boris Zaitsev, from a letter to Ivan Bunin
For the past three days the Germans have been making their way toward us. . . . [A friend] came by with a bottle of Château-neuf-du-Pape which we polished off quietly; all the while anti-aircraft artillery was sounding around Paris. . . .

November 11, 1939
Boris Zaitsev, from a letter to Ivan Bunin
This afternoon . . . the siren sounded and we all "gathered" in the cellar . . . for an hour. But we are getting quite used to such things. . . .

I also read that the Nobel Prize was finally awarded to an old Finn[3] who has long been angry that he had not received the honor.

November 16, 1939
Vera Muromtseva-Bunina, from her diary
I decided to spend the day amidst nature . . . in complete solitude . . . and silence.

November 21, 1939
Ivan Bunin, from a letter to a friend
Do not think that anyone in Europe needs Russian writers. No one buys their works; not even Russians read them. The old writers live on charity; and the young ones also receive funds from philanthropic gatherings and grab any kind of work they can. . . . The (spiritually) sick Balmont has received a great deal of help this past year. . . .

December 1939
Nina Berberova, from her memoirs
Bunin has been troubled by the question: Has he accomplished everything that he could? . . . He said that Rachmaninoff was tormented by the same thing. . . . Bunin wants to express himself in his works to the fullest extent of his powers. He also wishes to savor "the mysterious and rosy-white flesh of a woman, before which everything

---

[2]Balmont's *We Will Be Like the Sun* (*Budem kak solntse*) appeared in 1903.
[3]The "old Finn" was the novelist Frans Eemil Sillanpaa, who was fifty-seven years old at the time. (Bunin was sixty-three when he was accorded the honor.)

[else] is nothing." He says: "My life has passed me by, like a dinner that has not been eaten. . . . How very stupid I was! Now I want my youth, the charm of the world." . . .

From a letter of a [friend] in the south of France:

"We were once part of a nasty, poor, pitiful (emigré) Russia. Russian newspapers, Russian magazines, Russian rumors, Russians coming from there—sometimes we were alienated from the homeland, but we always had an opinion about what was going on there. But now there is nothing. We have been cut off. There are no newspapers or magazines, there are no arrivals or opinions. . . . My generation will be killed [in war] and the old will die off in quick order.

"I view all of world history with suspicion. There has never been justice or good or beauty. . . . I write nothing. I cannot, nor do I want to. What for? For whom? I have always loved people, but now I am deprived of those who are dear to me. . . . Who has died, who has left, who is distressed by his fate? But the most terrible thing is that I do not even feel like seeing them. . . .

"I thought of writing some [of the above] . . . to Bunin. But I am afraid that I will distress him even more, he is so miserable. . . . Zaitsev agrees with me." . . .

One night [when the Bunins were still in Paris] my husband, N. Makeev and I got stuck in Paris . . . so we spent the night at their place. . . . Bunin was alone. Vera Nikolaevna was off somewhere. . . . We talked until quite late (about 3 a.m.). On the desk in Vera Nikolaevna's room was her famous diary. (Aldanov once said to me: "Beware! . . . She's going to put you in there!") . . . One page was open. On it in the roundish handwriting of a child was written: "Tuesday. It rained. Ian has a stomachache. [A friend] stopped in."

This reminded me of the diary that Chekhov's father kept in Melikhovo:[4] "A peony blossomed in the garden. Maria Pavlovna came by. The peony faded. Maria Pavlova left."

We sat in Bunin's study. He told us everything, from beginning (and to the end) of his love [for Galina Kuznetsova] which still tormented him. Toward the end (both he and Makeev continued to drink), he really got upset. Tears flowed from his eyes, and he kept repeating: "I understand nothing. I am a writer, an old man, and I understand nothing. How can this be? Tell me, how can this be?"

Makeev embraced and kissed him. I stroked his head and face and

---

[4]Melikhovo was an estate that Chekhov bought in 1892, and is located about forty-five miles south of Moscow.

also got very upset. All three of us faltered terribly. In the end we went to bed. In the morning we left, but Bunin was still asleep.

December 3, 1939
Vera Muromtseva-Bunina, from her diary
Yesterday Ian and I talked about pilots. Do they know that they will perish?
Ian is very upset over Finland.[5]

December 9, 1939
Boris Zaitsev, from a letter to Vera Muromtseva-Bunina
It would be a very good idea if you could manage to get back here [to Paris]. Life is slow, but it is slowly returning to normal. The mood now is different from what it was three months ago. But all the same, it is still very sad. We are still saddened by what has happened to Finland.[6] . . . Just think of all our friends there. . . . It is just like Russia twenty years ago! . . .
The barbarians are coming! And we are the "last of the Romans." But no matter, for we will not surrender but will die with all that is sacred to us. . . .

December 29, 1939
Boris Zaitsev, from a letter to Ivan Bunin
Our letter about Finland is not worth much, but you should sign it nonetheless.[7] . . .

---

[5]On November 28, 1939, the Soviet Union, outraged that the Finns had allegedly fired on Russian troops from their border near Leningrad, renounced the 1932 nonaggression pact between the two countries. On November 29, the Soviet Union broke off diplomatic relations with Finland, and on the following day, Russian troops invaded the country.
On December 2 the Finns appealed to the League of Nations to mediate their quarrel with the Soviets. They were also putting up a desperate but heroic defense of their land. In the struggle, they inflicted heavy losses on the Russians not only because the Finns attacked ponderous Soviet tanks from quick-moving bicycles and skis but also because they hurled into Soviet tank turrets a type of incendiary grenade that would become famous as the "Molotov cocktail"—a bottle filled with gasoline, with a lighted rag in its mouth.
[6]At this stage in the Russo-Finnish War, the Russians had advanced to the so-called Mannerheim Line, the main Finnish defense line along the isthmus of Karelia.
[7]Bunin, together with Teffi, Gippius, Berdyaev, Merezhkovsky, Zaitsev, Aldanov, Remizov, Rachmaninoff, and Nabokov, published a letter in *Latest News*, protesting the Soviet invasion of Finland. The missive read:
"In these days, when the government of the USSR is bringing falsehood, death, and destruction across the borders of peaceful Finland, we, the undersigned, consider it our duty to register a most impassioned protest against this insane transgression.
"The Stalinist government has again covered itself in shame; but in vain are its mis-

✳ 1940 ✳

Circa 1940
Vera Muromtseva-Bunina, from a letter to Alexander Bakhrakh

Do not think that I am living in this ivory tower of my own free will. If I had had the freedom and strength, I, perhaps, would have gone . . . to Finland. But I have already lived thirty-three years, refusing to arrange life according to my tastes and tying my existence to that of Ivan Alexeevich, a very original individual. For *twenty* years I lived in close spiritual proximity with him, trying to merge our desires and strivings. We did everything together. But then I understood that such a thing was no longer possible. So I started to seek new paths for myself. Why was it no longer possible? If you read *Lika*,[8] you will have your answer.

Of course, I am not Lika and Ian is not Arseniev. . . . A woman who is married to a creative individual, but who does not live for his ambition . . . will never receive the attention, the response to her own inner life that she desires. She knows that her mate is greedy, that he is never satisfied with what he has, that he loves to take from everyone

---

deeds shouldered by an enslaved Russian people who bear no responsibility for their actions. After all, the very same people who are committing crimes in Finland have brought about countless and even worse transgressions in Russia itself.

"Further, we assert that the Russian people never had or can have the slightest hostility toward their Finnish neighbors who now defend their homes so heroically. We also believe that between Russia and Finland, there can never be any questions that cannot be decided hospitably, in a peaceful way. Furthermore, the Stalinist government has no right to speak in the name of the Russian people, since, with Hitler's blessing, it is shedding both Russian and Finnish blood. In their dark designs, and for reasons that are both fleeting and insignificant, Stalin and his group are preparing Russia for a catastrophe; and they are committing crimes for which the Russian people will pay heavily.

"We also note that when Russia is freed from the Communist dictatorship, it will come to a peaceful accord with Finland . . . and that it will show enduring respect for both the interests and mores of a country for whom we now express our deep sympathy." See "Protest protiv vtorzheniia v Finliandiiu," *Poslednie novosti* (December 31, 1939), 4.

Russian exiles were not the only ones to register their outrage over Soviet aggression. On December 14, 1939, the League of Nations expelled Russia from its ranks. (Such a course of action was one of the few decisive acts of an organization that was founded to guarantee world peace.) Additionally, the League asked member countries to render all possible assistance to Finland.

Such a request, however, seemed almost perfunctory. By the end of December, the Finns were still resisting their invaders, having scored a resounding defeat against the Russians at Suommuslami.

[8]*Lika* was the fifth and last "book" in *The life of Arseniev.* Like Muromtseva-Bunina, Lika strikes out for independence, seeking her own life and interests.

around, and that he gives himself only to his work and never to anything else.

Here it is already the thirteenth year that I have been searching;
and at long last I have found God. I am very happy with that inner
freedom which is especially easy to have when one lives with a creative
individual. In no way does my freedom from Ian destroy my friendship
with him. I am always ready to listen to everything. But I do not suffer
when there are aspects of my life that only *I* find interesting.

1940
Tatyana Loginova-Muravieva, from her memoirs
In Grasse, the Bunins entertained occasional acquaintances and
friends. At their table one met people who had nothing to do with art,
nor had anything special about them other than the fact that they were
"Russian."

For Ivan Alexeevich, there was no such thing as an "uninterest-
ing" person. "From childhood on," Vera Nikolaevna often said, "Ivan
Alexeevich had a spontaneous feeling for people. His favorite occupation was to discern an individual's character by his hands and legs or by
the type of umbrella he carried. I have never known a more insightful
eye than his. No matter what one said, he replied, 'I can see it already!'
I never understood how he did it." . . .

Everything was "interesting" for Bunin's "booklike memory,"
something he filled constantly and used as needed.

"All things are good," Bunin said. "Everything has something remarkable and unique about it. For instance, what can be more usual
than the color grey? But I once saw such a rare form of grey that it
stopped me dead in my tracks. A man had come to me. Not only were
his shirt and pants grey, but his very self, the very ends of his hair—
were grey." . . .

Bunin needed different kinds of people as much as he needed different types of nature. . . . Without people and nature, Bunin could not
live . . . or write. But he used up "human material" very quickly. He
grew cold suddenly, and his face, which had been so expressive, took on
a tired look. He would get up and go to his room, and the conversation
would go on without him.

It would be wrong, though, to say that Bunin looked upon individuals only as "material" for his writing. He had a lively interest in
their fates. He was never "dry" with people, though it sometimes
seemed that he was.

"Many people knew that Bunin's soul could be extremely tender,"
Vera Nikolaevna told me. "He was particularly solicitous of children

and old people who reminded him of his family. He loved his mother without end. 'No one loved me like Vanya did,' she often said. 'No one had a more tender soul than he.' Bunin remembered his father with ineffable love; he waxed eloquent over the man's artistic giftedness, his merry disposition, his expansive nature, and, most of all, his expressive language which he passed on to his son. Bunin also loved his brothers and sister with all the passion of his soul. He was 'passionate' in everything he did; he was never 'lukewarm' or 'cold.' Indeed, he could 'hate' with a passion."

Vera Nikolaevna was similarly disposed toward people. To everyone she gave a piece of her loving heart. How many she surrounded with her maternal affection and care! And to whomever needed help, she showed her remarkable talents. Tirelessly she arranged collections and benefits and wrote "teary letters" to people with means. She could touch the hearts of the most callous and miserly people.

In their genuine humanity, the Bunins very much complemented one another. . . .

January 21, 1940
Vera Muromtseva-Bunina, from a letter to Tatyana Loginova-Muravieva
From childhood on, my heart has always been pained by the sight of a Christmas tree lying in a snow-covered yard [after the holidays]. It always seemed to me to be a sign of ingratitude: we got the tree because it gave us so much joy, but we threw it out when we did not need it anymore. . . .

February 27, 1940
Boris Zaitsev, from a letter to Ivan Bunin
Yesterday evening turned out to be a rather anxious one. . . . About nine o'clock there were whistles and a great deal of hustle and bustle. . . . The radio announced that the Germans were approaching. From my window I saw a beautiful sight: searchlights were flashing a web of silver-golden rays: geometrical figures. The top of one polygon seemed to move as if it harbored a "beast." There were also the sounds of guns, but they did not last long. . . .

Today the newspapers reported that German air squadrons had been advancing toward Paris but had been repulsed.[9] . . .

I have been rereading *Dry Valley*, and I find it enchanting! As I

---

[9]This is not true. The so-called "phony war" that marked the early days of World War II continued unabated.

see it, it is the closest thing you have to Turgenev. *The Village* is still alien to my tastes, but its scenes are without equal. . . .

April 3, 1940
Ivan Bunin, from his diary
  [At a bar] I behaved very stupidly—I had a shot of whiskey followed by three glasses of gin. . . . *I should not drink.*
  I am rewriting excerpts from previous diaries. I also tore up and burned a great deal.

April 4, 1940
Ivan Bunin, from his diary
  [Today I saw] a dreadful-looking old man, with nails and fingers that looked completely gravelike. . . . Does he ever think that his terrible corpse is about to be carried off to a cemetery?

April 4, 1940
Ivan Bunin, from a letter to Maria Karamzina
  I have begun to think endlessly and as never before . . . about the vanity of all things and also about death . . . as something that is real and close at hand. Say that I still have five or, at the most, ten years left. But they will pass by so quickly that I will not even have the time to look around. . . . I keep spreading my hands in despair. As I see it, the fact that someday I will no longer exist is such a savage stupidity! Why, I still feel only thirty years old. Forgive me, dear God, but I also think about the other vile things that go with death—the coffin, the sprinkling of earth [on the lid] . . . and so forth. . . .

April 16, 1940
Boris Zaitsev, from a letter to Ivan Bunin
  You know what is most important in life: *to live and love.*

April 17, 1940
Ivan Bunin, from his diary
  This I know without a doubt: I will never go . . . to Tahiti or the Himalayas; I will never see Japanese groves and temples; I will never again see the Nile, Thebes, Karnak,[1] its ruins, palm trees, mud-covered

---

[1]Thebes, on the Nile about four hundred miles south of Cairo, was one of the famed cities of antiquity and the capital of the Egyptian Empire at various intervals between the twentieth and twelfth centuries B.C. At Thebes is Karnak, the site of a complex of temples on the banks of the Nile, including one to the state god, Amon-Re.

buffalos, or silt-covered ponds. . . . Never! All of this will exist for all time, but for me it is finished—*forever*. This I find incomprehensible.

April 21, 1940
Ivan Bunin, from his diary

Today has been a splendid and very warm day. . . . The lilacs . . . are in bloom . . . (just like Yalta at Eastertime). . . .

The grass is already tall. . . . Everything is in bloom, with soft, delicate, pale rose, and very feminine-like leaves. . . . [I delighted in] the irises . . . and the cherry and apple trees. . . . A branch from a dogrose tree is an exquisite scarlet with a dusty yellow in the center. . . . There are also some poppylike flowers . . . with a bright orange hue. . . . I sat on a dilapidated wicker chair and looked at the mountains behind Nice . . . light and dim like smoke. . . . A picture of paradise! How many years have I looked at them and felt such a thing! I feel lonely and awkward here, but to move to Paris . . . with its sparse nature and wretched climate! . . .

As is almost always the case these days . . . I am the only one in the house. . . .

It is a holiday today. The sun is out, the sea seems empty and vast, and church bells keep ringing in the town. . . . But I cannot express what is *behind* such things. . . .

Multitudes of butterflies fly around lilacs . . . with a white, greenish tinge. Once again the bees and flies multiply. . . .

This April flowering of trees, grass, and flowers . . . these first spring days—there is nothing more chaste, festive, and wonderfully splendid in the world.

But, as Faust once said about himself, "a dog should not have to live the way I do." I agree totally. . . .

Yesterday was Hitler's birthday.[2] Today I heard on the radio that Mussolini had sent him a congratulatory telegram wishing that "Hitler emerge victorious from the heroic battle that he and the German people were waging."

April 27, 1940
Mark Aldanov, from a letter to Ivan Bunin

A celebration to honor Merezhkovsky is under way (he is 75 years old); and, foreigners are being approached for money on his behalf. . . .

_____

[2]Hitler was fifty-one years old at this time.

Zaitsev's reading was very pleasant. There were a lot of people there, and the collection for him was good. In about three weeks, Sirin-Nabokov will leave for America, apparently forever.[3]

May 7, 1940
Ivan Bunin, from his diary
   I am going to Paris tomorrow, but as always, I am anxious and sad. What a pity to abandon my home, my room, my garden. . . .
   "The individual and his body are two different things. . . . When the body wants something, one should ask if that is what *You* also want. For *You* are God. . . . Go deep into yourself to find God. . . . Do not see your body as your self. . . . Do not succumb to endless worries about those trifles that occupy the time of many people. . . ."
   "I am one who knows no peace from my desire for happiness. . . ."
   This, it seems, has been the story of my life (right to the present day).

May 7, 1940
Zinaida Gippius, from her diary
   I have such a terrible headache because Vera Bunina chattered all evening long.

May 9–10, 1940
Ivan Bunin, from his diary
   Vera has been in Paris for a month already [visiting a sick friend]. She met me at the Lyons station there. On the way to our apartment, I was struck by the fact that the searchlights were on, and that rays of light were constantly crisscrossing the *entire* black sky. "Something is going to happen!" I thought. I was right. . . . The next day Vera . . . returned home with a newspaper. During the night, the Germans had

---

[3]Even before news of the new German push toward Paris, Nabokov was preparing to leave France. By April 20 he had obtained a passport for himself and his family and was expecting to receive an American visa within the week.
   There were several reasons why Nabokov felt little loyalty for France. For one thing, the French officials had refused to grant him a work permit, thereby condemning his family to near-poverty. Also, they had made America as difficult a place possible for the writer to reach. Finally, Nabokov did not wish to be drafted into the French army and to leave behind a wife and son who, as foreigners and Jews, would have been gravely at risk as residents in a country that was so vulnerable to Germany's military might. While Nabokov's biographers are uncertain about the actual date of the writer's departure from France—they cite it as around May 20—they know that he arrived in the United States on May 28, 1940. See Boyd, 520–521.

rushed into Luxemburg, Holland, and Belgium, and were moving forward.[4] . . .

Mid-May 1940
Ivan Bunin, from his diary
   The sirens sound more often and terrible (though they make al-
most no impression on me). . . .

May 19, 1940
Zinaida Gippius, from her diary
   Bunin is in a panic about things. . . .

May 22, 1940
Ivan Bunin, from his diary
   We left Paris today. . . .

Late May 1940–1945
Georgy Adamovich, from his memoirs
   Bunin spent the greater part of the war years in Grasse, in the
"Maritime Alps," as he loved to write it along with the date at the end
of the stories and pieces that he wrote there. At that time I was living
in Nice, and so I saw him rather often, especially in the early years of
the war. . . .
   [One time] in a café . . . Bunin ordered cognac and began drinking one glass after another. . . . Little by little he became tipsy, excited. . . .
   Bunin talked about his wife with passionate devotion and gratitude, as if he realized that he was not an easy person to live with. . . . I
did not need him to tell me that Fate gave two of our greatest Russian
writers—Pushkin and Tolstoy—wives who were precisely what they
needed.[5] . . . Thinking of them, I remembered Nekrasov's lines: "Do
with me what you will! My heart is weak from loss of blood, but it is
full of enduring love for you." . . .
   The war, the military setbacks, the situation in Russia, the vast
Russian losses distressed Bunin deeply, especially in the first year or
two of the conflict when it seemed that Hitler might win. There have
been many stories about Bunin's moods at that time and even later,

   [4]On May 10, 1940, the Germans invaded the Low Countries, their goal being to gain
a preemptive strike against France and to deliver a knockout blow to Allied forces in the
West.
   [5]Contemporaries of Pushkin and Tolstoy, along with biographers of both writers,
would take serious exception to Adamovich's statement.

when the war was over. . . . Without hesitation, though, and in the name of truth, I must say that in all my meetings with Bunin in the last fifteen years of his life, I did not hear a single word from him which would lead me to believe that his political views had ever changed. . . .

The war stunned and frightened Bunin. He feared for the fate of Russia decades and centuries into the future; and it was his deep fear [for his country] that allowed him to close his eyes to all that he found unacceptable about the Soviet system. Bunin hoped that the war . . . would bring new features and qualities to the Soviet Union; and he was bitterly disappointed when . . . such things did not happen. . . .

Bunin followed the course of the war feverishly; and he lamented the fact that the Allies were so slow in opening up a second European front.[6] He hated the Nazis, and he came to hate them with an even greater frenzy when . . . they occupied the southern part of France. Every day we saw firsthand the Nazis' disciplined inhumanity; every day they gave us the chance to see how they would change the world if they had won.

Bunin was not the type to restrain himself. One time we were having breakfast in a Russian restaurant. . . . The place was crowded; and the people there were mostly Russian. As was his custom, Bunin was talking very loudly and almost entirely about the war. Several of those present were avidly listening to his words; perhaps they knew who he was. Wishing to change the topic of conversation, I asked Bunin about his health. . . . As if in defiance, though, he exclaimed for everyone to hear . . . "You are asking me about my health? I cannot live so long as those two lackeys intend to rule the world!"

The two lackeys were Hitler and Mussolini. What Bunin did was extremely risky; but, luckily, his boldness brought no consequences. It could have been otherwise, though. After all, there were many informers throughout Nice, paid ones and volunteers. . . .

When we left the restaurant, I reproached Bunin for his carelessness. He answered: "You be the nice guy, I cannot be silent." And with a sly smile, as if laughing at himself, he added: "I'm just like Lev Nikolaevich [Tolstoy]!"[7]

---

[6]The delay of a "second front"—Stalin had first called for such an offensive on July 17, 1941—was a bitter and enduring complaint of Russians on both sides of the border.

[7]Bunin is referring to Tolstoy's most impassioned anti-government tract, "I Cannot Remain Silent" (*"Ne mogu molchat'"*), published in 1908.

June 2, 1940
Ivan Bunin, from his diary
   Today, at nine a.m., we had our first air alert.

June 4, 1940
Boris Zaitsev, from a letter to Ivan Bunin
   Today we were sitting [in a restaurant in Paris] . . . when suddenly there was an alert. But our [former Russian] generals and colonels remained calm and kept on eating. . . . One of them . . . claimed to have heard two bomb explosions. . . . The Germans were repulsed. . . .
   Later we learned that over a thousand bombs had been dropped . . . in less than fifteen minutes. . . . But this is only the beginning (for both you and me). It is hard to say what will happen; but we must endure. Of course, we are nervous . . . but none of our friends has been wounded or killed. . . .
   I am reading the Bible and have been very struck with the personage of King David. I feel like writing something about him. He arouses poetic sensations in me. . . .
   Perhaps tomorrow . . . there will only be dust from what was once us and our paltry way of life. But it is all the same. So long as I'm alive . . . "I will sing to the Lord . . . I will proclaim His holy name."[8] . . .

June 8, 1940
Ivan Bunin, from his diary
   We began collecting things to escape from Grasse. But where should we go? . . . I do not know how we will get on.
   These are terrible, decisive days—[the enemy] is marching to Paris, and getting closer with each passing day.[9]

June 9, 1940
Ivan Bunin, from his diary
   We are all leaving here.
   The lilacs have begun to bloom, but the birds have taken flight. . . .
   It is terrible when I think about it—17 years have passed since we

   [8]Zaitsev is quoting from Psalm 96:2.
   [9]Only the day before, the Germans were only twenty-five miles from the Seine at Rouen. On June 9 the Germans captured the city and were fewer than fifty miles to the northwest of Paris.

first settled in Grasse . . . again right after the lilacs had bloomed. Did I ever think I would spend a quarter of my life in a place called Grasse? I was still a young man at the time![1] Now this part of my life has disappeared—exactly as if it had never occurred.

For almost a decade, many Frenchmen had been expecting war, seeing it as a worldwide catastrophe. But now France is completely ill-prepared for it![2]

As usual, all kinds of things have been running through my head, God knows why. I now suddenly think that the names, patronymics, and last names of the characters in my stories must have a free and harmonious sound—for example, Maria Vikentievna or Boris Petrovich.

June 10, 1940
Ivan Bunin, from his diary

This evening Italy entered the war. . . . But the Italians did such a thing knowing full well that the Germans have smashed France, are descending into the Rhone valley, and are threatening the French army in the Alps. . . .[3]

At 1 a.m. I opened the window—[and saw] a single nightingale in the emptiness, the void, the inertia, the nonexistence of all life.

June 10–15, 1940
Ivan Bunin, from his diary

We have had a week of anxious packing, getting ready to leave Grasse. We thought we now would be leaving for at least several months. I collected all our pitiful belongings. I was afraid to leave and to rush into the sea of refugees . . . to the Pyrenees where of all France was running—and with six people and some thirty pieces of luggage to boot. . . . But the air alerts helped along with the thought that we would be occupied by Italians. . . .

---

[1]Bunin was fifty-three years old when he first came to Grasse.

[2]Before and during the German attack on the West, French officers and soldiers suffered from inertia, malaise, and defeatism: the result of their disastrous loss in World War I. At a meeting of British and French military leaders in the winter of 1935–1936, British generals were struck not only by the age and poor physical shape of their Gallic colleagues, but also by their preening pride and self-satisfaction. The British were also horrified by what they saw as French disinterest in the new methods of warfare, and by their willingness to cling to previous methods and strategies. See M. Dziewanowski, *War at Any Price: World War II in Europe, 1939–1945* (Englewood Cliffs, N.J., 1987).

[3]On June 10, 1940, the French Military Command, believing defeat was imminent, urged surrender to Germany.

June 16, 1940
Ivan Bunin, from his diary

We left Grasse at 10 a.m. . . . and arrived in Nimes[4] at sunset. We looked for a hotel for an hour . . . but all the rooms were occupied. . . . In full despair . . . we thought we would have to spend the night on the sidewalk next to the train station. . . . But we came across a Russian Jew and spent the night at his place.

June 17, 1940
Ivan Bunin, from his diary

[On the road] a French peasant . . . approached us and said with tears in his eyes: "You can go back—an armistice has been signed!"[5] But we cannot return as we do not have the necessary documents. . . .

July 5, 1940
Ivan Bunin, from a letter to Boris Zaitsev

It has been almost three weeks since we abandoned Grasse and have taken up residence in La Française.[6] I do not have words to describe all that we have endured (and are enduring). . . .

July 14, 1940
Vera Muromtseva-Bunina, from a letter to Tatyana Loginova-Muravieva

Our trip cost us dearly and sapped much of our physical and spiritual strength. La Française had no conveniences, and we had to choose between a stable and an open field! Food was also hard to find. There was no place to cook, and the restaurants were way beyond our means. Vegetables were in short supply, and fruit was expensive. . . .

I am so very tired from the shock of all that we have experienced. It was all so sudden. . . . But we are coming to our senses little by little.

July 22, 1940
Boris Zaitsev, from a letter to Ivan Bunin

The past month has been relatively calm. We are eating normally . . . though we both have lost a great deal of weight. . . . [A friend] has lost her husband and has been left with three small chil-

---

[4]From Grasse to Nimes, Bunin and company had traveled 120 miles directly west.

[5]On June 14, 1940, the Germans entered Paris. Three days later France, under Marshal Pétain, sued for peace.

[6]From Nimes, the group traveled first one hundred miles north to Montauban, then ten miles northwest to La Française.

dren! The memorial service for him was the most heartrending thing I have ever attended. The widow and her children were on their knees during the entire service. . . .

Many Russians have been awarded medals for their valor. . . .

Food prices are normal. One can walk the streets until 11 p.m. People are behaving well, and we do not feel constrained in any way. . . .

On July 7th, Paris had only 1 million people—2 million have left the city. A veritable desert!!!! What we will do next and *how* we will live . . . are anyone's guess. . . . But so far we are still breathing . . . and news from [our friends] in America has restored our spirits. . . . We wait for manna from heaven! . . .

July 23, 1940
Ivan Bunin, from his diary

Everyone in Paris is stunned. They do not understand how France could have been defeated so monstrously.

July 30, 1940
Ivan Bunin, from his diary

It is one and the same thing—pilots from fighter planes are beating each other up. The Germans are scaring everyone with rumors that they are making "gigantic preparations" for a decisive attack.[7]

News . . . America may enter the war. No, it will not!

I read about an experiment that two students from Vienna conducted two years ago. They decided to hang themselves, but also to extract themselves from the noose right before death so that they could tell about what they experienced. It turned out that they heard a clap of thunder and saw a blinding light.

August 9, 1940
Ivan Bunin, from his diary

Aldanov kept insisting that France will succumb to "civil war."[8] He has firmly decided to leave for America.

There is no rice or macaroni or oil or laundry soap.

[7]On July 29, Hitler told his military leaders that it was his "intention," but not yet his "decision," to attack the Soviet Union. See R. Goralski, *World War II Almanac, 1931–1941: A Political and Literary Record* (New York, 1981), 127.

[8]At this time there were two Frances—Vichy France, under Marshal Pétain, and the Free French Government, which came into being when Britain recognized Charles de Gaulle as the leader of Free France on June 28.

August 10, 1940
Ivan Bunin, from his diary

On the 8th there was huge battle between German and British planes over the shores of England. The Japanese . . . are carping at England. Stalin is getting captious with Finland; and Spain, with England. . . . Anti-Semitism . . . is beginning in France.[9]

The oleanders are thickly covered with scarlet leaves.

August 11, 1940
Vera Muromtseva-Bunina, from a letter to Tatyana Loginova-Muravieva

Ian keeps going to Cannes, but does not have enough energy to take walks with me. . . .

I bought some remnants . . . and made two skirts and a jacket. . . . I hope Ian does not notice [what I have done]. . . . Everything else is worn out. . . .

August 17, 1940
Ivan Bunin, from his diary

Today I finished reading Ertel's "The Lipiags."[1] It was terrible. Lyuba must marry a "*Mr.* Karamyshev," a gentleman of the bedchamber, who, wealthy and vulgar, insists upon the "superiority" of the Russian gentry . . . as well as its guardianship of the people—the "well-being of the folk." . . .

All morning long, the valleys and the mountains have been wrapped in bright steam. There is an indistinct, barely warming sun, and a slight bitter smell in the air—the smell of autumn.

The Germans have conducted a huge raid ("with remarkable accuracy!") on London, on the banks of the Thames. "Everything is smoke, in flames. . . ." It seems that war has truly begun. . . .

We went shopping. . . . The stores were almost empty. For the past month or so, people have been buying things at a frenzied rate. Lard has disappeared (and we have not had butter in ages). Laundry soap is being rationed in small chunks and weighed as if they were pre-

---

[9]In the first few weeks of the Occupation, the Germans began broadcasting anti-Semitic propaganda, thereby nullifying a 1939 French decree prohibiting media attacks on individuals based on religion and race. The Germans also moved against the Jews in Occupied France with laws to review recent grants of citizenship as well as to intern individuals whom they considered dangerous to national security. See S. Zuccotti, *The Holocaust, the French, and the Jews* (New York, 1993), 52, 53.

[1]Ertel's "The Lipiags" appeared in his collection, *Notes from an Inhabitant of the Steppe* (*Zapiski stepniaka*), published in 1883.

cious stones. When vegetables and fruit disappear this fall, there will be nothing to eat.

August 19, 1940
Ivan Bunin, from his diary

A recent conversation [with friends] sounds as if it took place in Soviet Russia—how we will feed ourselves in the fall and winter.

August 20, 1940
Ivan Bunin, from his diary

I awoke at 8 a.m. . . . and, as always, with a secret pain in my heart. As I do every morning, I went to the cathedral of the Virgin Mary and of the Little Flower[2] to pray. . . . I opened the Bible . . . and read: "My quarrel is with you, Arrogance. It is the Lord Sabaoth who speaks: 'Your day has come, the time when I must punish you' " (Jeremiah 50:31).

August 21, 1940
Ivan Bunin, from his diary

There is news that Trotsky is dying—someone fractured his skull with an iron bar in his home in Mexico.[3] In another time I would have

[2]The reference is to Saint Thérèse of Lisieux, who wrote that after her death she would "let fall a shower of roses," i.e., miracles and favors to believers who asked for her intercession. As a result, Thérèse is the patron of florists and is commonly known as "the little Flower."

Interestingly, Thérèse was popular with Russian emigrés abroad. Gippius wrote both articles and poems about the saint; and Merezhkovsky, in his 1941 biographical novel *Malen'kaia Tereza* (*Little Thérèse*), insisted that Thérèse would follow in the footsteps of Saints Teresa of Avila and John of the Cross in initiating internal reform in the church.

See T. Pachmuss, *D. S. Merezhkovsky in Exile: The Master of the Genre of Biographie Romanceé* (New York, 1990), 204, 252, 267–278.

[3]Trotsky, in exile in Mexico since 1936, was the object of two assassination attempts, presumably by Soviet agents. The first, a machine-gun attack on his house in May 1940, failed, despite the fact that assassins pumped seventy-three bullets into the room just a few feet from where Trotsky had been sleeping.

The second, by Ramon Mercader, was successful. Mercader was a Spanish Communist and Moscow-trained agent of Stalin's secret police who had won the confidence of the Trotsky family by convincing them that he was the fiancé of a woman who worked in the household. (Mercader later claimed that he had been a former disciple of Trotsky's, but that he had been horrified by Trotsky's request to kill Stalin in Moscow.)

On August 20, 1940, Mercader attacked Trotsky with an ice pick, which fractured his right cranium and penetrated three inches into his brain.

He later recalled of his deed: "On purpose I put my raincoat on the table to that I could take out the ice pick which I had in my pocket. When Trotsky began reading my article which I had given to him as a pretext for meeting with me . . . I decided not to lose the brilliant opportunity which had come my way.

"Having taken the ice pick from my raincoat into my fist, I closed my eyes and gave Trotsky a tremendous blow on the head. He screamed in a way that I will never forget as felt delight that this bloody reptile finally got what he deserved. Now I am rather indifferent to the whole thing.

August 22, 1940
Ivan Bunin, from his diary

Trotsky's skull was so split that one could see his brains. His murderer passed as one of his friends who often visited him.

I heard on the radio that Trotsky has died.

August 23, 1940
Mark Aldanov, from a letter to Ivan Bunin

I have received a summons from the American consul in Marseilles; and I assume that I have obtained visas to go to the United

---

long as I live. . . . A cry that was infinitely long . . . and pierces my brain still now. Trotsky got up like a madman. He threw himself at me and bit my hand. . . . Look, you can still see the marks of his teeth. . . . But I pushed him back, and he fell to the floor. He lifted himself as best as he could, and, then, running or stumbling—I don't know how—he got out of the room."

Trotsky's (common-law) wife, Natasha, also remembered: "There was a piercing cry. . . . Leon Davidovich appeared, leaning against the door frame. His face was covered with blood, his blue eyes glittered without his spectacles, and his arms hung limply by his side."

Although a doctor did not judge the wound to be serious, Trotsky died peacefully on August 21, 1940, but not before having admitted that, at the time of the incident, he had thought: "This man could kill me." Intriguingly, Trotsky had had a premonition of his end. Four years earlier he had written about Stalin that the Soviet leader "seeks to strike not at the ideas of his opponent, but at his skull."

Four days after the assassination, *Pravda* gloated: "When in 1929 the Soviet government expelled from its territory the counterrevolutionary and traitor Trotsky, he was embraced by the capitalist circles of Europe and America. . . . Such a response was no accident . . . for Trotsky had long since entered into the service of those who exploit the working class.

"Trotsky reached the depths of human depravity and became entangled in his own machinations. He was killed by his own supporters—the same terrorists whom he had taught the treachery of murder, treason, and villainy against both the working class and the land of the Soviets. In organizing the atrocious murders of Kirov, Kuibyshev, and Gorky, Trotsky became the victim of his own intrigues, betrayals, acts of treason, and evil deeds.

"Thus did this contemptible person ingloriously descend into his grave with the seal of an international spy and murderer on his brow."

The Soviets, though, disclaimed any responsibility for Trotsky's murder, and Mercader was sentenced to prison for twenty years, the maximum term under Mexican law. Eventually he moved to Moscow, where he lived in seclusion until 1977. He also worked in the Institute of Marxism-Leninism and co-authored a book on Spanish communism. A year later he died in Cuba. Sometime between 1940 and 1961—sources differ—Mercader was named a "Hero of the Soviet Union" ("*Geroi sovetskogo soiuza*").

Trotsky's house in Mexico became a museum, the scars from the bullets of the first attempt on his life still remaining on the walls. For more on the assassination of Trotsky, see V. Serge and N. Sedova-Trotsky, *The Life and Death of Leon Trotsky* (New York, 1975), 267, 268, 271; D. Volkogonov, *Trotsky: The Eternal Revolutionary* (New York, 1996), 466–469; Glad, 301–302.

States. Earlier I cried when I did not have one. Now I cry that I do. In any case, I am embarking on the greatest adventure of my life. Since I have nothing here in France, I must go. . . . Once I get to New York, though, the first thing I will do is to get money together to found a journal.[4]

August 24, 1940
Ivan Bunin, from his diary

Moscow, Berlin, and Rome are expressing their satisfaction over the anniversary of the German-Soviet pact.[5] Yes, Moscow has not made a bad bargain.

Trotsky's body will be burned and his "ashes" will be thrown into the sea—he requested such a thing in his will.

August 25, 1940
Ivan Bunin, from his diary

I went to Cannes . . . and ran into Maria Tseitlina in a café. . . . She is still trying to persuade me to think seriously about coming to America. "We cannot live here," she said. . . . Hence our second exodus, our second emigration!

August 29, 1940
Ivan Bunin, from his diary

Coffee will also now be rationed—100 grams per person per month. Our situation is starting to look like a joke.

The other day I was stunned at the thought that I am living in a conquered country for the first time in my life. . . .

These days I have been reading . . . *The Journal of the Brothers Goncourt*.[6] It is very good, except for the last years when Edmund sometimes writes genuine nonsense (for example, about Russian literature).[7] . . .

---

[4]In 1942, Aldanov and Tseitlin founded *New Review* (*Novyi zhurnal*), a major literary-political journal that still exists today.

[5]On August 23, 1939, the Soviets and the Germans signed a nonaggression pact which, among other things, divided Poland equally between the two countries. In addition, Germany was to control Lithuania; and, the USSR, Finland, Estonia, and Latvia. Later the pact was revised to place Lithuania in the Soviet sphere and more of Poland in the German one.

[6]Edmond and Jules Goncourt wrote their *Journal* from 1851 to 1870. After Jules's death in 1870, Edmond continued writing it until his own passing in 1896.

[7]Bunin must have been greatly disturbed by this excerpt, dated September 7, 1888: "The present success of the Russian novel is due to the annoyance which devout, respectable folk have felt toward the success of the naturalistic French novel. Such readers searched for something which they could use to counter that success. For, beyond a doubt,

September 5, 1940
Vera Muromtseva-Bunina, from a letter to a friend

I am reading Herzen in English, Pascal in French, and Bunin in Russian.

September 6, 1940
Ivan Bunin, from his diary

I often think how great events can sometimes pass unnoticed. Three entire governments have disappeared—Latvia, Lithuania, and Estonia![8] Was it all that long ago that I saw all the national pride of these countries, their presidents, their "flowering" and so forth! They were alive and well for more than twenty years—and now it is as though they have never existed at all! . . .

And what about Czechoslovakia, Poland, Bessarabia, Denmark, Holland, Norway, Belgium, and what was once France? It is beyond comprehension! . . . .

I am writing and looking at the sunny "lantern" of my room, with its five windows. Outside a light fog covers everything with such beauty . . . together with a huge whitish-bright sky. And amidst all of this is my lonely, eternally sad "I." . . .

---

it is the same kind of literature: the realities of life seen in their sad, human, and unpoetic aspects.

"Furthermore, neither Tolstoy, nor Dostoevsky, nor any of the other Russian writers invented this kind of literature! They took it from Flaubert, from me, from Zola, and added a strong dose of Poe. Oh, if one of Dostoevsky's novels, whose black melancholy is regarded with such indulgent admiration, were signed with the name of Goncourt, what a beating it would get all along the line!" See R. Baldick, *Pages from the Goncourt Journal* (London, 1962), 337.

[8]Estonia, Latvia, and Lithuania had all gained their independence from the Soviet Union in the aftermath of the Russian Revolution and civil war. In October 1939, though, roughly six weeks after Germany and Russia signed a nonaggression pact, Moscow demanded that all three Baltic states sign pacts of mutual assistance that allowed the stationing of Soviet garrisons on their territory. Feeling isolated in the international scene and realizing the futility of military resistance, Estonia, Latvia, and Lithuania agreed to the Soviet demands.

On June 14, 1940, the day Paris fell to the Germans, Stalin presented an ultimatum to Lithuania, insisting that the country admit an unlimited number of Soviet troops on its soil and that it set up a government acceptable to the USSR. With the flight of President Smetona to Germany, a "people's government" was installed immediately. Two days later, Latvia and Estonia faced similar ultimatums—and fates.

Sovietization proceeded at a rapid pace. In all three countries, the formerly small (and outlawed) Communist parties emerged as the leading political force. The new Soviet regimes in Estonia, Latvia, and Lithuania organized elections to so-called "people's assemblies" with only a single slate of candidates. Predictably, these new assemblies voted by acclamation to seek incorporation into the USSR; and on August 25 such a "request" was "accepted" by the Supreme Soviet.

September 7, 1940
Ivan Bunin, from his diary

Today I had to climb up to our home on foot. . . . Taxis have disappeared completely! . . .

Decrees and more decrees. . . . Yesterday there was a particularly noteworthy one. [Because of rationing] it is now forbidden to drink coffee from 3 p.m. on. Yes, if it had not been for the Germans, everything would have gone to hell a long time ago—people would have "pillaged what others have already stolen!"

Why, in their diary, do the brothers Goncourt call Turgenev a "lovable barbarian"?[9] What French obtuseness, what conceit! . . .

How devilishly hale and hardy are these Lenins, Trotskys, Stalins, "führers," and "duces"! . . .

For a long time now, I cannot help but be repulsed by beards and hairy people.

Behind me are seventy years. No, behind me is nothing.

September 13, 1940
Ivan Bunin, from his diary

From one of Flaubert's letters:

"I am the most avid liberal. That is why I hate despotism. That is why I also find socialism to be horrible and pedantic, a [system of belief] that brings a deathly blow to morality and art." He also wrote: "Women seem mysterious to me. The more I study them, the less I understand them."

September 13, 1940
Mark Aldanov, from a letter to Ivan Bunin

Apparently you have decided to stay [here] in France. I will not try to dissuade you. But I will tell you this. Yesterday I received a letter from [another Russian writer]. He reports that he has received a visa

---

[9]Edmond Goncourt made such a statement in his diary on March 2, 1872. In truth, the Goncourt brothers admired Turgenev greatly. On February 28, 1863, Edmond wrote: "Turgenev is a delightful colossus, a gentle, white-haired giant, who looks like a druid or the kindly old monk in *Romeo and Juliet*. He is handsome, but in an awe-inspiring, impressive way. . . . In Turgenev's eyes are the blue of the heavens. . . . Also, with the kindliness of his gaze goes the gentle caress of the Russian accent, something like the singing of a child or a Negro. A modest man, untouched by the ovation we gave him, Turgenev spoke to us about Russian literature, saying that, from the theatre to the novel, it was tending toward realism. He also said that the public in Russia were great readers of periodical literature and blushed to confess that he and a dozen others whom we did not know were paid 600 francs a sheet. On the other hand, he noted that a book brought in very little: 4,000 francs at the most." See Baldick, 82, 197.

for the United States without any trouble (*via* the American Federation of Labor,[1] just like I did). He also tells me that he can do the same for other writers. I wrote to him right away about you. I strongly advise you to write to him immediately, before the day is done. . . .

September 25, 1940
Vera Muromtseva-Bunina, from a letter to a friend
Thank God, Ian is writing, sometimes for days on end. His mood is pleasant and even. We can now hear Moscow at 9:30 each evening.

Circa October 1940
Alexander Bakhrakh, from his memoirs
During my initial stay with Bunin[2] . . . he began a long conversation, whining about his fate, or as he put it, about the "rise and fall" of Bunin—the glory and fame of a Nobel laureate who had shaken the hands of kings but who was now a "destitute old man," abused by an impudent house gardener for no reason at all. "Interviewers once swirled about me like bees around honey," he said, "but now I'm as poor as Job and needed by no one." . . .
He suddenly exclaimed:
"Why don't you like my verse? After all, I'm not such a bad writer. . . . But you, of course, find it insufficiently spicy and *recherché*. Blok has eaten away at you." . . . He immediately added that . . . Leo Tolstoy "himself" had praised his verse even though Tolstoy generally "turned his nose up" at poetry. . . .
"Ivan Alexeevich," I replied, "we had this conversation in Paris. When a volume of your verse came out in print, I begged you for a copy; but you, it seemed, did not want to give me one as a gift. It was only later that you took pity on my 'tears' and pulled out a copy from somewhere, from under your bed, I think."
"Ah, you villain," he interrupted, "so you remember that I love to

---

[1]Aldanov's statement is true. The American Federation of Labor, responding to calls for help from members of the Jewish Labor Committee, appealed both to Eleanor Roosevelt and to individuals from the departments of Justice and State for hundreds of "emergency visas" to enable prominent political and cultural leaders to leave Europe for America.
[2]About the arrival of Bakhrakh into the Bunins' home, Zurov wrote to the Bunin scholar, Alexander Baboreko, on July 29, 1965: "During the war, the Bunins gave refuge to the French writer Alexander Vasilievich Bakhrakh. Bakhrakh appeared in Grasse after the retreat of the French army [from Paris] and lived with them during the entire course of the war. . . . During one very dangerous moment, Vera Nikolaevna baptized Bakhrakh in a small church in Cannes-la-Boque, and I obtained a baptismal certificate from the priest there." See Baboreko, 302.

put new books under the bed so that no one will take them; no one would think of looking there."

"And then you wrote in it something like: 'Alex, why do you need my verse?' and followed it with a whole stream of exclamation points." . . .

[Bunin replied:] "But is my verse any worse than hurling pineapples, and into space to boot![3] . . . You would probably be more likely to accept a poem . . . that I wrote when I was still in grade school. . . . I do not know what prompted me to write it; I only remember that it was full of populist tendencies which, to tell the truth, were about as close to me as the [constellation] of the Great Bear. But such tendencies were in the air at that time, and I unwittingly became infected by them. I guess I thought that with this populism, my poem would be more 'tasteful.' At that time I was so very proud of my creation, but it seems I was completely alone in what I thought of it. . . ."

Bunin then asked me if I had read Saadi . . . and if I had ever come across his line "that a thousand-headed dragon guards every treasure."

"What is this leading up to?" I thought to myself.

Having guessed my thoughts . . . Bunin said, "No, my dear, take heart in the fact that you do not yet know what flashes before old men at night when they cannot sleep. . . . There are all kinds of dragons around us, even if there is no treasure around. There are big, huge dragons who sometimes howl on the radio, but there are also little ones who scramble along and cause a great deal of harm. . . . Remember the words of an old man!"

[He continued]: "You think that everything goes swimmingly around here . . . and that you have found yourself a quiet refuge. But that is only on the surface. In this godforsaken place, evil people, thank God, have forgotten about us. You have no idea how many such people there are in the world."

(This was one of Bunin's favorite sayings, which he often injected into his conversation if it belonged there or not.)

"True, so far life here has been an oasis where everything is peaceful and quiet. . . . But now we are entering upon . . . sacred 'fatal minutes'—may the devil take them! . . . From stubbornness, I do not want even to think about them. . . . I would rather be like an ostrich and

[3]Bunin is referring to Andrei Bely, who in his 1903 poem "In the Mountains" ("*Na gorakh*") "hurled a pineapple into space" ("*v nebesa zapustil ananasom*").

hide my head, if not in the sand, then in my pillow, and take a mild sedative." . . .

[As regards the war] Bunin did not understand strategic movements or offensives. . . . Very much the civilian, he kept getting angry that events were unfolding at such an extremely slow pace. . . .

I do not remember why, but one time I began declaiming some very bad verse by Ilya Ehrenburg:

I love the wind on upper decks
And the job of a gunner.
And also the scandals on the street,
On the 25th of October.[4]

"And to what refined pen does that little masterpiece belong?" Bunin asked. "It is both flat and false. God knows why you people have been reading the same things for twenty-five years now, without making any distinction at all."

And, mimicking me, he declaimed:

They'll put me in a vegetable bin.
As witness to so much treachery. . . .

October 14, 1940
Ivan Bunin, from his diary
Today is the feast of the "Protecting Veil of the Mother of God."[5] Vera went to mass in Cannes; it is also her birthday.[6] I feel so sorry for her. She is sick, weak, nervous, and takes comfort in whatever God sends her way. Indeed, my pity for her is unbearable.

October 17, 1940
Vera Muromtseva-Bunina, from her diary
Ian talks often and well about what Europe has fallen into. . . . why it fears Jews and welcomes dictators. . . .

---

[4]That is, the day (old-style calendar) that marked the beginning of the "second" Revolution of 1917.
[5]The feast of the "Protecting Veil of the Most Holy Mother of God" ("*Pokrov presviatoi bogoroditsy*") is one of the major festivals of the Orthodox church. Its origin draws from this legend: In 910 the Mother of God allegedly appeared in Constantinople to a "God's fool," Andrew and his disciple, Epiphany. As the two prayed, the holy Mother covered them with a white veil and prayed that the world be saved from suffering and disaster.
[6]Muromtseva-Bunina was fifty-nine years old at this time.

October 18, 1940
Alexander Bakhrakh, from his memoirs

I recall that right before Aldanov left for America, Bunin and I had gone to Nice to say goodbye to him. The three of us were sitting in a café that, though large and depressing, greatly appealed to Bunin. He was extremely sad that Aldanov was leaving. . . . We drank some cognac which Bunin had thoughtfully carried in a flask in his pocket, since he knew that liquor would not be served. He began telling Aldanov that he was writing with immense pleasure, something that he had not experienced for a long time. He also noted to Aldanov that he was . . . working on a cycle of stories that were so explicit that he did not know whether he could ever publish them.[7] "The time has come," Bunin said, "for us to start calling things by their real names. After all, we are not kids anymore!" . . .

"I trust Aldanov more than anyone else on earth," Bunin once told me. And when Aldanov left France, he said bitterly:

"Now I am completely alone." . . .

October 23, 1940
Ivan Bunin, from his diary

On this day, seventy years ago, *at dawn* (so my deceased mother told me) I was born in Voronezh.[8] . . . How many years do I have left?[9] In any case, not many, and they will go by quickly. . . .

I woke up late (at 9 a.m.). It started off grey and cold; then it rained all day. Nonetheless, we celebrated my birthday—a shoulder of lamb and wine.

October 23, 1940
Vera Muromtseva-Bunina, from her diary

Today is Ian's birthday. As a gift, I gave him the last of my coffee—a gift [from someone else].

October 23, 1940
Galina Kuznetsova, from her diary

From morning on, Bunin pretended that there was nothing unusual [about this day] . . . and that there was nothing to celebrate. On purpose, he went around in his old greasy robe. The rest of us, knowing full well his superstitious fear of all birthdays and especially this, his

[7]The work in question is *Dark Alleys* (*Temnye allei*).
[8]Voronezh is a city about four hundred miles south of Moscow.
[9]Thirteen, to be exact.

seventieth one, also pretended that today was nothing special. . . . The only thing we did to mark the occasion was to set a clean tablecloth on the table. . . .

October 30, 1940
Ivan Bunin, from his diary

For about a month now, I've been writing nonstop, sometimes late into the night before I go to sleep.

November 14, 1940
Ivan Bunin, from his diary

All day long I have been reading the stories that I wrote in the fall and have been putting them into two folders—one [of these] I should place in a safe.

The Italians write that Molotov has spent two days in Berlin, and the Germans and Russians are deciding a new structure for Europe "on the ruins of the old one."[1]

---

[1]Hitler, seeking to ease mounting tension between Germany and the Soviet Union, invited Vyacheslav Molotov, foreign minister of the USSR, to Berlin for talks on November 12 and 13, 1940. (Molotov's trip to Berlin was the first official visit of a Soviet statesman to the Nazi capital.)

During their meeting, Hitler suggested that, given the imminent defeat of the British Empire and the Commonwealth, the Soviets should participate with the Axis in partitioning the world. Specifically, they should abandon their interests in the Balkan and Baltic areas, and seek hegemony in the Persian Gulf, the Middle East, and the Indian Ocean, i.e., spheres of British influence.

Molotov accepted the German proposal eagerly, but he also stressed the primacy of Russia's interests in regions from Finland to Turkey and the Black Sea. Additionally he protested the increasing presence by the Axis in Rumania and Bulgaria, and stated a desire for Soviet bases in the Bosphorus and the Dardanelles.

While in Berlin, Molotov was privy to an amusing if poignant incident. During a speech by the foreign minister of Germany, Joachim von Ribbentrop, on the certainty of an English defeat as well as on the benefits to the Soviets in joining the Axis to partition the British Empire, Berlin was host to a massive air raid by the Royal Air Force. In the air shelter, Ribbentrop repeated his argument that Britain was finished as a great power. To such an assertion, Molotov replied: "If that is so, who is dropping bombs on us?" Ribbentrop did not respond.

Not surprisingly, Molotov returned to Moscow, angry and empty-handed. If anything, the meeting in Berlin only revealed to him the widening gap between Russia and Germany. He was not alone in this view. Hitler, dismayed by Molotov's stubborn if "parochial" insistence on the primacy of Soviet interests in Eastern Europe, now believed that Stalin's price for continuing cooperation between the two countries was too high. Reaffirming his July decision to prepare for a military showdown with the Soviets, he issued, on December 18, 1940, directives for operation "Barbarossa": a short campaign against Russia which would begin on May 15, 1941 and end by the autumn of that year. Hitler believed he would thereby eliminate the USSR as an enduring menace to Germany in the east. See Dziewanowski, 148–149.

December 1, 1940
Ivan Bunin, from a letter to Mark Aldanov

Where are you? Have you truly left once and for all? And whom have I been abandoned for? Seriously—I cannot think about my future without horror, genuine horror.

Today I received a letter from Grebenshchikov (a writer who has already lived in America for almost twenty years), who answered my questions about life in that country. He writes:

"My English novel[2] finally came out on May 16th. From the enclosed reviews, you can see how brilliantly it has been received by the press. Its publication was even cause for a reception at Columbia University. But as of July 31st, it has sold only 300 copies. America is not at all interested in literature. You cannot imagine how slavishly materialistic Americans are. For all our incessant labor, my wife and I have neither health, nor freedom, nor money, nor readers. If a lasting peace were to be concluded in Europe, we would head for France.

"I am afraid that life in America will seem to you so hurried and coarse, and also so hopeless as regards money for your works, that you would long for Europe even as it is now. All our dreams of giving lectures, of publishing books here—have led to one disappointment after another. Our literary foundation is powerless to help us, and there is crying and gnashing of teeth from all sides. A gathering to aid Teffi came up with only 29 cents—not dollars, but cents. It is a nightmare."

So, my dears, that is America for you. . . .

December 15, 1940
Vera Muromtseva-Bunina, from a letter to a friend

It is a great luxury for me to write letters. My house chores have increased . . . not to mention my trips to town for provisions. . . . I lie down a great deal, and I find it difficult to write from that position as my hand gets tired quickly. . . .

Teffi needs help greatly. . . . The Merezhkovskys receive 8 francs apiece from the mayor's office. . . . The Remizovs are also without any means. . . .

Thank God, Ivan Alexeevich is healthy. He suffers from the cold, but he has written a great many stories. I hope that he continues writing. . . .

I keep getting thinner . . . and lines have formed on my face—a feature that calls forth fear from the men in my life. . . . But I am still

[2]The novel in question is *The Turbulent Giant: An Epic Novel on Russian Peasantry.*

hale and hearty in spirit. As long as everyone is heathy, I can go on living.

When we have money, we can still eat well, despite the fact that the market has no eggs and is almost always without meat, rice. Also, the amounts we get on ration tickets are small. . . .

I get up with the sun. Thank God, it does not rise very early these days; and often at dawn, I head for the market through some ineffably beautiful surroundings. There is a good side to everything; one just has to find it. . . .

December 25, 1940
Ivan Bunin, from his diary

Christmas was poor and sad—unhappy France!

December 27, 1940
Mark Aldanov, from a letter to Ivan Bunin

Prospects in America are not bright. . . . But I keep thinking that we will adjust. . . . Your news about writers in need . . . is depressing. . . . If I can earn some money in America, I will try to help those who have remained [with you]. . . .

PART THREE

Watching Russia in Agony
1941–1942

BUNIN, 1933

On the morning of June 22, 1941, Bunin and the world awoke to startling news: some two hundred German divisions had invaded the Soviet Union. The Nazi advance to the east was almost as stunning as the blitzkrieg had been in the West.

The Nazi objectives were threefold: in the north, to overrun Latvia, Estonia, and Lithuania, to seize Leningrad, and to isolate Russia from the Baltic sea; in the south, to take hold of the agricultural and coal-producing regions in both the Caucasus and the Ukraine; and in the center, to pursue the route used by Napoleon to capture Moscow and to disrupt the system of transportation that converged there. All along the way, the Germans hoped for support from Russians and others who hated Stalin and communism.

Initially the Germans were successful. By October 1941 they had surrounded Leningrad, threatened Moscow, and secured most of the Ukraine. Two months later, nearly 40 percent of the Russian population had fallen under German control, and with it, vast segments of industries ranging from coal and steel to sugar and grain.

For the Soviet Union, things went from bad to worse. By late summer 1942 the Germans had seized the Donets coal basins, the entire coast of the Black Sea, and parts of the Caucasus. A month later they had also reached Stalingrad, the gateway to the lower Volga basin.

It was at Stalingrad, though, that the tide turned. In what would be the psychological watershed of the war, the Russians under Marshal Zhukov defeated the invaders in a heroic but bitter five-month struggle. The entire German VI army was captured, and the remaining Nazis began a slow but steady retreat.

By the summer of 1943 the Russians were on the offensive. They not only stopped a massive Nazi assault in the south but also launched a huge counterattack which, by mid-1944, ousted the Germans from most of Russia. By early May 1945 the Red Army was engaging the enemy on the steps of the Reichstag itself.

The reasons for the Russian success in the war were many. For one thing, Stalin had restored prestige to the military, giving to unit commanders authority over political commissars and reviving traditional military honors, ranks, and insignia. For another thing, he had reconciled with the Russian Orthodox church, curtailing anti-religious propaganda and bidding the patriarch to call upon the faithful to defend the country.

It was Stalin's appeal to the nation, though, that proved to be decisive in the crisis. Here the Russian leader asked the populace to safeguard the homeland as Russian patriots, not as Soviet citizens. Such a request fired the hearts, minds, and souls of Russians on both sides of the border. Whatever their feelings for communism, both groups sought to purge the enemy from Mother Russia.

When the conflict was over, Russia had suffered more than twenty million casualties. If one accepts the figure of Western historians that fifty million people died in both the Western and Eastern theatres of the world conflict, the sad if overwhelming conclusion is that 40 percent of these victims were Russian. Even worse, if one adds the ten million victims of Stalin's purges in the previous decade, a still more shocking judgment is that Russia experienced a "holocaust" all its own.

✳ 1941 ✳

Circa 1941
Alexander Bakhrakh, from his memoirs

Bunin was repulsed by the poems of Tsvetaeva and indifferent to the lyrics of Akhmatova, Pasternak, and Mandelshtam. . . .

The main corridor at "Jeanette" was always dark; something had happened to the switch there. I had fussed with the wires for a long time, but of course nothing came of it. The very next day Bunin repaired it somehow. He was unusually proud of his accomplishment and kept running around like a little boy.

"I am a genius," he kept screaming throughout the house, "Take that, Leonardo da Vinci! You see, I can still do something useful with my hands. Just imagine what I still can do!" . . .

Bunin used to say to me: "Someday I will write a story about your ancestors, the Philistines, today's Bedouins, an especially obscene story that I will dedicate to you."

But whenever I pestered him: "Well, how is my philistine heroine doing today?"—he answered: "No, I cannot do it. I truly wanted to keep my promise to you, but nothing came of it. I do not know their life well enough; I cannot crawl into the skin of their women. So how I can write about them?" . . .

As if by chance, Bunin said:

"Our [Russian] ancestors were good people. Great fur coats down to the floor, hats rising up to the skies, grand sable collars and brocades—in a word, they looked like idols. Thank God that pure Russian blood runs through my veins. . . ."

Bunin once told me: "The title of a story should never explain anything, since such a thing will ruin the piece. Why give the reader the key to the story right away? Let him crack his head a bit on the title." . . .

[Bunin said:] "Have you ever thought about the saying—'Laziness is the mother of all evils'? . . . As I see it, though, it is not laziness, but stupidity. . . . I simply cannot imagine how the individual can come with as many stupidities as he does. It is beyond anything I can think up." . . .

I loved taking walks with Bunin. We usually climbed up to Napoleon's road, the very same path by which the deposed emperor went from Elba to Paris for his "hundred days."[1] Bunin always chose a small place where, in the summertime, huge quantities of fireflies flew about. He followed their phosphorescent trails passionately. Having sat down on a wide tree stump . . . he avidly told me about his former love conquests. For instance, he confessed that as a young man at his father's estate, and despite the fact that his family was ruined financially, he still regarded himself as a "gentry youth." Such a distinction opened many doors to him, he continued, but he was too inexperienced to take the initiative. Later, when he began to become a well-known writer, women clung to him, but he was still too shy and terrified of becoming involved. Incidentally, Bunin insisted that he was drawn to women who had defects in their speech. A woman who stuttered or pronounced a letter incorrectly, he found irresistible! . . .

Once Bunin suddenly began quoting from Byron: "It is often easier to die for a woman than to live with her." . . . I wondered why he said these words in such an exaggerated and agitated way. . . . Could there have been a sincerely tragic nuance here?[2] . . .

January 1, 1941
Ivan Bunin, from his diary

We "greeted" the New Year, with each member of our household being host to a small piece of loathsome, bluish-grey sausage, a small dish of watery mushrooms with onion, two pieces of terribly tough meat, some fried potatoes, two bottles of red wine, and a bottle of the cheapest Asti. We also listened to Moscow radio; and, as always, we heard the "Soviet Union" being praised for all its various joys and love of labor and work.

---

[1]On March 1, 1815, Napoleon, having escaped from exile on Elba, landed with fifteen hundred men at Cannes and immediately marched on Paris. The "Hundred Days" refers to the period in French history between March 20, when Napoleon arrived in Paris, and July 8, 1815, when Louis XVIII returned to that city.

[2]Bakhrakh was apparently unaware of Bunin's tempestuous affair with Varvara Pashchenko which almost ended in his suicide.

The newspapers have published Hitler's greeting for the New Year: "Providence is with us. . . . We will punish the criminals who are responsible for this long war. . . . In the coming year, we will stun the world with our victories. . . ."

The mountains above Nice are beautiful.

January 16, 1941
Ivan Bunin, to a Russian correspondent of the New York Times

My wife has acute anemia, and her liver is not good. As regards finances, both of us are in absolutely *dire* straits. Through no fault of our own, we are completely ruined. We live in absolute hunger and savage cold; we do not have the slightest help here.

Perhaps good and kind people in America can help us? I earnestly implore you—if you can, to do something in this regard, and write about me in your newspaper.

January 29, 1941
Ivan Bunin, from a letter to a friend

I have never been in such total despair. . . . I cannot write because my hands are all chapped from cold. . . .

January 29, 1941
Vera Muromtseva-Bunina, from a letter to Tatyana Loginova-Muravieva

Marina Tsvetaeva once told me that I always turn my back on what I want most. This is true.

Right now my life is like this. From Friday morning to Monday, I have house chores until three p.m.; but during the second half of the week, I am free. Of course, I wear myself out working, and almost all the free time I have away from the kitchen I spend lying down. But I cannot write in such a position as my hand becomes tired very quickly. On Monday afternoon I also lie down, or sometimes retype something for Ian. On Tuesday, Wednesday, and Thursday I am besieged by all kinds of things, including a pile of letters which I most often dash off.

Once every two weeks, I have to go somewhere, either to Cannes . . . or sometimes on "business" or to celebrate someone's name day. Add to this the fact that I get up early, often have to rush all over Grasse, stand on lines at stores . . . and carry heavy bags home.

I should add that everyone has to endure this prosaic life, and that if I were younger and healthier I would even enjoy it. My existence also has some poetic moments. For instance, when I get up early, nature gives me all these wondrous impressions . . . perhaps a thought that passes by "in a flash" is more valuable that one that is fixed [in time]. . . .

I do find time to read some wonderful books, though. Right now, I am enjoying Florovsky's *Paths of Russian Theology*.[3] It is a very useful book, a survey not only of Russian theological thought but also of that secular thinking that has attended this religious search: Khomyakov, Soloviev, K. Leontiev, Yury Samarin, and others. Of course, one should study such a book or, more accurately, use it as a guide to study those whom it talks about. That would be the ideal way to go about it, but so far I thank God that it has fallen into my hands for me to read first. . . .

For relaxation I am now reading Aksakov's *Family Chronicle*[4] and others of his works. He is a wonderful writer. . . . I have also taken up reading Shestov. . . . So, as you see, my life here in Grasse is often more enjoyable than [the one I had] in Paris. Only one thing distresses me: I cannot write, I have no energy to do so. But perhaps I can overcome such languor soon.

Ian got ahold of four bottles of bull's blood for me. I have finished one, and I feel stronger. . . . I eat little, though . . . and I am thin as never before. My entire body has lines! Such a situation very much frightens the men in my life who, very touchingly, try to get me to "take some nourishment," or even to cram food down my throat. But they do not try all that hard, and I get thinner and thinner. . . .

Ivan Alexeevich, thank God, is well. He is rereading the stories that he wrote last fall. He sometimes suffers from his usual illnesses and gets irritable, but such things pass, and he is in comparatively good spirits. . . .

I am very glad that you are working well. . . . Everyone has his own fate, and artists have it better than others in that they can do more than one thing. . . . Take Leonardo [da Vinci], for example! One must not only have an appetite for food . . . but also for work. One should also try to do everything well, and leave the rest to God. . . .

January 30, 1941
Ivan Bunin, from his diary
    I received 889 franks from Switzerland—someone heard something of mine on the radio. . . .

---

[3]Florovsky's *Paths of Russian Theology* (*Puti russkogo bogosloviia*) was published in Paris in 1937.
    [4]Aksakov wrote *Family Chronicle* (*Semeinaia khronika*) in 1856.

Today in a speech, Hitler said . . . that *"in 1941 history will know a new order—one without tyranny or privileges."* . . . He is both an idiot and a madman. . . .

February 1, 1941
Ivan Bunin, from his diary

I have to change the way I live. There is nothing to drink at night, and day and night I go about as in a dream. . . .

Yes, spring is already here. But my heart tightens suddenly—it feels youthful and tender and sad. And, for some reason, I recall the time of my first love, deceptive and unhappy—but nonetheless right *for its time* . . . for at that time, this *it*, this love, was remarkably winsome, enchanting, touching, passionate, and chaste. . . . But I am saying all this in a very poor sort of way.

February 3, 1941
Ivan Bunin, from his diary

Each return home [from town] is a genuine torment. I have to climb our steep hill with a heavy bag over my shoulder (wine, fruit, and vegetables).

I am reading Shakovskoy's (Father Ioann's) *Tolstoy and the Church.*[5] . . .

I often react with surprise and sorrow, even horror (for I cannot undo what I have done), when I think about how dully and inattentively I regarded women in my first years in France (yes, and even earlier). That amazing, ineffably splendid entity, that very special something in all things earthly—i.e., the body of a woman—[this is a subject] which *no one* has *ever* written about. And not only the body. I should, I have to try. I have tried—but the result was vulgar and base. I have to find different words.

February 6, 1941
Ivan Bunin, from his diary

Today we saw Italians—dandies bordering on pimps. We had a "luxurious" breakfast and lunch. Each of us had a piece of pork (one was fatty and tough) . . . and a salad.

---

[5]Shakovskoy's *Tolstoy and the Church* (*Tolstoi i tserkov'*) appeared in Berlin in 1939.

February 12, 1941
Vera Muromtseva-Bunina, from her diary

Ian just came into my room with a banana. He is very attentive to me. He tries to feed me something whenever he can. Yesterday he [and a friend] brought home an entire kilo of macaroni. . . . Thank God!

I can do little about the cold. For a while it seemed that my bones were getting stiff. Domestic life is hard, with few joys. . . . I just finished reading *The Village* . . . and *Dry Valley*. One should read them in one fell swoop, as if listening to a symphony. . . .

Our generation turned their backs on everything that was spiritual. Positivists[6] reigned, seized by reflections and thoughts. Even Tolstoy turned his back on the church. Few people read Vl. Solovyev, and almost no one knew about Konst. Leontyev. Even the Slavophiles were relegated to the shadows. Herzen took possession of people's souls. Then, at the beginning of the century, the socialists and materialists began making inroads, Plekhanov at their head. . . . The "waftings" of Merezhkovsky and Gippius never reached anywhere. We were "eternal wanderers"—who got carried away with everything we did. . . .

February 23, 1941
Ivan Bunin, from his diary

Postcards from friends. . . . [One writes:] "Life is shit. Be well." . . . [Another adds:] "We are eating plants. Be well." . . . Never in my life have I experienced anything like this. There is nothing to eat except cabbage and dates. The stores are completely empty!

March 6, 1941
Ivan Bunin, from his diary

This morning I had lunch in Cannes. . . . Very stupidly I drank almost an entire bottle of red wine there. I next went to an English café and had some gin . . . and then to another café . . . for some more wine. . . . I fell asleep only at night, lying in bed, afraid that I might die. . . .

Having listened . . . to a spring bird in the garden, I again thought that one cannot conceive of God in any other way than Tolstoy did (in his later years), i.e., the divinity of this bird's life, its song, its mind, its feelings.

---

[6]Loosely speaking, Positivism is any system of thought that focuses on the data of experience at the expense of metaphysical speculation. As a philosophical movement, Positivism assumed its distinctive features in the work of August Comte.

March 8, 1941
Ivan Bunin, from his diary

I rewrote several things from the rotting notes that I had written at the end of 1885, the beginning of 1886, and the end of 1887. It was a miracle that they have survived at all. With pain in my heart, I kissed them. Then I tore them up and burned them. I continue to remember and write down the days and years of my life. . . .

March 8, 1941
Ivan Bunin, from a letter to Mark Aldanov

From America we have received only 1,100 francs (from A. Tolstaya) . . . but a thousand of that was instantly eaten up a long time ago.[7] . . .

March 8, 1941
Mark Aldanov, from a letter to Ivan Bunin

Why haven't you still told me anything about your plans? . . . The first thing *everybody* asks me is—are you coming and when; and, I cannot answer them! I repeat, I cannot and do not want to advise you. I am satisfied with the United States. . . . If my journal becomes a reality, we want to publish the beginning of *Dark Alleys* in the first issue (and include you among our list of contributors). Is that all right? For God's sake, send us at least one copy of the book. . . . But also for God's sake, remember that laws exist in the United States! (as regards the propriety of subjects). . . .

If I cannot get the journal off the ground, things will be bad in all respects, for we will have *no place* to publish in our language. . . .

March 9, 1941
Ivan Bunin, from his diary

Three times in my life I have suffered from nervous illnesses that were both intellectual and spiritual, and that persisted for two or three years straight. That is why I wrote so poorly when I was a young man. Then there was the poverty and wandering that has attended me

---

[7]Bunin is referring to a gift from the Tolstoy Foundation, established in New York in 1939 by Tolstoy's youngest daughter, Alexandra, together with Sergei Rachmaninoff and other Russians in exile. Initially the purpose of the Tolstoy Foundation was to help members of the diaspora and to preserve Russian culture in America. During World War II and later, however, the foundation expanded its efforts to assist victims of revolution, war, and political persecution throughout the world. Under Alexandra's forty-year leadership, the Tolstoy Foundation enabled more than fifty thousand individuals to begin new lives in America. It still exists today.

throughout most of my life, not to mention the unhappy lives of my father, mother, and sister! Generally speaking, what have I not had to endure! Revolution, war, another revolution, another war—all with unheard-of savagery, unspeakable baseness, and monstrous falsehoods! Now I face old age, new poverty, and terrible loneliness—and what lies ahead?!

March 12, 1941
Ivan Bunin, from his diary

Yesterday . . . I was in the same movie house where I was a full seven years ago . . . when I was sitting in the darkness and suddenly [a friend] appeared and said: "You have received a telephone call from Stockholm."[8] . . .

I fell asleep at 1 a.m., having drunk—again!—five glasses of vodka. . . . But this morning I feel rather good. . . .

March 20, 1941
Ivan Bunin, from a letter to Mark Aldanov

I do not plan on going anywhere, because what can I use for money? I swear to you that I have never been so poor, and that I look at the impending future as a slow death from hunger. From herbs boiled with only hot water and salt (what we call soup!) . . . I have become as thin as Gandhi, and Vera Nikolaevna sees "spots" before her eyes. Our home is like ice, we do not heat it, and for the kitchen we have only a hundred logs. We cannot buy wood anywhere. Furthermore, the government here is now demanding that we pay taxes of almost two thousand francs on the house.

But what will happen to me if I do leave? After all, so far you yourself have earned only 125 dollars [since you arrived in America]! What can I do? Can I also not expect something akin to the beastly indifference which America shows me now? Whom have I not written to? But not a dollar from anyone! . . . A Nobel laureate is perishing! . . .

March 21, 1941
Mark Aldanov, from a letter to Ivan Bunin

Most likely a journal will become a reality. . . . You must be in the first issue. . . . Write me once and for all and tell me if you are com-

---

[8]See Marullo, *Ivan Bunin: From the Other Shore*, 279–280.

ing [to America] or not. There are visas and tickets for you and Vera Nikolaevna—of this I have been assured.

March 25, 1941
Vera Muromtseva-Bunina, from her diary

Ian is again starting to write and again about love. . . .

God has punished me for all my "illicit" attachments, for not wanting children. I would have had grandchildren by now. . . .

Our generation was cursed with many distorted emotions. We were greedy in life. We took a great deal from our parents . . . but we did not understand what was important. . . .

April 6, 1941
A friend, from his memoirs

Over tea, Bunin and I talked about the war. He was very disturbed by the capitulation of France. Bunin said: "If Russia would declare war on Hitler, I would walk to Moscow on my knees to thank Soviet power. . . ."

The conversation turned to Merezhkovsky and Gippius. Bunin said:

"Merezhkovsky went to see Mussolini. He told me: 'As soon as I entered Mussolini's huge study in the Venice Palazzo, I felt that I was in the presence of Christ.' . . . After this meeting, Merezhkovsky and his wife lived in Italy for an entire year at Mussolini's expense. A year later he returned to Paris and told me: 'Mussolini has deceived me, that son of a bitch! He is not giving me any more money. . . .'

"Now there are rumors that Merezhkovsky is feeling Christ's presence in Goebbels's foyer."[9]

April 11, 1941
Ivan Bunin, from his diary

Today is Good Friday for Catholics. When I woke up this morning, I thought . . . if God gives me life, I have to live and accept whatever He sends me. . . . I was somewhat comforted by this thought. . . .

_____

[9]The rumors were both outrageous and untrue.

April 11, 1941
Ivan Bunin, from a letter to Mark Aldanov

Tickets and visas to America are good things to have, but how, how am I going to live [once I get there]?

April 12, 1941
Ivan Bunin, from his diary

Austria, Czechoslovakia, Poland, Norway, Denmark, Holland, Belgium, Luxemburg, and France. Serbia and Greece are in line. If Germany wins [the war], how will it suffer from the hatred of all the countries it has defeated! But if it is not victorious, it is even more terrible to think how the German people will suffer. . . .

April 13, 1941
An acquaintance, from his memoirs

Bunin and I were talking about life, death, and Gorky. Suddenly he recalled: "I was once sitting with Aldanov [in a café]. The waiter brought me a note which said: 'Vanya, I am here and want to see you! Alexei Tolstoy.' I showed it to Mark Alexandrovich. 'How can this be?!' I said. He replied: 'It's your business, but if you want to, go see him.'

"I got up and was taken off guard, for there he was coming straight toward me. We met. Tolstoy asked: 'May I kiss you?' I said: 'Go ahead.' We kissed. . . . He continued: 'What is there to say? Should we drink something to celebrate our meeting?' 'We can if you wish,' I replied. So we drank a bottle of champagne.

"Tolstoy then said: 'Why are you sitting here [in France]? Come and visit us [in Russia].' I answered: 'But I don't ask you: "Why are you sitting there [in Russia]!" Besides, what would I do there?' He replied: 'You would live and write. You would be published and get royalties. I don't live half badly there.' I answered back: 'What are you telling me! How can you tell me such things! What nonsense!'

"Nothing came of our conversation. We sat there and then parted. . . ."

April 15, 1941
Mark Aldanov, from a letter to Ivan Bunin

I repeat: I cannot and do not want to advise you [about leaving France]. The responsibility is too great. But if you are eating only herbs, and if Vera Nikolaevna is, as you say, "seeing spots," why are you staying in Grasse? Think, dear friend, while there is still time to do so. *The possibility still exists* for the both of you to leave [France]. How will you live here [in America]? I do not know. But . . . we will not allow *you*, as you say "to die from hunger." You will live here like you lived in France before you were awarded the Nobel Prize. . . .

I have just called Alexandra L'vovna [Tolstaya]. She told me that people here have already collected *five hundred* dollars [on your behalf], 200 of which have already been sent to you. . . . We also have sent you a package. Furthermore, Alexandra L'vovna told me that you have been taken care of. . . . There are two tickets for a trip from Lisbon to here. . . .

April 16, 1941
Ivan Bunin, from a letter to Mark Aldanov
I have just received a letter from [an acquaintance] in New York . . . who writes that she wishes to publish two collections of stories by Russian emigré writers . . . but she is offering to pay me only *one* dollar a page! . . .

April 19, 1941
Ivan Bunin, from a letter to a friend
After my many letters to Alexandra L'vovna [Tolstaya], the Tolstoy Committee has begun to send me some money, and promises to send me 25 dollars monthly. . . . But how am I going to pay for coal for the kitchen, electricity, bread, vegetables . . . taxes, and everything else? . . .

April 20, 1941
Ivan Bunin, from his diary
Today is (Orthodox) Easter. Christ has Risen! Help us, O Lord! . . .

April 27, 1941
Ivan Bunin, from his diary
Yugoslavia and Greece are no more. In one month, everything has perished.

April 27, 1941
Vera Muromtseva-Bunina, from a letter to a friend
As of late, we have begun to get various edibles from Lisbon and immediately felt a new surge of energy. We had been like grass-eating animals, eating only vegetables. Now we have meat sometimes once, sometimes twice a day. We also have something that looks like sausage

once every two weeks, but as of late only in portions of 50 grams per person. But we are happy with what we have. For Easter we even had ham! True, it was only a thin slice, but it was very pleasant nonetheless. We even had a few colored eggs. That was all we had for our holiday table. . . .

Waiting on line tires me out greatly. Last Saturday I stood in line for three hours and then had to go to the pharmacy because my head was spinning.

Of course, Ivan Alexeevich does not wait on line, but he often has to walk to town and stop at the stalls. . . .

But I am still hale and hearty in spirit, and I even find a good side to this difficult existence. Everyone has become less demanding and capricious. My life is difficult physically, but it is good spiritually.

May 2, 1941
Ivan Bunin, from his diary

A Swedish newspaper reported that 12,000 Germans in tanks and other vehicles are in Finland. . . . Is this a warning to Stalin? Is Petersburg in danger?

May 2, 1941
Ivan Bunin, from a letter to Alexei Tolstoy

I am in such a terrible position, the likes of which have never happened to me before. I am in complete poverty (not from my doing), and I am perishing from hunger together with Vera Nikolaevna, who is ill.

Several of my books have been published in Russia.[1] Help me, please—not you personally, but perhaps your government and publishing houses who have printed my books will pay me something for my works? Appeal to them on my behalf if you think it possible to do something for an individual who has done a thing or two for Russian literature.

For all the differences in our political views, I have always been impartial in my evaluations of contemporary Russian writers. [So I ask that you] treat me in a similarly impartial and humane way.

---

[1] A volume of Bunin's collected works was published in 1918; *Mitya's Love* appeared in 1926, and *The Elagin Affair* in 1927. In addition, three anthologies of Bunin's stories, his memoirs of Chekhov and Tolstoy, and an edition of his 1898 translation of Longfellow's "The Song of Hiawatha" were published by the Soviets in 1927 and 1928.

P.S. I have written an entire book of short stories, but where can I publish it?[2]

May 6, 1941
Ivan Bunin, from a letter to Mark Aldanov

Regarding *Dark Alleys* . . . you told me about how strict mores are in America. But can that be? . . . For if that were the case, how could people there have read *Lady Chatterly's Lover?*[3] . . .

Two weeks ago I received a letter [from New York] dated March 19th, saying: "Dear Mr. Bunin . . . [This is] to . . . inform you that your application for a special visa was sent to Washington on March 6, 1941. We trust that you will receive your visa very shortly."

Now what am I to do? I am very grateful to you [for your help]. . . . But how can I decide to go? . . . You write: "We will not let you die from hunger." Well, perhaps, not from hunger . . . but what about from indigence . . . from misery, humiliation . . . and ongoing uncertainty? Maybe I will be taken care of for *two or three months* . . . but then *I will be abandoned, forgotten*—of this I am firmly convinced.

How am I going to make some money? You say: "You can give readings and sell your books and stories. . . ." But how many times can I give a reading? . . . And I can't keep cooking up stories and books without end. . . . After all, I'm not a kid anymore . . . and Vera Nikolaevna *is very sick and weak.* . . .

You write: "You will be given temporary rooms at a place forty-five miles from New York." And how, given our age, will we live even "temporarily" among foreigners, dependent on their kindness, getting used to a new life, and so forth!

Simply put, we cannot decide on anything *right now*. We will be glad to have visas, if *any kind* of extreme emergency should arise. Also, if we could get ones that *would be good for half a year*, we might, perhaps, use them.

May 8, 1941
Ivan Bunin, from a letter to Nikolai Teleshov

I have not written to you for a long time—about twenty years. You, probably, are a very old man.[4] Are you in good health? I kiss your hand—and you—with undying love.

---

[2]Bunin's appeal to Tolstoy was in vain.

[3]*Lady Chatterly's Lover* was published privately in Florence in 1925 and 1928; it appeared for public readership in New York in 1930 and in London in 1939.

[4]At this time Teleshov was seventy-four, three years older than Bunin.

We are in Grasse (next to Cannes), where we have spent 17 years (alternating with Paris); we are now in a very bad way. By the will of fate, if I had been "rich," I would now be like Job. I was "known throughout the whole world"; but now no one needs me, and the world could care less. Vera Nikolaevna is very sick . . . and we are very hungry. But I am still writing. I have finished an entire book of new stories; but what should I do with them? Are you writing?

P.S. I am grey, dried up, but still filled with poison. I very much want to go home.

May 8, 1941
Alexander Bakhrakh, from his memoirs
[When Bunin wrote his letter to Teleshov], it was a boring May day. It had not stopped drizzling; everything around had a dead look; and there seemed no end to the war. Material concerns—which Bunin always was inclined to exaggerate—were ever present. He was also tired of the meager, monotonous food and even more bored by the faces that flashed before him. He began to recall his previous existence, God knows where, but apparently a place where he could visit his colleagues and go for coffee. . . . He suddenly felt like being at his familiar but not very comfortable apartment [in Paris] which truly was his "home"—he never had any other. . . .

May 16, 1941
Ivan Bunin, from his diary
On Russian radio . . . I heard a "folk singer" . . . who lived in some "out of the way place," singing: "Stalin's words to the people flow like a golden stream." . . . How could anyone go to such a vile and deceitful country! . . .

May 16, 1941
Vera Muromtseva-Bunina, from her diary
I have never been so tired as I am now. My entire body, shoulders, and back are in constant pain. It is difficult to do anything. . . . People are always criticizing me because I think so little about myself. But how should one think, given our circumstances and way of life? Deprivations . . . bother me but little.

May 17, 1941
Ivan Bunin, from his diary

I continue to marvel how France has gotten into such an unprecedented situation, in such hunger and shame!

May 25, 1941
Ivan Bunin, from his diary

This morning Vera came in with a piece of white bread which she got for free. It was made out of white flour, a gift to France from America. It was splendid! The bread that we have been eating has been repulsive: sour and yellowish-grey.

June 15, 1941
Galina Kuznetsova, from her diary

Yesterday Pushkin's granddaughter, Elena Alexandrovna Rozenmayer, spent the day here. She is fifty-five years old, petite, courageous, short-haired, with round bright eyes. She was dressed very modestly and conducted herself with dignity and restraint. Her face and the lines of her nose . . . were undoubtedly Pushkin-like. . . . Apparently she is in very dire straits. She is clearly suffering from the effects of malnutrition, but everyone goes hungry now. She also loves to talk. Ivan Alexeevich was especially attentive to her, asking her many questions about her family and about Pushkin. . . .

June 16, 1941
Ivan Bunin, from his diary

[I keep thinking] how the early Christians looked upon life with distrust, how revolted they were by its cruelty, coarseness, and bestiality. Then came the barbarians; and the Christians founded monasteries and retreated into crypts and caves. . . . Will this also be the case in the twentieth and twenty-first centuries?

June 18, 1941
Alexei Tolstoy, from a letter to Joseph Stalin

I have just received a postcard from the writer Ivan Alexeevich Bunin, who is in occupied France. He writes that he is in a terrible situation, that he is starving, and that he is in need of help.

Several weeks ago the writer Teleshov also received a postcard from him in which he says straight out: "I want to go home."

Bunin in our literature is an extremely important example as to how one should treat the Russian language, perceive a subject, and express it in a supple way. We should study Bunin's mastery of words, his imagery and realism.

Bunin is now about seventy years old. He is still full of energy and has written a new book of stories. As far as I know, he has pursued an active anti-Soviet policy in emigration. He has also kept to himself, especially after being awarded the Nobel Prize. I met him in 1936 in Paris, where he told me that no one needed his art, that he was not being read, and that his books were being published in very small quantities.

Dear Joseph Vissarionovich, I come to you with an important question that has been on the mind of many Soviet writers. May I answer Bunin's postcard, and extend to him the hope that he can return to the homeland?

If such hope does not exist, could the Soviet government at least render him material assistance through our consulate in Paris? After all, Bunin's works have often been printed by the State Publishing House.

With great respect and love.[5] . . .

June 21, 1941
Ivan Bunin, from his diary
There is anxiety everywhere: Does Germany want to attack Rus-

---

[5]In an earlier draft of this letter, Tolstoy had also written: "Allow me to express to you my opinion of this writer. As an artist, Bunin belongs to the post-Chekhov generation. When Russian literature (with the exception of Gorky) was frightened by the rumblings of the people's fury and dashed headlong into God-seeking . . . mystical anarchism, and symbolism (with its platonic conception of an ideal world), Ivan Bunin—also frightened by the events of 1905—began to portray the village with merciless realism, stripping from it the veneer of populist idealism.

"After Chekhov's ironic impressionism, Bunin's cruel, weighty, and palpable fiction was a significant step forward [in the national written expression]. Later, in connection with his trips to Europe and the East, Bunin wrote stories about the heartless world. As an emigré . . . Bunin has retained his mastery [as a writer], but he has lost his creative energy. He is not only repeating himself, but his horror at the world is also rote, and his poison no longer burns.

"In 1936, Bunin and I met by chance in a café. He was friendly and animated . . . still fresh and capable of work. His mood, though, was burdensome. . . . No one was reading him . . . and he did not know whom to write for. . . . He said nothing about returning to the USSR; but he did not bear it any malice. Generally speaking, he has kept himself aloof from emigré life.

"Bunin has influenced Soviet literature to a great degree. Both Sholokov and I value him . . . for his sharp and precise vision . . . for the way he depicts the typical details in life. . . . Others are studying his mastery as an artist. . . .

"His fate as an artist affects us Soviet writers deeply. . . ." See Iu. Krestinskii, "Pis'mo A. N. Tolstogo o Bunine," in V. Shcherbina *et al.*, eds., *Literaturnoe nasledstvo. Ivan Bunin. Kniga vtoraia* (Moscow, 1973), 394–395.

sia? Finland is evacuating women and children from its cities. Will the front against Russia be from Murmansk to the Black Sea? I cannot believe that Germany would embark on such a terrible adventure, although only the devil knows what they are capable of. For Germany it is either now or never—Russia is preparing for war at a frenzied pace.[6] . . .

For some time now, a cow has been mooing somewhere in Grasse on a daily basis. I recall Russia and its fairs. What can be more irritating than the mooing of a cow! . . .

June 22, 1941
Ivan Bunin, from his diary
    This morning Germany declared war on Russia.[7] . . .

After breakfast (sparse soup made from mashed peas, and a salad), I lay down to read some of Flaubert's letters. . . . Suddenly [a friend] cried out: "Ivan Alexeevich, Germany has declared war on Russia!" I thought he was joking, but then [another friend] cried out the same thing. I ran into the dining room and turned on the radio. Yes, we are terribly upset. . . .

Now it is truly either all or nothing.

---

[6]On June 19, 1941, German forces massed along the Russian border. In truth, Soviet officials should not have been surprised by such a move, since warnings to Moscow of a German attack on the Soviet Union had become almost commonplace in the month or so before the actual onslaught.

On May 19, 1941, a Soviet spy in Tokyo advised Moscow that Germany was preparing to invade Russia on June 20 with a force of between 170 and 190 divisions. (On June 15 this individual named the precise day of the attack.) On May 21 the Soviet deputy military attaché in Berlin warned Moscow that "the attack of the German army is reportedly scheduled for June 15, but may begin in the first days of June." A month later the Soviet Embassy in London cabled Moscow: "As of now, the British Ambassador to Moscow is deeply convinced of the inevitability of armed conflict between Germany and the USSR which will begin no later than the middle of the June. According to him, the Germans now have concentrated 147 units (including air force and service units) along the Soviet borders."

Equally routinely, though, the Soviets were so convinced of German operations against Britain that they refused to believe in a Nazi invasion of their country. On June 13, TASS, the Soviet news agency, denied a split between Berlin and Moscow. On the following day, eight days before Germany attacked Russia, Molotov rejected intelligence reports of an imminent German offensive, saying: "Only a fool would attack Russia." See Goralski, 160, 161, 163.

[7]On June 22, 1941, Germany and its Axis partners launched the greatest military attack in history when they invaded the Soviet Union along an 1,800-mile front from the Arctic to the Black Sea. More than 3 million troops, 600,000 vehicles, 750,000 horses, 3,580 tanks, and 2,770 planes were hurled against the Russians. At the same time, Rumanian and Finnish troops also crossed into Soviet territory. The Russian defenders, 4.5 million men along the frontier, were taken completely by surprise. They were also totally unprepared for the struggle.

June 23, 1941
Ivan Bunin, from his diary
So far the newspapers report only one new item of news, i.e., a declaration by those who are advancing on Russia that this is a "most holy war to save world civilization from the mortal danger of bolshevism." . . .

June 24, 1941
Ivan Bunin, from his diary
This morning the newspaper reported the first Russian communiqué: The Russians are supposedly trouncing the Germans. But the Germans are saying just the opposite.[8]

June 25, 1941
Vera Muromtseva-Bunina, from her diary
All these days are like living in a fever. . . . The Russians here are sharply divided into two camps.[9] . . .

June 27, 1941
Vera Muromtseva-Bunina, from her diary
What will happen to Russia? The Communist "song" has been sung. People in Moscow now talk only about patriotism. Their spirits are strong. . . .

June 30, 1941
Ivan Bunin, from his diary
So now the Germans, Slovaks, Hungarians, Albanians (!), and Rumanians have all declared war on Russia.[1] And they keep saying that this is a holy war against communism. How late have they all come to their senses! They have put up with it for almost 23 years! . . .

June 30, 1941
Galina Kuznetsova, from her diary
I heard the sound of the bell at the gates. I looked out and saw . . . the local police chief. . . . It turned out that he wanted to see all the

[8]The German successes against the Soviet Union were nothing less than spectacular. For instance, in just seventy-two hours of fighting, the Germans destroyed two thousand Soviet planes, thereby reducing what had been the largest air force in the world to an ineffective fighting unit. Also, on June 24, 1941, the Germans took both Vilna and Kaunas in Lithuania.
[9]That is, for or against Hitler.
[1]To this list must be added the Finns, who declared war on Russia on June 25, 1941.

men who were living in the villa. He interrogated Ivan Alexeevich first.... [When he saw Vera Nikolaevna] he asked: "Are you White Russians?" She replied: "We are emigrés." He then said that he had an order to check on all the Russians in the area.... For a long time we did not understand what he meant.... He then said that he had to bring the three men who were living in the villa to a special commission for verification. Ivan Alexeevich was in his robe. Terribly pale, he suddenly began acting as though he did not understand French. I told the police chief that Bunin was sick ... and could not go anywhere. He immediately told his assistant to write this down, that he would take responsibility, and that Bunin would be placed under house arrest for twenty-four hours. Bakhrakh was not at home; but he was ordered to appear at the police station as soon as he returned. ...

The police chief again began speaking very carefully and in a roundabout way, saying that he would have to "take a look through Monsieur Bunin's desk." At first, Ivan Alexeevich did not understand what he meant, but when the police chief explained what he wanted a second time, Bunin sent him with me into his study, where the police chief opened several drawers and briefcases. The search was purely formal. It was quite apparent that such a course of action was not the police chief's idea. He said he knew full well who Bunin was, laying the blame on his superiors as well as pleading ignorance to what was going on. Nonetheless, they took Zurov off to police headquarters. When they left, we could not come to our senses for a long time. The radio, though, reported that today France broke off diplomatic relations with the Soviet Union. It thus became clear why such "measures" were taken, despite our well-known situation as "emigrés." ... Of course, Ivan Alexeevich got so upset after he visited police headquarters that he called the doctor.

June 30, 1941
Ivan Bunin, from his diary
    It seems as if about 200–300 Russians in the area were arrested and taken to camps outside of town. ... [Friends] went to one camp and saw a long line of unhappy, crestfallen people (most of them were in rags), guarded by gendarmes. ... It is a cruel and senseless act.[2]

[2]In the wake of the Nazi attack on the Soviet Union, French authorities so feared that Russian emigrés in both Vichy and unoccupied France were actual or potential fifth columnists that they arrested large numbers of expatriate men in both regions. In most cases the "prisoners," who ranged in age from fourteen to sixty-five, were detained only momentarily, with little or no unpleasantry.

Circa July 1941
Ivan Bunin, from the memoirs of a friend

The hell with the Bolsheviks! Russia will not suffer under them much longer. People say that Stalin killed the "best revolutionaries." No, it is the punishing hand of God [that is at work here]. It is the Bolsheviks who are the enemies of the people. But God grant that the people prove victorious over Hitler!

July 1, 1941
Ivan Bunin, from his diary

I have been drowning my sorrows in cognac. . . . Vera went to a [prisoner-of-war] camp (about 5 or 6 kilometers from the city) and saw [several of our friends] there. . . .

I do not remember such a dull, burdensome, and repulsive *Angst* as the one that has oppressed me all day long. I recall the spring of '19 in Odessa and the Bolsheviks—what I feel now is very similar to what so distressed me then.

[Our friends] are still in the camp. . . . One is worried about his dog. He says, "I hope that that son of a bitch of a son of mine remembered to feed it today, but what about tomorrow? That son of a bitch should drop dead."

The town has sent beds and food to the camps. The local Frenchmen are very upset as to what is going on.

Terrible battles are going between the Russians and the Germans.[3]

Yes, we are again living through the "Cursed Days"![4]

Of these arrests, Sedykh recalled: "[When the Germans invaded the Soviet Union] several Russians, including myself, were living in Nice. We were all arrested and imprisoned in some medieval dungeon. After an hour a police commissioner asked in a solemn voice:

'Is there anyone among you who has been awarded the Great Cross of the Legion of Honor? If so, I am by law obligated to free you.'

I look at my imprisoned comrades. All of them were drunk. . . . One of them asked what the commissioner wanted. I translated. The tramp advised me in a cold-blooded way:

'Why not just send him to the devil?'

'What did he say?' the commissioner asked anxiously.

'He said that he has not the fortune of being awarded the Great Cross of the Legion of Honor.'

How Bunin laughed when he heard this story!" See A. Sedykh, *Dalekie, blizkie* (New York, 1962), 210–211.

[3]The Germans were now two hundred miles into the Russian frontier.

[4]Bunin is referring to his time in Moscow in 1918 and in Odessa in 1919 and 1920.

July 2, 1941
Ivan Bunin, from his diary

I woke up . . . feeling sick. Vera got up earlier—and apparently went to the camps. I fell asleep again and had several erotic dreams. . . .

[A friend] says that . . . the Russians have just surrendered Riga and Murmansk.[5] Truly, Stalin's kingdom is coming to an end. Kiev will probably be taken within a week or two.

We arrived in Paris on March 28, 1920. I remember the chestnut trees and the charm and novelty of everything around us (right up to the people who were selling sausage at the stands). . . . Oh how young we still were! What festive days we all had then![6]

July 3, 1941
Ivan Bunin, from his diary

About eight this evening, Bakhrakh and Zurov returned home from the camps.[7] It was all very burdensome; the place where they were imprisoned was dirty and filled with cockroaches. Roughly thirty people slept in the same room. They all sat around and waited to be interrogated. But no one asked them anything. But today some commission . . . let them all go. It is extremely stupid and shameful.

July 4, 1941
André Gide, from a letter to Ivan Bunin

Over the past few days I have been very distressed, thinking of you as regards certain administrative measures affecting Russians in our country. I heard that you would be left alone. . . . But I want to be fully assured that you will be left in peace. In any case, if you encounter any unpleasantness or difficulties, inform me immediately. My admiration for the author of *The Village* and my respect and sympathy for him are so great that I cannot remain neutral to his misfortunes. Rest assured of my complete devotion to you.

July 6, 1941
Ivan Bunin, from his diary

I was deeply touched by Gide's letter. . . .

[5]On July 1, 1941, the Germans captured Riga but were halted about thirty-five miles west of Murmansk.

[6]Again, Bunin's memory has failed him. He was not young, and the days were not festive.

[7]Zurov, in the already mentioned letter to Baboreko, maintains that the baptismal certificate he had earlier obtained for Bakhrakh was instrumental in saving Bakhrakh's life. See Baboreko, 302.

How terrible not to know how the war is *really* going in Russia. . . .

July 9, 1941
Ivan Bunin, from his diary
   The newspapers report that the Russians are taking a savage beating.[8] . . .

July 10, 1941
Vera Muromtseva-Bunina, from her diary
   [A friend] told me how the old men around here had been predicting that "a great deal of blood would flow," that "birds with steel beaks would take flight," and that everyone had laughed at them. . . .

July 13, 1941
Ivan Bunin, from his diary
   The Germans *have taken Vitebsk.*[9] A sickening feeling. . . .
   How could this have happened? What does Vitebsk look like now? We know nothing! *All* the communiqués—on both sides—are so boastful and false. The Russian reports are particularly distorted and short.
   [A French newspaper] says that things are going terribly for the Russians.
   The Russian All-Military Union[1] has offered to serve in those parts of Russia that are occupied by the Germans. Apparently there are many people who are willing to do so. They also broke into stormy applause whenever someone spoke about the downfall of the Bolsheviks.

---

[8]On July 8, 1941, the Germans captured Pskov in northwest Russia and were advancing toward Novgorod and Leningrad. On the following day they overran Minsk and Vitebsk, eliminating more than 40 Soviet divisions, taking at least 300,000 Russians as prisoners, and destroying 2,500 Soviet tanks and 1,500 artillery pieces.
   [9]Vitebsk is a city roughly three hundred miles southwest of Moscow.
   [1]The Russian All-Military Union (*Russkii Obshchevoennyi Soiuz*) was founded in 1923 by General Wrangel and counted more than 100,000 members, the majority of them having served with him in the Russian civil war. Fiercely anti-Bolshevik, the group was headquartered in Paris, included 1,500 members, and maintained branches in almost all the important centers of "Russia Abroad."
   It is ironic that the Russian All-Military Union believed itself capable of armed action in Russia, since its existence was marred by at least two public disasters. On January 26, 1930, its president, General Alexander Kutepov, was kidnapped in broad daylight on a busy Paris street and never seen again. Kutepov was a well-known figure among Soviets and emigrés. He had been an iron-willed commander during the domestic strife in the homeland as well as in the Gallipoli camps following the evacuation of the White Army from the Crimea. With Wrangel's death in 1928, Kutepov had left his post as head of the Association of Gallipoli Veterans to direct the Russian All-Military Union. Although the

July 14, 1941
Ivan Bunin, from his diary

The Germans are saying that they have completely routed the enemy, and that *the taking of Kiev is just a "matter of hours."*[2] They are also on their way to Petersburg. . . .

July 17, 1941
Ivan Bunin, from his diary
    Smolensk has fallen.[3] Can it be true?

July 24, 1941
Ivan Bunin, from his diary

This is the third day that Moscow has been bombed.[4] This is something completely new for that city!

August 2, 1941
Ivan Bunin, from his diary
    Vera is doing poorly. She is thin and *aging terribly.*

---

group was concerned primarily with the welfare of its members, in particular with providing them with gainful employment, Kutepov was also involved in numerous murky schemes involving "active" anti-Soviet agitation. He was less than successful with his efforts, though, since none of the agents he dispatched to Soviet Russia on missions of intelligence or sabotage was ever heard from again.

Witnesses of Kutepov's kidnapping spoke of a short struggle between the general and three men; and, later that afternoon, observers on a beach on Normandy noted the mysterious transfer of a bulky, oblong parcel by a motorboat to a steamship which was later identified as the Soviet freighter *Spartak*.

On September 24, 1937, General E. K. Miller, the next president of the Russian All-Military Union, together with an aide who was heading the counterintelligence section of the group, vanished. The parallels to Kutepov's kidnapping were striking. This time witnesses reported that a grey truck had arrived at Le Havre with three passengers, but that it had left with only two. Later that morning the Soviet vessel *Maria Ulianova*, which had been anchored at Le Havre, left port unexpectedly early. (The story goes that Miller was taken to the Soviet Union and shot.)

Needless to say, the French took a dim view of such shenanigans. "France is not a no man's land," the newspaper *Le Matin* exploded. "Our country belongs to the French. If there are foreigners here who have scores to settle between them or quarrels to fight out, let them do it in their own country, not in ours. We are as little interested in the difference of their opinions as we are in the color of their emblems. . . . Indeed, not only do we not clean our own doormat, but we also even hold it out for the entire world to muddy and wipe their feet on." For more on the "Kutepov" and "Miller" affairs, see Johnston, 101–104, 141–143.

[2]On July 10, 1941, the Germans had advanced to within ten miles of Kiev.

[3]On July 16, 1941, Smolensk fell to the Germans, trapping 600,000 Russians in the encounter. Although the defeat was a disaster militarily, it also signaled a stiffening of Soviet resistance to the enemy for the first time since the invasion.

[4]The Germans first bombed Moscow on July 12, 1941. In a second attack on July 21, the Germans dropped 100 tons of high explosives and 45,000 incendiaries on the Russian capital.

For the past two days I have been rereading and rereading the first volume of *War and Peace*. The first part is particularly remarkable.

August 2, 1941
Mark Aldanov, from a letter to Ivan Bunin

I have received *Dark Alleys* and I am terribly grateful to have it. The stories in it are superb, and many of them have left me enthralled. You are a brave man, Ivan Alexeevich! People will scold you for the boldness of several scenes. They will say that it is "pornography" and that you are holding "laurels to Lady Chatterly." . . .

August 3, 1941
Ivan Bunin, from his diary

[At friends'] I had a very full breakfast. I ate with the barbaric thought of eating as much as I could.

Today I read the first volume of Sholokhov's *Quiet Flows the Don*. It was talented in spots, but there was not a simple word in the entire thing. It was very difficult to read because of its affected language and the abundance of local words. . . .

August 6, 1941
Ivan Bunin, from his diary

"The wind mercilessly tore a cotton bandage from the moon, and its deathly light flowed like yellow pus. . . ." Almost all of *Quiet Flows the Don* is written like this. Sholokov is very talented.

August 7, 1941
Ivan Bunin, from his diary

The Germans report monstrous losses among Russian citizens. . . . They have achieved "complete victory."

August 11, 1941
Vera Muromtseva-Bunina, from her diary

As of late, Ian has been very kind, tender, and attentive to me. He has even let me have his sugar and butter. He has also stopped reproaching me for expenses—the main cause of all the unpleasantness between us. God grant that it continue. . . .

August 12, 1941
Ivan Bunin, from his diary

Country after country is distinguishing itself by lies and servility.

No one supposedly "fought" [against bolshevism] for twenty-four years. Finally people have opened their eyes. . . .

I continue to cut out and gather news about the various Russian fronts. . . .

Yes, do not look back—otherwise you will turn into a pillar of salt. Do not be carried away by the vision of the past! . . .

August 17, 1941
Ivan Bunin, from his diary
The Germans explain their incredibly cruel assault on Russia as distinct from the war they are waging in France, Bulgaria, and elsewhere. What is going on in Russia, they say, is a war with savages who do not value life and are insensitive to death. . . .

August 22, 1941
Ivan Bunin, from his diary
The Germans say they have taken Kherson; and, the Russians, that they have surrendered Gomel'.[5] . . .

So far the war in Russia has lasted 62 days. . . .

As if on purpose, I am rereading the third volume of *War and Peace*. Borodino, the abandoning of Moscow.[6] . . .

August 24, 1941
Ivan Bunin, from a letter
The Germans write that they have killed *more than 5 million* Russians.[7] . . .

August 24, 1941
Boris Zaitsev, from a letter to Nina Berberova
I have just received news from Paris that . . . what is left of the

[5]Kherson is in the northern Crimea, 100 miles directly east of Odessa. Gomel' is in southeastern Belarus, approximately 450 miles southwest of Moscow.

[6]Bunin is referring to the Battle of Borodino, which took place on September 7, 1812, in an area roughly 70 miles west of Moscow. On that day, 130,000 French troops, under the command of Napoleon, narrowly defeated 120,000 Russians headed by General Kutuzov. Casualties from the struggle were 45,000 Russians and 30,000 French. A week later, Napoleon occupied Moscow, unopposed.

Even more poignant, perhaps, the Germans won a victory over the Russians at Borodino on October 20, 1941.

[7]Not quite, but the death and destruction were stunning nonetheless. German sources claim that Russian losses in the first two months of the invasion were over 3.5 million, together with 1,250,000 prisoners, 14,000 tanks, 15,000 guns, and 11,250 aircraft. Soviet sources cite lower figures. They also claim that for the same time period, German losses on the Eastern Front were 86,000 dead, 20,000 missing, and 292,000 wounded.

Turgenev library[8] has to be moved off the premises before October. . . . For me, the most important thing is Ivan's archive. . . . [There are] nine suitcases . . . with his manuscripts and letters![9]

Can they be kept at your place? . . . I know that you love Ivan and that the matter is a serious one. The money to move the books, we will get in one way or another. . . . Do you know of another reliable place in Paris where we can put them? (I have not seen one so far.)[1]

August 28, 1941
Ivan Bunin, from his diary

André Gide was here. He made a very pleasant impression. He is subtle and smart; but then he suddenly exclaims that "Tolstoy is Asiatic." He is also enraptured by Pasternak, saying that "Pasternak has opened his eyes to the current situation in Russia." Sologub also enthralls him. . . . Gide also saw Gorky, but when he was lying in state. . . .[2]

---

[8]The Turgenev Library was founded by Ivan Turgenev and others in 1875 for Russian students and political emigrés who, in the writer's words, "wished to escape loneliness in a big city." (Lenin had worked there during his time abroad.) Eventually it housed some sixty thousand volumes, including the archives of Russian emigré writers; works by Turgenev with his own markings in the margins; many pamphlets, brochures, and periodicals that had been illegal under tsarist rule; and, at the beginning of World War II, the archives of many Russian emigré writers who had given their personal and professional writings to the Turgenev Library for their protection.

Throughout the 1920s and 1930s, the "Turgenevka" was a center of intellectual and cultural life for Russian emigrés. In 1940 the Nazi ideologist, Alfred Rosenberg, seeing himself as a connoisseur of things Russian, ordered that the holdings of the Turgenev Library be relocated in Germany for an "Institute for Eastern Europe" there. On the way, though, they were destroyed in a bombing. (Some sources claim that the books actually reached Germany and that they later wound up in Minsk.) Berberova reports that in 1945 a German officer brought her a letter that she had written to Tseitlin in 1913 and that had been housed at the library.

Berberova continues: "The officer related that at a certain German railway station, he had seen some gutted boxes, and that Russian books, manuscripts, and letters were scattered on the ground. Picking up some letters by Gorky, the officer by chance noticed my signature on a crumbling sheet and decided to give me some pleasure. That was the end of the Turgenev Library."

In 1959 determined librarians and volunteers reopened the Turgenev Library at a new location. Beginning with six hundred books that had been stored in the basement of the original building and that had escaped the notice of the Germans, it now consists of some thirty thousand volumes. Since 1972 the Turgenev Library has been subsidized by the Mayor's Office in Paris. For more on the Turgenev Library, see N. Berberova, "The Disappearance of the Turgenev Library," *Journal of Library History,* No. 1 (1992), 95–101; Glad, 325.

[9]At this time Bunin's archives were hidden in the basement of the Turgenev Library.

[1]At her home in Longchêne, Berberova had many things that Russian emigrés had entrusted to her keeping, including a number of valuable paintings.

[2]After his death on June 18, 1936, Gorky lay in state in the Hall of Columns in Moscow. He was attended by a guard of honor that included Stalin, Khrushchev, and other high dignitaries of the Soviet state.

August 28, 1941
André Gide, from his journals

    While in Grasse . . . I saw Bunin. It was a rather disappointing visit. Despite cordial efforts on both sides, we did not establish any genuine contact. One esteems too little what the other admires. His cult for Tolstoy embarrasses me as much as his scorn for Dostoevsky, Saltykov-Shchedrin, and Sologub. We decidedly do not have the same saints, the same gods.

    But Bunin was charming. . . . His handsome face, though very wrinkled, is still noble; his eyes are filled with enthusiasm. He was wearing dark-red pajamas, open at the chest and with a fine gold chain on which, I suppose, hung a holy medal.

    Bunin told me that he had just finished a new book, but that he does not know where or how to get it published. I was somewhat embarrassed that I knew nothing of his *oeuvre*, except *The Gentleman from San Francisco* and *The Village*, a youthful piece of work which, he told me, represents him little and poorly, and which I was quite wrong to like so much. He almost disowns it. I do not know what he knows of my work, nor was I able to make out why he liked me.

August 29, 1941
Ivan Bunin, from his diary

    Today I finished the second volume of *Quiet Flows the Don*. Sholokhov is still a boor, a plebeian. . . . I feel the return of my hatred for bolshevism.

August 30, 1941
Ivan Bunin, from his diary

    Tonight I had a splitting headache and a palpitating heart. I again drank away the night (with vodka that I had made myself)!

    The Germans have taken Tallinn.[3] . . .

August 30, 1941
Vera Muromtseva-Bunina, from her diary

    I have just had a bad attack. I did not sleep all night. . . . Today I was at the market, but there were no vegetables there. . . . [In town] I happened to catch sight of Gide and got a very good look at him. He

---

[3]Tallinn is the capital of Estonia. Even worse, perhaps, on August 30, 1941, the Germans captured Mga, approximately twenty miles southeast of Leningrad; in so doing they cut the last railway connection between that city and the rest of Russia. Two days later the enemy was within artillery range of Leningrad itself and, to the east of the city, it was also advancing toward the southern shore of Lake Ladoga, the last link of Leningrad to the homeland.

has a pleasant, interesting face . . . with distinguished features. Sharp wrinkles marked the middle of his neck and the space between his nose and lips. He had a bald spot which showed off his skull. . . . When he visited us at "Jeanette" . . . [I was told that] he went into raptures over Russia's landscape.

Early September 1941
Tatyana Loginova-Muravieva, from her memoirs

The more I came to know Vera Nikolaevna, the more I admired her internal force, her rare self-sacrificing love. Having confessed my admiration for her, I added:

"But all the same, I find your patience to be incredible. How can you endure so much? Always to stay in the background when you should be in first place alongside your writer-husband. After all, he needs you so, like a pillar that holds up the entire edifice. How can he leave you even for a short period of time?"

"It is not easy to be the wife of a writer," she answered. "No, it is a very, very difficult thing. One has to understand, accept, and forgive all a writer's passions, not only those that have occurred but, in advance, all those that will come. One must understand the writer's thirst for new sensations and emotions, things which necessarily intoxicate him, without which he cannot create, and which are for him a means, not a goal. After all, the goal of a creative person is his creativity itself."

"So such means are good? Do they justify the ends?"

"Your analogy is not appropriate, for it cannot be applied to the writer. A writer is made of different stuff. He sees and hears things that we do not see or hear. He also feels in a different way. . . . Bunin said in his poem, 'In the Memory of a Friend':

How close this yearning and *Angst*
To be the universe, its fields, its sea, its sky!
How sharply you and I loved the world
With a love that was blind, mysterious, and wry!

That nameless sweet pain, those causeless joys and sorrows
That you alone shared with me, our merging with heaven and
     earth. . . .
To my death I will carry those moments when you vaunted anew
Your power, your love, your charm, your mirth. . . .'"

[I replied]: "Does that mean that for all these sharply feeling people, one has to forget herself, to offer herself as a sacrifice for them?"

"There is no sacrifice here—something you will understand later. I always knew and continue to know that the 'prince' will die only with me in attendance. He has always needed me, and to the end of his days he will need me for the most important thing in life . . . his creativity. Right now I am again sorting through Ian's archives. . . . Here is what he says about Varvara Pashchenko, his first great love: 'Varvara acted correctly when she refused to join her life to mine. Such a woman cannot be the life of a creative person. Her nature does not have the necessary qualities. First and foremost, a creative person lives for his creativity, and he must arrange his life so that it accommodates his work.'

"Later, he continued: 'It is difficult to say why one or another circumstance is needed so that a writer, an artist, a composer, or a scholar can work. . . .'

"But is it the wife of a creative individual who creates this 'circumstance' when she rejects anything that is her own and finds happiness in her sufferings!"

September 5, 1941
Ivan Bunin, from his diary

The Russians have begun their counterattack.[4]

I am reading Pearl Buck's Chinese stories. The first was very pleasant and noble. . . .

Today is the 76th day of war in Russia.

September 7, 1941
Ivan Bunin, from his diary

The newspapers and radio comfort their own people with the same hopeless drivel. "In Petersburg people are dying from sickness and hunger"[5]—this is from Helsinki. How do the reporters know what is going on there?

---

[4]Nowhere in the homeland, though, were the Russians able to halt the German advance.

[5]On September 5, 1941, the Germans began a violent shelling and bombing of Leningrad, causing many deaths. For Russian defenders, though, the main problem was how to feed the three million people in the city, especially when, three days later, the enemy captured Petrokrepost', roughly thirty miles to the east of Leningrad, encircling that city completely by land.

Although some supplies were brought into Leningrad by boat on Lake Ladoga, there was, even with ration allowances, only enough food in the city for about a month. On September 21 what had been the daily ration of bread made from rye, chaff, flax, soya, and/or malt—21 ounces for workmen, 12 ounces for clerical workers, and 10-1/2 ounces for others, including children—was reduced by an additional 1-1/4 ounces. There was no heat or light; people concealed their dead to use the ration cards of the deceased.

September 14, 1941
Ivan Bunin, from his diary

Last night I was awakened by banging at the door. I was very afraid, thinking that something had happened to Vera. But it turned out that there had been two terrible strikes. The English had dropped bombs [not far from here]. . . . From my window I saw a soft moonlit night and . . . a raspberry-colored oval hanging low in the sky. It was awesome, like a miraculous icon. Its light showed the results of the bombing. . . .

The news from the various fronts is the same—demonic but pointless bloodletting. The enemy is putting pressure on Petersburg and has taken Chernigov.[6]

September 16, 1941
Georgy Adamovich, from his memoirs

After lunch Gide and Bunin finally began talking about literature. Host and guest clearly liked each other, though they had little in common. Bunin was garrulous, noisy, and mocking. Gide was restrained. He laughed at Bunin's jokes politely but responded to them as if they were serious comments. Bunin spoke French poorly. Gide did not know a word of Russian.

Sooner or later [the topic of] Tolstoy and Dostoevsky was bound to touch these writers. . . . Bunin knew Gide's admiration for Dostoevsky and began to tease him. Gide answered him curtly and evasively. . . . In response, Bunin uttered Tolstoy's name in such a way as if once and for all to vanquish and disgrace Dostoevsky. Gide shrugged his shoulders . . . and kept repeating: "A genius, yes, Tolstoy is a great genius. . . ." But then he said that *War and Peace* was a monstrously boring book.

"What? What did he say?" Bunin asked over and over again in Russian; and, having seized a huge cutting knife, and with a deliber-

---

The Germans were convinced that they could starve Leningrad into submission. Indeed, they did not want the city to surrender; they preferred to avoid the burden of feeding the population there. German troops were ordered to shoot people who fled Leningrad toward their lines, but to spare those who escaped the city toward the east where, presumably, they would add to the chaos. The vicelike grip that the Germans held on Leningrad had almost immediate effects. In November 1941 alone, 11,000 of its citizens died of starvation; in the following month, the figure rose to 52,000.

The German siege of Leningrad was not lifted fully until early 1944, after several hundred thousand citizens had died of starvation. For more on the German assault on Russia's European capital, see H. Salisbury, *The 900 Days: The Siege of Leningrad* (New York, 1969).

[6]Chernigov is situated in northeast Ukraine, about one hundred miles north of Kiev.

ately beastly face, he began to wave it, as if intending to kill Gide. Gide burst out laughing; and for a long, long time his whole body shook with laughter.

September 19, 1941
Ivan Bunin, from his diary
    The radio reported that *Poltava . . . and Kiev have been taken.*[7] . . .
    First one place falls, then another. . . . But *à quoi bon?* Will Russia be defeated? I find that rather difficult to imagine.

September 22, 1941
Ivan Bunin, from his diary
    The Germans are suffering monstrous losses. But where will they go next? They are already at the Sea of Azov,[8] but they are taking a tremendous risk.

September 23, 1941
Ivan Bunin, from a letter to Nina Berberova
    I wrote to [the people at the Turgenev Library in Paris] that "if possible, I would prefer it that the (approximately nine) suitcases [containing my writings] be moved to my apartment in Paris." . . . There is nothing new in my sad life. I kiss you from the depths of my soul.[9] . . .

---

[7]Both Poltava and Kiev had special significance for Bunin as well as for all Russians. On July 8, 1709, Poltava was the scene for the decisive victory of Peter the Great over Charles XII of Sweden in the Great Northern War. The conflict not only ended Sweden's status as a major power but marked the beginning of Russia's supremacy in Eastern Europe.
    Kiev was the "mother of Russian cities," the political and cultural center of Rus' until its destruction by the Tatars in 1254; but at this time it was also the third largest urban area in the Soviet Union. In the forty-day assault on the city, and despite a defense of "stand-and-die" ordered by Stalin, German forces destroyed five Soviet armies. They eliminated more than 500,000 Russians, captured another 600,000, and lay claim to 2,500 guns and 1,000 tanks. To the Germans, the fall of Kiev was the single greatest capitulation of the war, but to the Russians it represented the nadir of their struggle with the invaders.
    [8]On September 21, 1941, German forces reached the Sea of Azov and isolated Soviet forces in the Crimea. Four days later they attacked the peninsula itself.
    [9]In her memoirs, Berberova adds: "Of course, [I knew] that it would be too risky to send Bunin's suitcases to his flat in Paris. . . . So Zaitsev and I decided to take the writer's archives to the Rue Lournel, where there was a Russian dormitory and a cafeteria. The place was hardly safe, and within a year people there were arrested. But it seems to me that when Bunin returned to Paris [in 1945], he got back his suitcases." See N. Berberova, *Kursiv moi*, vol. 2 (New York, 1983), 438. (When Bunin returned to Paris, he did in fact receive his suitcases.)

September 28, 1941
Vera Muromtseva-Bunina, from her diary

I am content with my life with Ian. Indeed, if I were to begin existence anew, I would live it exactly the same way that I am doing now. I could not have a better companion in life. No one else can call forth such feeling from me. No one else, besides my brother Pavlik, can bring me to such fullness. Pavlik is my tragedy. I will feel guilty before him for all time. . . . [My other brother], Mitya, is a different story. He also greatly loved me, but we were very different people. . . .

October 9, 1941
Ivan Bunin, from his diary

[I heard] a report by the Russians, saying that Oryol has fallen to the Germans.[1] "Things are very serious," they say. It looks as though the Germans are going to win. But, perhaps, this is not a bad thing? . . .

October 17, 1941
Ivan Bunin, from his diary

Yesterday the radio reported that the Germans have taken Kaluga, Tver (Kalinin to the "Soviets"), and Odessa.[2] It seems as if the Russians have been dashed to pieces. Most likely first Moscow and then Petersburg are also on the verge of surrendering.[3] . . . Most likely the

---

[1] The report is true, the German assault on Oryol being the first stage in the formal German offensive on Moscow. (It will be recalled that the region around Oryol was the site of Bunin's childhood, adolescence, and youth.) With the surrender of Oryol, Hitler predicted an early victory in the struggle on the Eastern Front. On October 3, 1941, he announced to the German people that Russia "has already been broken and will never rise again."

[2] On October 12, 1941, the Germans captured Kaluga, an important railway center about one hundred miles southwest of Moscow. Two days later they took Kalinin, roughly one hundred miles northwest of the capital. On October 16, German and Rumanian troops seized Odessa after a two-month siege. Almost immediately, Rumania renamed the conquered Russian territory as "Transdniestria" and incorporated it within its borders.

It should also be noted that October 16, 1941, was the day of the *bol'shoi drap* or "great panic" in Moscow. When Muscovites learned that Lenin's coffin had been removed from Red Square and that the Germans were about 60 miles from the city gates, they fled eastward amidst widespread looting and chaos. The people's commissars and the entire diplomatic corps were evacuated beyond the Volga, 525 miles east to Kuybishev; many senior party members made a less official if dignified exodus in cars and trains. (Stalin was the only high-ranking official to remain in Moscow.) In their place, more than a half-million children, women, and old men completed the defenses around the city with 60 miles of anti-tank ditches, 5,000 miles of trenches, and 185 miles of barbed wire and felled trees.

[3] On October 19, 1941, Stalin informed his compatriots that he was still in Moscow. Having proclaimed the city in a state of siege, he ordered: "Moscow will be defended to the last." Reports of Russian losses, though, continued to be grim. At this point in the strug-

war will last all winter—and perhaps longer than that. We will die from hunger.

October 17, 1941
Vera Muromtseva-Bunina, from her diary

Ian came into my room . . . and together we listened to the radio. . . . Ian was quiet, then he left. . . . After fifteen minutes or so, I . . . went to see him. . . . He was lying in the darkness. I told him: "[Russian] troops were able to get out of Odessa even as late as yesterday.[4] . . . The city was taken by Italians and Rumanians . . . but they did not set it on fire."

October 18, 1941
Ivan Bunin, from his diary

Yesterday I finished reading *Oblomov*.[5] It was long, but almost all of it was good. . . .

October 19, 1941
Vera Muromtseva-Bunina, from a letter to a friend

We are being allowed to buy 10 kilos of potatoes at a time. What tremendous happiness! . . .

October 23, 1941
Ivan Bunin, from his diary

Today was my birthday. I was very weak and made my way to the dining room only with great difficulty. I ate a couple of spoonfuls of soup (as always, water with all kinds of inane and repugnant green things thrown in). After that I made my way over to the chair by the radio. When I got there, I felt even worse, with my head being more and more like ice. I had to rush out . . . onto the porch—I was sick to my stomach. I then dragged myself back into the house . . . and collapsed next to the sofa. . . .

---

gle, the Russians had lost 600,000 square miles of territory, embracing a population of 6 million. German sources claim that the Russians lost 3.2 million as prisoners of war, along with 19,000 tanks, 28,000 guns, and 14,600 aircraft. On October 31, the Luftwaffe carried out at least four air raids on Moscow in a single day.

[4] About 35,000 Russians were evacuated from the city. With the German bombings of Soviet transports, though, not all of these troops reached Sevastopol, about 200 miles to the southeast.

[5] Goncharov wrote *Oblomov* in 1859.

October 23, 1941
Vera Muromtseva-Bunina, from her diary

Ian started gasping for breath . . . and said he was having pains in his chest. . . . He also said he "was dying" . . . and that he had "not managed to take care of everything." . . .

The doctor was very sweet . . . and did not take any money from us. He told Ian only things to keep up his spirits. But the doctor told me that the matter was serious, and that perhaps one of Ian's arms would be paralyzed. And today is Ian's birthday.

October 24, 1941
Ivan Bunin, from his diary

Today I found out that it was Galina [Kuznetsova] who dragged me in from the porch, although she also took a spill when she tried to get a hold of me. I remember being on the sofa . . . and writhing about because of my asthma and also because of a mortally repulsive something that kept attacking and slicing away at my throat. . . . People tell me that my face was terrible, like that of someone who was truly dying. I myself thought I was done for, and that I would leave all my manuscripts in a state of disorder. . . .

The doctor, a very sweet Hungarian Jew, was very concerned when he saw me. . . . He later told me that it was only my strong heart that had saved me, and that at one point he could barely hear my pulse.

October 29, 1941
Ivan Bunin, from his diary

I have been in bed for three days—weak with both fever and chills. For some reason my temperature keeps going up and down. Perhaps my illness was from food poisoning. When I had lunch at Nice, I was given, instead of liver, some vile clump of meat . . . which was soft, crimson-black, and oozing with pus. But I was so hungry, I ate half of it. . . .

Late Fall 1941
André Gide, in a conversation with Alexander Bakhrakh

You do not realize what a major contemporary you have in Bunin.

November 1941
Alexander Bakhrakh, from his memoirs

[Bunin said:] "My right arm used to be so splendid. My left one was never as nice. But look at what has happened to it. It has become flabby and looks as though it is covered with buckwheat. Cursed old age. . . ."

November 11, 1941
Ivan Bunin, from his diary
The newspapers report a speech by Hitler, saying he will found "a new Europe that will last *for a thousand years.*"

November 23, 1941
Vera Muromtseva-Bunina, from a letter to a friend
I get bored and anxious when I do not receive any letters, but it never occurs to me that anyone has forgotten me or is not writing to me "out of spite." I may not write letters for some time . . . but daily I call to mind those I have not written to. . . .

Ian and I are getting along. The atmosphere has seemingly gotten better. It is as though we are looking at life more seriously and giving less importance to trifles. . . .

People keep telling me that they have nothing to spare. . . . There are few vegetables in the market . . . and I often have to stand in line . . . for more than an hour [to buy what is available]. Fish touches our lips rarely . . . and fruit has disappeared completely. I "treat" myself to coffee . . . but I will so less often, since I do not have enough sugar. . . .

[At a friends'] I saw a rare sight: wood burning in a fireplace. How I love to look at the burning logs, to be quiet and think about things—no, not to think, but rather to feel.

November 25, 1941
Ivan Bunin, from his diary
This is the 157th day of war in Russia.

December 5, 1941
Ivan Bunin, from his diary
The Russians are beating the Germans in the south.[6] In Africa the battle "first goes one way, then another." There is snow and cold in Russia.[7]

[6]On November 29, 1941, the Russians recaptured Rostov, which the Germans had taken only a week before. It was the first setback for the enemy on the Eastern Front.
[7]On December 3, 1941, high winds from the Arctic, coupled with heavy blizzards and temperatures of minus 38 degrees centigrade, forced the already badly frostbitten German units to retreat from the suburbs of Moscow. The frigid conditions reduced some battalions to fewer than 100 men. Two days later, Hitler ordered a halt to the German offensive on the city.

December 7, 1941
Ivan Bunin, from his diary

I am rereading Baudelaire's collected works, his *Small poems in prose*.[8] They are paltry, melodramatic, and mannered à la Balmont. . . .

December 8, 1941
Ivan Bunin, from his diary

The Russians are . . . making it hot for the Germans.[9]

December 10, 1941
Ivan Bunin, from his diary

The Swiss radio reports that Merezhkovsky has died.[1]

December 13, 1941
Ivan Bunin, from his diary

The Russians have taken back Efremov.[2] . . . Germans had been in Efremov! It is beyond all understanding! But what does Efremov look like now, where my brother Evgeny used to live, and where he, Nastya, and *our mother* are buried!

December 14, 1941
Ivan Bunin, from his diary

Today is a splendid day. . . . Just like early September in Russia. . . .

I am not at peace, though, and have not been able to do anything. I keep thinking about Merezhkovsky.[3]

---

[8]Baudelaire wrote *Small poems in prose* (*Petits poèmes en prose*) in 1869.

[9]On December 6, 1941, three fresh Soviet armies, headed by Marshal Zhukov and consisting of more than a million men positioned along a five-hundred-mile front, launched a surprise, violent, and successful counteroffensive against the now exhausted and overextended German troops.

[1]Merezhkovsky died in Paris on December 9, 1941.

[2]Efremov is in southern Russia, about 180 miles southeast of Moscow.

[3]It should be noted, though, that Bunin and other emigrés did not attend Merezhkovsky's funeral, for two reasons. First, Merezhkovsky published his own works during the Occupation, an act that for many exiles was tantamount to "collaboration" with the enemy. More important, though, was a radio broadcast that Merezhkovsky had made the previous summer in support of the Nazi invasion of Russia—the "enormity of the heroic feat" of the German "crusade" against the Soviet Union. The text of Merezhkovsky's speech first appeared in *Parisian Herald* (*Parizhskii vestnik*) on January 8, 1944; it was republished in "Bol'shevism i chelovechestvo. Posmertnaia stat'ia D. S. Merezhkovskogo," in *Nezavisimaia gazeta* (June 23, 1995), 5.

December 23, 1941
Ivan Bunin, from his diary

The Russians are beating the Germans . . . [who] keep retreating, losing a great many people and war materiel.[4]

Hitler has named himself supreme commander of the forces on the Russian front.[5] He has told the army and his country: "*I am postponing the Russian offensive until spring.*"

Tomorrow is Christmas Eve. We are preparing a meager "gala" dinner. . . .

December 24, 1941
Ivan Bunin, from his diary

Today is Catholic Christmas Eve. We made vodka and something like a hot pot (I bought some cabbage that was rotten and grey). Each of us also had a piece of meat and some reconstituted fish.

December 28, 1941
Ivan Bunin, from his diary

The Russians have taken Kaluga and Belyov.[6] . . .

I wake up every morning with something akin to a bitter *Angst*, (for me) the finality of everything. "What still awaits me, O Lord?" My days are numbered. If only I knew what still lies before me—if only for the next decade! But what will these years be like? All kinds of helplessness, the impending death of everyone who is close to me, the most terrible loneliness. . . .

But in the unfortunate event that I die suddenly, I am forcing myself to organize all the notes I have written during the various times of my life. . . . But I am constantly seized by the thought: whatever for? I will be forgotten almost immediately after my death.

December 30, 1941
Ivan Bunin, from his diary

We wanted to "greet" the New Year, but our preparations for the holiday were pitiful. We took a walk into town, but there was absolutely nothing to buy. . . .

My fingers are cracked from the cold. I have not been able to wash

---

[4]On December 16, 1941, Russian forces recaptured Kalinin. At the same time, however, the Germans launched a new offensive against Sevastopol in the Crimea.

[5]Hitler also told one of his generals: "After all, anyone can do this little matter of operational command."

[6]Kaluga and Belyov are located about ninety miles southwest of Moscow.

or take a bath; we have revolting soups made from turnips. . . . Today I wrote on piece of paper: "I want to be cremated when I die. . . . No matter how terrible, how repulsive it sounds, it is better than rotting in the grave."[7] . . .

People want me to love Russia. Its capital is now called *Leningrad.* Nizhnyi-Novgorod is now Gorky; Tver is now Kalinin.[8] All are named after nonentities. . . . What a farce.

December 31, 1941
Ivan Bunin, from his diary

Another year has passed. How many more do I have left?!

I woke up . . . and not for the first time, I felt a heaviness and some pain in the top of my head. Could it be some kind of poison coming forth from the fire in the fireplace? . . . My right arm is also cold. . . .

The Russians have taken Kerch and Feodosiya.[9]

✳   1942   ✳

Circa 1942
Alexander Bakhrakh, from his memoirs

"You once insisted," Bunin told me, "that every person, over the course of his life, has wanted to do away with himself at least once, or at the very least has been carried away by the persistent thought of suicide."

"Yes," I answered, "but these are not my words. I read them in Galsworthy, and it seemed to me that they were indisputable."

"Perhaps," Bunin replied, "such a thing happened to me once. It was a very long time ago—way before the Flood. It was late fall in

---

[7]Muromtseva-Bunina was able to change her husband's mind, persuading him to agree that his body would be placed in a coffin made of zinc and that he would be laid to rest in a burial vault. She recalled: "Bunin was always afraid that snakes would crawl into his skull." See Baboreko, 300.

[8]Tver was named Kalinin in 1931; it resumed its historical name in 1990.

[9]On December 29, 1941, Kerch and Feodosiya were recaptured by Russian amphibious forces in eastern Crimea. The Germans, however, maintained their drive on Sevastopol. To date since June, losses for the Russian army included at least 5 million casualties, 3 million prisoners, 20,000 tanks, and 30,000 guns.

Yalta, during the 'Chekhov' epoch of my life, when I was friends with the writer.[1] I was young, free, and at the flowering of my talents; I was also just becoming known as a writer. Some acquaintances had introduced me to an enchanting and still quite young maiden—a Georgian beauty, a real Tamara,[2] with huge, lively, dark eyes, extremely long eyelashes, and a barely noticeable down over her upper lip. She had a splendid, sound body with a lilac tint to it which made a tremendous impression on me. Right away I began courting her, pursuing her with all . . . the determination I had at that age. I chased her for a long time. I was literally at her heels, but it was all in vain. . . . My beauty was inflexible. But her indifference to me excited me even more, and I became utterly exhausted from my ardor. . . .

"One time around evening, after she had rejected me yet again, I left my hotel in a gloomy frame of mind. I felt like wandering through the town, to breathe the sea air; but in truth I had absolutely no idea of what I was doing. I found it simply unbearable to be alone. On the embankment I unexpectedly met a woman—striking and elegantly dressed. I had run into her several times before when I was with other people. I knew that she had performed as a singer in a café in Odessa and that she did not have a definite profession.

"On that ill-starred night, my inflexible Tamara weighed on my soul so heavily that I was genuinely happy to come across this woman. I gallantly went up to her, and for the sake of appearances began talking to her about the weather. I then invited her to dine with me at the City Garden, which at that time was a favorite hot spot for tourists. To my woe, I drank a great deal of vodka and champagne. The next morning found me in the bed of this happy and flighty woman. . . .

"After that evening's adventure . . . I began to pursue my big-eyed Tamara with ten times the energy I had shown previously. Finally my efforts met with success. Trembling, she fell into my arms. I am ashamed now to confess that I do not even remember her name, though perhaps she too may sometimes recall our tryst as her first.

"Another day passed by. Again walking along the embankment, I ran into an old friend, Doctor A. . . . He said:

"'Listen, Ivan. As a friend, I have to tell you a medical secret. God forgive me for not observing ethics, but the matter is extremely serious. Once, in the City Garden, you were seen in the company of a certain lady. I have to warn you: she is sick. . . .'

[1]Bunin was friends with Chekhov from 1894 until the writer's death in 1904.
[2]Bunin is alluding to Lermontov's poem "Tamara," written in 1841.

"I thought the sky had fallen in on me. I also thought I was the worst scoundrel. The image of an enchanting young girl loomed indistinctly before my eyes. What was I to do? I resolved to shoot myself—I saw no other way out of my situation.

"That very same hour, without saying goodbye to anyone or even packing my suitcases, I rushed off to Moscow to liquidate my affairs and accounts with life.

"On the road there I almost froze to death, but my brother convinced me to visit specialists. I made the rounds of all the most famous ones. No one found anything. I was at a loss.

"Several years passed by, and I had almost forgotten about what had happened. I had been invited to some dinner, and the person next to me turned out to be none other than my doctor friend from Yalta whom I had not seen since that fatal day. Seeing me, he smiled sarcastically. After dinner, he . . . came up to me and, in an edifying way, mumbled through his pointed, shovel-like beard (I have hated such beards from that day on!):

" 'It seems, young man, that I really gave you quite a scare. Let that be a lesson to you. In the future be more careful whom you associate with.'

"I was struck dumb.

"How that stupid joke could have ended so tragically. . . ."

Several days later, Bunin said: "Yesterday evening I was reading a book of Tyutchev's verse, and by strange coincidence I came upon some lines I had forgotten:

And who in the rush of emotions
When the blood boils and then grows cold
He does not know your temptations—
O Suicide and Love untold!"

He read these lines quietly, but my whole body shook as if in a shiver. Then he added:

"That old boy knew something . . . what a smart boy he was!" . . .

Bunin said: "I do not know anything more splendid than the metallic sound of Latin. But only when someone has matured, only when he has a solid grounding, can he genuinely go into raptures over Virgil. How can a high school student be interested in Sallust or Cornelius [Nepos] or remember the details about some ubiquitous 'spies'? On the other hand, how can one read Latin texts in the same enthralled way that we read a Russian book, even if it be one by Tyutchev?" . . .

I had the fortune to observe Bunin when he was writing *Dark Alleys*. . . . Most of the stories in this work he wrote with abandon, as if he were rushing off somewhere, afraid that he would not have time to finish them, or that the events of the war would keep him from completing what he had begun. There were weeks when . . . he holed himself up in his large room—he actually locked the door!—a place that was very comfortable and "gentrylike," but that he had also reduced to an indescribably unreal and chaotic condition. Four huge Italian windows looked far out onto the sea; on particularly clear days, one could see the outlines of the Italian coast. . . . When Bunin rested from his writings, he went up to these windows, looked out on the azure sea . . . or on the terraced garden that ran alongside the villa . . . and waited for the irregular deliveries of the newspapers. Bunin always . . . read the newspapers with fervor . . . and he would be very offended if someone in the house got to them before he did. . . . He kept insisting that if someone read the paper before he had a chance to do so, it would lose all its freshness and interest for him.

When he was writing, Bunin left his room . . . only for "sparse suppers" (how else would you call them?), which were announced by a gong that gave them a certain out-of-place solemnity. Invariably these suppers were accompanied by curses at the "Führer" (thank God the walls did not have ears!), Pétain . . . writers who . . . had agreed to collaborate [with the fascists] in publications that he considered unacceptable . . . and the members of the household who did not meet his gastronomic demands. There were also sporadic "arguments" on how to divide the macaroni which, though repulsive, always seemed to be the most delicate of all the dishes. Each time Bunin first cursed up a storm because of the poor food; next he recalled the wonderful pheasant with sauce that used to be served at the Prague in Moscow; then he would take his bottle of red wine, go up to his room, lock himself in, and write until late evening. He broke his routine only rarely, e.g., trips to Nice or Cannes . . . for a change of scene, to see one or two of his friends, and to take advantage of the "black market." . . . In summer, trips to Nice would be more frequent so that he could go swimming in the sea. . . .

Whenever Bunin left Grasse, it was as if by magic that he became younger, merrier, and more alive. . . . Sitting in a crowded bus, he began to look at all the passengers and to assert that, just as Cuvier could fashion the skeleton of a prehistoric animal from just one of its bones, he could establish the biography of each passenger with a glance—by the way he wore his hat, or by some other insignificant detail that had escaped the notice of an "ordinary" person. He insisted that his talent for seeing things had turned him into a writer, and that his plot lines arose solely from the sober observations of his mind. As he himself said, he was unable to indulge in fantasies. . . .

Bunin jotted down all kinds of words: bits and pieces of dialogues for works that he had not yet written, lists of local expressions that he recalled from memory . . . even inventories of curses. These he entered into different notebooks with cardboard covers of different colors, which he loved greatly. He even made up lists for the names . . . of future heroes . . . asserting that an unsuccessfully christened character could destroy any work with his name. I recall . . . how he loved to make fun of Chekhov's Simeonov-Pishchik.[3] Even now I can see before my eyes those long columns of first and last names, all arranged in categories: merchants, noblemen, Tatars, Jews, teachers, doctors, writers, and the like. . . .

Such notebooks, though, were often sacrificed in *auto-da-fés* which Bunin periodically held in his small stove, for, as he often said, he feared that some "hard-working monk" . . . would penetrate into his creative laboratory . . . root about in his manuscripts, and arrive at conclusions . . . that he would consider absurd or infuriating. . . . Painstakingly he tore his drafts into small pieces . . . stuffed them into the fireplace, and did not leave it until the last page had turned into ashes.

"Tolstoy preserved his manuscripts," he often said, "and now anybody with half an urge can go through his dirty laundry. One should destroy all his drafts without fail. The same thing goes for his letters." . . .

"I can handle a pen . . . but I never have been any good at writing letters. . . . Without fail, I must note in my last will and testament that my letters never be published. But will anyone listen to me? . . ."

Bunin worked on his stories and tried not to think about what was happening around him, until the external, unfriendly world burst into his life with a vulgarity that was common to that time . . . e.g., he had to save someone, keep his home from being requisitioned, or even fight to get packages [from abroad]. . . . He was stubborn, but it was easy to change his mind—though inevitably he returned to his previous opinion. . . . He was uncomfortable with numbers . . . and did not have the patience to count something or do some types of arithmetic.

---

[3]Boris Simeonov-Pishchik is a character in *The Cherry Orchard*.

When it came to single digits, he . . . sensed the weight and importance of every number. But when it got into hundreds and thousands . . . he could not fathom the reality of such magnitudes. . . .

Like many Russian writers, Bunin was afraid of the "evil eye." He also feared walking under open ladders . . . and he shuddered whenever a black cat crossed his path. He would not sit at a table if it was numbered "thirteen." But it also seemed that he did such things more for the sake of "theatre" than from any genuine emotion or belief. . . .

Bunin was also extremely mistrustful by nature. . . . For instance, a well-known critic, a contemporary of Bunin's . . . once paid a visit to "Jeanette." He was quite neat, without a single grey hair, and smelled of eau-de-cologne. With relish he began telling Ivan Alexeevich about his recent love intrigues. . . . Although Bunin listened attentively, he was laughing at the speaker in secret and giving him an ironic look. After the guest had left, he said: "What a liar!" That evening, though, he came down from his room, annoyed and upset over something.

"Ivan Alexeevich, what's the matter?" I asked.

"You know, I have been thinking all day, and suddenly it seems that everything that today's guest told us is true!"

The possibility that a contemporary might have been so triumphant in love aroused in Bunin a feeling of envy. . . .

I never knew Bunin to covet another's glory . . . or money . . . or physical gifts, but stories about someone's success with women invariably depressed and perturbed him. He wanted to be seen as a Don Juan, and he sometimes loved to talk at length about his past adventures. Incidentally, I must mention that . . . Bunin's flights of fantasy were rather limited. Of course, I was not acquainted with his "Don Juan file," but judging by his stories, it seemed to me that his list was not very long, and that in matters of love he was somewhat shy and not overly aggressive toward women. Like most men . . . he was more talk than . . . action. . . .

There was also a whole series of regrettable incidents with the gloomy old gardener of "Jeanette." This individual had agreed with the owner of the house to take the fruit from the trees and to keep his own garden. . . . From the very beginning, Bunin took an instant disliking toward the gardener of "Jeanette." . . . He amused himself by teasing the old man or by sometimes swiping an unripe apricot or some other vegetable from the "forbidden" garden. Usually the gardener kept silent, but sometimes he got angry, and then there would be no end to the wrangling. Bunin often let loose with the most vile Russian, and the gardener answered back in the language of Provence. Although

Bunin saw such shenanigans as entertainment, his heart always beat more forcefully after one of these episodes. But, no matter, he started all over again the next day! . . .

We all had specific duties in the kitchen (except, of course, Ivan Alexeevich). Each had his or her turn to light the stove or to prepare dinner. (There was no great art to this, and one did not dare cede to fantasies—macaroni or lentils were luxuries!) . . .

During the time I lived with Bunin, potatoes were a very great luxury. It was almost impossible to get them on the black market. We sometimes got hold of some . . . but only when some Russian chicken farmers living on the outskirts of town gave them to Bunin as a gift, a sign of respect, making it clear that such an elegant vegetable was for him alone. . . . Each time Bunin carried them upstairs, hid them under lock and key, and, of course, did not share them with anyone. . . .

As a conversationalist, Bunin could be brilliant, witty, and caustic. . . . But he almost never responded to abstract themes. . . . With foreigners he involuntarily shriveled up and became momentarily dull. Bunin was extremely conscious of the fact that his inadequate command of foreign languages was an insurmountable obstacle not only for extended intercourse but also (and more importantly) for him to "shine," to utter some witty word, one of those *bon mots* with which he so loved to adorn his conversations and which, truly, gave them their spice and unforgettable charm.

That is why Bunin was not genuine friends with any foreign writer. He had an "inferiority complex," a feeling that he was not their equal socially, or, more to the truth, materially. . . . [Such uneasiness] explains why he was not friends with Rilke, who was said to have knocked on his door, or Thomas Mann,[4] or Henri de Régnier who wrote about him,[5] or Mauriac who praised his writings to the skies, or even young French writers of Russian descent with whom he could talk in Russian. . . .

Bunin insisted that since he had been an avid hunter, he most likely would not fear lions. . . . He also was not afraid of rats. Indeed,

---

[4]The fact that Mann did not give his unqualified support to Bunin's candidacy for the Nobel Prize, especially when Thomas's brother, Heinrich, was also a competitor for the award, did not endear the German writer to Bunin. See Marullo, *From the Other Shore,* 251, 278.

[5]Henri de Régnier particularly liked Bunin's *The Village* and such "peasant stories" as his "Night Conversation" ("*Nochnoi razgovor,*" 1911) and "Spring Evening" ("*Vesenii vecher,*" 1914). See L. Kuvanova, "Anri de Ren'e o proizvedeniiakh Bunina, 1921–1924," in Shcherbina, 376–378.

more than once I was witness to this epic picture: Bunin chasing after rats in the cellar, armed only with a stick, and the things . . . rushing at him from all sides, and filling the house with the most unbearable and depressing screams. . . . Bunin, though, panicked over anything that coiled or crawled on land, not only snakes, but even . . . small lizards which, on sunny days, crawled out on the warm rocks on the terraces of Bunin's villa. . . .

"You do not know them," Bunin explained to me. "You do not think about the fact that their ancestors were the most terrible monsters and iguanas. . . . Very likely they still have the instinct of their ancestors; and when they grow up, God knows what they'll be capable of!" . . .

Bunin did not usually get dressed before breakfast but appeared . . . in a tattered velvet housecoat with a skullcap on his head. He would be smoking a cigarette in an unsightly cherry-colored cigarette-holder. . . .

Bunin, of course, had his literary likes and dislikes. . . . For instance, he was an avid fan of Flaubert, but he told me that he fell asleep whenever he read Stendahl's novels, and that he never bothered to find about what happened to Balzac's heroes. He responded to Blok and his poetry with undisguised—almost pathological—enmity, saying that Blok's derangement was the only thing that merited attention, and that even that was overrated. It seemed to me that Bunin was somewhat jealous of Blok. After all, Blok had been the acknowledged trendsetter for several generations, whereas Bunin's glory rested on his prose.[6] [Such a state of affairs] annoyed him, for he always wanted to be known primarily as a poet. . . .

[Bunin said:] "How can I be indifferent to my writing when it is my craft? Not for nothing does it say *'homme de lettres'* on my passport! After all, writing is the only thing I can do in a genuine way. Writing nourishes me. It not only affords me a break from routine . . . it also gives me a joy that helps me live in today's cursed circumstances, when in the morning, one does not know what will happen in the evening. I always have something in my head, i.e., how to finish writing something, or how to say something I had written in a better way, or how to describe something I had experienced or witnessed in my life. After all, I do not dream up things; I write only about what I know. But, of course, like every writer, I also have an element of pride—I will not

---

[6]Bakhrakh was not alone in making such an assertion. See similar remarks by Kataev in Marullo, *Ivan Bunin: Russian Requiem*, 260.

deny such a thing. Sometimes a nasty little review will drive me into a frenzy, even though I know that it has no significance or that it will not damage my reputation." . . .

"Yes," I interrupted, "like when you snapped at me in print when I hinted at a certain autobiographical quality in *Arseniev*. . . ."[7] . . .

In my time with Bunin, I spent literally every hour . . . talking with him. . . . But not once in those terrible years . . . did I ever hear from him even the remotest suggestion of his wish to return to the Soviet Union. I also never heard that he had written to Alexei Tolstoy, even though I served as his "postmaster."[8] . . . There were, of course, days when Bunin wanted to leave "repulsive" Grasse. . . . He even once thought about going to Portugal or . . . taking a trip across the ocean. . . .

During the war Bunin tried not to think about events. He was deeply optimistic about the outcome of the war; but he was easily panicked by events. Any defeat of the Soviet army . . . he saw as a tragic and irreparable loss. . . . I remember how upset he was when Roosevelt was running for [another term as president]. He had everyone convinced that if Roosevelt were defeated, such a situation would mean the end of Europe. . . . I also recall how upset Bunin was during the Battle of Stalingrad. At first he thought that all was lost; several hours later, though, he moved from extreme pessimism to high-blown optimistic hopes. Bunin was extremely impatient in life; he wanted the events of the war to match his temper.

Bunin was deeply perturbed by any new order of the Vichy regime or the occupying forces. But he never thought of how to get around them or to find loopholes. . . . At times Bunin was rather cowardly and indecisive when the matter was not worth fighting for; but there were other times when he could be almost heroic when the issue was truly essential or involved principle. The invaders, with their insolent faces, guttural speech, rapping gait, cruelty, and lack of human appearance, Bunin hated not only for political or humane reasons but also for aesthetic ones as well. . . .

In the evenings . . . Bunin went into the dining room where there was a big radio, and tried to catch a broadcast from London or Switzerland. He became especially interested in the course of the war after Hitler had attacked Russia. He hung enormous pictures of the Soviet

---

[7]The article in question is "Sovremennye zapiski, XXXV," *Dni* (June 10, 1928), 4.

[8]The Soviets routinely maintained that it was Bakhrakh who brought to the post office Bunin's request to Alexei Tolstoy to "return home."

Union in his room, following summaries of events attentively and becoming angry when he could not find a place on his maps. . . .

But the activity at Bunin's "headquarters" did not go on for long. When Hitler's armies penetrated deep into the homeland, Bunin announced that he could no longer keep moving the ribbon that marked the line of the front. He also said that he could no longer believe the German news sources, since he could not find the places they mentioned on the map. "It would be better," he added, "to take the maps off the wall. After all, who knows what will happen. Maybe the invaders will someday stick their heads in here. . . ."

January 1, 1942
Ivan Bunin, from his diary

Yesterday at 6 p.m. Vera went [to a friend's], and so we "greeted" the New Year without her. . . . Everyone had an orange (the local kind and very sour) and a small handful of vile-looking raisins. Bakhrakh also got hold of two bottles of wine (which used to cost 5 francs but now cost 20). . . .

Yesterday Hitler told the army and his people: "We are winning the greatest victories in the history of the entire world. . . . The Soviets will be crushed in '42. . . . The blood, which will be spilt this year, will be the last to be spilled in Europe for generations."[9]

January 1, 1942
Vera Muromtseva-Bunina, from her diary

Ian was angry that I was not home [to "greet" the New Year with him].

January 22, 1942
Vera Muromtseva-Bunina, from a letter to Tatyana Loginova-Muravieva

We celebrated the New Year (old style) in a very nice way. . . . Happily, there was meat . . . [and other items]. In a word, we have not eaten like that in a long time. . . . Indeed, outside of the New Year

[9]Such sentiments remained unchanged even after Hitler, on February 20, 1942, received a report on the staggering number of German casualties suffered thus far in the Russian campaign: 199,448 dead, 708,351 wounded, 112,627 cases of severe frostbite, and 44,342 missing. Optimistically, Hitler told the German people: "Now that January and February are past, our enemies can give up the hope of our suffering the fate of Napoleon. . . . Now we are about to switch over to squaring the account. What a relief!" See Goralski, 20.

merrymaking with my own family in Moscow, I have never had a more pleasant time. . . .

These days I take a walk before dawn and feel the poetry of an early rising, of pre-morning stars, and of the town arising from its sleep. . . .

I am feeling better . . . though I have been losing weight. . . . Ivan Alexeevich has also gotten thin. . . .

February 19, 1942
Ivan Bunin, from his diary
Vera was at the doctor's . . . for a swollen stomach. . . .

February 26, 1942
Ivan Bunin, from his diary
There are rumors that the Russians have inflicted a great loss on the Germans . . . [and that] the German sixteenth army has perished.[1]

February 28, 1942
Vera Muromtseva-Bunina, from her diary
Marina Tsvetaeva has hanged herself.[2] It is very sad.

Spring 1942
Helen Iswolsky, from an article
Russian literary works abroad can be divided into two categories: the works of the older generation, uprooted from Russia yet still

---

[1]The rumors were true. On February 24, 1942, the Russians surrounded the Number II corps of the German 16th Army just south of Lake Ilmen on the northern front, about one hundred miles south of Leningrad.

On the day before, Stalin had affirmed that the war against Germany had turned in favor of the Soviet Union. He stated: "Now the Germans no longer possess, by virtue of their sudden and treacherous attack, the military advantage which they had in the first months of the war. The momentum of unexpectedness and suddenness which constituted the reverse strength of the German fascist troops has been fully spent." See Goralski, 205.

[2]The forty-eight-year-old Tsvetaeva committed suicide on August 31, 1941, in Elabuga, Russia, about six hundred miles east of Moscow. She was buried there in an unmarked common grave; to this day the exact spot of her resting place is unknown. Tsvetaeva's death was not reported in the Soviet press. It was only several years later that the outside world learned of the poet's passing, and more than a decade later that Tsvetaeva's suicide could be mentioned in print in the Soviet Union.

In truth, Tsvetaeva had long been in a poor frame of mind. She wrote in June 1941: "I have been trying on death for a year. Everything is ugly and terrifying. . . . I do not want to escape people (posthumously). I think that posthumously I am already afraid of myself. I do not want to die, but I do not want to live. Nonsense, [I want to live] as long as I am needed. . . . But, Lord, how tiny I am. I can do nothing at all. Dragging it out—drinking the dregs. Bitter wormwood." See E. Proffer, ed., *Tsvetaeva: A Pictorial Biography* (Ann Arbor, 1980), 35.

closely linked to the former Moscow or Saint Petersburg literary world and having preserved its atmosphere, and the works of the new, "Western" school of young writers and poets. We call it the "Western" school not because it has consciously abandoned purely Russian traditions and adhered to Western European culture, but because it is both intellectually and geographically situated in the Western European milieu. . . . It has therefore inevitably submitted to the influence of Western literature, especially to that of modern French and English masters.

This new, "Western" school has also—and this is natural enough—a less clear and vivid reminiscence of Russia than that which their elders have retained. The young writers are still in many ways typically Russian; but they do not breathe that acute melancholy, that burning nostalgia so characteristic of the senior school, whose representatives still vibrate to the voice of their lost homeland and shall ever continue to do so. The young authors . . . are "citizens of this world," born in one country, bred and educated in another. Even those who spent their childhood or youth in Russia have undergone too many foreign influences, have seen too many lands, and have roamed through too many cities to preserve a unique attachment to a soil they have trodden long ago. Many have not even known this soil and have learned about it only from their families or out of books.

On the contrary, the memory of Russia forms the keynote of the works produced by the older generation. Its representatives still live exclusively by this memory; they long to see once more their native land and fear lest its image be dimmed or forgotten.

Ivan Bunin, who is the most prominent writer of this group and who today is internationally famous, is a typical example of this deep, poignant attachment. . . .

Indeed, for Bunin that Russia of long ago is still "terribly alive" . . . and he has almost completely detached himself from the world he is living in at present, in order to dwell in the enchanted past. . . .

Bunin's descriptions of men and landscapes, and even of psychological moods and human tragedy . . . are not mere recollections; they are a mysterious resurrection of the past, they are daydreams fixed by the pen of a great master; they recreate life *exactly as it was*, with its dimensions of time and space, its sounds and colors, its very atmosphere and odor. . . .

One can quote whole pages of Bunin's novels where this strange past, which cannot die, is conjured up and becomes more alive and genuine than the world which lies immediately before our eyes. And, thanks to his great gift, Bunin has been able to write during these years of exile a remarkable chronicle of Russian life. Much of his writing is autobiographical, and his descriptions of his native town of Oryol and of the Russian country belong to the best pages of classical Russian literature. If Bunin had not been "uprooted," if he had not known the pang of separation and exile, he would perhaps have never reached this lauded if lonely pinnacle. . . .

March 31, 1942
Ivan Bunin, from his diary
Fighting rages on in Russia. The Germans keep threatening a spring (more likely, summer) offensive.[3] Will they suddenly smash everything to pieces? It seems more and more likely. . . .

April 4, 1942
Ivan Bunin, from his diary
Our Easter table will have four colored eggs and a bouquet of hyacinths—that is all! . . .
We broke our fast [after midnight]: each of us had a tiny piece of sausage and one-tenth of an egg. . . .

April 12, 1942
Ivan Bunin, from his diary
I finished rereading Babel's *Red Army* and *Odessa Tales*.[4] His *Odessa Tales* are the best ones. He is very capable—and a remarkable scoundrel. Everything he writes is so flowery and also often vile enough for the latrine. He also has a pathological weakness for blasphemy, and for things that are ignoble and purposely base. . . .
All these writer "comrades" and "warriors" [of that time] give me such a sinking heart! What filthy boors they are, physically and spiritually. I hate them all to the point of nausea. How they are all alike—for example, Babel and Sholokhov. The same assuredness, the same filthy boors and pigs, with their foul-smelling bodies and their loathsome minds and hearts.
For example, Babel writes:
"Everything was slain by silence, and only the moon, having

---

[3]On March 1, 1942, Hitler predicted: "The Bolshevik masses which could not conquer the German soldiers and their soldiers in the winter, will be beaten in every direction in the summer." See Goralski, 209.
[4]Babel published *Red Cavalry* (*Konarmiia*) in 1926 and *Odessa Tales* (*Odesskie rasskazy*) a year later.

seized its round, shining, and carefree head in its blue arms, wandered over the ocean."

"Gedali (a Jew) circles me with several belts of his smoky eyes."

"The shrine of Saint Valentine had been destroyed. Lying about were pieces of rotten wool and the ludicrous, chickenlike bones of the saint. . . ."

"The moon burst through the window, and jumped into the clouds like a lost calf. . . ."

And about the Mother of God (the icon in the Ipatievsky Monastery[5] that was occupied by "textile workers"): "The thin-looking hag sat with her knees spread apart, and with breasts that were long and green like snakes. . . ."

April 26, 1942
Andrei Sedykh, from an article

War had broken out, we had fled Paris, it was the end of an entire epoch. We were living in Nice and counting the days until our departure to America. We wondered: would we ever get there, or would the door of the mousetrap bang shut forever.

Ivan Alexeevich had come from Grasse to say goodbye, and also to pass on instructions to friends on the other side of the ocean. We had agreed on a rendezvous beforehand, and my wife prepared for him what at that time would have been considered a "kingly" breakfast: herring, scrawny-looking mutton chops (an entire week's worth of rations!), real cheese that we had gotten from Portugal . . . and even coffee with sugar. When Ivan Alexeevich saw all these riches laid out on the table, he was simply stunned:

"Good Lord!" he said. "Just like we had [when I was awarded the Nobel Prize] in Stockholm!"

Bunin had become severely emaciated in that winter of '42. He was thin, and his face looked even more like that of a Roman patrician. . . .

[Before I left France] I asked Bunin how well he knew Tolstoy.

"We drank home-brewed vodka and even ate some meat together," Bunin replied. "After all, I was a Tolstoyan. . . . Don't you laugh at me. What is there to laugh about? His lessons contained many

[5]The Ipatievsky Trinity Monastery was founded *circa* 1330 in Kostroma, at the site of an alleged appearance of the Virgin Mary there. It was also at Ipatievsky that Michael Romanov agreed on March 14, 1613, to be tsar, thereby putting an end to the notorious "Time of Troubles," an interregnum on the Russian throne that lasted from 1598 to 1613.

things that were splendid, chaste, . . . and captivating for a young heart.[6]

"What a shame that I do not have a picture of myself at that time. I had these romantic eyes, so blue and dreamy-like. My cheeks had such a light down on them that people sometimes took me for a young Jew. . . ."[7]

A thin veil of sadness hung over this farewell gathering. . . . When we accompanied Bunin to the bus . . . he asked that when we got to America we not send him books or journals with his writings in them. . . . Never before had I seen him treat his writings with such indifference. . . .

Bunin, who did not like talk about death and even feared the word itself, said with solemn sadness:

"Well, goodbye. Most likely I will die here. But it is a good place to do so."

We embraced. Bunin walked ahead quickly—somehow agile, unusually erect, and suddenly festive.

May 1942
Ivan Bunin, his Last Will and Testament
To whom it may concern: There exist all kinds of letters to me in Russia. If these have been saved, destroy them all *without reading them*, except for those that were written by well-known writers, editors, public figures, and the like (and only if these letters are interesting).

Do not print or publish any of *my* letters. . . . This I ask of all my correspondents. Circumstances almost always forced me to write hastily, and in a bad and careless frame of mind; what letters exist rarely reflect my actual feelings at the time. (For example, my letters to Gorky, which he published without my permission.)

I also implore all literary grave diggers not to exhume and publish those poems and stories . . . which I did not include in editions of my works. Many of them I wrote when I was very poor: a frequent occurrence in my life.

The most terrible thing would be to have my good things crammed together with my poor ones.

---

[6]Bunin is lying shamelessly here. His meetings with Tolstoy were brief and unsatisfying encounters. Also, his time as a Tolstoyan was short and his hatred of the group severe.
[7]In his "Tolstoyan" period, Bunin was twenty-three years old.

May 2, 1942
Vera Muromtseva-Bunina, from her diary

[A friend] gave me a copy of Dostoevsky's *Diary of a Writer*.[8] I read it in one sitting. [My friend] was correct when he said that Dostoevsky had an unusual feeling for Russia, for the people. I gave it to Ian. He also liked it. "It is very intelligent," he said.

May 6, 1942
Ivan Bunin, from his diary

At the movies I saw *La grande farandole*[9] with Fred Astaire and Ginger Rogers. Their dancing was so astounding that I was enthralled to an extreme. . . .

I am reading Comte de Las Cases's *Le Mémorial de Saint-Hélène*.[1] I also feel like I am on Saint Helena.[2] How terrible to think what Napoleon had to feel. But he lived, dictated, lived on his former glory, and hoped. . . .

May 23, 1942
Ivan Bunin, from his diary

For about two weeks now, terrible battles have been raging around Kharkov.[3] . . .

I again think: there is nothing more beautiful in this world than flowers and birds.

May 26, 1942
Ivan Bunin, from his diary

Vera is so poignant-looking now. . . . My tenderness toward her torments me to the point of tears.

---

[8]Dostoevsky wrote *The Diary of a Writer* (*Dnevnik pisatelia*) from 1873 to 1881.

[9]Bunin is referring to the 1939 American film *The Story of Vernon and Irene Castle*.

[1]Las Cases's *Le Mémorial de Sainte-Hélène*, published in 1823, was the first defense of Napoleon after his defeat and abdication in 1815. *Le Mémorial* was so popular that it became known as the "Koran of the Napoleonic cult."

[2]Saint Helena, an island with an area of only forty-seven square miles, is located in the South Atlantic Ocean, roughly twelve hundred miles west of the southwest coast of Africa. Napoleon was exiled on Saint Helena on October 15, 1815, and died there May 5, 1821.

[3]On May 12, 1942, the Russians began a major drive toward Kharkov, which the Germans had captured on October 24 the preceding year. Five days later their offensive was halted by the Germans in increasingly bitter fighting.

At this time the Germans reported that since the beginning of the invasion, the Russians had lost 7.3 million men, killed, wounded, missing, or permanently disabled.

May 26, 1942
Mark Aldanov, from a letter to Ivan Bunin

Good Lord, what a mistake not to come here [to America]! . . . Here you would not be starving. . . . I am constantly asked about you, not only by Russian writers but also American ones. . . .

June 1942
Vera Muromtseva-Bunina, from a letter to Tatyana Loginova-Muravieva

Lately I have had to do a lot of darning: I have to wear stockings all the time to help support my waist and stomach. . . .

June 3, 1942
Ivan Bunin, from his diary

May was very unusual—absolutely monstrous battles. . . . But now there is a lull. . . . As always, the Germans keep lying on the radio. How amazingly whorelike is their "song," their language! I keep thinking: what lies ahead! Either the Germans win or they are completely destroyed. If they win—how can a country exist when it is hated by almost all the world? . . . What will happen to a country when the very strongest from ages 15 to 50 have perished! Millions have perished and will continue to perish.

The French radio is also amazing. We are drowning in slavery and lies.

I am also not getting any better—my health has been broken. I can hardly move my legs. Will it really be the same thing as last year? I cannot even remember that far back. Perhaps I have forgotten it?

I have been reading poetry—G. Ivanov and Gippius. Ivanov has the beginnings of a genuine poet. Gippius is terrible. She is a scoundrel.

July 1, 1942
Ivan Bunin, from his diary

The radio reports that the Germans *have taken Sevastopol*.[4] But the costs must have been great! . . .

I reread the first volume of *The Brothers Karamazov*. Three-quarters is the most absolute pulp fiction and farce . . . but written by a very deft and remarkably capable scribbler.

---

[4]Sevastopol is located on the southwest tip of the Crimea. The Germans, after a costly ten-month battle, captured the city, taking 90,000 Russians as prisoners and losing 24,000 of their own men.

How will the war end? The next month or two will be fatal for Europe. . . .

July 14, 1942
Ivan Bunin, from his diary
I read (more accurately, reread) the second volume of *The Brothers Karamazov*. It is remarkably intelligent and skillful—but the implausible nonsense of the work is often extremely stupid. Generally speaking, it is boring and leaves me cold.

July 18, 1942
Ivan Bunin, from his diary
The Germans keep moving deeper into Russia.[5] . . .
The radio reports that "Timoshenko's situation is catastrophic."[6] Something new and huge must be about to happen. But I still cannot believe that all is lost.

July 19, 1942
Ivan Bunin, from his diary
On July 6th the radio reported that the Germans had taken Voronezh;[7] but it turned out to be nonsense. The city is still in Russian hands.

July 28, 1942
Ivan Bunin, from a letter to Mark Aldanov
My dear friend, I ask you to do everything possible to obtain visas for Vera and me [for America]. . . .

Mid-August 1942
Alexander Liberman, from a letter to Alexander Baboreko
I remember a hot summer day in August 1942. The resistance had informed us that all foreign Jews would be arrested that night. . . . We immediately started packing several small suitcases to go "underground." At that very moment Ivan Alexeevich walked in. In a sur-

[5]On July 5, 1942, German forces occupied the Crimea; two days later they were destroying Russian forces in the Donets region. On July 11 the Germans moved to swift and successful drives toward Rostov and Stalingrad.
[6]On July 12, 1942, the Russians, under the command of Marshal Timoshenko, established the "Stalingrad front." Five days later they were putting up a desperate resistance on the Don to prepare defenses for the city. On July 30 the Germans were within eighty miles of Stalingrad.
[7]On July 7, 1942, the Germans captured Voronezh, the place of Bunin's birth.

prised tone of voice, he asked us what we were doing; and when we told him what we had heard, he insisted that we stay with him. At first we refused . . . but he said that he would not leave us until we gave him our word that we would be at his home that evening.

We spent several anxious days with him. The battle of Stalingrad[8] had just begun. Trembling, we listened to the English radio, forgetting completely about our own fate. Ivan Alexeevich spent most of the time in his study, working on his latest stories. . . .

After about a week, we returned to our home in Cannes. Ivan Alexeevich was a hundred percent Russian patriot. He thought only about saving Russia from the barbarians.

August 23, 1942
Vera Muromtseva-Bunina, from her diary
    We have received an invitation from America: visas, a free (or almost free) passage, money for travel, and so forth. But as far as I'm concerned, it is an "invitation to a beheading."[9] I pray to God that we do not have to leave here.

September 3, 1942
Ivan Bunin, from his diary
    The battles in Russia are horrendous.[1]

September 16, 1942
Ivan Bunin, from his diary
    Already summer is coming to an end, and perhaps this one will be my last. . . .
    The Germans keep "advancing" on Tsaritsyn.[2] All the attacks of the Russians are invariably "repulsed." For a month and a half now, monstrous battles have been raging day and night—and, of course, the

---

[8]On August 15, 1942, the Germans opened a major offensive toward Stalingrad.

[9]Muromtseva-Bunina is referring to Nabokov's 1938 work, *Invitation to a Beheading* (*Priglashenie na kazn'*).

[1]On August 26, 1942, an estimated one million German troops attacked the Russian defenders at Stalingrad. By September 3 they had penetrated into the western suburbs of the city. In addition, over one thousand German planes made constant raids on the area.

[2]Volgograd is in southeastern Russia, about five hundred miles southeast of Moscow. Before 1925 the city was called Tsaritsyn; from 1925 to 1961, Stalingrad; and after 1961, Volgograd (its present name). On September 10, 1942, Russian forces retreated from the western suburbs of Stalingrad. Six days later they gave way to German forces who had entered the northwest environs of the city. Russian defenders, holed up in factories, continued to hold out against the enemy.

Germans are suffering tremendous losses. By the end of the war, Germany will have only little boys and old men. It is complete madness!

All right, let's say that the Germans take Tsaritsyn—then what? Only a crazy cretin [like Hitler] could think he could rule over America, Brazil, Norway, France, Denmark, Poland, Czechoslovakia, Austria, Serbia, Albania, Russia, and China—twelve countries whose citizens, not counting the Jews, hate Germany and will continue to hate it with an unprecedented hatred that will last for almost a hundred years. Why, the force of that hatred is unprecedented—even now.

September 18, 1942
Ivan Bunin, from his diary

What a disgrace—in this entire time, people in America have collected only about 500 dollars for me!

September 22, 1942
Ivan Bunin, from his diary

In a certain way, my father, mother, brothers, and [sister] Masha exist—in my memory. But when I die, that will be the absolute end for them. My past is becoming more and more alive for me. . . . Good Lord, how I see and feel it all!

I keep cleaning up my desk, hoping to sit down to work. But, most likely, it is a vain hope!

The newspapers feature such stories as "The Hopeless Situation of the USSR." . . . People say that the "deed is done" in Tsaritsyn, and that one must wonder what the Germans will do next. . . .

The radio is a nightmare. The only thing the broadcasters do not lie about is the time.

September 23, 1942
Ivan Bunin, from his diary

The Germans have smashed through Tsaritsyn and the Caucasus.[3] The past few days they have said nothing other than that they "are taking building after building. . . ." The Russians, of course, are slaughtering them in great numbers. . . .

---

[3]On September 17, 1942, Russians and Germans engaged in fierce hand-to-hand (and house-to-house) combat in Stalingrad, with Russian women fighting alongside Russian men. Six days later, stiff Russian resistance brought the Germans to a virtual halt in the city. But the broad front that the Germans had launched in the Caucasus on September 9 proceeded unimpeded.

But we know only one-hundredth of what is really going on in the world. . . . France has never encountered such destruction. . . .

September 24, 1942
Ivan Bunin, from his diary

I took a walk at 11 p.m. . . . and I saw my dark shadow ahead of me. I was seized by terrible thoughts—that I would suddenly be alone. Where would I go? How would I live? Would I commit suicide?

October 1, 1942
Ivan Bunin, from his diary

Yesterday was Vera's name day. We had a lavish dinner . . . the sausage was called "Canine Joy." . . .

October 14, 1942
Ivan Bunin, from his diary

Today is Vera's birthday. . . . She went to church and took communion. The dinner was festive. Everyone had three pieces of rotten boiled potatoes. But the tea had real ("prewar") jam—a gift [from a friend]. . . .

Today is the feast of the Protective Veil of the Virgin. Protect us, O Mother of God.

The Germans' advance is lackluster. This is the 76th day they have been trying to take Tsaritsyn.[4]

October 23, 1942
Ivan Bunin, from his diary

A terrible day—I've turned 72!

The radio reports about Tsaritsyn: "All Bolshevik attacks have been repulsed!"[5] But soon it will be three months that the Germans have been trying to take the city!

---

[4]Bunin's remark aside, there was nothing "lackluster" about the German advance. On September 28, 1942, the Germans brought fresh reinforcements to Stalingrad; two days later, Hitler vowed publicly that his troops would take the city. On October 3 the Russians improved their position in Stalingrad, but at an immense cost in lives and with no outside assistance from their countrymen.

One day later, General Paulus began a new series of attacks on the city, the fiercest and most enduring of the German offensives. On October 8 the German High Command announced that it would no longer assault Stalingrad frontally but that, by means of heavy artillery, it would level the city into submission. Six days later, newly arrived Russian Guards joined the defending troops.

[5]On October 20, 1942, German forces began a new offensive on Stalingrad (Tsaritsyn) but were repulsed by the Russians. On the following day, though, the invaders made headway into the city. On October 22 early winter snows fell on the hills outside the area.

October 27, 1942
Ivan Bunin, from his diary

Tsaritsyn is still holding.[6]

I have been feeling poorly. . . . Truly, this is the end of my writing. Deliver me, O Lord.

November 12, 1942
Ivan Bunin, from his diary

Fatal news: The Germans have seized control of our coastline.

The Italians took Nice yesterday afternoon, and Cannes last night. And two thousand Italians entered Grasse this evening.[7] . . . Truly, there is *nothing* left in my life!

Mid-November 1942 and after
A friend, from his memoirs

Bunin's villa was somewhat away from the road, but the Italians . . . decided to requisition it. Local French officials and an Italian officer came to Bunin with the requisition papers.

Ivan Alexeevich lost his temper, saying that what they wanted to do was both outrageous and illegal. He flatly refused to go to the Italian's office and ask that the requisition be canceled.

"Leave me alone! I will not go there! I will not stoop or beg!" he shouted . . . at Vera Nikolaevna who had been persuading him to go. . . .

He then went into to his study. . . . The Italians, having learned that Bunin was a Russian writer and a Nobel laureate, left him in peace. . . .

I did my best to help Bunin. For instance, I managed to find food for him. He always asked how much it cost, and sent me the money. An Orthodox priest in Marseilles, a relative of the artist Leon Bakst, helped me get food parcels to him. . . .

At Villa "Jeanette" . . . Ivan Alexeevich could work undisturbed. On his desk was his well-known ashtray, heavy and somewhat burned . . . as well as a pile of books and files with manuscripts in

---

[6]Soviet historians see the "defensive period" of the Battle of Stalingrad as taking place between July 17 and November 18, 1942, and the "offensive period" of the struggle as occurring between November 19, 1942, and February 2, 1943.

[7]On November 11, 1942, Hitler informed Marshal Pétain that Germany could no longer preserve the "armistice" with France, and that all measures had to be taken to "arrest the continuation of Anglo-British aggression." As a result, German and Italian forces marched into all of unoccupied France.

them. . . . There was nothing superfluous in his room: a comfortable armchair . . . and three or four chairs. When Bunin was working, no one entered this room, not even Vera Nikolaevna. . . .

As there were no servants in Grasse, Vera Nikolaevna did all the housework herself. Those who knew Vera Nikolaevna or had met her, never forgot her. . . . She was not young, and her hair was completely white. Ivan Alexeevich once wrote a charming poem about such old age:

> All in snowy curls,
> With fragrance and grace,
> You hum with blissful buzz
> Like wasps and bees, envious and base. . . .
> Are you getting old, dear friend?
> Put aside your fears!
> Others should have
> Your young old years!

Vera's delicate, amazingly tender features, her large, light, and endlessly kind eyes, her high clear forehead, the pale color of her skin which blushed slightly when she was worried—everything about her was harmonious . . . like the finest Chinese porcelain.

Miraculously, the years had spared her, and she remained as beautiful as when she was young, but her beauty . . . had become more spiritual and defined. Her hands were small, with fingers that were flexible, like those of a pianist. She herself typed Ivan Alexeevich's manuscripts—he was a strict and exacting "customer"—"wife-secretary," she jokingly called herself. She carefully guarded his peace; and, like no one else, she knew how to calm his fits of (sometimes unreasonable) anger. Bunin was sometimes very hot-tempered and, having lost his calm, he was not very careful about his choice of words.

The dearest thing for her was Ivan Alexeevich's manuscripts and books; she was his first reader and critic.

In his declining years, Bunin himself was amazingly handsome, graceful, and elegant. . . . He was not tall, but well proportioned, making him . . . look bigger than he actually was. His hands were small, nervous, and dry; his fingers were thin, flexible, and restless, as though they were constantly looking for something.

Even in old age, Bunin held his head straight and would even throw it slightly back, giving him that proud look which many took for haughtiness and arrogance. His dry, long face had a distinctive dark tan, the result of time spent every summer under the hot sun of Côte d'Azur. . . . His eyes were sharp, young. Calm and strict, they fixed intently upon a person, a thing, an object, though not for long. They laughed seldom, very seldom, and, even when he was merry, an indistinct bitterness and pain . . . would hide in the depth of his pupils. . . .

November 25, 1942
Ivan Bunin, from his diary
  This morning I thought I was dying. Blood rushed from my head.

December 25, 1942
Ivan Bunin, from his diary
  Today is Catholic Christmas. . . . Yesterday we went to dinner with friends . . . and the bill was more than 2,500 francs! But [our friends] picked up the tab. We certainly ate well! . . .
  But I am still sad. There is *nothing* left in my life!

December 27, 1942
Ivan Bunin, from his diary
  Since I did not leave with Tseitlin and Aldanov for America, I have signed a death sentence for myself. To end my days in Grasse, in poverty, cold, and bestial hunger!

December 31, 1942
Ivan Bunin, from his diary
  Vera and I "welcomed" the New Year. . . . When the clock chimed twelve, we drank a glass of wine and "had dinner": each of us had a piece of salted red fish, a slice of potato, and a very thin piece of sausage which smelled like a dead dog. . . .
  Yet another year of trifling human life has gone by!

PART FOUR

Putting Pen to Paper

1943–1944

BUNIN, 1938

It is a sad truism that, in the first half of the twentieth century, Russian writers in and out of the country were fated to ply their craft amidst conditions of revolution, war, and other chaotic events. Bunin was no exception. He had written *The Cursed Days* behind locked windows and barricaded doors in both Moscow and Odessa during the Russian Revolution and civil war. Twenty years later he wrote his last great fictional work, *Dark Alleys* (*Temnye allei*), with German and Italian troops stationed on the doorstep of his home in Grasse. To many critics, Bunin's muse inhabited peaceful steppes and Elysian fields; more truthfully, his inspiration often drew from the tyranny, anarchy, and terror from which he never seemed to escape.

In *Dark Alleys*, Bunin's response to world cataclysm contrasted markedly with his outlook on revolution and war that informed *Cursed Days*. This time Bunin did not comment on sociopolitical events; rather, he pursued a theme that had lurked just beneath the surface of his earlier fiction: the often murderous tie between love and death.

Dark Alleys is a collection of almost forty short-story vignettes, many of which are only a few pages in length. Although the characters in *Dark Alleys* come from all walks and stations in life, they share a common bond: they are individuals who, lonely and bored, seek—and sometimes find—momentary happiness in sexual union before they die or wander down the "dark alleys" and "shadowed paths" of their lives.

With *Dark Alleys*, reviewers and readers were troubled by several things. For one, they were distressed by what they saw as the "pornography" of the work. The Bunin of more than seventy years was for them a "dirty old man." Many of the women in *Dark Alleys* appear as modern-day Eves who relish their nakedness. They admire their bodies in mirrors, sunbathe in hidden gullies and bays, and throw themselves on their lovers with abandon. Equally problematic, Bunin's audience was upset by the "tragedy" of love, particularly the fact that in *Dark Alleys* couples entered the stories merely to mate before they died from war and accident, suicide and disease.

As they had with most of Bunin's writings, readers and reviewers missed the point of *Dark Alleys*. Caught between world upheaval and the mundane business of living, they might have responded more intuitively, if not positively, to the message of Bunin's stories. In *Dark Alleys*, more than in any other work of his fiction, Bunin made clear what he saw as the difference between life and love. For him life was sorrowful, tragic, and grey; but love was joyful, triumphant, and sparkling. In *Dark Alleys*, love was the catalyst for intense, almost out-of-body experiences which, however fleeting, brought to its participants consummate happiness and freedom, and which, as the stuff of memory, made their time on this earth both unforgettable and unique.

"Is there really such a thing as an unhappy love?" the heroine in "Natalie," a story in *Dark Alleys*, asks in an introspective moment. Bunin would say no. Simply put, and however trite the adage, he believed that having loved and lost was better than never having loved at all. In a more philosophical vein, Bunin agreed with Socrates that the unexamined life was not worth living. As he saw it, though, the impetus for such a life review was physical, not philosophical—those times in life when individuals, through the magic mystery of love, created their own version of "paradise."

✳ 1943 ✳

Circa 1943
Alexander Bakhrakh, from his memoirs

[Bunin said:] "My brother writers write and write, but how many things they do not know. . . . They know nothing about clouds, and trees, and even people. . . . They are ignorant of the most elementary laws of physics; they do not know anatomy, the parts of the human body. . . .

"The woman [standing at the bus stop] next to us has blue veins on her legs. No one knows what this means. Writers, though, do not take note of such things or other barely discernible markings. But I can describe for you her appearance, the many details of her face, her life.

"I was once sitting in a restaurant with Boris Zaitsev. A certain bald gentleman was having dinner not far from us. I said to Zaitsev: 'Boris, look at his ears, at the way he is sitting and eating, and tell me something about him.' Zaitsev looked, thought hard, and, laughing, changed the topic of conversation. But I could have written the life story of this individual. . . ."

"If the Goncourt brothers had Lermontov's knowledge of life, they would have become first-class writers. There is much talent and sparkle in their writing, but it is uneven and dry, and this is what kills them.

"Gorky is guilty of the same thing. . . . He is essentially a great talent, but only for vulgar literature. Take any one of his books . . . and one begins to notice the incongruities. . . . For example, his story, 'The Birth of Man'[1] is replete with physiological details which even nature

---

[1] Bunin seems to forget that it was he who convinced Gorky to write "The Birth of Man" (*"Rozhdenie cheloveka"*) in 1912. See Marullo, 179.

197

does not know about. . . . In all seriousness, Gorky writes: 'The leaves of the maple tree swim downstream like chopped-off human arms, like pieces of salmon flesh. . . .' Where did he ever see such thing? And what was he thinking when he wrote about 'the laughing sea' or how 'one eye drinks you in, while the other winks at you slyly'? Does this tell the reader anything, even the slightest detail?

"When we lived together at Capri, I always told Gorky: 'You write as though you have been in a dissecting room and that you have dragged everything there into your stories—here a face, there a torso, over there a leg—truly are such things possible in nature?' Gorky scratched his head and said: 'Yes, of course . . . you are right.'

"Then there's Leonid Andreev with his Judas climbing a mountain in Jerusalem at sunset.[2] His hands are outstretched and 'his shadow seemed like a black crucifix.' That is a cheap shot. But I also told him, 'Leonid . . . the sunset is on the other side, on the Black Sea.' 'You're always talking trifles,' Andreev objected, annoyed, at my criticism. But it is not trifles at all. . . ."

[Bunin said:] "Last night, Chagall appeared to me in a dream; he was a big man with an even and smoothly clipped beard that looked like a fluffy necklace about his face."

"But, Ivan Alexeevich," I answered. "Chagall is clean-shaven."

"You are always correcting me. I am sure it was Chagall. I even remember that green bits and pieces of Jews were swimming in the background behind him. Then some German officers appeared, looking so terrible that I woke up." . . .

"Garshin was such a splendid writer. How unfortunate was his untimely death for Russian literature.[3] . . . Without a doubt, his literary freedom and bold images gave witness to a very profound and genuine talent . . . for example, his stories 'The Red Flower' . . . 'Four Days' . . . and 'Attalea Princeps.'[4] . . .

"No Western literature of the period has risen to the poetic heights of *The Lay of the Host of Igor*,[5] but one has to be Russian to appreciate its beauty. . . ."

[Bunin said:] "I should have taken Stanislavsky up on his offer to

---

[2]Andreev wrote "Judas Iscariot" ("*Iuda Iskariot*") in 1907.

[3]At age thirty-three, the mentally unstable Garshin committed suicide by throwing himself down a stairwell.

[4]Garshin's "Four Days" ("*Chetyre dnia*") appeared in 1877, "Attalea Princeps" in 1880, and "The Red Flower" ("*Krasnyi tsvetok*") in 1883.

[5]*The Lay of the Host of Igor* (*Slovo o polku Igoreve*), written in the twelfth century, is Russia's most famous medieval epic.

join the theatre.[6] Most likely I would have been somebody. Be so kind as to tell me who reads me now?"

But Bunin knew that he would not be forgotten.

"Do you often reread Pushkin's *The Tales of Belkin*?"[7] Bunin once asked me.

"About once a month," I answered.

"Yes, everyone should do this. To me they are like oxygen. I literally suffer when in the hustle and bustle of leaving for somewhere, I forget to take something by Pushkin along with me. . . . Pushkin's prose is dry, but so unusually splendid. One should read him throughout one's life. No sooner should he finish the last page of a work than he should start again on the first [page of another]. . . .

"Gogol, of course, is a writer genius. . . . But I do not like him. Much about him is vulgar and false. Take the first page of *Dead Souls*, for instance (A 'poema'? How is it a 'poema'?).[8] . . . And where did he dig up such stillborn names for his characters? 'Yaichnitsa,' 'Zemlyanika,' 'Podkolesin,' 'Derzhimorda,' 'Borodavka,' and "Kozopup'[9]—they are stupid, not funny. Even 'Khlestakov'[1] is false and unpleasant, even somehow shocking. . . . No, that a character has a successful family name—this is one of the most important things for a writer to think about. Take, for example, the last names of Tolstoy's characters—they are real gems. . . .

"Yesterday I was again leafing through a volume of Fet's verse . . . and I thought that the editor should be flogged. . . . Whose idea is it that everything a writer wrote should be included in his posthumous editions? God forbid that that should happen to me. I will crawl out of the coffin and demolish everything that is superfluous, childish, immature, and unpolished. . . ."

Everyone thinks that Bunin had an extremely ironic attitude toward his literary brethren, and especially to young and beginning writers. This, of course, is not true. Whenever the conversation touched upon some . . . "yet to be noticed" author from the next generation, or

---

[6]According to Bunin, both Stanislavsky and Nemirovich-Danchenko made such an offer after a 1910 lecture on Chekhov in which Bunin recalled the writer in Chekhov's "own voice and intonations." See Marullo, *Ivan Bunin: Russian Reqiuem*, 117.

[7]Pushkin wrote *The Tales of Belkin* (*Povesti Belkina*) in 1830.

[8]Loosely translated, a "poema" is a verse epic.

[9]"Yaichnitsa" is the Russian word for "omelet"; "Zemlyanika" for "strawberry"; "Podkolesin" for "axle"; and " 'Derzhimorda" for "fierce mug."

[1]"Khlestakov" derives from the Russian verb *khestat'*, to whip, and the adjective *khlestkii*, meaning cynical or sharp.

when someone let loose a caustic comment on a novice writer, Bunin immediately bristled . . . and defended the "accused." . . .

"It is easy to criticize," he would say. "But you yourself try to write. But if one has talent, it will express itself. No one wrote *War and Peace* in a day." . . .

His pronouncements about "Alyoshka" Tolstoy were especially tender. Bunin forgave him many things, something he did not do for anyone else. He readily recalled his meetings with Tolstoy "in the dawn" of the emigration.

"When Tolstoy and I were together in Paris," Bunin said, "he often told me in a strained type of way: 'If there should ever be a new tsar, I will fall on my knees before him and say: 'Father-tsar, I am your slave, do with me what you will.' . . . But that did not stop him from sitting and drinking . . . with the Bolsheviks—even though he hated them. . . ."

"Do you like the now deceased Kuprin? Not long ago I wrote an article about him for *Contemporary Notes*.[2] . . . Many people were very unhappy with what I wrote. But I wrote what I thought . . . so I cannot help if it did not turn out to be a 'posthumous panegyric.' . . .

"During his last years in Paris, Kuprin started to seem more sympathetic and complaisant, though he was always morbidly rancorous. . . . For a long time I courted M. K. Davidova, who later became Kuprin's first wife. . . . One time at a gathering, Kuprin got drunk and began taking out after me with insults, snickering, and double entendres. I endured such abuse a long time, but then I got angry and said loud enough for everyone to hear: 'Look here, you damned platypus, if you don't shut your mouth, I'm going to crash this bottle on your Tatar-like head. . . .' I thought there would be a fight . . . but nothing happened. Kuprin looked at me with surprise. He quieted down immediately . . . but then he burst our crying, 'So I am a platypus,' he said. 'Brothers, look at how I'm being insulted!' . . .

"Another time . . . [Kuprin said to me:] 'It is you who has kept me from being elected to the Academy [of Sciences in Saint Petersburg].' . . . 'It never even occurred to me to do such a thing,' I replied.[3] . . . At that time Kuprin was renowned throughout Russia. Editors would seek him out . . . and give him 2,500 rubles a page. . . . But he never forgave me for not being elected to the Academy. . . ."

[2] *Contemporary Annals (Sovremennye zapiski)*, published in Paris from 1920 to 1940, was one of the most influential journals in the diaspora.

[3] Kuprin was never considered for membership in the Russian Academy of Sciences.

Bunin always responded to the Symbolists with extremely passionate . . . and also seemingly inopportune polemics. He had not forgotten the old battles of the past. More and more, he kept pretending that he did not like Blok's writing, that it was all alien to him. He even kept an entire "dossier" on Blok with clippings from his articles, letters, and diaries. (That means that Bunin was genuinely interested in him!) . . . Some of these clippings were rather funny. . . . For instance, on the day the *Titanic* sunk,[4] Blok wrote in his diary: "But there is still the Ocean" and "I, who have thirsted for destruction, have been drawn into the grey purple of a silver star . . . into the amethyst of a storm." Bunin was always greatly amused by Blok's dedication to Bryusov: "To a helmsman in a dark raincoat—to a guiding green Star." "The grain merchant[5] is now a helmsman in a dark raincoat," Bunin tittered. . . .

Sometimes Bunin would sing like a *chanteuse*, taking lines from Blok's *The Twelve*,[6] growling that it was "all vulgarity" and insisting that the ditty-type style of the poem was a crass forgery, a cheap wish to humor the undemanding reader. . . . Bunin's dislike of Blok extended even to the poet's physical image.

"I just came across a portrait of Blok and I'm giving it to you as a present," he once told me. "Put it next to you, so you can admire his baggy lips."[7]

The mere mention of Andrei Bely would irritate Bunin even more. He acknowledged Bely's charm, but he also wailed that Bely was "half devil, half clown." He continued that he and Bely had once been friends, but then he again became annoyed when he recalled Bely's portrait of him in his memoirs.[8]

"*The Silver Dove*[9] is the apex of bad taste and pretentiousness. It is all a world of wax cupolas, doing God knows what. . . .

"Balmont once told me: 'I've just read your . . . what did you call it? . . . *The Man from San Francisco*?'

" '*The Gentleman from San Francisco*,' I corrected him coldly.

[4]The *Titanic* sunk on April 14–15, 1912, claiming about fifteen hundred passengers and ship personnel as victims.
[5]Here Bunin's "aristocratic" bias is painfully evident. In fact, Bryusov was the scion of a family of merchants. His paternal grandfather was a former serf who, having purchased his freedom, founded a cork (not a grain) business in Moscow. Although Bryusov's father, Yakov Kuzmich, had been a youthful atheist and a radical, he eventually returned to the family business and became a very wealthy individual.
[6]Blok's *The Twelve* (*Dvenadtsat'*) appeared in 1918.
[7]Blok's lips were rather pronounced.
[8]Bakhrakh is referring to Bely's *The Beginning of the Century* (*Nachalo veka*), published in 1933. See Marullo, *From the Other Shore*, 85.
[9]Bely published *The Silver Dove* (*Serebrianyi golub'*) in 1910.

" 'Oh, yes, *"The Gentleman"* . . . you really do have a feeling for a ship.' . . .

"[Bryusov also told me:] 'You won't believe this—but I had to force myself to finish *War and Peace.* . . . It is not bad at all, and even very good in spots. . . .'"

[Bunin once asked me:] "How many Russian words do you know for 'ass' (he said something even more vulgar!)? . . . There are some wonderful words . . . 'drop-seat,' for example. Remember—no, of course, you wouldn't remember—Benediktov's [poem] about a woman rider who was proud of her 'pretty and ample drop-seat.' What a pity that I do not have a copy of Benediktov's poems! I would read some of them aloud right away. They are much more sonorous that anything that Balmont would write, and much more intelligent, to boot." . . .

[Bunin said]: "I met Merezhkovsky rather late in life. I remember that I had walked into an editorial office in Petersburg . . . and that [I saw] a small man who was just finishing a lively argument. I heard only one phrase: 'The art of the lie is the greatest of all the arts.' . . . [Later] in Grasse I had with [Merezhkovsky's wife] Gippius something akin to an *amitié amoureuse.*[1] I had this sudden feeling that she liked me. At that time I had just published a small story in which an unknown admirer had sent an anonymous letter to a famous writer. . . . Gippius gave me a good dressing-down. She indignantly rushed at me, saying, 'You trample on the most pristine and sacred things. You have no tact. You are ready to debase everything. . . .'

"I could not understand her anger, but the lyricism of our relationship began to fade away. . . .

"In the first years of our emigration, we were still 'exotic birds' who were invited everywhere—Merezhkovsky always sidled up to some famous guest and introduced his wife as . . . 'the famous Russian poetess.' . . ."

[Bunin said]: "It is a pity that you never met Vyacheslav Ivanov. He was a most interesting fellow, though he was muddleheaded and kept one in a state of constant tension. I very much loved several of his poems . . . but I could not accept his 'Dionysius.'[2] Also, this religion of

[1]Bunin is fantasizing here.
[2]Dionysius is the Greek god of wine, vegetation, and religious ecstasy, as well as the force of life in all living things. Not surprisingly, the followers of the so-called "Dionysian cult" were often drunk, lawless, and noisy.
Dionysius was also a key facet in Ivanov's life and work. In 1895 he wrote "Funeral Rites in Memory of Dionysius" (*"Trizna Dionisa"*), in which he celebrated the death and resurrection of the god. His lectures on Dionysius in Paris in 1903, entitled "The Hellenic Religion of the Suffering God" (*"Ellinskaia religiia stradaiushchego boga"*), were serialized in

a suffering God is some kind of salon-type scholasticism. It comes from Merezhkovsky, not me.[3] . . ."

[Bunin said]: "You equate Khodasevich and Pushkin. Khodasevich once called himself 'an old hazel-hen.' What an apt description. I will not argue that Khodaesvich has written some very precise poems—even intelligent ones. But he walked through life with a very small suitcase, pretending that he had mountains of baggage.

"Nabokov keeps going higher and higher, and there are few like him among the younger generation. Truly, he is one of the most adroit writers in all of Russian literature, but he is also a circus clown. . . . Sinner that I am, I love the talent of clowns." . . .

Whenever Bunin was in a bad mood, he loved to curse out someone violently, to make fun of him, and to seize upon his "opponent's" weak spots in a very precise way. . . . He first said something profane about someone, then he calmed down, and his mood improved. . . .

"Who should I tear to pieces today?" he sometimes asked the people around him.

We were once talking about the poetess Berberova. "Now, there's someone I can take out after. She's starting to look like a sea slug!"

Such a cruel comparison truly delighted him.

"My father knew really how to curse out people. I remember that my mother often said to him in reproach: 'Good Lord, how all the Bunins can abuse and insult people!' " . . .

Whenever Bunin began swearing or speaking openly about things which would have been better to have been passed over in silence (and he truly loved doing this), Vera Nikolaevna remarked with pain in her heart:

"Ian, it is as though the devil is standing right by you. Do not sin."

"What is so sinful about what I am saying?" Bunin would reply. "After all, I am talking about [love], the most splendid thing in the world. For this alone, it is worth being born. . . . In love, in the very act of love itself, there is something divine, mysterious, and terrifying, something we do not value at all. One has to be as old as I am to feel to

---

the Russian press in 1904 and 1905. And at the University of Baku in 1923 he completed a doctoral dissertation, *Dionysius and Pre-Dionysianism* (*Dionis i pradionstvo*).

In his studies on Dionysius, Ivanov objected to Nietzsche's claim that Dionysius and his cult were alternatives to "weak-willed" Christianity. Rather, Ivanov saw the god and his sect as essentially religious phenomena: the spiritual antecedent and historical basis of the new Christian mystical ideal that he was proposing for his time.

[3]Bunin is grossly simplifying Merezhkovsky's understanding of the Deity.

the very depths all the ineffable, mysterious charm of love. Such charm is impossible to describe in words. . . . The essence of love always manages to escape me. No matter how much I try—I cannot capture it. . . . But I am not the only one who has failed. No one has yet expressed [the true nature of love]. . . ."

[Bunin told me:] "I want to read you just one phrase from Flaubert's correspondence." (He carried Flaubert's works with him constantly and made certain that no one else was allowed to read them). "Just listen how he writes to his long-standing friend and lover, Louise Colet:

"'Yes, there is something missing in the life of one who has never awakened in an anonymous bed, who has not seen a head on a pillow that he will never see again, and who, when he leaves that room at sunrise, would not cross some bridge without wanting to throw himself into the water. . . .'"[4]

I was aware of [Flaubert's] extremely remarkable letter, but I did not understand why it made such a lively impression on Bunin.

"Ivan Alexeevich," I asked him, "why have these words affected you so strongly, why have they agitated you so?"

"The letter is remarkable," he answered, "because it is the sincere and incomparable cry from the soul of a thirty-year-old youth. It is also unlike anything that any writer could ever make up, even if he is greatly talented. What Flaubert writes is noteworthy also because I myself have never had such an encounter . . . though. . . ." But he did not go into details. . . .

Bunin began telling me that he was keeping a diary; and, almost with an embarrassed air, he added that he was doing it unconsciously but with an eye to having it published. "It is a professional deformation," he said smilingly, and he also noted that he would be ashamed if he saw this diary in print. "After all," he said, "there is a great deal that I cannot write about, like my relationships with several women. . . ."

He then began talking about Rousseau's *Confessions*,[5] as well as about the "official" and private diaries of Tolstoy, insisting that telling everything about oneself is appropriate when the goal is confession. "But can you imagine me in the role of a repentant sinner?" he asked. Then he recalled the words of Saint Augustine: "O Lord, give me the gift of chastity, but not now. . . ."[6]

---

[4]Flaubert wrote this letter to Colet on June 1, 1853. For the complete text of this missive, see G. Flaubert, *Selected Letters* (New York, 1997), 210–213.

[5]Rousseau's *Les Confessions* appeared in 1784.

[6]More accurately, Saint Augustine wrote in his *Confessions* (397–398): "As a youth,

[Bunin continued:] "Zinaida Nikolaevna [Gippius] will die someday . . . and her diaries will be published.[7] In them will be all her thoughts on all kinds of meetings and conversations—and, invariably, very 'serious' ones at that—encounters that she will describe with malice and spite. She loves to prophesy *post factum* and on all kinds of things to boot. Then she will dry the ink by the light of a candle so that all her notes look alike, as if they were all done at the same time. Even her handwriting is remarkable; for seventy years she has not changed it in the slightest way so that no one can ever make out when and where her notes were written." . . .

The radio was broadcasting an aria from *Tosca*[8] from Milan—"In the star-filled twinkling of night."

Ivan Alexeevich listened to it with rapt attention. Then he said:

"What a pity that the audience there did not demand an encore. After all, that is my favorite aria. I myself sometimes sing it when there are no 'discriminating witnesses' around." . . . Then he began to hum some of Puccini's bars—"here it all is: the bliss of love, the sweet torment of happiness, the poison of love. . . ."

[Bunin said]: "I do not believe that when people are asked the stupid question—'What book would you take with you if you had to live on a desert island?'—respond by answering, 'Something by Dante.' This is hypocrisy. Dante, of course, is a very major, world poet, but one cannot be 'nourished' by him in our time, for he is boring. . . .

"When Cervantes was alive, people wrote in a general, allegorical style, without psychological flourishes. Perhaps people were simpler then. *Don Quixote*[9] is a most splendid book, but we, its late descendants, have given it a deep, eternal meaning, something that Cervantes himself did not intend." . . .

[Bunin spoke] for a long time about French literature. He first discussed Anatole France:

"It is, of course, nonsense," he exclaimed, "that France's sun has set and that he is doomed.[1] Much of what he has written cannot die.

---

particularly in early adolescence, I had been woefully at fault. I had prayed to you for chastity and said, 'Give me chastity and continence, but not yet.' For I was afraid that you would answer my prayer at once and cure me too soon of the disease of lust, which I wanted satisfied, not quelled." See Saint Augustine, *Confessions* (London, 1976), 169.

[7]In truth, Gippius had already published selections from her diaries in 1908, 1922, 1925, and 1929.

[8]Puccini's *Tosca* was first performed in Rome on January 14, 1900.

[9]Cervantes wrote *Don Quixote* in two parts in 1605 and 1615.

[1]Although Anatole France was awarded the Nobel Prize in Literature in 1921, he was continually faulted by his younger colleagues for what they saw as his thin plots, sparse imagination, limpid style, and polished wit.

Read only his 'Red Lily.' What freedom, what ability to see things, how easily and without a trace of tension does he render a French atmosphere. And with what flawless art and sense does he depict individual characters. Take, for instance, his sculptor or his Englishwoman. They are living people; I can feel them breathing. Of course, France did not make up his Englishwoman. He had to have met her somewhere . . . for there is very little that is stylized about her. . . . I am sure that Lev Nikolaevich [Tolstoy] would gladly sign his name to France's books." (Bunin loved to say this when he especially wanted to praise a literary work . . . but when words failed him.) . . . "No, without a doubt, France created eternal treasures, and it is only fashionable snobbism to poke fun at him now. . . ."

Flaubert was one of Bunin's favorite writers. He would often cite passages from *Madame Bovary*; even the word "bovarism" delighted him.

"Everyone should read Flaubert's *Three Stories*[2] at least once a year," he would say. "The change of rhythm in [his story] 'Saint Julian,'[3] when at the end of the narrative the work transmutes into legend, into a saint's tale, is simply the stuff of genius. There is no other word for it. Remember how Flaubert's wounded deer cries out: '*Maudit, maudit.*'[4]" (Here Bunin stretched out his neck and tried to mimic the agonized animal.) "The prolonged 'au-au' in 'maudit' gives such a remarkable sense of a pre-death wail. . . .

"There are also excellent spots in [his story] 'The Temptation.' Flaubert worked long and hard on this story, writing several variants [of it]. His *Éducation Sentimentale*[5] is also good, though wordy. . . .

"But I cannot read Balzac at all. I get forever confused in his genealogies—who is related to whom; and I cannot force myself to read on, when on the fiftieth page [of the work] he begins describing the who, what, and where of how some inherited mill or textile factory was sold. I find these details boring; and I avoid boring literature. That is why I am also ready to say . . . that Molière is a very good and valuable writer . . . but that I cannot find it in myself to read him, for his plays do not amuse me, even when I see them staged.

"Remember how you used to bring me one volume after another

---

[2]Flaubert wrote his *Three Stories* between 1875 and 1876.
[3]Flaubert's *The Life of Saint Julian the Hospitaller* (*La Légende de Saint Julien l'Hospitalier*) appeared in 1875 and 1876.
[4]That is "Cursed, cursed."
[5]Flaubert wrote *L'Éducation Sentimentale* in 1869, and *The Temptation of Saint Anthony* (*La Tentation de Saint Antoine*) in 1874.

of *Remembrance of Things Past?*[6] At that time I had read a great deal of Proust, though not everything of his, of course. I find him somewhat artificial, but in spite of this and also his endless digressions, he is very good. No one before him has written so well and charmingly. I open one of his books, and from the very first page I fall into a Proustian atmosphere. From childhood on, though, he was a doomed individual, and, like all doomed people, he knew and felt a great deal. No one can write page after page about jealousy and lies like he does." (Bunin apparently had in mind the chapter on the relationship between Swann and Odette, since he had gone into raptures over it earlier.)

Having momentarily thought about what he had said, he suddenly got hold of himself and added:

"Well, Tolstoy could, if he had wanted to, but he did not. . . ."

Several times I gave to Bunin Stendhal "for the night" . . . but he always said to me on the following morning: "I tried to read several pages, but I found it so difficult to get through that I had to set it aside." . . . Even a reference to Tolstoy's admiration for Stendhal did not help. . . .

[I once asked Bunin]: "Have you ever tried to compile a list of your love conquests?"

"Alas," he answered, "that was all a very long time ago, but it is an excellent idea. If I had some free time, I would set about such a task without fail. Only now I do not remember all the names. . . . But your 'tactless' question has aroused all kinds of memories. Youth—what a golden time! How many conquests there were, how many splendid and captivating women did I meet then. Life goes by so quickly, and we do not value it when we should. We begin to take stock of it, only when things are way far behind us, only when it is too late. . . .

"[As regards women] it would be easier for me to compile a list of . . . lost possibilities. That list would most likely be much longer! . . .

"When I was in the third, or fourth grade . . . [I knew] a certain Drakovtsev, a dandy with blue eyes. He was a few years older than I, since he saw it as his duty to be left back first one year, then two. He was a repulsive, pathological individual . . . a bully. He was much more experienced than I, and kept bragging about his knowledge of life. Most likely he made it all up, but he made an impression on me. No matter what girl I looked at, he would tell me in a free and easy way: 'Oh, I was with her last year' or 'Not long ago I . . .'

[6]Proust wrote *À la recherche du temps perdu* between 1909 and 1922.

"Although I didn't believe him, I nonetheless envied him!

"One time he whispered to me: 'Meet me today after nine behind the green wall.'

"I, of course, rushed off to meet him there. There were about six of us students there. Suddenly a huge bottle of vodka appeared, and we all kept taking swigs. . . . It was loathsome, vile. . . . But I was afraid that everyone would laugh at me, and so I forced myself to drink. . . .

"After we finished off the bottle, we hailed a cabbie. . . . 'To Anisya Petrovna's,' Drakovtsev commanded, having decided beforehand that it was time for me to 'fall,' and that he should be my mentor. . . . We arrived at a low small house with the symbolic red light at the entranceway. Drakovtsev pretended that he was a welcome visitor. Some plump girls circled us. . . . Stammering, I ordered a bottle of wine. Suddenly, and without any encouragement on my part, a well-endowed, middle-aged woman plopped down on my lap, almost crushing me. . . .

" 'Let's have some vodka,' she said in a voice that tolerated no objections. She then tried to kiss me. I turned both hot and cold, not knowing how to act or what to talk about. . . . But toward this sweaty woman, with her hoarse voice and dirty underwear, I felt nothing but revulsion. The vodka had made me sleepy. My eyes kept closing, the walls around me began to spin, and the ceiling merged with the floor.

"I ran outside . . . and I don't know how I made it to my own bed. . . . But my expedition had come to an abrupt end!" . . .

[He continued:] "When I was about fifteen . . . I met [a girl]. She was swarthy and plump, with merry blue eyes. . . . Within a few days I had fallen hopelessly in love with her; and, of course, I imagined that no one else had ever experienced such a feeling as I! . . . But I was too shy and bashful to tell her, and she, in her perfidy, pretended that she did not know what was going on. . . . [One time] I was sitting next to her in a carriage. . . . An unexpected jolt suddenly brought our faces together. Without thinking, without even being conscious of what I was doing, I kissed her firmly. . . . I have yet to experience anything more splendid, more delightful than that first kiss, that almost innocent touch . . . of a woman's body. I remember it all as though it had happened yesterday. . . . Later on, our time together became more frequent. . . . But I lacked the courage to proceed [with my passion]. . . .

"About twelve years later . . . I let this same girl know that I was in town. She visited my hotel under the cover of night. She was no longer as enchanting as before. Indeed, she had stopped being my femme fatale, though she was still rather appetizing. . . . Looking at those familiar blue eyes, I regretted that I had wasted so much time earlier, and without any futile introductions I . . . turned down the lamp and perhaps said something vulgar like 'so things will be more cozy.' . . .

"After she left . . . I did not feel like sleeping. . . . So I got dressed and went out into the street. . . . I hailed a cabby and ordered him to take me for a drive.

"He understood me in his own way and hurriedly . . . took me to some out-of-town dacha. . . . I entered . . . [and saw] a small lamp burning before an icon.

" 'I'll wait for you here,' he told me.

"I went on further . . . [and came across] two half-dressed girls who were sleeping on a wide bed . . . and looking like two huge, motionless fish. One was wearing a dirty corset, its black color catching me by surprise. Whalebones were sticking out all over it. . . . You have never seen such tightly laced-up corsets, nor can you imagine the joy it is to untie them! . . .

"The sleeping girls unwittingly opened their eyes. . . . I sat down and talked with them for a few moments and then got up to leave. They were clearly indignant. . . . [When he saw me] the cabby exclaimed: 'Done already?'

"I returned to my hotel, philosophizing on the vanity of the world. . . . So ended my first love."

[Bunin said:] "At one time I passionately collected folk ditties, sayings, and catchphrases . . . about eleven thousand of them in all. . . . I don't know if all these materials are still intact, but they are in my archives in Moscow."

Bunin used to make up humorous ditties and, pleased with what he done, he would declaim them in a joyous way.

"Ivan Alexeevich," I once said to him, "the last two lines limp along."

He was almost offended.

"But Pushkin, too, had . . . weak rhythms. And your friends rhyme 'whore' with 'floor.' . . . You may not like my poetry, but do not poke fun at my rhythms." . . .

[Bunin said:] "There are no people more deceptive than those with noble grey beards!" . . .

I once told Bunin that I could not get used to the idea that I was spending time with a person who had visited Tolstoy and was friends with Chekhov. For me that was such a long time ago that I could not imagine how one could be a contemporary of both Tolstoy and Hitler. . . .

According to Bunin, Parisian anti-Semites from [the newspaper] *Renaissance*[7] called him "the kike father" because he was friends with Jews. . . . He was not above poking fun at them—but no more than he did Poles, Finns, and Latvians. He sometimes loved to go to a Jewish restaurant; and he was extremely well informed about the many patriarchal Jewish customs which only highly Orthodox Jews practiced. I do not know where he picked up such information.

"Now here is a splendid custom for you," he once told me. "After a holiday meal, the head of a family, a venerable old man with a grey beard and a skullcap, solemnly dips his finger into a glass of wine from Palestine—something I find very strong—and then, with a sharp movement, shakes the drops from his fingers and pronounces: 'May the enemies of Israel perish!' "

He often did that himself, showering colorful curses on political enemies. . . .

[A radio announcer] once happened to be quoting large excerpts from an article by Charles Maurras which, full of anti-Semitic attacks, irritated Bunin greatly.

"People say that Maurras is a very intelligent person. Perhaps this is true, but his brains are muddled. Can he, fully and sincerely, advocate the restoration of the monarchy?[8] Such an idea has become hopelessly obsolete. Never again can there be a monarchy either here or in Germany or even more so in Russia. Every vegetable has its own season. Now one has to be to powerful and cruel; one has to bang his fist on the table and not wax nostalgic over overturned traditions."

He then began singing:

Hey, hey, rotten potato,
Return Nikolai[9] to me. . . .

[Bunin said:] "When I was a kid . . . [formal] education was so dim and dull. . . . For example, take the word 'participle.' . . . What a

[7]*La Renaissance* ("*Vozrozhdenie*"), published in Paris from 1925 until 1940, did have an anti-Semitic bent. In the 1930s it rejoiced openly at the electoral victories of Hitler in Germany and of pro-fascist parties and organizations elsewhere. The publication also supported Mussolini's war in Ethiopia, acclaimed Franco's rebellion, and defended appeasement.

[8]Chalres Maurras was indeed an ardent monarchist.

[9]Bunin is referring to Nikolai II, the last tsar of Russia.

stupid word. Or 'adverb of manner.' Try explaining that to a fourteen-year-old booby. To this day I still do not know what it is, and I have managed to do without it.

"As you know, I never finished grade school, nor did I attend the university, but I turned out no dumber than others and no less educated than they. What counts is not the diploma but the desire to learn. . . .

"The director of my school was a little old man . . . a Baltic German . . . bald, with a pointed skull. To my misfortune, he once came to my mathematics class, a subject I profoundly hated since birth. I was absentmindedly sitting behind my desk, bemoaning my bitter fate and waving my notebook in the air because my neighbor's shoes smelled of tar, and because he was spewing some millet out of his mouth. I was suddenly called to the blackboard. [On it I saw] some triangles . . . which no one needed, along with some mysterious markings on their tops. I was asked several questions . . . but I stood there as if rooted to the spot, silent and understanding nothing.

"The director looked at me in pity and muttered loud enough for everyone to hear:

"'Boy, are you dumb!'

"That was the last straw. I could not stand it anymore. I looked at him with an arrogant air, and, as if suddenly inspired, I answered him in a similarly haughty tone:

"'And you are so smart!'

"The scandal was unimaginable. They wanted to expel me from school. They summoned my father from the village for an explanation. But I was not perturbed. I knew that my father would . . . stand up for me. He was a stubborn and very proud individual, and was much seized by a sense of 'family honor.' Somehow things got taken care of, and I soon left the school on my own volition.[1] . . .

"On my way home that day . . . I happened to come across a group of cabbies [who knew what had happened to me in school]. One of them immediately began pestering me:

"'Hey there, *barin*'s son, buy a math book from me. . . . I just so happen to have plenty of cheap ones right here. . . .'

"Curiously, I stopped . . . but then he lifted up his horse's tail and said:

"'Here's your math book for you!'

---

[1]More accurately, it was the state of the family's finances that caused Bunin to leave school.

"Everyone burst out laughing, and I wanted to die from shame." . . .

[Bunin said:] "At a reception . . . I was introduced to Paderewski. . . .

" 'You probably want to speak Russian with each other,' [my host] said to me.

"But Paderewski kept wincing. Dryly, with stony pride, he extended his hand to me, muttering *'Enchanté'* in a very official tone. Then he immediately vanished into thin air. How he dislikes Russians!" . . .

Bunin once started writing a story with a prostitute as a heroine.

"I began writing it in the first person," he told me. "But because of this, I could not give any details. How awkward for an 'I' to convey details. A pity. The story was very well conceived, but nothing came of it."

[Bunin repeated a line from Tyutchev's verse:] "Happy are those who visit this world in its 'fatal moments.'[2] . . . But during my life, these 'fatal moments' have been painfully many. . . ."

1943
A Bunin scholar, from an article
During the *Stalinshchina*, praising Bunin's talent could have the most unexpected and unfortunate consequences. V. Shalomov told me that in 1943 he was sentenced to ten years . . . for asserting that Bunin was a classic of Russian literature.[3]

1943
Nikolai Teleshov, from his memoirs
Ivan Alexeevich Bunin died [in France] in May 1942. He was 72 years old. . . . Kuprin's return to Russia . . . aroused in Bunin a wish also to return to the homeland, but the sudden outbreak of the war prevented him from doing so. Of this wish there remains only a letter with this clearly expressed desire: "I want to go home!"

January 1, 1943
Ivan Bunin, from his diary
Lord, save us and help us.

[2]Bunin is quoting from Tyutchev's poem "Cicero" (*"Tsitseron"*), published in 1832.
[3]The statement is true.

January 3, 1943
Ivan Bunin, from his diary

Balmont has died.[4] . . . He has disappeared from the world and my life! But I see him so vividly in Moscow, in the Madrid hotel on Tverskaya Street! His hair was reddish and cut like a hedgehog's; blue blood poured through his veins; his neck and cheeks were marked by big abscesses. . . .

January 27, 1943
Vera Muromtseva-Bunina, from a letter to a friend

Today I got up before dawn and left the house in the light of the moon. It was very nice out. I like . . . greeting people in the dark and wishing them a good day. Standing in line at the market, I saw the sun rise. I loaded myself down with meat, macaroni, and all kinds of vegetables . . . [with] as many things as I am allowed to buy. . . .

[A friend] . . . will be performing Russian love songs here in Grasse. I do not know if I will go or not, though I really do want to. I have not heard such songs in a long time. . . .

February 1, 1943
Ivan Bunin, from his diary

Paulus . . . surrendered at Tsaritsyn along with seventeen generals. Tsaritsyn is almost entirely free. Thirteen hundred people are said to have perished.[5] But in Berlin people talk about Hitler's ten years in power.

February 2, 1943
Ivan Bunin, from his diary

The last of the enemy have surrendered. Tsaritsyn has been liberated completely.[6]

---

[4]Balmont died on December 23, 1942, at Noisy-le-Grand, ten miles east of Paris.

[5]In the struggle for Stalingrad, the Russians lost roughly 1.1 million men, and Axis casualties amounted to 800,000 troops. Hitler, furious that Paulus preferred surrender to suicide, said of his general: "Paulus has done an about-face on the threshold of immortality."

[6]On February 3, 1943, Berlin acknowledged the German defeat at Stalingrad but said that "the sacrifices of the Army, the bulwark of a historical European mission, were not in vain." While Germany began a three-day period of national mourning for the casualties of the city, Soviet forces advanced on all fronts in Russia.

February 8, 1943
Ivan Bunin, from his diary

The Russians have taken Kursk and are advancing on Belgorod. Will they break through?[7]

February 17, 1943
Ivan Bunin, from his diary

I had a dream that the top of my head had been broken open.

February 24, 1943
Ivan Bunin, from his diary

I was once intelligent and still am. I am also talented and seized by something divine. Can it be that my life, with its individuality, thoughts, and feelings, has disappeared? No, it cannot be!

Circa March 1943
Nikolai Roshchin, from his memoirs

A mutual friend . . . told me how he once saw Bunin wandering on the slope alongside his home, cutting the grass with scissors to make soup. When I heard this, my heart did a flip-flop, although I myself, like so many others, was so hungry that I could barely move my legs. In deserted Paris, though, I had the good fortune of getting hold of about half a pound of lard, a little sugar, some plums, and a little bag of groats. The entire package easily fit into a coat pocket. I added a pouch of tobacco and an amber cigarette holder, which I happened to buy by chance. I sent these meager gifts to my dear old friend.

March 12, 1943
Ivan Bunin, from a letter to Nikolai Roshchin

You have touched me so terribly deeply with your card and package. I had forgotten how good these things can taste (and the cigarette holder was a delightful addition). . . .

You cannot imagine our life here . . . oppressive monotony, aimlessness, hopelessness, terrible loneliness, boredom, tormenting winter cold, together with incessant vile hunger and the despicable, sickening, arch-beggarly food that has driven Vera Nikolaevna to such thinness. It is simply terrible to look at her. I am also ashamed to look at

---

[7]Kursk is located about 300 miles south of Moscow. The city had been captured by the Germans on November 11, 1941, and was serving as a military base. Belgorod, situated approximately 370 miles from the Russian capital, was retaken by the Russians on February 9.

myself when I get undressed. . . . My health is shattered. The steep hills have worn out this dark grey horse in both a real and figurative sense. . . . I am at the end of my strength; and I have begun to sell one or two of our things. . . . What else is there to tell you?

March 16, 1943
Vera Muromtseva-Bunina, from a letter to Tatyana Loginova-Muravieva
You are right: unfinished letters are the most talented ones, since they do not risk offending the addressee and contain many spontaneous and unexpected things. I have also written such letters to you; but unfortunately you will never receive them. . . .

I am very happy that you have resumed your beloved art. . . . But I do not agree with you when you talk about the "time you have lost." . . . You could not have devoted yourself to art earlier. Such creativity cannot be done halfway . . . and you loved your family way too much . . . to do your own thing. The conditions of your life were ill-suited for the study of art. And as soon as you found yourself in more suitable circumstances, you again took up the brush. But as for "time you lost," this I do not understand.

Moreover, you keep forgetting the wise aphorism of Koz'ma Prutkov:[8] "One cannot embrace the unembraceable." But you have always wanted to do just that, making yourself a nervous wreck . . . and further preventing you from studying science and art. It is always harmful to hurry. . . .

Life is getting expensive . . . and I have to turn my back on many things. At the market, for instance, I pass by the line for grapes and try not to look at them. . . . But sometimes good people dress up our table with a thing or two.

Ian also does not feel very well. He reads a great deal, right now, Plutarch. We are also immersed in Shakespeare's tragedies. It is suitable reading. . . .

March 28, 1943
Ivan Bunin, from his diary
The radio reports that Rachmaninoff has died.[9]

---

[8]Koz'ma Prutkov was a fictitious poet and playwright, the creation of two poets, Alexei Konstantinovich Tolstoy and Alexei Zhemchuzhnikov. The character gained fame throughout Russia for attacking the bureaucratic and mundane aspects of national life in the mid-nineteenth century.

[9]Sergei Rachmaninoff died at age seventy in Beverly Hills, California.

March 29, 1943
Vera Muromtseva-Bunina, from her diary

Rachmaninoff's death casts a pall over everything. He did not live to see the end of the war . . . or the possibility of returning to the homeland.

April 2, 1943
Ivan Bunin, from his diary

I'm continuing to read . . . the diaries of S. A. Tolstaya (two volumes).[1] She is possessed!

I often think about returning home, but will I live that long? And what will I find when I get there?

April 10, 1943
Ivan Bunin, from his diary

I have just finished *1918* by A. Tolstoy.[2] . . . It is vile and almost completely pulplike. He could have done better, after all he himself lived through that year. And he is one to talk about "dens of White Guards!"[3] He himself said that, if the monarchy would be restored, he would kiss the shoes of the tsar and poke out the eyes of the Bolsheviks with a rusty pen. . . . I remember well how Tolstoy spent 1918 . . . we were both in Odessa at that time. He served as an elder to the gambling dens there . . . and all the base things that were going in them.[4]

April 11, 1943
Ivan Bunin, from his diary

Milyukov died (very quietly) on March 31st.

So ends a long—and also a very brief—life.[5] I cannot believe it. . . .

---

[1]The diaries of Sofya Tolstaya were published in Leningrad between the years 1928 and 1932. In truth, both husband and wife were to blame for the bitter wrangling in the later years of their married life.

[2]Tolstoy's *1918* (*Vosemnadtsatyi god*), published in 1928, was the second book in a trilogy entitled *Road to Cavalry* (*Khozhdenie po mukam*), written between the years 1921 and 1940.

[3]White Guards were the monarchist, anti-Revolutionary forces in the Russian civil war of 1918–1922.

[4]See Marullo, *Cursed Days*, 63–64.

[5]Pavel Milyukov was 84 years old when he died at Aix-les-Bains, about 275 miles southeast of Paris.

April 14, 1943
Ivan Bunin, from his diary

Tonight [we heard] a quick, furious bang. I thought [someone] had crashed into the wall. It turned out to be shooting from an English plane. There was an alert.

April 14, 1943
Ivan Bunin, from a letter to Nina Berberova

When you tell me that you are writing "little, slowly, and with difficulty" . . . I get very angry with you. After all, you are at the height of your powers. . . .

P.S. I was very touched by the fact that you sent me a package (even though someone stole it along the way). . . . I even regret the ties that were in it, though they would have gone very poorly with the rags that I wear for pants. . . .

Circa April 18, 1943
Boris Zaitsev, from a letter to Ivan Bunin

Christ has risen. . . .

We have not been home for two weeks. On April 4th [the area where we live in Paris] took a tremendous beating. Fortunately, [our daughter] had invited us to lunch after the Mass and the memorial service for Rachmaninoff. We left the church at 1:30; the bombing began at 2. If we had headed straight for home . . . we would have been hit! We got to our apartment at 4, finding it full of broken glass and refuse. All the windows had been blown out. . . . Again some hand had saved us from catastrophe. . . .

We stayed at [our daughter's] for several says. But then Nina Berberova suggested that we stay with her. That is why I have a different address. She has a huge place, and we are living in a back room which no one needs. Nina spends little time in Paris . . . 1-1/2 days a week. . . . She has been very gracious and hospitable. . . . We have to find a new place in Paris . . . but there are no places just now. . . . So we will live here for a while, though I do not know what we will do. . . .

I found it both terrible and sad to leave our apartment. . . . It may not have been much, but it was mine. . . . What a pity that you are so far away. . . . The only thing in my future is death. . . . But God does not forget us. . . .

April 25, 1943
Ivan Bunin, from a letter to Nadezhda Teffi

How sad that you are not well. I feel all the more sorry for you as I am also experiencing increasing ill-health, weaknesses, hopelessness, the burden of time, and the like. But . . . you are as delightful as ever. What you say is priceless: "Not for nothing do the words 'devil' and 'man' begin with the same letter."[6] . . .

I am very, very grateful for your attention to me and that you are reading my works. I would have to look long and hard to find a reader like you. "My writings and their fate take up my time," as Plutarch wrote in his old age, but to what lengths I have fallen! Just a year ago I could write for eight hours a day without getting tired. . . . But now I cannot write for more than two hours at a stretch. I keep thinking the same thing: Why am I doing this now? Who needs it? And then everything becomes unpleasant and cold.

May 2, 1943
Ivan Bunin, from his diary

I do not recall anything about yesterday other than I was cleaning up things like a madman. We may have to leave here. . . .

May 2, 1943
Ivan Bunin, from a letter to Tatyana Loginova-Muravieva

Do me a favor. If you wish that I continue enriching both Russian and world literature, send me two boxes of [medicine] which is sold where you are but which I cannot find here. . . . Also let me let know how much it costs. . . . For *in no way* will I accept them as a present. . . .

May 4, 1943
Vera Muromtseva-Bunina, from her diary

We cannot leave the house after 11 p.m. . . . or spend the night in any other place but our home . . . or go anywhere without permission . . . . Across from our home someone has built a warehouse for machine guns.

---

[6]The Russian word for "devil" is "*chort*"; for man, "*chelovek*."

May 7, 1943
Ivan Bunin, from his diary
    The Germans are making arrests among the French and are taking hostages. . . .
    The Russians are attacking the Kuban. Yesterday they took back the Krymsk.[7] . . .

May 10, 1943
Vera Muromtseva-Bunina, from a letter to Pyotr Struve
    Ivan Alexeevich is sad, but also rather calm. We are living in a very isolated way. People rarely climb up to visit us on our mountain. Sometimes we go down to the sea . . . so that we can learn something from the local newspapers. Now we spend nights at home and cannot go out after 11 p.m.
    It is very difficult to ride buses because they are so crowded, and if one wants a seat, he or she has to be at the ticket office at 6 a.m. two days in advance. . . . One also has to be the first or second one in line to get a return ticket home. . . . Of course, I do this for Iv[an] Al[exeevich], who goes to Nice once every ten days. I would not have the patience to do such a thing had it not been for all those years that we stood in lines and went through the good "school of patience." I can stand without complaining for an hour and a half. . . .
    People of our circle, we almost never see. . . .
    I read a great deal, though I must read lying down to keep my health. . . .

May 17, 1943
Ivan Bunin, from a letter to Nikolai Roshchin
    The most marvelous airplanes keep flying over us, almost touching the ancient trees in our garden. And below us, just under our gates, Italians sing enchanting songs. . . .

May 23, 1943
Vera Muromtseva-Bunina, from a letter to Pyotr Struve
    During this time, the Third International[8] has been destroyed; it serves it right.

    [7]The Kuban is a river in southern Russia; Krymsk is twenty miles to the south of it.
    [8]The Third International, also known as the Comintern, was founded in March 1918 to advance the cause of revolutionary workers throughout the world. It was disbanded by Stalin in May 1943 to allay Western fears that associated the Third International with "world revolution."

May 26, 1943
Ivan Bunin, from his diary
   [We have received word] that Nilus has died. I am numb.

June 1943
Vera Muromtseva-Bunina, from a letter to the Zaitsevs
   Every day I thank God that we are doing relatively well in such an extremely difficult time. I live much more monotonously than Ian does. But the Kingdom of God is within us. I think that Ian is doing poorly not from external circumstances. He would do poorly anywhere.

July 17, 1943
Vera Muromtseva-Bunina, from her diary
   A representative from the mayor's office notified us . . . that perhaps we will have to be evacuated and that such a thing could happen within a week or two. . . . We were given three hours to pack our things.

July 25, 1943
Ivan Bunin, from his diary
   This morning an Italian quartermaster inspected our house—perhaps to take over several of our rooms. . . .

August 2, 1943
Ivan Bunin, from a letter to Boris Zaitsev
   My one joy is the sun and the beauty surrounding me.

August 4, 1943
Ivan Bunin, from his diary
   I have just learned that Oryol has been taken [by the Russians]. . . . There are large numbers of Germans in Nice. . . . They are badly and slovenly dressed. Their boots weigh tons.

August 9, 1943
Ivan Bunin, from a letter to Nadezhda Teffi
   We literally "hung" on the radio, trying to get Paris—but alas, we got nothing. Static, thunder, and earthquakes! . . .
   As always, I am glad and grateful that you found time to write me another wonderful letter. I am also extremely happy that you are feeling better. As for myself, I am weak all the time. I often have to stop

and catch my breath on the stairs and the like. I take comfort that all of this is from a poor diet; I still do not wish to acknowledge my old age.

I am also both very touched and distressed that you are reading my early works—distressed because one-third of the works that were published in the *Niva* edition [of my writings][9] is one of the most burning wounds in my heart. How much in there is so offensive to me. At that time I just wrote any old way—and then sold it immediately. I was poor and did not care what I published. I was also hitting the bottle on a pretty regular basis.

August 22, 1943
Ivan Bunin, from his diary
   [The doctor] says that my health is not bad.

August 22, 1943
Vera Muromtseva-Bunina, from her diary
   [When the doctor informed Ian about his health] he immediately livened up, made it home with ease, and sat down to lunch with an appetite for the first time in months.

August 27, 1943
Boris Zaitsev, from a letter to Ivan Bunin
   This evening I read aloud [your story] "Saints"[1] to my wife. I was deeply moved, of course, to both laughter and tears. . . . This evening I heard your voice in a dream. You were talking to me from Grasse, giving me your views on events. . . . You had a very clear idea of what was going on, and I agreed with much of what you were saying, though you are more of an optimist than I. . . . I awoke with the feeling that I had just talked with you on the phone. I am not going to make any "secret" conclusions from [our encounter], only that I was left with a feeling of great closeness to you. . . .
   I started to tell my wife [what had happened with you], but then the sirens went off and we had to go downstairs. But there were no attacks. The planes flew over us—they were not German fighter planes but American humanists.
   Many people, though, are losing their lives in the surrounding areas. . . . These days more and more average citizens are being slaughtered.

   [9]Bunin is referring to the first collection of his works, published in 1915.
   [1]Bunin wrote "Saints" ("*Sviatye*") in Capri in 1914.

But we have gotten used to such things. Death is all around us . . . but we are becoming calmer. There is no way out, it is all the same, and the "end" [of the war] is in sight. . . .

[A friend] keeps intending to return to Russia and hopes to wind up around Petersburg. . . . He has hopes (delusions).

I am so grateful to you . . . for being such a splendid writer.

September 2, 1943
Ivan Bunin, from his diary

[A friend] says that the Germans are coming to Grasse.

September 7, 1943
Ivan Bunin, from his diary

We have received a letter . . . saying that Elena Alexandrovna Pushkina (Rozenmeyer) died on August 14 after a second operation. Yet another pathetic human life has disappeared from Nice—and whose life to boot? The granddaughter of Alexander Sergeevich Pushkin! And perhaps only because she, in her poverty, had to drag around heavy things which she sold and resold so as not to die from hunger. . . .

September 8, 1943
Ivan Bunin, from his diary

Tremendous news . . . Italy has . . . surrendered.[2] . . . What will happen to us now?

It is 12:30 a.m. . . . . The Italians are fleeing [Grasse].

September 8, 1943
Vera Muromtseva-Bunina, from her diary

I remember Pushkina as a little girl with her governess in Moscow. . . . Who would have guessed such a fate for her?

She was an intelligent woman, but she also had a difficult disposition. Her views were like those [of other Russians] in Nice: faith in the Germans, hatred for Bolsheviks and Jews. She was very proud of her origins. . . . She often talked about dinners in a Moscow palace where the tsar's family often came and dined. . . .

---

[2]In truth, Italy had signed a secret armistice with the Allies, ending its participation in the war as a member of the Axis on September 3, 1943. The surrender was made public five days later.

September 9, 1943
Ivan Bunin, from his diary

During the night the Italians were disarmed and arrested. . . . The higher-ups had tried to flee, but they were caught on the road to Nice. . . .

September 12, 1943
Ivan Bunin, from a letter to Boris Zaitsev

I am becoming more and more weak, physically and spiritually. . . . But I still have cause for joy if only because you the are one reader who understands every word I write, and who makes me feel that I am not writing in vain. Allow me to ask that you praise me a bit more. . . .

September 17, 1943
Ivan Bunin, from his diary

This evening there was bombing close to us.

September 24, 1943
Vera Muromtseva-Bunina, from her diary

[A friend writes] that Merezhkovsky's grave now has a marker on it—a white marble cross with a copy of Rublyov's icon[3] on it. . . . Gippius said that she is very grateful to the French for the tombstone, and also that she had never been separated from her husband during their fifty years together. She also hopes they will soon be together again. . . .

September 25, 1943
Ivan Bunin, from his diary

The Russians are taking city after city. Now it is *Roslavl and Smolensk.*[4]

September 25, 1943
Boris Zaitsev, from a letter to Ivan Bunin

The smoke [from battle] has been so bad that the Eiffel Tower has been closed. . . . But I am becoming calmer . . . indifferent and resigned. My outlook on the future is so poor . . . but I keep saying, "Thy Will Be Done." Everyone here is very nervous. Every day there are

---

[3]Most likely the icon in question is "The Trinity" ("*Troitsa*"), which Rublyov painted *circa* 1400.

[4]Roslavl and Smolensk are located roughly two hundred miles southwest of Moscow.

alerts, sometimes two of them. The other day the shooting was so bad that I could not sleep. Planes were flying somewhere over Paris to further the bloodletting and suffering. This morning in town I saw a plane that had fallen right on the Louvre store, imagine that! During one bombing, we looked out from the windows of our apartment and saw how two planes were brought down and burst into terrible flame in the clear, azure-blue sky! Pieces of burning wreckage fell all over Paris. . . .

But what will we still have to see? We have to be prepared for anything. As I child I could not bear to see a smashed peasant nose, but now, without hysterics, I "contemplate" how people burn to death in the sky, and how, on earth, tens and hundreds of others perish from bombs: all of them "noncombatants." . . .

This letter is becoming extremely gloomy, but this is how I feel.

But I also find it pleasant to have before me six volumes of your works. . . . What you write about various types of people is very true. . . . I myself belong to those who, relatively speaking, have been spared much in life. . . . I always thank God for His mercy, but I am sad just the same. . . .

P.S. I am very happy that so far you have been left in peace.

October 8, 1943
Ivan Bunin, from a letter to Boris Zaitsev

I am so bored that I just want to sit on my ass and howl. . . .

I dreamt today that I was at a station in Prague . . . and that because I did not have a ticket, I was served only a ham sandwich, though it was huge.

October 23, 1943
Ivan Bunin, from his diary

Lord, save and have mercy on me. Today is my birthday.[5]

October 29, 1943
Ivan Bunin, from his diary

Ekaterinoslav has been taken [by the Russians]. . . . The place now bears the vile name: "Dneprodzerzhinsk."[6]

---

[5]Bunin was seventy-three years old.
[6]Bunin is mistaken here. In 1926 Ekaterinoslav was renamed Dnepropetrovsk, not Dneprodzerzhinsk.

November 1, 1943
Ivan Bunin, from his diary

Today is "All Saints' Day," but tomorrow is a most terrible holiday—"The Feast of All Souls."[7] . . .

November 6, 1943
Ivan Bunin, from his diary

Kiev has been taken.[8]

November 6, 1943
Vera Muromtseva-Bunina, from her diary

Six hundred Russians wearing German uniforms have appeared in Grasse. . . . They sing Russian songs, visit cafés, and loudly talk Russian. . . . Who are they? Where are they from?[9]

November 8, 1943
Ivan Bunin, from a letter to Boris Zaitsev

I am rereading Flaubert's letters. . . . Many of them are *remarkably* splendid. . . . Flaubert was a very special kind of Frenchman. What an exalted and romantic heart! What a noble and genuine mind! That night of love . . . that he spent in Egypt with the former concubine of some pasha![1] Not your typical French adventure in an exotic land! . . .

---

[7]"All Souls' Day" is a feast day celebrated by the Roman Catholic church to commemorate the souls of the faithful departed who are believed to be in purgatory, and who thus need the prayers of believers here on earth to cleanse their souls and to prepare them for the vision of God in heaven.

[8]Kiev had been under German occupation since September 19, 1941. Before the invaders withdrew, they burned most of the ancient buildings in the city.

[9]Most likely these Russians were fighting with German forces to put an end to Stalin and communism in the homeland; or, as will be seen, they were prisoners-of-war who performed menial work for the Germans stationed in France.

[1]Flaubert wrote to a friend on March 13, 1850: "[In Egypt] I walked through the streets . . . letting all the women call me and grab hold of me, taking me by the waist and trying to pull me into their houses. . . . One night we visited Kuchek Hanem . . . a famous courtesan. . . . The party lasted from six to half-past ten, with intermissions for fucking. . . . Later I went downstairs with Kuchek to her room. We lay down on her bed, made of palm branches. . . .

"I fucked her furiously, and her body was covered with sweat. . . . The *coups* were good—the third was especially ferocious, but the last was tender—we told each other many sweet things—and towards the end there was something sad and loving in the way we embraced." See F. Steegmuller, ed., *The Letters of Gustave Flaubert, 1830–1857* (Cambridge, Mass., 1980), 115–117.

November 9, 1943
Ivan Bunin, from a letter to Boris Zaitsev

Today we had a gala dinner in honor of Nobel:[2] macaroni (more accurately, sticky dumplings made from raw, moldy flour) and a bottle of wine that made my mug wince as if the devil himself had made it. I collected and tore up all my cigarette butts, put them together and . . . and smoked them. Now I am sitting and writing. . . .

My dear, dear "old boy," I fervidly remember the nobility, sincerity, and selflessness with which you . . . responded to my good fortune on that day! You were the only one of all my literary colleagues to do so. I will never forget you for this!

November 10, 1943
Boris Zaitsev, from a letter to Ivan Bunin

Exactly ten years ago I read in [the newspapers] . . . that you had received the Nobel Prize. What great joy you gave me then. I have already told you that on that evening [when I heard the news] I was setting up an article on you in typescript. . . . Immediately I made the rounds of all the bistros . . . drinking a cognac in each and repeating in Russian: "Way to go, Swedes!" (Gone are the times when it used to cost next to nothing to do such a thing!) Yes, it was a rare occasion, a holiday. Our twenty years of life here—is the one victory for the emigration (but of course, one which is not very well understood or valued). But now when this emigration is coming to an end—if it has not done so already—I still hail you and embrace you from afar. . . .

In a letter, your wife takes my wife to task for her "hatred." . . . But hatred is necessary, or indifference will be the result. Revenge is one thing . . . but sacred anger—sacred anger at evil—is another. To think that evil "no longer exists" is to close one's eyes to life . . . or to know less about events in the homeland. No, evil is not finished. No, multitudes of henchmen exist and celebrate. . . . You, as the author of *The Cursed Days*, can hardly object to what I am saying. . . .

[A friend] is leaving for Pskov tomorrow to work as a teacher among the people there. . . . He thinks that if he has to die somewhere, it would be better there than here. . . .

By contrast, my wife's niece and two children have just arrived in Prague. . . . About her life in Russia she writes that her "twenty-five-year nightmare is over." . . .

---

[2]It was on this day ten years earlier that Bunin was informed that he had been awarded the Nobel Prize in Literature.

November 11, 1943
Ivan Bunin, from his diary

At eleven o'clock, on a marvelous moonlit night, the bombing . . . began and continued for about forty minutes. . . . A rare, marvelous sight. The house kept shaking.

November 11, 1943
Ivan Bunin, from a letter to Boris Zaitsev

Again there is an alert, that gloomy and pleading howling! This is the third day in a row that it has sounded and always at noon, amidst bright and cold sunlight. But God be with it, though it is somewhat terrifying just the same. I can already hear very loud rumbling and booms. . . .

My book bears the title of the first story in the collection, *Dark Alleys.* All the other pieces also focus on the dark and more often extremely cruel "alleys of love." . . .

November 15, 1943
Ivan Bunin, from a letter to Boris Zaitsev

Today at 11 p.m., in the presence of a wondrous moon, I saw—for the first and God grant the last time—an absolutely wondrously beautiful but also horrific sight—how the enemy was hammering a nearby town. From where we are, we could see absolutely everything.

November 19, 1943
Ivan Bunin, from a letter to Boris Zaitsev

I keep sending my stories to you . . . so that I can share with you my thoughts and days, and . . . that, no matter what will happen to me, there will be duplicates of my work. . . .

November 21, 1943
Ivan Bunin, from a letter to Boris Zaitsev

I was just about to fall asleep, when the alert sounded. I looked out the window and was privy to a storm, and such a downpour and darkness, the likes of which we used to have in the village in Russia, at midnight in late fall—a regular inferno. . . .

November 28, 1943
Boris Zaitsev, from a letter to Ivan Bunin

I have just received your stories . . . and read them right away, with my well-known eagerness. . . . But, old man, I will tell you the truth. . . . All that "between the legs" stuff, and the pants with the split in them, and references to menstruation and to girls' asses, add nothing to your stories. As you know, I am in no way a prude . . . I myself have been a great sinner who "got around" a lot in his time. . . . But literature does not gain anything from such details. . . . I should say that it is hard for me to write this. . . . But I think you understand me. I should also add that I am alluding to *aesthetics*, not morals. . . .

Your letter . . . made me very sad. . . . It seems that we should take pity on each other in a very brotherly way, but that we should also feel sorry . . . for half of humanity. . . .

Gippius is getting very old.[3] She showed me a huge notebook that she had filled up—a life of Merezhkovsky—they were together for 52 years! . . . But such work is good for her; it keeps her busy. . . .

I am glad that you are alive, writing, and interested in things. . . . This is great at your age. I can feel your vigor in every line you write to me. . . .

Late November 1943
Alexander Bakhrakh, from his memoirs
I remember that during the days of the Teheran conference,[4] Bunin said: "Just think of what things have come to! Stalin is flying to Persia; and I shudder that, God forbid, something might happen to him along the way!"

Circa December 1943 and after
A Soviet correspondent, from a later article
One time several strangers appeared at the gates [of Bunin's villa], addressing the people who lived there in Russian. Bunin saw them though a window . . . and, after some hesitation, went out into the yard. He was silent for a moment but looked attentively at their weather-beaten faces. Then he suddenly exclaimed:
"What are you doing here? Are you defending the homeland?"
The strangers blushed and frowned.
"No, sir . . . we are guilty [before our country]! But we will make amends for our guilt, by God, we will make amends!"
Bunin's face softened a little, but he was still very serious and sad.

---

[3]Gippius was seventy-six years old at this time.
[4]The Teheran conference took place between November 20 and December 1, 1943, and centered on the plans of Roosevelt, Stalin, and Churchill for a "second front" in Europe.

"Well, if you are guilty," he said, "tell me what happened."

They began a long and sometimes contradictory conversation in which each explained his own complex predicament. They had been taken captive near Novgorod[5] and had been placed in a camp. . . .

"But do not think, dear sir, that everyone is as downcast as we are. There are upbeat people dying in the camps. They do not sign any papers, and they are immediately taken out and shot. But we did so because we were weak. Three hundred and fourteen of ours have died from hunger. The fascists threw their bodies behind the wire of the camp as if they were beasts. We are an unhappy lot, dear sir! We hate the fascists with a passion, and we have to serve them against our will. But we are only waiting for the right moment to settle accounts with them."

Bunin was silent; he was deeply lost in thought.

The Russian soldiers visited the Bunins every Sunday. The Germans allowed them to stroll outside the camp since they did not know French and could not escape from Grasse. The captives were from Leningrad, Moscow, the Donetsk basin, Byelorussia, and the Ukraine. . . . They were drawn to the writer. They also wanted approval from someone abroad. They all yearned for the homeland. Bunin understood such feelings very well and did not turn them away.

There were several bakers among the captives. . . . Ivan Alexeevich was particularly fond of a certain Andrei . . . who took Bunin aside and promised him with tears in his eyes:

"We are at your service, dear sir. Only give us the chance and we will prove ourselves to you!"

Small loaves and flat cakes were deftly "appropriated" from the bakery. The Bunins received fresh bread every Sunday, and such deliveries helped to sustain the gravely weakened writer. Together Bunin and the prisoners drank tea with the sugar they had brought. The soldiers quietly sang "Moscow," "Katyushka," and the marches of the pilots and the tank crews. Sometimes they cried when they talked about everything they had gone through. When it grew dark, the Bunins carefully closed all the doors and windows of their home, turned on their six-lamp radio receiver, and listened to the Soviet airwaves. Everyone present held their breath as they listened to the military reports. . . .

[5]The Germans captured Novgorod on August 17, 1941. The city is located roughly 120 miles southeast of Saint Petersburg and 300 miles northwest of Moscow.

After the liberation of Grasse, the soldiers . . . returned to Russia.[6]

Circa December 1943 and after
A friend, from his memoirs

In a letter to me, Bunin wrote about his meetings with Soviet prisoners-of-war who worked in a bakery in Grasse. . . . Ivan Alexeevich received them first with some distrust, then with unabashed curiosity. He was pleased to learn that . . . even though these simple country fellows had not read his books, they knew his name and that he was the first Russian writer to receive the Nobel Prize. . . .[7]

December 3, 1943
Ivan Bunin, from a letter to Boris Zaitsev

It is impossible to write without gloves, but I cannot write with them. . . . You should see my hands. Besides the devilish pain . . . of rheumatism, they are all cracked and dirty like those of a chimney sweep. We rarely have hot water. . . . Most of the time it is like ice! . . . Now (it is evening) I decided to stoke the fire in the fireplace; but I have to be careful about that, too, for there is hardly enough wood for the kitchen. A very kind neighbor gave us some pieces as a gift; otherwise we would have perished! . . .

I am glad that you liked . . . my stories. But I think you are wrong as regards your opinion of "menstruation" and of the other "woman's problems" that my female characters have. . . . Think about it. What role do these "everyday feminine things" play in the love life of each of us, particularly in the lives of our own women! As I see it, it is far more tasteless to write about a head cold or that some Ivan Ivanovich blew his nose loudly into a checkered handkerchief. . . .

---

[6]Later letters by Zurov and Muromtseva-Bunina repeat many of the details of the interviewer's story, most notably the prisoners' shame at being captured by the Germans. In a missive to Baboreko, written on April 2, 1962, Zurov adds: "Was it dangerous [for the Bunins to be on such friendly terms with the prisoners]? Yes it was, for three hundred and fifty meters from our villa was the headquarters for German transport in the area. The place was guarded by soldiers with hand grenades and automatic rifles. . . ." See Baboreko, 302.

It should be noted here that many Soviet prisoners-of-war resisted repatriation to the homeland, their reasons being a distaste for Stalin's dictatorship, the material advantages of the West; and/or a history of prior mistreatment under the Soviet system. They also feared official reprisal for collaboration with the Nazis; for surrender to the enemy (which Soviet pronouncements equated with treason); and simply for exposure to the West. Such qualms were well founded. The 5.2 million repatriates to Soviet Russia were often welcomed with execution, forced labor, renewed military service, or strict surveillance.

[7]Such an assertion is somewhat surprising, since the Soviet government never acknowledged Bunin's award in any public way.

You say that "such details add nothing to literature" and that "they do nothing to expand upon the matter at hand." But I contend that it is not a matter of "gaining" or "expanding upon" anything . . . especially as regards mercenary goals. Simply put, I wished to write precisely about things that are truly "fatal." . . .

Must one write only things like: "their lips came together in a passionate kiss"? Perhaps, things "between the legs" are excessive. . . . But I repeat: they correspond fully to the bitterness of my characters. . . .

Thank you for writing about Zinaida [Gippius]. I think of her often. It is a terrible thing! Fifty-two years together (with Merezhkovsky)! And now she is alone! God knows what she will write about him. [There will be] thousands of thoughts along with knives in the backs of many, many people; but you are right in that such an undertaking will be her salvation.

December 3, 1943
Boris Zaitsev, from a letter to Ivan Bunin
These days the public is against artists, art, and poetry. The fashionable interest in Russian things is fleeting and will not amount to anything. And Comrade Stalin has turned out to be our ally!

December 10, 1943
Ivan Bunin, from his diary
Ten years ago I almost became a millionaire. I remember the banquet and the Crown Prince. Today for dinner, each of us had a bowl of thin cabbage soup and three boiled potatoes. . . .

December 18, 1943
Ivan Bunin, from his diary
On the radio today I heard Provence music and the singing of girls. Again I think how quickly their youth will pass, that they will soon wither and become sick, and that they will then face death and old age. . . . People have such unhappy lives! No one has yet to write about such a thing as he should!

December 30, 1943
Boris Zaitsev, from a letter to Ivan Bunin
Exactly twenty years ago tomorrow I came to Paris, and on that very same evening I visited your home. . . . Yes, an entire span of life

has passed by. Personally speaking, life too has passed by. Should we prepare for the finale? Keep us safe, O Lord.

Ivan, dear one, return [to Paris]! All your friends are here. . . . You still have your apartment. And it is easier to live here. We are eating more or less well, and the heating situation continues to improve. Generally speaking, conditions here are incomparably better than those in the south. . . . [Other people] very much want you to come back here. "We will take care of him," they say. "He will have everything he wants; he will not want for a thing." I also make such promises to you. . . .

✳ 1944 ✳

Circa 1944
Alexander Bakhrakh, from his memoirs
Bunin became especially gloomy when the newscasters began to mention places that were familiar to him: Elets, Oryol, Tula. But he fell into a genuine fury when a sign appeared on a small tree . . . next to "Jeanette": a picture of a skull and the inscription: "Beware—this forest has been mined."

"Now they have really gone crazy," he said indignantly, "to mine *our* forest; this is truly pathological."

So the time went . . . slowly, sullenly, and . . . monotonously. Ivan Alexeevich stopped going to Nice or Cannes. There was no more reason for him to go; all his acquaintances were no longer there.

January 1, 1944
Ivan Bunin, from his diary
Lord, save and protect us. . . .

I have been doing nothing other than to worry about things that are beyond my control.

January 2, 1944
Ivan Bunin, from his diary
There were two alerts today. After the second, there was a loud thundering somewhere, as well as smoke behind Cannes.

Now there is another alert!

January 3, 1944
Ivan Bunin, from his diary

Yesterday the Russians took back Novgorod, Volynsk, and Olevsk.[8]

Terrible days are just ahead!

January 6, 1944
Ivan Bunin, from his diary

We "celebrated" Russian Christmas Eve ... with a mushroom soup made with small pieces of lard, cutlets, and mashed potatoes!

At midnight we took a walk in the garden. From the road we heard cries and saw the bright lights of flashlights. A patrol was out. We hurried back into the house.

January 7, 1944
Ivan Bunin, from his diary

Today is our Christmas. There were two alerts today.

I have been reading Zoshchenko's 1937 stories. They are monotonous and poor. The only tolerable thing about them is the idea that life in Russia is superficial and vulgar. Not for nothing does Zoshchenko use such a wretched, half-savage language, for this is the tongue of ... what Russia has become.[9]

January 8, 1944
Ivan Bunin, from his diary

All of Europe is being destroyed savagely. The last "great war" was absolutely trifling by comparison. Beyond the fact that Germany will be shorn of its skin, the country has already lost three-quarters of its strongest citizens.[1] And what will be the fate of Bulgaria, Hungary, Rumania, and unhappy Italy, all of whom have been gouged by this German bull!

---

[8]Olevsk is northwest of Kiev, ten miles from the 1939 frontier between Poland and the Soviet Union.
[9]Bunin is referring to Zoshchenko's use of *skaz*, i.e., "the oral folk narrative" of Russian workers and peasants.
[1]German casualties during the war amounted to more than 6 million, of which 3.2 million were members of the armed forces.

January 17, 1944
Ivan Bunin, from his diary

The war continues to drag on without any end in sight! Good Lord, when will something decisive happen?[2]

January 18, 1944
Ivan Bunin, from his diary

We live, chewing our cud, but our situation is terrible. Alerts now sound three times a day, almost without stop.

January 19, 1944
Ivan Bunin, from his diary

[The Russians] have retaken . . . Peterhof[3] . . . a huge success. But about 20,000 men have been killed.

January 20, 1944
Ivan Bunin, from his diary

[The Russians] have taken Novgorod. . . .

Almost every morning, as soon as I open my eyes, I am filled with sadness—my aimlessness, the *finality of everything* for me. I have looked through my notes on bygone Russia. I keep thinking: if only I can live that long, if only I can get back to Russia! But why? Everyone who has survived there is old . . . the cemetery of everything that once lived.

January 22, 1944
Boris Zaitsev, from a letter to Ivan Bunin

Generally speaking, it is rather quiet. . . . No one is writing. . . .

January 31, 1944
Ivan Bunin, from his diary

The peasant in my story "Spring Evening"[4] truly said it well when he noted: "The Good Lord gives us life, but all kinds of reptiles take it away."

---

[2]Bunin, of course, is overlooking the stunning successes of Soviet forces on the Eastern Front, as well as the ongoing victories of the Allies in Italy.

[3]Peterhof (also known as Petrodvorets) is the site of Peter the Great's Summer Palace, and is located twenty-four miles west of Saint Petersburg.

[4]Bunin wrote "Spring Evening" ("*Vesenii vecher*") at Capri on January 31, 1914.

Circa early February 1944
Ivan Bunin, from a letter to Boris Zaitsev

Alerts now sound three times a day. [The authorities] want to evacuate us . . . but where? but where? I do not have many more years to live; so every day I write one story and drink five bottles of wine.

February 2, 1944
Ivan Bunin, from a letter to the Zaitsevs

I was still a young man when I used to visit Capri.[5] I would drink five bottles a wine and write a story every day. . . .

February 8, 1944
Ivan Bunin, from his diary

The Russians have taken Nikopol[6] and a great amount of war materiel. They have also taken about 2,000 of the enemy captive, and killed about 15,000 more. . . .

February 12, 1944
Boris Zaitsev, from a letter to Ivan Bunin

Your poetry is enjoying great success. I read it to [a friend]—and her eyes became very moist. The same thing happened to [two other people]. . . .

I am tired of the alerts. They occur almost every day. . . . And when they do happen, we have to run down to the first floor. (We live on the seventh with the sky *right* above us.) Like everyone else, we do not have *the slightest idea of what will happen next.* But, at sixty-four years old, I do not think about such things. . . .

February 15, 1944
Ivan Bunin, from his diary

The Germans have taken two of our rooms upstairs. Today is the first day they have occupied *all* of the Maritime Alps.

February 23, 1944
Ivan Bunin, from a letter to Nadezhda Teffi

The Zaistevs and others criticize me for the fact that [in *Dark Alleys*] I decided to mention (only mention!) women's monthly

---

[5]Bunin was in his early forties at that time.
[6]Nikopol is situated approximately two hundred miles northeast of Odessa.

illness. . . . Why, for example, can one describe or paint a picture of birth, but one cannot say a word about [menstruation], even though the Bible talks about it. (Rachael says to Lavan: "Excuse me, I cannot get up, for I have my usual feminine woes.")[7]

I have another question: Why can artists and sculptors describe the feminine body . . . and all kinds of satyrs and fauns with extreme "naturalness," but we writers cannot? . . .

February 25, 1944
Boris Zaitsev, from a letter to Ivan Bunin

I know that you cannot stand Dostoevsky, but I will not yield to anyone, even you, in my view that he is a tremendous writer (even though I personally find him to be absolutely alien to my tastes). After all, I unconsciously learned [my craft] from Turgenev, Chekhov, and you, and nothing from him. But that does not mean that Dostoevsky is a bad or poor writer. . . .

March 1, 1944
Ivan Bunin, from a letter to a friend

About two weeks ago we received a package from the Swedish Red Cross. What a pity that its contents will soon disappear.

We almost cried from happiness over the sausage and butter and canned fish.

March 4, 1944
Vera Muromtseva-Bunina, from her diary

We have learned that Pyotr Struve has died. I cannot be at peace. . . .

So far we have not been summoned to the police station.

March 6, 1944
Ivan Bunin, from a letter to Boris Zaitsev

I am dead from exhaustion. We have been informed that all foreigners will be evacuated from Grasse. So for the past week, and without any rest at all, I have been working twelve hours a day, straightening up the house and packing my suitcases with the most necessary items.

I have sent off requests and entreaties everywhere, asking that our

[7]The citation is from Genesis 31:35.

exile be postponed, if only for a few days. But as we do not know what will come of all this, we are living out our days in anxious expectation. People tell us that it is not easy to return to Paris, that we need permission from the Germans. But where else will we go, if we are, in fact, chased out of Grasse. The terror and uncertainty are horrible! . . .

When I fall into bed after a hellish day of work, I smoke one of my last cigarettes and read a few words from a wonderful new translation of *A Thousand and One Nights*.[8] . . . Here is a wonderful line from it: "Even Abraham said to Sarah: 'Woman is created round and firm like a rib.' "

March 9, 1944
Boris Zaitsev, from a letter to Ivan Bunin
Tomorrow you will receive a letter . . . from the Office for Russian Emigré Affairs here in Paris . . . to be given to the German authorities in Grasse who *will approve* your petition to return to Paris. They will take into account your fame, age, and the fact that you have an apartment in the city. . . .

March 12, 1944
Vera Muromtseva-Bunina, from a letter to a friend
If we have to leave Grasse, we hope to wind up in Paris and settle somewhere in a village nearby. We already have an invitation there.[9] But travel there terrifies us. God knows what is going on in the trains. . . .

At present everything has been packed up, but we do not want to leave. . . . What a strange feeling! Not to know what will happen to you tomorrow.

March 27, 1944
Boris Zaitsev, from a letter to Ivan Bunin
The other day . . . I saw a translation of your works in a bookstore . . . in a wonderful morocco binding . . . and costing 250 francs! Your works were much cheaper earlier. . . .

---

[8]*A Thousand and One Nights*, also known as *The Entertainment of Arabian Nights*, is a collection of oriental stories of uncertain authorship and date, which includes the tales of such well-known figures as Aladdin, Ali Baba, and Sinbad the Sailor. Earliest references to the work date back to the mid-tenth century; its stories draw from the cultures of India, Iran, Iraq, Egypt, Turkey, and possibly Greece.
[9]Nina Berberova had invited the Bunins to live with her in Longchêne.

March 30, 1944
Ivan Bunin, from a letter to Boris Zaitsev

It is simply terrible how Cannes, this innocent little city, has been turned into a fort. There are no direct paths or routes anywhere. One keeps going around in circles; not one street leads to the embankment. Also, the ends of all the streets are barricaded with giant concrete posts held together with rusty barbed wire. . . .

This morning I read that "all of Grasse might be evacuated. . . ." So we continue to sit "on our suitcases," without the slightest idea of what will happen tomorrow.

April 27, 1944
Vera Muromtseva-Bunina, from a letter to Tatyana Loginova-Muravieva

We keep living "out of our suitcases." . . . Ian has again started to write a little. . . . Thank God, I was able to attend church twice during Holy Week. . . . Keep us safe, O Lord. . . .

May 2, 1944
Vera Muromtseva-Bunina, from a letter to Tatyana Loginova-Muravieva

We have been very distressed as of late. Too many bombs have been falling everywhere. People in Paris are writing to us about terrible things.

In Grasse . . . signs are again being posted as to the number of people that can be accommodated in one or another bomb shelter. . . .

There are many Russian soldiers here right now . . . and their language is good and unspoiled. They are all smart-looking and healthy. . . .

Several times now I have stayed in bed for twelve hours at a clip . . . and this helped me from becoming tired. . . .

[As regards the bombings in Paris] one newspaper was correct in reporting that "it has been a night of Apocalypse!" . . .

May 4, 1944
Boris Zaitsev, from a letter to Ivan Bunin

On May 1st, we had an air alert. And bombing every evening at midnight—if not Paris itself, then the surroundings close to it. . . . Helpless people are being killed.

May 8, 1944
Ivan Bunin, from his diary

It is 1 a.m. I got up from the table. I still have to finish [writing] the last few pages for [my story] "The First Monday in Lent."[1] I turned off the light and opened the window to ventilate the room. The evening was perfectly still. There was a full moon out, the most delicate fog had enveloped the entire valley, and the sea had a muted rose-colored shine. Everything there was quiet. The leaves of the trees were young, soft, and fresh; here and there one could hear the trilling of the first nightingales. . . . O God, let me continue my lonely, poor life to enjoy this beauty and my work!

May 10, 1944
Ivan Bunin, from a letter to Nina Berberova
     I was very touched and grateful for your invitation [to join you at Longchêne]; but I still have not lost hope that we will be allowed to remain here [in Grasse]. But if we have to leave, and if we cannot find a place in Paris, we will stay with you, but only for a short period of time.

May 19, 1944
Ivan Bunin, from a letter to Nadezhda Teffi
     What kind of "teacher" am I? Especially for someone like yourself who has sung like a nightingale all your life, and who continues to do so without even noticing the radiance that shines from your soul? . . .
     It seems . . . that all we do is exchange compliments. . . . You value a thing or two in me, and I—I repeat and swear to God—have always been in awe of you. I have never met anyone like you in my life. What genuine happiness God has given me to know you! But enough . . . all the more since it is 2 a.m. and the night is pitch-dark, cursed . . . and marked by a deathly silence broken only by the sound of machine guns.
     You praised me in your last letter . . . but then you fell silent for some time, and to tell you the truth I was afraid that you did not like my stories at all, and that you had written such kind words only to be nice to me. Now you praise me again . . . and I, like a schoolboy, proud, ambitious, and vile . . . blushed from joy and pulled out my notebook to read my things again. . . .
     The stories [in *Dark Alleys*] have absolutely nothing to do with the present time. Perhaps they have an eternal quality, akin to what happened during the plagues of Egypt, and about those things that the uncomparable He spoke of, and whose shoes I would kiss gladly. . . .

---

[1]Bunin finished "The First Monday in Lent" ("*Chistyi ponedel'nik*") on May 12, 1944.

May 19, 1944
Nadezhda Teffi, from a letter to Ivan Bunin

When I think of the remarkable stories in your *Dark Alleys*, I often recall a scene from our provincial life. One time when I visiting in the area around Novgorod, I came across a customs officer who was looking though an album. Suddenly he smirked and handed the album over to a friend of his. Both began looking . . . at a picture of Canova's famous sculpture, "Cupid Awakening Psyche."[2] . . . When I approached, the officer said, "Young ladies should not see such a thing!" and slammed the album shut. Many people relate to your new stories in a similar way. . . .

May 20, 1944
Boris Zaitsev, from a letter to Ivan Bunin

Your "First Monday in Lent" is simply charming. . . . Moscow, olden times, and their undying beauty, is written with such marvelous liveliness and spiritual freshness. It is as if you are exactly thirty years old! Yes, without any sluggishness or apathy. Good for you!

"Madrid" and "A Second Coffeepot"[3] are also very sweet; the girls in it are drawn with such tenderness. Generally speaking, these pieces are "philanthropic" stories. Ivan, you have turned out to be a humanist in your old age, though earlier I loved it when you sometimes wrote exposés of life. Aldanov rates your "Loopy Ears" highest of all.[4] . . . But such people never understood you as a poet, one who praises God for creation. . . .

The siren has just sounded, the streets are deserted, and little boys are running from school into the basement of our building.

May 21, 1944
Boris Zaitsev, from a letter to Ivan Bunin

Again there are sirens and shootings. Will I finish writing to you this time? . . .

---

[2]Canova sculpted "Cupid and Psyche" in 1793. The officer and his friend were not alone in their chagrin over the erotic qualities of the work. In fact, "Cupid and Psyche" exerted an extraordinary influence on poets and writers throughout the nineteenth century. The poet Wordsworth withdrew from the sculpture in outrage, exclaiming, "Devils!" Flaubert, though, responded to the work differently. After kissing Psyche's armpit, foot, head, and face, he exclaimed: "Forgive me, but it was my first sensual kiss in a very long time. Indeed, it was something more, for I was kissing beauty itself." For more on Canova's "Cupid and Psyche," see G. Pavanello and G. Romanelli, eds., *Canova* (Venice, 1992), 234–241.
[3]Bunin wrote "Madrid" on April 26, 1944, and "A Second Coffeepot" (*"Vtoroi kofeinik"*) four days later.
[4]Bunin's "Loopy Ears" (*"Petlistye ushi"*) appeared in 1916.

Zinaida [Gippius] has taken ill. Something like a stroke.[5] She can barely move her arm and leg. No one is allowed to see her.

May 25, 1944
Ivan Bunin, from a letter to Boris Zaitsev

Less than thirty minutes after the sirens had sounded, [we heard] the incessant rumbling thunder of bombs tearing through the entire embankment around Nice. I am sitting here like a helpless idiot, knowing that at any minute, two or three of these missiles can fly over us down to the valley below. . . . But God is with us. From our heights we can see the cathedral in the deep and far-off distance below. We can also see the marble statue of the Mother of God on its portal. Whenever we enter this church, we also see the charming marble statue of little Thérèse, and I always pray to both of them, wanting passionately to believe in their help and protection.

"An artist needs praise like a violin bow needs resin." It seems that I have already told you such a thing. Again, I repeat how much you comforted me when you told me that "people do not understand that you are a poet who praises all of God's creation" . . . or that I write "stories filled with love for humankind." . . . In fact, you said it so well that sometimes when I write . . . I smile a kind smile and feel something akin to the onset of tender, happy tears. Thank you, thank you, my dear friend. How intelligent you are! . . .

Again I hear the siren and again all of Grasse, the embankment, and our home shake and tremble with the thunder of bombs. I also see green fires breaking out between Nice and Antibes. . . . Again also, I hear a terrible thunder, and I see fire near the port or station in Cannes. I try to write, but for the past two hours I keep running to the windows and get nothing done. . . .

P.S. Zinaida's condition is serious. If she dies, it will be very heavy in my soul. . . .

May 30, 1944
Vera Muromtseva-Bunina, from a letter to Tatyana Loginova-Muravieva

Frequent air alerts have begun, and Ian will not let me leave the house.

[5]In late March 1944, Gippius complained of creeping paralysis. Doctors diagnosed sclerosis in several areas of her brain; but two months later, Gippius had recovered so completely that she was again able to write.

June 8, 1944
Vera Muromtseva-Bunina, from a letter to Tatyana Loginova-Muravieva
We are prepared for anything. The times are such that there is only one thing one can do—pray. . . .

June 19, 1944
Boris Zaitsev, from a letter to Ivan Bunin
If you want to keep your "archive" with me, I will be very happy to do so. I will do everything possible to keep your things safe. . . . I also passed on your directives to Teffi that she keep a second group of things with her. . . .

A notice has now appeared on the doors of our building. As we are now in a *zone très dangereuse*, the mayor of the city has ordered women, children, and old people to leave from here if they can. . . . It seems as though the English have announced that they will be bombing bridges near us. . . . Maybe it is all nonsense. In September they threatened to blow up [a number of places] . . . but nothing happened. Maybe they are doing this on purpose, so as to upset people and incite anarchy. . . .

The last few days have been quiet—God, let it last!—but the alerts have been endless. During the nights, too. Everywhere one sees explosions of shrapnel in the sky, downed planes, and other charming items.

June 21, 1944
Ivan Bunin, from his diary
Vyborg has been captured.[6]
On this night three years ago, Hitler, as he loved to say, "fell like lightning" . . . on Russia. This is something he should not have done!

June 22, 1944
Ivan Bunin, from his diary
We have had an alert. . . . There was something red and huge over by Nice, with flashes here and there.
It is 1 a.m, but I feel like writing.

June 27, 1944
Ivan Bunin, from his diary
Vitebsk, Zhlobin[7] . . . and *Odessa* have been taken. I am so happy. How everything has been turned around!

---

[6] Vyborg is in southern Finland, roughly eighty miles northwest of Saint Petersburg.
[7] Vitebsk and Zhlobin are located in Belarus, some 300 miles southwest of Moscow.

June 28, 1944
Ivan Bunin, from his diary

[The doctor] has examined me. He found nothing wrong, and I am in better shape now than I was last year. My heart is good; the same thing can be said for my blood pressure.

July 1, 1944
Ivan Bunin, from his diary

All day long the Germans have staged a noisy celebration [in a neighboring villa]. Germans in Grasse! And for some reason, *I* am in the middle of all this!

July 11, 1944
Ivan Bunin, from a letter to Boris Zaitsev

Again, we worry about you, since today both the radio and newspapers report that the "region around Paris" is again taking a beating. . . . We hope that God will spare you. We have alerts here [in Grasse], but so far, God preserve us, the city has been left untouched. But we keep living in the same boring, prisonlike way because we are not allowed to walk or drive anywhere. . . .

July 14, 1944
Ivan Bunin, from a letter to Boris Zaitsev

The ribbon on our typewriter is fading fast, and there is only a little carbon paper left. . . .

July 15, 1944
Boris Zaitsev, from a letter to Ivan Bunin

Today we had a burial service for Father Sergei Bulgakov. . . .

We do not go anywhere these days. . . . We cannot. Of course, I do not have much longer to live, and I do not see anything good ahead. It is not pleasant always to take cover from bombs, airplanes, and bullets. You cannot imagine what is taking place on the roads outside Paris! . . .

When Vitebsk fell to the Russians on June 26, 1944, Stalin ordered salvos from Moscow's 224 guns to mark the first major victory of the summer offensive. Stalin had additional cause to rejoice: Vitebsk was a key stronghold which Hitler had ordered to be defended at all costs to avoid the fall of Minsk in the west.

July 22, 1944
Ivan Bunin, from his diary

I have had a dream about my death. It was twilight, there was a church, and I was choosing my grave. . . .

I am rereading *The Death of Ivan Ilyich*. The end is incomprehensible. Everyone is lying, except Ivan Ilyich himself. . . . Everything around him is genuine, but nothing is taken from life. . . .

July 23, 1944
Ivan Bunin, from his diary

Pskov has been taken. *All* of Russia has now been liberated.[8] Truly it has been a gigantic undertaking! . . .

The Milky Way is smoky and phosphorous, as if made from jelly. . . . There are millions and millions of stars in the sky!

July 25, 1944
Vera Muromtseva-Bunina, from a letter to Tatyana Loginova-Muravieva

Air alerts have been occurring in the morning; so we do not go anywhere. . . .

July 25, 1944
Boris Zaitsev, from a letter to Ivan Bunin

Your last letter upset us terribly. What kind of life have you been living? [It sounds like] a total disaster. Is there really no way that you can escape from it? I have never heard anything like it. You need peace, love, and affection. . . . I do not want to continue this missive, as I am feeling irritated and helpless. What I can do for you? . . .

Do not concern yourself over the shooting going on around us in Paris. So far it is nothing bad. We have grown so used to the alerts . . . that we are even indifferent to them. . . . They have just sounded the "all-clear," though right before it there was a terrible crackling: fighter planes sounded as though "they had broken from a chain." . . .

The more we head into fall, the more we feel our cavelike existence. . . . We are as if in jail, living only on bread and water. . . . We do not even want to think about the winter. To tell the truth, we think little these days. But I am ready for anything: if I get sick, I get sick; if I die, I die. Least of all do I want to fall into the paws of these bastards—but [if I were in Russia] I would soon die just the same. . . .

---

[8]Pskov was the last Russian city held by the Germans.

Early August 1944
Vera Muromtseva-Bunina, from a letter to Boris Zaitsev

Please tell Father Kiprian that I am very close to everything that he wrote to Ian regarding the transformation of the flesh. . . . Things that I had felt vaguely before I read his letter now burst into light as I reread his lines. From childhood on, my favorite holiday was that of the Transfiguration [of the Lord],[9] perhaps because it was during that time that the apple and pear trees came into bloom. . . .

When I was in the Holy Land, I was far from any religious consciousness. But the surroundings there made such an impression on me that my soul was filled with faith. I often lived with childhood religious feelings, a faith that was tied to my father who was a great believer, and who, when I was small, imparted so much to me as regards belief in God. But alas! I fell under the sway of "great minds"; and for many years I abandoned the most important things in life, things for which we had been sent into this incomprehensible world. But like an onion skin, I have been shedding everything that is alien to life. I am beginning to feel like a child again, now that I have found things that I had lost, and have regained the same fondness for the Feast of the Transformation that I had had when I was an eight-year-old girl. . . . Now suddenly, in my loneliness, I receive a letter on this theme. Thank Father Kiprian for me. . . .

August 1, 1944
Ivan Bunin, from his diary

Today I talked to a German and also to a Russian captive, a "student," both of whom were standing guard. . . . When I said goodbye, the German shook my hand firmly.

August 3, 1944
Ivan Bunin, from his diary

There have been five alerts a day. . . .

Yesterday Churchill said the war would be over no later than October. We will see.

[9]The Transfiguration of the Lord, celebrated on August 6, commemorates Christ's revelation of his divinity to the Apostles Peter, James, and John on Mount Tabor. See Matthew 17:1–9.

August 5, 1944
Ivan Bunin, from a letter to Boris Zaitsev

My Vera is so weak, pale, and terribly thin. But sometimes she is so unusually charming and splendid that I am ready to do anything in the world for her. But I am not good for anything. . . .

August 12, 1944
Ivan Bunin, from his diary

There were two alerts today. . . . For the first time I am truly fearful. The strikes are getting very close . . . and right now several places are on fire.

August 15, 1944
Ivan Bunin, from his diary

I slept fitfully, in an anxious frame of mind. I kept hearing planes all night long. Starting at 7 a.m. I heard horrifying booms beyond the Esterel that lasted into the afternoon. At 1 p.m. the radio announced that the Allies had landed [close by].[1] I cannot describe my excitement.

August 15, 1944
Alexander Bakhrakh, from his memoirs

One fine morning . . . the sirens began howling in a melancholy way. There was nothing particularly strange about such a thing. Air-raid alerts were quite common, and one could sometimes see the black dot of a bomber in the skies. We usually did not have to wait long for the all-clear signal.

This time, though, something was amiss. An hour passed, then a second, and a third, but there was no all-clear signal. . . . Bunin was getting more and more upset. Whenever the sirens sounded, he put on his tattered robe, went out into the garden, and "sat out the siege" in a boxlike stall. . . . This stall could barely be seen, and, for Bunin, it was a type of "bunker," a genuine bomb shelter. . . . But today he ran from the stall . . . and into the dining room, trying to find out from the radio what had happened.

But the radio had gone dead. Only by chance did he learn later that on that afternoon the air-raid alert had signaled that the Allies had landed on the beaches of the Mediterranean . . . about a hundred kilometers from Grasse.

---

[1] On August 15, 1944, American and French forces landed near Toulon and Cannes in southern France.

We spent the next few days in nervous anticipation. We had no real information, only the most contradictory rumors. . . .

Sometimes we could hear artillery firing or see small clouds of smoke rising over the islands near Cannes. But for Bunin this was not enough. He was on the verge of despair because he thought the offensive was moving too slowly. "You see, there is nothing to wait for, all has perished," he would say angrily.

August 18, 1944
Ivan Bunin, from his diary
The Allies have taken [an area] near Cannes. I keep making out six ships out on the sea. And every so often, I hear the dull roar of gunfire.

August 24, 1944
Ivan Bunin, from his memoirs
At dawn today the Americans entered Grasse. . . . Freedom after so many years of servitude! . . .

In the afternoon I took a walk into town. . . . The rejoicing was indescribable. . . .

August 24, 1944
Vera Muromtseva-Bunina, from her diary
I was in town today. There was excitement everywhere. Everyone was dressed up, with national ribbons, bows, and belts. Everyone was happy. . . . Where the police used to be in the mayor's office, women, who had cooperated with the Germans, were getting their hair shorn and made to look like idiots. People were also saying that they would be led out and shown to the crowd. . . .

I went to the cathedral to pray to Theresa the Little Flower, to thank her for saving us from all kinds of misfortune.

The barber shop has been blown to smithereens. For the first time I saw what a pogrom was like.[2] The place where I get my hats . . . all the windows were broken and there was nothing left in the store. Its owners had escaped with the Germans. They were Italians.

---

[2] Muromtseva-Bunina's allegation is not true; she had also seen pogroms in Odessa in 1919.

August 24, 1944
Alexander Bakhrakh, from his memoirs

Finally that joyous day for which we had been waiting more than four years—the dawn of August 24th. The Germans had retreated from Grasse without any resistance. We could see the last of them going past our villa . . . in full disarray. Several hours later the first detachments of the Canadian Air Force were landing . . . near the beachheads.

August 25, 1944
Ivan Bunin, from his diary

At 2 p.m. today the radio triumphantly announced that five hundred thousand partisans, together with the population of the city, *had liberated Paris.*

This evening the Germans began blowing up something (shells?) in Grasse. Then, on the hills nearby, there was firing in a small forest— crackling, firing, the launchings of flares—all this lasted for an hour and a half. The twilight was hazy, and we looked for a very long time at this terrible and glorious sight with sinking hearts. . . . But it is clear that the Germans are fleeing from Grasse!

Today I again went into town. There was drinking everywhere . . . dances, music. . . . All the faces of the people had become transformed with joy. Suddenly they all seemed more attractive. I was struck dumb when . . . having entered a tavern for a double shot of cognac to "celebrate the liberation," the owner announced that "today drinks were on the house." . . .

But I did see something that made me despair—our wayward girls with the Americans. . . .

"Fedya," one of the Russian soldiers who used to visit me, escaped from the Germans two days before the Americans arrived. He hid in the bushes, not far from the bakery where he worked.

August 27, 1944
Vera Muromtseva-Bunina, from her diary

[A friend] saw how the crowd was marching through the streets those women who had allegedly gotten mixed up with the Germans. They were wearing only pants and bibs . . . and were being beaten on the heads with rifles. Thank God, the American authorities have forbidden public mockings. . . .

On the radio one can hear the excitement in Paris. People are shouting and singing the Marseillaise. . . . But all of Paris is in ruins. . . .

August 29, 1944
Vera Muromtseva-Bunina, from her diary
Ian said: "If the Germans had occupied Moscow and Petersburg, and if they had asked me to go there and given me the best of everything, I would have refused. I could not see Moscow occupied by Germans, or how they would run things there. I hate many things about Russia and the Russian people, but there are also many things that I love, respect, and hold sacred. But for foreigners to give the orders there—no, this is something I could not endure! . . ."

August 31, 1944
Ivan Bunin, from his diary
I am rereading Gogol—his "Rome" and "The Portrait." His "word-weaving" and endless use of periods are intolerable. "The Portrait" is something that is absolutely dead, cerebral. "The Nose" is pathologically repulsive.[3] Imagine! A nose in hot bread! And one could choke on the literary affection and bombast in "Rome." . . .

Will I get to Rome one more time before I die? Dear Lord, if only I could!

September 9, 1944
Vera Muromtseva-Bunina, from her diary
Our soldiers [from Russia]—15 of them in all—have been taken away by truck. . . . At four this afternoon they came by our house. . . . [A friend] had given them three bottles of wine. When I got there, they were already back on the truck, in high and heady spirits. I made the sign of the cross over them. . . .

September 21, 1944
Ivan Bunin, from a letter to Boris Zaitsev
It is impossible to describe everything that has gone on in this town and in our souls! Yes, over the past few years I knew that Germany would perish. It has done so, but it also has covered all of Europe in blood!

---

[3]Gogol's "The Nose" ("*Nos*") appeared in 1836, "The Portrait" ("*Portret*") in 1835, and "Rome" ("*Rim*") in 1842.

September 23, 1944
Vera Muromtseva-Bunina, from her diary

This year the Nobel Prize in Medicine will be awarded to Professor Alexander Fleming for his discovery of penicillin.[4] I wonder what that is?

October 13, 1944
Vera Muromtseva-Bunina, from her diary

It seems that we will have to spend winter here—something I find very burdensome.

October 22, 1944
Ivan Bunin, from his diary

Tomorrow is my fatal day. I will be seventy-five years old. Lord have mercy!

Bakhrakh will leave tomorrow at 8 a.m. He has been with us for four years. Four years have gone by!

The night is cold, but blue Orion shines in the sky. But soon I will never again see such a thing, for I have been condemned to execution.

October 26, 1944
Ivan Bunin, from a letter to Boris Zaitsev

The house has become rather empty. . . . Quite often Vera and I are the only ones home. Zurov has begun to be more and more absent. Now he is a key organizer for the local (Nice and Cannes) chapter of the "Union of the Friends of the Soviet Motherland."[5] Tomorrow he is again going to Cannes to prepare for celebrations commemorating the October Revolution on November 7th. In Nice, also, people have formed a "Union of Russian Patriots"[6] . . . The day before yesterday I received a letter from [its president], inviting me to participate in the "solemn proceedings of the twenty-seventh anniversary of the October Revolution," and to deliver a speech along with the other speakers there. I answered that since I am completely alien to any kind of political activity, I could not come and take part. . . . There will be more than enough speakers, and besides, a Russian choir will sing the Soviet

---

[4]Alexander Fleming discovered penicillin in 1928.
[5]Earlier this group had called itself "The League of France for the Return to the Motherland."
[6]The "Union of Russian Patriots" ("*Soiuz russkikh patriotov*")—later called the "Union of Soviet Patriots" ("*Soiuz sovetskikh patriotov*") and then the "Union of Soviet Citizens" ("*Soiuz sovetskikh grazhdan*")—was a pro-Soviet and initially clandestine emigré group,

national anthem and choral songs "from Soviet Russia" and the like. . . .

Yesterday I heard Radio Moscow announce that N. D. Teleshov will be awarded the Order of the Worker's Red Star on the occasion of the fiftieth anniversary of his career as a writer. . . .

My soul is very sad. . . .

October 28, 1944
Boris Zaitsev, from a letter to Ivan Bunin

I can finally write to you like a human being! Life is getting better little by little. . . . We now have electricity, gas, and the streets are getting a bit more cheerful. These are the things that make one's heart glad. . . . Paris is coming more and more alive. . . .

We keep thinking about the day when we will clink glasses with you and Vera. . . . By that time we should have some wine, though we don't have it now. . . .

But the heating situation is still poor. In Paris there are no coats at all. And everyone is afraid of winter. . . .

You will see a lot of very burdensome things when you come back here, but we will talk to our hearts' content! It will also be difficult to write. . . .

October 29, 1944
Vera Muromtseva-Bunina, from her diary

[A friend] writes that [another friend] has been seized, and has had her hair shorn. She also has been put in jail, and, even more tragic, cannot get out because her "dossier" has been lost.

My hands are completely tied. I cry a great deal when I am alone [and thinking about her]. I have written a ton of letters [on her behalf]; but I do not know if anyone will respond to them. . . . I blame myself that I did not tell her not to go near the Germans under any circumstances. . . .

---

founded by Dmitri Odinets in Paris on October 1, 1944. It eventually included more than eleven thousand members. Its purpose was to promote reconciliation between an "infinitely glorious, magnanimous motherland and her errant, remorseful children abroad." The existence of the Union was rather short-lived, if only because on November 25, 1947, the leaders of the group were deported to the Soviet Union.

Odinets was a legal historian and a professor at both the Sorbonne and Russian People's University. He had headed the Turgenev Library from 1925 to 1940, and was part of the delegation that had visited Bogomolov at the Soviet embassy in 1945.

In March 1948, Odinets was deported to the Soviet zone of German occupation. He immediately returned to the Soviet Union where, for the next two years, he lived in Kazan and taught at the university there. See L. Liubimov, "Na chuzhbine," *Novyi mir* (No. 4, 1957), 173.

November 4, 1944
Ivan Bunin, from a letter to Boris Zaitsev

Today we received an official announcement . . . informing us that our apartment [in Paris] will be free by January 1st, but how will we get there if the city will be frozen in ice like Nansen's *"Fram"*?[7] . . .

Congratulations on finishing [your book]. God grant it success! But where will you publish it? And, generally speaking, where will all of us "appear" in print? After all, the emigration is no more. . . .

[Coming across a note from a relative] I read: "How many wonderful things Zhukovsky has! But all my life I have always been somewhat offended that out of a thousand educated people, only one knows that *Zhukovsky is not a Zhukovsky, but a Bunin!*"[8] . . .

November 8, 1944
Boris Zaitsev, from a letter to Ivan Bunin

"My dear Uncle Vanya. . . . I have before me a picture of our [group] "Wednesday" with Teleshov . . . but for the hundredth time I rejoice that I did not stay [in Russia] but have lived 22 years as a free Cossack here! And I want to die a free man. . . .

> I hate humankind
> I run from it as fast as I can
> For it the desert of my soul
> That is my native land.

Who said this? I think it was Balmont, and he was right to do so. I have always been repulsed by those places where we suffered so many Russian disasters. That is why, perhaps, even the Bois de Boulogne now

---

[7] In 1890 the Norwegian explorer, Fridtjof Nansen, proposed to the Norwegian Geographical Society that he build a ship which, when trapped by ice, would be lifted above the floes, not crushed by them. Nansen also proposed that the ship be left to freeze in the waters off eastern Siberia, and that the currents carry it across the Arctic Ocean to Spitsbergen, an island in the Svalbard archipelago north of the Arctic Circle. With funds from the Norwegian Parliament as well as from King Oscar II and other individuals, Nansen built the *Fram* (the Norwegian word for "Forward").

With a crew of thirteen men, Nansen sailed the *Fram* from Kristiania (now Oslo) in southeastern Norway into the open sea on June 24, 1893. Three months later the ship was completely enclosed by ice but bore the pressure of the floes without difficulty. On March 14, 1895, Nansen, convinced that the ship would continue its safe passage, left the *Fram* in an unsuccessful attempt to reach the North Pole. He returned home by ship to Norway on August 13. A year later the *Fram* also reached its destination. (The *Fram* is now preserved outside of Oslo.)

[8] Vasily Zhukovsky was the illegitimate son of a wealthy landowner, one Afanasy Ivanovich Bunin, and a captive Turkish woman. The liaison speaks volumes about Russian society in the eighteenth century. Afanasy had asked a servant-serf who was going to fight

seems dearer to me [than places in Russia]. There is less violence. Here [in France] there are many ruins, cemeteries; here many people have perished from human rage, but in a different way [than they have in Russia].

November 11, 1944
Ivan Bunin, from a letter to Nikolai Roshchin

These are terrible, fatal, and great years for Russia. . . . No less than others do I gnash my teeth . . . at these "base invaders"; and no less than others do I rejoice that the Russians and the Allies are breaking their heads. . . .

November 17, 1944
Boris Zaitsev, from a letter to Ivan Bunin

We are arranging a literary-musical benefit for Russian prisoners of war. . . . May we read something of yours? It would be wonderful if we could. . . . The whole evening will be about Russia. . . .

Also, the event will be purely "literary-artistic," without any "political" biases. . . . Perhaps the whole thing will turn out to be boring . . . that is why we wanted something . . . from your writings. It will raise the tone [of the affair] and enhance the *spirit* of the gathering. . . .

November 23, 1944
Ivan Bunin, from a letter to a friend

If God allows us to see each other, I will tell you about the [Russian] captives and how they often visited us (even when the Germans were here). Several of them were so charming that we hugged and

---

in a Russian campaign against the Turks to bring back a good-looking Turkish girl, since his wife was getting old. Although Afanasy had meant such a request to be a joke, the serf fulfilled his master's wishes. In 1770 Bunin found himself to be the owner of a Turkish girl, Salkha, who, despite her youth—she was only sixteen years old—was already a widow, her husband having been killed in the war. Salkha was christened as Elizaveta Dementievna Turkhmanova (from the Russian word for Turk) and installed in an outlying part of the manor. To Afanasy, Salkha-Elizaveta bore the future poet, together with three daughters, all of whom died in infancy.

The child, Vasily, was given the family name of his godfather, Andrei Grigorievich Zhukovsky, a relative who lived on the charity of the Bunins. He was also raised by Bunin's wife, who had lost all but one of her offspring in infancy.

Even more bizarre, perhaps, Salkha-Elizaveta was employed as a housekeeper at the estate. When Afanasy Bunin died in 1791, he left the boy nothing in his will, though his stepsister, Maria, treated him as a member of the family and promised never to sell his mother. See C. Rydel, ed., *Dictionary of Literary Biography*, vol. 205 (Farmington Hills, Mich., 1999), 363.

kissed each other like family. They themselves told Vera and me: "Papasha, mamasha, we will never forget you. You are like family to us!" One Tatar was the most delightful of all. He was so noble in everything he did, so noble, so polite, well kept, and respectful to his elders. Truly the Koran had entered into him heart and soul. . . .

The group often danced and sang—things like "Moscow, My Dear, Unconquerable City" and the "Japanese Will Grovel at Our Homeland's Border" and the like. After the Germans fled, most of them went their separate ways. . . .

November 27, 1944
Boris Zaitsev, from a letter to Ivan Bunin

When neither of us is among the living, children will study your things in school. . . .

The other day I read "A Cold Autumn" and "Mistral"[9] [to friends]. [One woman] was so moved by what you had written that she burst out crying; that I found to be a very pleasant thing.

December 1, 1944
Ivan Bunin, from his diary

Come to my aid, O Lord. I fear sickness, and I keep wanting to live in greater health than I have now. . . .

Suddenly, all the Russians [around here] are becoming "redder" than red. Some are fearful, others are cringing, still others are following a herd instinct.

December 2, 1944
Ivan Bunin, from a letter to Boris Zaitsev

How unhappy is our Russian emigration! What has it not endured! . . . Now we hasten to take new measures. Everyone is being pressured to sign up as "patriots" and as members of the "Union of Friends of the Soviet Fatherland" . . . (what a rather strange title—"Soviet Fatherland"!) . . .

December 8, 1944
Nikolai Roshchin, from a letter to Ivan Bunin

Our people [in the Soviet homeland] not only accept but also love their strength . . . for otherwise they would not struggle for their fu-

---

[9]Bunin wrote both "A Cold Autumn" (*"Kholodnaia osen'"*) and "Mistral" (*"Mistral"*) in 1944.

ture. . . . [As regards our stance to the Soviet Union] we cannot wait any longer, or delay, or take sides, or bargain, or avoid the issue altogether. What has happened [to our country] and what is going on there is simply too crucial and huge. We must understand and accept [the Soviet homeland] even if we find it personally difficult, unpleasant, and risky to do so. Otherwise we will fall victim to inertia, to old self-deceptions, to live "like we used to." But the emigration cannot return to its previous ways. . . .

So, before your feet, I throw down all the heavy baggage which, I will not hide from you, I have carried with me for about twelve years. My grief will be bitter if you push me away; my face will be covered with tears.

December 18, 1944
Ivan Bunin, from a letter to Nikolai Roshchin
Please understand me. In no way am I opposed to your crossover or to that of others to the side of Moscow. But you should have acted more simply. You should have said: "Yes, we have made a mistake [in emigrating]. Russia has become a powerful nation, it has done many good things . . . and we now acknowledge its power and stand firmly on its side. . . ."

December 19, 1944
Ivan Bunin, from a letter to Mark Aldanov
Finally some news from you! I received . . . your telegram and money. But I almost burst out crying, because I got less than five thousand francs on the exchange. This is now *pennies* here. Do not send me any more money this way. If you still have some for me, it is better to wait. . . .

Also, thank you for the foodstuffs. We are perishing from hunger (and cold). We have lived terribly during these years; now it is getting worse. I have sold everything I could—even underwear. . . . My health has gotten much worse . . . and now my liver is acting up. We are still here in Grasse; we would have perished if we had stayed in Paris. . . .

December 27, 1944
Ivan Bunin, from a letter to Alexander Bakhrakh
You say that "joys are few these days!" But the galaxies and the stars are still there!

December 28, 1944
Boris Zaitsev, from a letter to the Bunins

Not long ago I took part in a benefit for some Russian prisoners-of-war. The entire first row . . . was filled with Soviet officers—a Paris military mission! Elsewhere in the hall were more modest, puny, and unprepossessing types. Right now the emigrés here are going wild over them. It is just like when everyone "went to the people" in the 1870s.[1] Without question, such individuals touch our hearts and call forth our fullest sympathy. But it is also beyond a doubt that they will exploit their popularity, for they are very good at catching people by surprise. . . .

You know, it was exactly this time twenty-one years ago when I came to your place on rue Offenbach, having just tumbled out of Italy. Truly, it was there that my life as an emigré began. And it is also there that it will end. We will not see Russia again. We are too old for our homeland; graves are the only things that we have there. Even [our friends] who have taken a close look at our country—and greatly sympathize with everything that is going on there—are extremely cold to the idea of returning there. . . .

December 30, 1944
Ivan Bunin, from a letter to Boris Zaitsev

Yesterday I found it very difficult to restrain myself, for I had to endure a most vile and base threat. [The person from the occupying forces who is staying here] is threatening to denounce me to the authorities. . . . He kept screaming that he has some "exclusive authority" to take over the entire house, not only the room he is in. Well, just let him try!

---

[1]Zaitsev is referring to the massive but abortive "going to the people" movement ("*khozhdenie v narod*"), which took place between the years 1873 and 1875, and sought a new level of populism in Russia.

The strange and convulsive *khozhdenie* has almost no parallel in modern history. Thousands of young, well-to-do students went into almost every province of European Russia to spread the gospel of socialism and progress, and, in particular, to educate the peasants or to incite them to revolt. (About one-fourth of this group were women.) Individuals who "went to the people" believed that the cooperative was the only just form of conducting business and trade. They also saw the village commune not only as the key political unit of social order in Russia but also as the means whereby Russians would gain a place of prominence in European civilization.

To their chagrin, the utopian-idealists who "went to the people" were met by a highly skeptical and often hostile populace. The students also had to face an even more antagonistic government which detained roughly four thousand of their group for suspected sedition, and which, in such major trials of the "Fifty" and of the "One Hundred and Ninety-Three," tried to suppress such activities in Russia.

PART FIVE

Returning to Faith

1945–1946

BUNIN, 1938

The citizens of "Russia Abroad" were no atheists in foxholes. No sooner had they entered into exile than they saw themselves as modern-day Israelites, a people who had worshiped false idols and whom God had now condemned to wander the world. With sincere repentance, Russian exiles confessed their many sins. They had revered materialism, positivism, and science; they had mocked "family values," particularly motherhood; they had deemed both God and the church as irrelevant or dead, the stuff of backwardness, superstition, and darkness.

In exile, Russian expatriates soon rediscovered their faith. They built churches, seminaries, and schools. They organized presses and publications, and established "believer" brotherhoods and societies.

The war and its aftermath only intensified the spiritual hunger of "Russia Abroad." During the war, Russian expatriates dodged bullets and bombs, facing death at every turn. After the conflict they resumed roaming alien shores amidst hunger, poverty, and despair. At the end of its exile, the diaspora's appeals to the Almighty for deliverance were even more frenzied and strident than they had been at its beginning.

As if to hedge their spiritual bets, latter-day members of "Russia Abroad" observed a peculiar if historic *dvoeverie* or "double-faith." They set aside nearly a millennium of enmity between Roman Catholic and Russian Orthodox churches, and borrowed freely from the dogma and ritual of both faiths. Even more interesting, perhaps, the approach of many Russian exiles to religion was as popular and devotional as it was serious and scholarly. Russian emigrés bowed before icons, lit candles to the Virgin Mary, and sought the intercession of the saints. (Not surprisingly, such "wanderers" as Francis of Assisi and "little people" as Thérèse of Lisieux were particular favorites.) In their consciousness, Catholic hymns, prayers, and holy days figured as prominently as Orthodox ones.

The members of "Russia Abroad" also read the Bible, especially the Psalms, as well as the weighty tomes of both Western and Eastern philosophers and theologians. They particularly relished the writings of Russian religious thinkers, not only on their own passage from darkness to light—many of them had been atheists and Marxists in their youth—but also on the mission and meaning of life.

Russian philosophers and theologians inspired the members of "Russia Abroad" with images and ideals that blazoned resplendently against their often harsh and bleak lives. Nikolai Berdyaev rejected bourgeois materialism as vehemently as he condemned Bolshevik atheism. He also saw humankind in near-Kierkegaardian terms—the individual was both a historical and an existential phenomenon whom God (not the state!) had created as autonomous, imaginative, and free. Sergei Bulgakov was influenced by Vladimir Soloviev, first to publish a Christian synthesis of philosophy, theology, and science, and later to posit a Sophia who was both cosmic and divine. Georgy Florovsky emphasized "ascetic creation" (*"podvizhennicheskoe delanie"*): the individual does not "build, posit, or give birth to his world"; rather, he "finds it" in the creative discovery of his surroundings.

Most poignantly, perhaps, Russian philosophers and theologians captured the minds and hearts of "Russia Abroad" when they insisted that the diaspora was the true covenant of national spiritual values, which would someday bring joy and peace to the world. In a 1935 article, Georgy Fedotov rejected the idea that the sins of Russian exiles in the homeland had condemned them to idle lives abroad. Rather, he insisted that exile was for the Russian emigrés a "feat" and a "creative act" by which they would preserve, for the future, the very best of *l'âme russe*, both present and past.

He wrote: "Perhaps no emigration in history has received such a powerful mandate from its homeland—to be the bearer of culture. We are here, abroad, to serve as the voice of all those who remain silent there [and] to reestablish the polyphonic wholeness of the Russian spirit. . . . We can become the living link between Russia's present and past."[1]

Anything else, Fedotov and the members of "Russia Abroad" agreed, was superfluous to their meaning and mission in life.

[1]Fedotov, 410.

Circa 1945
Vera Muromtseva-Bunina, from a letter to Alexander Baboreko

Ivan Alexeevich was comparatively hale and healthy in Grasse. He climbed a mountain easily . . . [and] was never seriously ill. . . . Of course, after we decided to stay in Grasse, Ivan Alexeevich immediately started begging to go "home"—to Paris, where we had rented an apartment since 1934. . . .

1945–1946
Antonin Ladinsky, from his memoirs

Even as a youth, Bunin was seized by contradictions. For instance, in his travel sketch "The Shadow of a Bird,"[2] he wrote: "I know well that one can love one or another way of life, but can one surrender all his powers to . . . one type of existence? Is that where one gets the idea of a 'homeland'? If a Russian revolution distresses me more than a Persian one, I can only regret such feelings. Truly blessed is each and every moment that we feel ourselves to be citizens of the universe."

Such a statement expresses a noble cosmopolitanism. But . . . when an individual is battered by life's storms, he finds it pleasant to remember that he has a home, a homeland, and graves for his forefathers. Bunin could not help but remember such things when he was abroad. . . .

To a certain degree, the duality [of nation and universe] remained with Bunin until the end of his life. It was with interest that he asked Soviet citizens who had come to France after the war about events in the homeland. But his questions did not reveal a filial love. Bunin was seemingly "offended" by something. . . . Was it the loss of his gentry

---

[2]Bunin wrote "The Shadow of a Bird" (*"Ten' ptitsy"*) in 1907.

estate or a self-consciousness of class? Quite possibly, even though Bunin was *déclassé*, with no estates to his name. Perhaps, it was also . . . a fear and an inability to cross the line that marked the beginning of the new world.

Despite Bunin's love for Paris and Provence . . . he never took root in life abroad. . . . Also, with all the hardships of his life in France, he realized that he had made a mistake [in leaving the homeland]. Indeed, it was only his arrogance that prevented him from admitting his error. . . .

[One time] Bunin and I . . . ordered a glass of a French peasant vodka. I remember how he sniffed the glass and said: "Good stuff. It smells just like new shoes!" . . . And, to tell the truth, the vodka smelled a bit like leather. . . .

At this time, also, the staff of *Russian Patriot*[3] . . . very much wanted to have Bunin write for them, since everyone knew his patriotic and anti-Hitler views. But for some reason, Bunin believed that he had to stay "above politics." . . .

January 1, 1945
Vera Muromtseva-Bunina, from a letter to a friend
1945 is here. What will it bring to us and the world?

January 14, 1945
Boris Zaitsev, from a letter to Ivan Bunin
My dear John the Landless[4] . . . [A colleague] is persecuting Nina Berberova [for her alleged pro-German sympathies]. But she never had a thing to do with the Nazis. She never wrote for them; she never participated in their meetings; she never was a member of Surguchev's and Zherebkov's Alliance.[5] Nevertheless, [this colleague] has written to the

---

[3]*Russian Patriot (Russkii patriot)*—later known as *Soviet Patriot (Sovetskii patriot)*—was the official publication of the "Union of Russian Patriots in France." With probable funding by the Soviets, it was published from 1943 to 1945, when it was closed by the French police. The newspaper, though, was resurrected as *Russian News (Russkie novosti)*, which existed from 1945 to 1952.

For financial reasons and to his eternal regret, Bunin was forced to collaborate with *Russian News*, having published in it six stories from *Dark Alleys*. See Johnston, 171.

[4]Zaitsev is referring to King John (also known as John Lackland and, in French, *Jean Sans Terre*), who ruled England from 1199 to 1219, and who, in a war with Philip II of France (1202–1204), lost Normandy and also all of his other possessions to France. It was also King John who, after a revolt of English nobles, was forced to sign the Magna Carta in 1215.

[5]With the German occupation of France, the Gestapo named Yury Zherebkov as *Leiter* ("Leader") of the Russian emigration there. Zherebkov was a naturalized German, the son

Union of Writers that she "engaged in German propaganda"! Do you realize how bad that smells these days?

Very badly. We know Nina very well. In no way has she ever collaborated with the Germans[6] . . . but her passionate nature has sometimes caused her to utter "heretical" opinions. (She likes force, discipline, and courage.) For instance, she prefers Russians to Jews and

---

of a tsarist general, and, if witnesses are to be believed, a professional dancer in the emigration. He was also a friend of Alfred Rosenberg, Hitler's theoretician on questions of race, and a member of the Committee for the Liberation of Peoples of Russia (*Komitet po osvobozhdeniiu narodov Rossii*), an organization connected with Pavel Vlasov, the famous Russian general who had cast his lot with the Germans, and who headed a volunteer army of Ukrainians seeking to free their land from Soviet rule.

Simply put, Zherebkov was a Russian Quisling who wished to chain "Russia Abroad" to the Nazi juggernaut. As he proclaimed to his fellow exiles both at public meetings and in articles printed in the *Russian Herald* (*Russkii vestnik*)—a journal published under the German aegis in Paris from 1942 to 1944—only Hitler could determine Russia's fate, only the National Socialist party could resurrect Russia from the Bolshevik grave. Zherebkov's plan was that Russian expatriates should not so much cooperate with the Germans as submit to them utterly. They should also abandon their patriotic instincts for their besieged country, no matter how great their hatred of Stalin. Russian exiles, Zherebkov insisted, must not see the German campaign in Russia as a "conquest"; and for a straightforward reason. After all, citizens in Russia, by their ready willingness to fight for Stalin, were showing their inner corruption under communism.

Zherebkov wasted no time in enforcing such views. Just thirty-six hours after the German attack on Russia, he issued a communiqué, rejoicing that the invaders were both "resurrecting" the Russian people and deflecting the "satanic sword of Judeo-Marxism" from Europe.

On July 25, 1941, Zherebkov summoned 250 prominent Russians to a meeting in Paris to inform them that he had jurisdiction over all emigrés in Vichy France and the Unoccupied Zone. (The Russian Jews were ominous exceptions in both areas.) Further, Maklakov's Office of Russian Refugees, which had helped expatriates almost from the beginning of the emigration, was replaced by a Nazi-run Bureau for Russian Affairs. All Russians in the country had to register with Zherebkov's agents; individuals who failed to do so would be seen (and treated) as Soviet citizens.

Needless to say, Zherebkov's program evoked only contempt from Russians in France and beyond. Although resistance was dangerous, many Russians regarded the new registration as the first step toward forced labor in Germany; thus they refused to comply. See Glad, 314, 315.

[6]Berberova wrote in her diary, *The Black Book* (*Chernaia kniga*), in July 1940: "Paris has become quite empty. . . . In this new quiet on the Champs-Elysées a voice rings out: this is a loudspeaker at a cinema commenting in German on the *Wochenschau*. I go in. The dark hall is almost full. On the screen we are shown how the Germans broke through the Maginot Line, how they took a million prisoners, how they struggled for the Loire . . . and how they were greeted with flowers in Strasbourg and Colmar. . . .

"Then Hitler comes to the Trocadero and from there looks at the Eiffel Tower. Suddenly he makes a gesture . . . of indescribable vulgarity and ugliness. . . . With full satisfaction he smacks himself on the rear end and pivots on one heel.

"At first I wanted to scream loudly out of shame and horror. But then, with the pealing of the Strasbourg cathedral and the music from a military band, the entire affair became ridiculous. . . . Nearby pairs giggled, embraced, and kissed in the half gloom." See N. Berberova, The *Italics Are Mine* (New York, 1982), 389.

places the interests of the former over the latter. But when the Jews started being tortured, she, like everyone else we knew, helped them as much as she could. But she did do one stupid thing: she wrote some careless thing to Adamovich.[7] And because he had nothing to do, he spread it around everywhere, and the nonsense even reached America. . . .

Yes, gossip will shorten one's life span. . . . But I think [the controversy over Berberova] is a tempest in a teapot, and that younger writers (all of whom have grey hair!) are reacting to these "accusations" rationally and quietly. But Nina is upset. . . .

P.S. I just remembered: John the Landless was an English king who was a bit of a shit.[8] But I called you that not because you are a shit, but because you own no land.

January 17, 1945
Ivan Bunin, from a letter to Mark Aldanov
[A friend] writes: "Your book is . . . a great success, but it has been published in a very limited edition." . . . Does that mean I won't get a kopeck from it? . . .

Early February 1945
Ivan Bunin, from a letter to Boris Zaitsev
Little by little, I am perishing in the precise sense of this word. I have this constant sharp pain, if not in the liver then somewhere close by. . . . There is also something unpleasant going on with my stomach and sense of taste that has now moved on to my intestines. . . . Add to that a bronchitis that has lasted two months, dull eyes, a face that has grown old, and pain coming from frozen arms. . . . I should have gone to Nice for an x-ray a long time ago, but I would have had to stay two days in an icy cold hotel, eating God-knows-what, and paying about two thousand francs for the x-ray—a sum that I do not even dare think about!

---

[7]Berberova was indeed careless in letters to friends. She wrote to Aldanov on September 20, 1945: "Yes, right up until fall 1940 . . . I, along with nine-tenths of the French intelligentsia, considered . . . cooperation with the Germans . . . [if only because] we were completely disenchanted with capitalism, parliamentarianism, and the 'third republic.'" See *Evrei v kul'ture russkogo zarubezh'ia. Stat'i, publikatsii, memuary i esse*, vol. 4 (Jerusalem, 1995), 286.

[8]Historians would contest Zaitsev's assessment of King John. During his reign he scored important advances in English systems of justice, taxation, and military organization.

So I am writing to you to ask if you can have the French again give us a regular allowance to live on? . . .

February 4, 1945
Boris Zaitsev, from a letter to Ivan Bunin

Your very sad letter distressed me greatly. I am completely incapable of helping you (financially). I would send you 10,000 francs if I could . . . but where would I get the money? . . . [Other organizations] can send you only very little. . . . But I will do what I can. . . .

Poor Mochulsky has been perishing from the cold.[9] He is all blue, a frozen little chick without feathers.

February 10, 1945
Ivan Bunin, from a letter to a friend

What is your opinion of the "patriots"? I really let Roshchin have it—not because he has moved over to the Communists, that is his business—but because he threw mud at the *emigrantshchina* (his name for it) in such a very coarse way. . . .

Berberova gave me a dressing down. Everyone is persecuting her because of something *I* supposedly did. One of her friends in America informed her that I had denounced her in writing to Mark Alexandrovich [Aldanov]—and that is why everyone is against her. I have to pity her. Her letter was so filled with suffering, so full of oaths that she had been slandered, that I answered her shortly but firmly that I had *never* written *a single line* about her to Mark Alexandrovich. . . .

February 12, 1945
Nina Berberova, from her memoirs

I do not like to look at decay . . . but for Bunin it began the day when S. K. Makovsky . . . took him to see the Soviet ambassador, Bogomolov, to drink to Stalin's health. . . . All of this had been arranged by A. F. Stupnitsky—the so-called eye of Moscow. First Stupnitsky had "brainwashed" Maklakov, telling him "there will be an amnesty for emigrés," and "everything has changed in the Soviet Union."[1] Then he

---

[9]Mochulsky was also suffering from the advanced stages of tuberculosis; he died in 1948.
[1]On February 12, 1945, Maklakov did the unthinkable. Heading a delegation of Russian emigrés, he was received formally by the Soviet ambassador, Alexander Bogomolov, at the Soviet embassy at rue de Grenelle in Paris. (Despite emigré rumors to the contrary, Bunin was not a member of the group. He did not return to Paris until May 1945. Neither accounts in emigré newspapers about the meeting, nor Bunin's own letters to family and friends at this time, mention any visit to Bogomolov or other Soviet personnel. In fact, the

entrusted Makovsky to bring Bunin and several others [to the Soviet embassy]. Bogomolov was there waiting with refreshments. [The meeting] had no political consequences; [but] it was the beginning of the decay of the emigrés in general, and of its individual representatives in particular. . . .

Before Bunin visited Bogomolov, he was a reactionary, but after . . . he was completely reconciled to Soviet rule. . . .

---

emigré delegation to the Soviet embassy was conspicuous for the absence of exile writers in the group.)

At the Soviet embassy, Maklakov and other emigrés declared that they now recognized the Soviet government as the legitimate representative of the Russian people, and that, as such, they were were willing to work with, rather than against, officials there. The tsarist admiral Mikhail Kedrov addressed Bogomolov: "Mr. Ambassador, I speak as an officer who commanded others to fight against you. Yes, it is true that we were enemies, but the years have thinned our ranks. Some have died; others have left us because they lost faith in that struggle. Those of us who remain are mere husks of men. As early as 1936 and 1937, we began to realize that a new generation had been born in Russia, one that was on your side rather than ours. [We also saw that] a new state and a new army had been created, and that a formerly destructive process had taken a constructive turn. There then ensued a great war. Initially the Soviet Union was an ally of Germany. We Russians living abroad hailed such a development, since we believed that the homeland, if spared war, would escape harm and grow strong. But Germany, in her pride, attacked the Soviet Union. Although we shed bloody tears when we learned of the first defeats in our country, we knew, in the depths of our souls, that the Soviet Union and the Russian people would be victorious." Such speeches were followed by toasts to the Soviet people, the Red Army, and Stalin.

Needless to say, the event caused the greatest sensation among Russian emigrés since the German attack on the homeland in June 1941. Of course, Maklakov knew that by crossing the threshold of the building where he had formerly ruled—he had been the official representative of Russia before France recognized the Soviet Union in October 1924— he was committing an act which many would find incomprehensible, if not treacherous. He spent the next few months fending off the wildest rumors about the visit, as well as explaining the reasons for his action, probably the most decisive act of his political career.

Maklakov, though, had no choice but to meet with the Soviets. As he wrote to Kerensky on June 21, 1945, it had long been time for Russians in France to face facts. The abject penury and isolation of their existence, coupled with growing lists of obituaries, pressure from Zherebkov's agents, and admiration for native Russians during the war, compelled him and other emigré leaders to consider the future of their dwindling community and, specifically, the possibility of the return of exiles to the homeland.

Both Russias had much to gain from the meeting. Emigrés could seek to reconcile the old and new Russia. The Soviets could restore Maklakov as the spokesman for "Russia Abroad." They could also promote unity between the pro-Moscow forces and nationalist anti-fascist groups in the diaspora, as well as thwart an alliance between Soviet wartime defectors to the West and the older generation of refugees from the USSR.

Although the meeting between the two groups was amicable, Bogomolov took a high hand with his guests. Russian emigrés, he declared, had no future in the West. They also had to accept that their native country would not return to its pre-1917 past, and that Soviet patriotism superseded any Russian longing for the homeland. Leaving open the possibility of return, Bogomolov invited his visitors to toast the Soviet people, its armies, and its leader. Different versions exist as to the unanimity of the response.

Also defying consensus was the response of emigrés in France and elsewhere to the visit. Some expressed hope, others hatred, with the now seventy-six-year-old Maklakov caught in the middle. Sergei Melgunov, editor of the conservative *Renaissance* (*Vozrozhde-*

February 23, 1945
Ivan Bunin, from his diary

Today is some anniversary of the "Red Army"[2] that is being cele-brated both in Russia and in France. . . . All the Russians here have gone out of their mind precisely over the victories of this army, "its love for the homeland, its spirit of sacrifice." But this is no cause for joy. If one thinks about it, should not one also go crazy over the Ger-mans? After all, their victories were legendary, having gone on for al-most four years. And "their love for the homeland, their spirit of sacrifice" was certainly no less. What about the Huns? And Mamai? . . .

February 24, 1945
Ivan Bunin, from his diary

The Moscow radio reports: [*Alexei*] *Tolstoy has died.*[3] Good God, was it all that long ago—our first years in Paris, when he was almost a young man and strong as a bull![4]

February 25, 1945
Ivan Bunin, from his diary

Tolstoy was cremated yesterday. He has completely disappeared from the world!

February 26, 1945
Ivan Bunin, from his diary

Tolstoy was only 62 years old. He could have lived 20 years more.

---

nie), compared Maklakov's visit to the Soviet embassy to the humiliating barefooted penance that Henry IV performed before the windows of Pope Gregory VII at Canossa in 1077.

"We are asked to forget," Melgunov raged, "about the hundreds of thousands of Rus-sian lives destroyed, not on the field of battle with a foreign enemy, but in the cellars of the GPU and in concentration camps. . . . Only people with an extremely short memory can spread so easily the foam of forgetfulness over the recent victims of forced collectiviza-tion. . . . Only those who are deaf to their political conscience can seek fictional justifica-tions and demand 'sincere reconciliation' with a dictatorship that has committed crimes against its own people. The voices of the dead do not cease to call to our conscience and horror. There can be no forgiveness for the exercise of violence over humankind." See John-ston, 175–178; Glad, 336–337.

[2] Bunin is referring to the so-called Army-Navy Day (*"Den' sovetskoi armii i voennogo-morskogo flota"*). On February 23, 1918, great numbers of Russians enlisted in the Red Army in response to a Soviet decree, "The Socialist Homeland is in Danger" (*"Sotsialis-tichekoe otechestvo v opasnosti"*), which had been published the day before.

[3] Alexei Tolstoy died in Moscow on February 23, 1945.

[4] Tolstoy was in his early forties at that time.

February 26, 1945
Ivan Bunin, from a letter to Boris Zaitsev
It seems as though Alyosha was not judged sufficiently worthy to be buried in the Kremlin Wall.[5]

Spring 1945
Ivan Bunin, from a letter to Gleb Struve
Forgive me, but I am forced by my poverty to remind you that the last time you wrote to me—June 19, 1934—you said: "I owe you 7-1/2 pounds, and I will try to get this money to you next month."

At that time, you did not do so. So please return this money to me now, even if it be in bits and pieces. I thank you in advance.

March 5, 1945
Boris Zaitsev, from a letter to Ivan Bunin
At a literary reading . . . the speaker cited a list of well-known writers. . . . *You and I are the only ones who are living!* . . .

For me everything is filled with you and Vera; everything is tied to you two, and without you, my life is a desert.

March 6, 1945
Yakov Polonsky, from a letter to Ivan Bunin
First things first—Russian patriots and your return home. I know that you have no taste for politics, but you cannot turn your back on such matters now.

With the exception of such people as Berberova, all of us writers are patriots of Russia. Moreover, all of us are patriots of *Soviet* Russia, of the *Soviet* Union. The latter is to be understood in the sense of Empire. Further, all of us have renounced any (imagined) struggle with the regime. Such views have ramifications, but people with little experience in politics can easily make mistakes. . . .

Most likely you assume that if you contribute to *Russian Patriot* it will be easier for you to return home. But I think that is the way *you* should proceed. Of course, should you not return to the homeland for good, you can always visit there for a period of time and be the focus of triumph and respect. But the road there (for you) is not through *Rus-*

---

[5]Tolstoy was buried in the "Cherry Orchard" of the Novodevichy Convent in Moscow, alongside the remains of such writers as Gogol, Chekhov, and Mayakovsky. Burial in the Kremlin Wall was an honor reserved only for the most eminent Bolsheviks and supporters of the Revolution. (The American journalist John Reed was buried there in 1920.) Gorky is the only Russian writer to have been accorded such a distinction.

sian Patriot. . . . It is only by returning home that you will become an authority for Russia and Russian writers.

We do not empathize or share your gospel-like temperance toward Berberova. She is in a class by herself. After all, she is one of Merezhkovsky's group, a fan of someone who got a promise from Goebbels that German propagandists in Munich would publish "trustworthy" emigré writers in Russian.[6] . . . She will be excluded—along with others who worked for the Germans—from the Union of Writers and Journalists.[7] . . .

We are very happy that you are returning to Paris. In no way should you remain in Grasse, and not only for reasons of health. There you are very isolated from everything. There you do not have enough confidence in yourself, but in Paris you will acquire it anew. The atmosphere here is quite different, and people have a different attitude toward your name. In the backwoods where you are now, you will bring yourself down, but—and I must be open with you—Paris harbors a personal danger for you. Do not look for unsolicited advice; many things will become clearer to you once you are here. It is now more impossible than ever to be indifferent politically, even more so with someone who is as well known as you. It will also be impossible to maintain personal meetings and relationships as before. I do not know if I am expressing myself adequately and clearly, but the line separating people is becoming more and more pronounced. Attitudes toward Russia and Germany determine everything. . . . You will be in a very delicate position. . . .

March 9, 1945
Ivan Bunin, from a letter to Yakov Polonsky
With regard to your statement that I "lack confidence in myself," you have been informed incorrectly—*I have always been and will continue to be confident.* . . . You also say that I think that if I contribute to *Patriot*, it will be easier for me to return home [to Russia]. But not for a single moment have I ever assumed such a thing. . . . Three times I was invited "home"—the last time *via* the graces of A. N. Tolstoy (whose death I truly took exceptionally hard—his talent, for all its diversity, was truly rare!).

At present I am rejecting the idea of returning . . . [for I fear] that

---

[6]There is no evidence for this statement.
[7]Berberova was not excluded from the Union of Writers.

my situation there will be like a mousetrap, and that I will have to be a humble servant without the freedom to go about as I please! . . .

March 10, 1945
Vsevelod Vishnevsky, from his diary

I am reading Bunin. . . . What a misanthrope he is! What a dull, burdensome, and hopeless life he portrays in *The Village*! Why, if all Russia were like that, could our current victory [over the Germans] be even thinkable?

March 21, 1945
Ivan Bunin, from a letter to Nadezhda Teffi

How can I thank you for all your letters to me, for your eternal kindness to me! I find it even a bit strange. All my life it seems that right after something nice happens to me, fate hits me on the head. . . . So I live in constant fear that you will suddenly say: "No, I was wrong about Bunin!" Do not think that I am joking, for I believe that evil lurks right behind the corner. . . .

March 23, 1945
Mark Aldanov, from a letter to Ivan Bunin

We have published *Dark Alleys*. But I have to tell you that Sedykh and I consulted a lawyer—*several* of the stories could not be printed. If we had done so, we would have been arrested and prosecuted as criminals. Believe me, I am not joking. Here [in America] morality is very strict. . . .

Your book is being very well received in reviews in Russian periodicals, but, generally speaking, the Russian colony here in America does not read books. . . . One of your stories, "Natalie," has been accorded a great honor. It is being included in an anthology of world literature published by the American firm Fisher.[8]

There are no Russian publishers in America. We got some money from "patrons" (loans). . . . All they have asked was for an advance of a hundred dollars and that their money be returned to them should sales exceed costs. So far this has not happened. . . .

---

[8]"Natalie" appeared in *Heart of Europe: An Anthology of Creative Writing in Europe, 1920–1940*, published by L. B. Fisher in 1943.

March 27, 1945
Ivan Bunin, from a letter to Boris Zaitsev

The spring here has been a poor one! But a sweet and edifying feminine voice from Radio Moscow reports that "in the air one already feels the wafting of spring through the great Soviet homeland. . . . In the south there flower the first Soviet violets, the first ice floes float along the endless shores of the great Soviet Union. . . ." So take your Maritime Alps and shove them!

April 7, 1945
Vera Muromtseva-Bunina, from her diary

People are again becoming divided in Paris. It is one group against another. Some have "to go underground"; others have taken it upon themselves to be policemen and detectives. In Paris I will associate only with those who do not engage in politics and interfere in other people's lives. I will keep my distance from everyone else. I have had quite enough of ruining my nerves and health over petty squabbles!

April 8, 1945
Boris Zaitsev, from a letter to Ivan Bunin

We are waiting for you to come [to Paris]! I imagine that, like you and Verochka, entire populations of countries are so tired of these endless packings and unpackings. . . .

I went to see Gippius the other day. She has had a second stroke. She is weak and can barely move her arm and leg. Her speech is *not* slurred. She is not taking any visitors. . . . Apparently she looked worse after she had her hair done up. She wanted to make herself *indéfrisable*, dye her hair, and the like. . . .

April 15, 1945
Ivan Bunin, from a letter to Mark Aldanov

Do not be surprised when I write to you about my returning [to Russia]. I repeat: I am so weak from need, hunger, cold, and all other types of deprivations (and especially at my age). I think of the future with horror. I have hardly anything to my name, I am head over heels in debt, and I have no way of making any money. I keep firmly to myself and turn down all invitations and requests. I will wait and look around, but most likely I will leave [for Russia] by the fall. We are heading for Paris on April 29th and leaving the south forever! How sad! . . .

Early May 1945
Ivan Bunin, from a letter to Mark Aldanov
We are finally here in Paris, having left Grasse forever.

May 2, 1945
The Soviet Ministry for Foreign Affairs, from a confidential report
Bunin, "the bard of the White emigration," hates Germans. . . . Having regarded Hitler and Mussolini as "insane monkeys," his behavior during the occupation was beyond reproach. . . .

At the present time, Bunin's political views are extremely unstable, but they seem to be relatively pro-Soviet. But as the "first writer of Russia"—so Maxim Gorky used to call him—Bunin knows his worth. Ambitious to a sickly degree, he loves to . . . distinguish himself from the emigré masses. . . .

Bunin, though, is a weak-willed individual who is easily influenced by . . . friends . . . for example, the writer B. K. Zaitsev . . . who is anti-Soviet . . . and I. S. Shmelyov . . . who is a closet fascist.[9] . . .

In light of Bogomolov's upcoming invitation to Bunin for breakfast [at the Soviet Embassy in Paris]—Bunin is a great lover of food—it would be a good idea to appeal to his love of attention and to single him out from everyday emigré circles. . . .

After May 1945
Alexander Bakhrakh, from his memoirs
[After Bunin returned to Paris] he felt that he was a "sick repulsive old man." In truth, his health kept worsening, and he always felt poorly. The smallest cold . . . would go on for weeks and always threatened to cause serious complications. . . . Even after he was operated on by the best medical specialists in Paris, he never regained his strength. . . .

Bunin had a great penchant for all kinds of patented medicines. He would hardly see someone with a box of pills that he did not know, then he would try to get the same thing for himself. He also studied the components of any medicine and insisted that he knew more about them than the best doctor. One can say without exaggeration that his collection of pharmaceutical bottles and boxes would be the envy of

[9]Shemlyov was held suspect by both emigré and Soviet Russians for having published several wartime stories and essays about tsarist Russia in the German-sponsored *Parisian Herald (Parizhskii vestnik)*. See Glad, 325.

any pharmacy, especially during wartime. In fact, he was so hostile to any kind of his requisitioning that he filled several suitcases to overflowing with his "collection." . . .

May 28, 1945
Ivan Bunin, from a letter to Mark Aldanov

I am trying to nourish Vera with better food. I buy butter (at 600 francs a kilo!). We need money terribly. . . .

[In answer to your second invitation for me to come to America] I repeat what I have already written to you: *How are we going to live there?* I simply cannot imagine that! On charity! And whose? We would be completely impoverished . . . and I simply do not have the strength to endure that. Then, too, how long would this charity last? Two, three months? And then what? [In America] we would have the same beggarly, tormenting, and *Angst*-ridden existence that we do now.

So, like never before, there is only thing left to do: go home [to Russia]. From what I hear, I very much want to go there, being promised mountains of gold in every possible form. But how can I decide on such a move? I will wait a bit and think about it . . . although, I repeat, what else can I do?

May 30, 1945
Mark Aldanov, from a letter to Ivan Bunin

[A friend] almost burst out crying when I read her your last letter to me. She kept saying: "Good God!" "The Bunins have lost their minds!"

I very well understand what it means to see "home" again, no matter where it is. We share this great sorrow. But if you consider the "pluses" and "minuses" of this decision calmly, then the "minuses" are overwhelming. I list the "minuses":

(1) Have you read Teleshov's memoirs? He . . . reports that you died in 1942 and that your last letter was that: "I want to go home." . . . Was that the letter you apparently wrote to Alexei Nikolaevich Tolstoy, about which there have been so many rumors? Teleshov's book . . . was nobly written, with love for you. But he also talks about Kuprin's torments [in Russia], which we did not know about.[1] I am afraid that such distress would have been the case no mat-

---

[1]In his memoirs, Teleshov wrote: "Kuprin died in 1938, shortly after his return from abroad. Although he was no longer young, he had left [Russia] as a strong and vigorous man, almost an athlete. But he came back [to the homeland] weak and worn out in mind

ter who would have been invited back and promised God-knows-what. You, as a well-known Russian writer, are responsible for your own biography.

(2) Precisely *who* is inviting you and what are they promising you [if you do return]? . . . I think that some of these promises will be fulfilled. Several of your books will be published, you will be given an apartment, and you will get a lot of money, but there is nothing to buy there. Indeed, the hunger and poverty there is almost the same everywhere in Europe. . . .

(3) It seems that there is not a single close friend of yours who is alive there. . . . Young writers there will greet you respectfully but coldly. . . . And some will remind you of *The Cursed Days*.

(4) If you still have any money coming to you from the Nobel Prize, you will never receive it. Surely what you will be given [by the Soviets] will not be worth much. . . .

You would be completely justified in asking: "But what could you guarantee me in America?" Truly, we, your friends, can only promise to try to do for you everything that we can, in any way possible. And I know that is not much.

I very well understand how burdensome all this is for you. My feelings for you cannot change, nor will they—no matter what you decide. . . .

I also must tell you that my efforts to have Knopf or Scribner's

---

and body, a helpless, aimless invalid. I was with him in the Metropole Hotel [in Moscow] about three days after his arrival [home]. He was no longer Kuprin—the brilliant man that we all knew. Rather, he was a shadow of his former self, weak, pitiful, and plainly dying. He forgot the names of his old friends; he kept confusing things from the past. One could feel that Kuprin was broken in spirit; he was trying to call up and respond to something, but the strength [to do so] was not there. I walked away [from my meeting] a sad man: a strong individual and brilliant writer was no more."

In recalling Kuprin, though, Teleshov was careful to pander to the Soviet regime. He continued: "In August 1937, Kuprin was invited to a reception for Red Army soldiers. . . . The people there had seated him in his favorite armchair in a place of honor to watch the fun. But Kuprin merely looked on, without saying a word. Every now and then Red soldiers came up to him to say how glad they were to see him there and how much they liked his writing. Kuprin thanked them curtly, but sat there deep in thought. It seemed to some that he was not 'there,' and that the merry spirit of the affair had not reached him.

"But when the men from the Red Army sang Russian songs—'Stenka Razin,' 'Down on the Mother Volga,' and the like—Kuprin seemed to change and come to life. And when they sang the song 'My Native Land,' he was moved deeply. Further, when the soldiers, in farewell, hailed Kuprin as a great writer, he broke down completely. All that he had lived through on that day, in silence and seemingly untouched, had suddenly found a release. 'I have been a great sinner before my country,' Kuprin said through real and scalding tears, 'and my country forgives me. The sons of the people, the Red Army itself, have forgiven me. Now I shall find rest.' See N. Teleshov, *A Writer Remembers: Reminiscences* (London, 1946), 58–59.

publish *Dark Alleys* have come to nothing. Both publishers said that such collections of stories have not done well in America, and will not do well now. . . .

Circa June 1945
Nikolai Roshchin, from his memoirs
    Bunin was thrilled by the successes of the Soviet army. Once at a performance of the Russian theatre in Paris, he happened to be sitting next to a young lieutenant colonel from the Soviet military mission. During the intermission, the young colonel got up and, turning to the writer, said: "Have I the honor of sitting next to Ivan Alexeevich Bunin?" Bunin, also having risen with youthful swiftness, answered: "Yes. But it is I who have the still greater honor of sitting next to an officer of our great army."

June 12, 1945
Ivan Bunin, from a letter to Mark Aldanov
    We have been besieged by visitors. . . . I will give a reading on June 19th. . . . Thank God, the hall will be filled to overflowing, and I will get about 30,000 francs from the event. (Do not think, though, that my financial situation is improving. I owe [a lot of people].) . . .
    We are not planning to go anywhere. . . . But *how* are we going to live?

June 29, 1945
Ivan Bunin, from a letter to Mark Aldanov
    Will you kill me if I ask you to change one word in my story, "First Monday in Lent"?!! In your copy, you have the hero "entering Annunciation Cathedral and seeing the marble slabs covering the tombs of the Muscovite tsars." . . . But the tsars are buried in *Archangel* Cathedral.[2] So I replaced "Annunciation" with "Archangel." Do not kill me. . . .

---

[2]The Archangel Cathedral (*Arkhangel'skii sobor*) was built in 1333 and houses the remains of both the princes of Moscow and the tsars of Russia (with the exception of Boris Godunov) until the founding of Saint Petersburg. The Annunciation Cathedral (*Blagoveshchenskii sobor*) was constructed between the years 1484 and 1489. It served as a private chapel for medieval Russian rulers and sometimes as a dungeon for dangerous political prisoners.

July 5, 1945
Vera Muromtseva-Bunina, from a letter to a friend

[Ian's] reading was very successful. . . . But I could feel how difficult it was for him up there. . . .

Besides taking care of the house . . . I am giving Russian lessons to a French student. I am getting paid rather well—180 francs twice a week. . . .

July 25, 1945
Vera Muromtseva-Bunina, from a letter to a friend

I am not a politician, and so I understand little about politics. But I know only one thing: without Faith and Kindness the world will not survive. I feel terribly for children, youth. You know that the cruelest Germans were the minors! . . .

July 31, 1945
Vera Muromtseva-Bunina, from a letter to a friend

I need socks most of all. . . . It is also difficult to find soap.

I do not know what Teffi is living on. . . .

August 8, 1945
Nina Berberova, from her memoirs

It was my birthday.[3] With difficulty I obtained half a pound of sausage. I set the table in the dining room, cut twelve pieces of dark bread, and put the twelve pieces of sausage on them. The guests came at eight and, as was proper, first sat in my room. . . . When I poured the tea, the guests came into the dining room. Bunin entered first, took a look at the sandwiches, and, without even hurrying, ate . . . all of the twelve pieces of sausage. So when the others came to the table . . . they found only bread . . . spread out on two plates . . . and looking rather strange and pitiful.

August 14–15, 1945
Vera Muromtseva-Bunina, from her diary

[Among our friends] only the Zaitsevs are happy—they have a new grandson, Mikhail. . . . I have not seen Gippius. But people say that her paralysis has defeated her. . . .

---

[3]Berberova was forty-four years old at this time.

August 16, 1945
Ivan Bunin, from a letter to Mark Aldanov

The way we are living now [in Paris] is simply tormenting: a small apartment, crowded with suitcases, children screaming and crying in the dirty yard below, the radio blaring over my head all day long, the vile weather outside. . . .

August 17, 1945
Ivan Bunin, from a letter to Mark Aldanov

Why is *New Review* engaging in strip-farming? One time it uses the old orthography, another time the "new," coarse, and vulgar one! Whom is the latter one for? . . .

August 27, 1945
Mark Aldanov, from a letter to Ivan Bunin

Do not be surprised that I am writing to you in the new orthography. My typewriter is being repaired, and I was given another one in the interim. . . . [In answer to your question] the editors of *New Review* have been assured that their circulation would double if they would use the new script. "You will have young readers," they have been told.

So we have to compromise. Several, including myself, will publish in the old orthography, but the majority of contributors will use the new one. . . . Your stories will be published exclusively in the old. . . .

I am so terribly happy that you are going "nowhere." I understand that your decision to remain [here in the West] is not sweet, but nonetheless I am happier than words can say. . . .

September 4, 1945
Ivan Bunin, from a letter to Mark Aldanov

Who do you think will win the Nobel Prize this year? Sholokhov or Leonov? They are very much alike![4] . . .

The newspapers say that the Academy of Sciences of the USSR will publish an edition of my works. I do not know whether this is true or not, but I do know this: the people there have not bought or paid me anything, and if they do print my works, they will, of course, not pay me anything. After all, I was never paid anything (nor will I be) for

---

[4]Gabriela Mistral of Chile won the Nobel Prize in Literature in 1945. She was the first Latin American woman to be accorded this honor.

editions of my works that have already been published in Russia (and in such great quantities, to boot)! But I should be paid something.

After all, forgive my lack of modesty here, but I am not bragging when I say that I have a great deal of proof to show that in recent times I am very greatly admired by readers in Russia. . . .

September 8, 1945
Ivan Bunin, from a letter to a friend
Enclosed please find a book of my verse. Read it and weep from delight.

September 9, 1945
Vera Muromtseva-Bunina, from her diary
[Coming home from a friend's] we saw that someone had pinned a note on our door: "Zinaida Gippius has passed away. The *panakhida*[5] will be at nine o'clock."

I . . . immediately rushed off [to her place], running down the quiet streets in a state of great distress. I have not seen her in more than five years.

[When I got there] someone had tidied up her apartment. There was cleanliness and order everywhere. The study no longer had her husband's bed in it; so it seemed more inviting. . . . In the salon . . . was a coffin covered with fresh, snow-white sheets. In a black dress and a plain black scarf lay Zinaida Nikolaevna. She was thin, with a peaceful face. I bowed to the ground before her and kissed her hand.

[Her secretary] Zlobin told me that right before she died, she opened her eyes and expressed her gratitude toward him. . . . She died without suffering. . . . "I think she is in purgatory," he said.

The priest arrived. . . . The bell rang again. I saw a white raincoat—it was Ian.

I was somewhat unnerved [by his arrival]. He has always been afraid of dead bodies and never goes to requiems or burial services.

He entered, very pale, and went up to the coffin. . . . He stood there for a minute, then went into the dining room, sat down on a chair, covered his face with his left hand, and burst out crying.

When the funeral service began, Ian went into the salon. . . . He prayed fervidly on his knees. At the end he went up to the body, bowed to the ground before her, and took her hand. He was pale, with a very strained look on his face.

[5] A *panakhikda* is the memorial service for the dead.

Ian said that he met Gippius fifty years ago, when he first came to Petersburg. She was all in white, wearing sleeves that hung down to the floor; and when she would raise her arms, she looked as though she had sprouted wings. She read: "I love myself as a God!" . . . to both whistles and thunderous applause. "Then she was so young and beautiful," Ian said, "but now she is a gaunt old woman. I am beginning to pity her greatly. It is a good thing that she is lying in a coffin and not on a table." . . .

Many people are wrong when they say that Gippius was not a kind woman. She was much kinder than she seemed. At times she could be wicked . . . [and] was never completely indifferent to things. Several times, though, I saw in her both kindness and sincerity. . . .

October 1, 1945
Ivan Bunin, from a letter to Mark Aldanov
I have just received a letter from the editors of *New Review*, rejecting my stories "Madrid" and "The Second Coffeepot" because, in their view, the characters were absolutely obscene!

October 11, 1945
Ivan Bunin, from a letter to Mark Aldanov
A visit to America . . . would be very interesting, but also very difficult. . . . Truly, I do not have the strength for such a trip, as well as for all the other "experiences" connected with it. . . .

Get this: I have just received a letter from [a publisher in Sweden who tells me] . . . that all my books in Swedish have sold out, but that it is not good *psychologically* to republish the works of an *"emigré"* there!

But in Moscow itself, people continue to publish me. Just the other day I read in *Literary Gazette*[6] that the Soviets have published an anthology of my "selected" works![7] In the spring, too, "Soviet" newspapers reported that the Academy of Sciences is likewise printing an edition of my writings. Such news disturbed and continues to disturb me greatly. God knows what will be heaped into this edition! Sensible pieces will be placed alongside trite, early ones. In a word, they will do things that have many writers with such "editions" turning in their graves!

---

[6]*Literary Gazette (Literaturnaia gazeta)*, first published in 1929, is still in existence today.
[7]In 1944 the Soviets published *Shadowed Paths*, an anthology of Bunin's works in English.

If you can, please send me some "Vitamins Plus." I am truly weak.
Vera too.

October 11, 1945
Nikolai Teleshov, from a letter to Ivan Bunin

I have learned that you are alive and well. I rejoice over such news
and send my fond regards to both you and Vera Nikolaevna. I received
your 1941 postcard, but I could not respond, since the fascists had attacked us and ended all contacts with Europe. Then came extremely
sorrowful news about your passing; and I, believing what I had heard,
published it my *Notes of a Writer*, which, according to a Russian saying,
promises you a long and happy life.[8]

My dear, write back! Write me right away!

As you know, our Homeland has emerged brilliantly from the
most difficult circumstances and disruptions. Everything here is sound
and prosperous. When Alexei Tolstoy and Kuprin returned here, they
were delighted to be back.

Here we also honor and revere the memory of Chaliapin and
Rachmaninoff. Such a respect we have for all great Russian talents.

October 13–November 1, 1945
Vera Muromtseva-Bunina, from a letter to a friend

Writing letters are for me the most difficult activity. I have so
many things to do and worry about them all. Besides caring for the
house and waiting on lines, I do exercises for the soul. . . . I am also
making money by doing some typing. One week I made more than a
thousand francs. . . .

One evening we and friends headed for Montparnasse, where
"those who survived the shipwreck" [of the Revolution] were sitting in
a café and talking quietly over some glasses of beer. Everyone has become kinder and more pleasant, but also more ragged and worn out.
They have all had to endure a great deal. . . .

Yesterday there was a gathering where Adamovich talked about
four poets: Mayakovsky, Esenin, Akhmatova, and Os. Mandelshtam. . . . This was a first evening of a seemingly past and forgotten
life. I knew everyone there . . . but how they have all changed! They
have gotten older, greyer. There were no young people there. Someone

---

[8]In Russian, people respond to an individual who has had a close encounter with death
by saying "he will live for a long time" ("*dolgo budet zhit'* ").

who has just arrived from Russia kept asking: "But where is your youth? Aren't they interested in literature?"

But for those of us who spent those wretched years in the south, the emotions were quite new. It would be difficult to express the joy we had at meeting people there: "You are still alive!" "You have survived!" It is also difficult to convey the sadness of learning that many people who used to come to such gatherings are no longer with us. . . .

The auditorium for Adamovich's reading was full, but the take was small—only several thousand francs in all. . . . But many of the people there had been invited to come. . . .

Thank you very much for the package you promised to send. The prices here are so astronomical that I look at the items in the store windows not as things to buy but more as exhibits in museums where things are not sold.

Our main concern now is how to keep ourselves warm. . . . I somehow do not worry about such a thing, even though there is no heat in my room and I have to give Ian the one real blanket that I had. So I am counting on my fur coat which I will wear when I go to bed. I will look like a bear sucking his paw. . . .

Your jacket keeps me warm so far, and it is good that it is wide . . . for I am starting to put on weight. . . .

October 24, 1945
Ivan Bunin, from a letter to Mark Aldanov
The obituary that you wrote for Merezhkovsky—pardon me, dear friend, but you have exaggerated his talent![9]

October 24, 1945
Mark Aldanov, from a letter to Ivan Bunin
I implore you: come to America. If you . . . were here, I would want nothing else from life. . . .

October 25, 1945
Vera Muromtseva-Bunina, from her diary
Mikhail Osipovich [Tseitlin] has died from leukemia. He was a rare type of individual, delicate, intelligent, meticulous, and educated.

[9]Aldanov's highly flattering obituary of Merezhkovsky appeared in *Novyi zhurnal*, No. 2 (1942), 368–373.

October 31, 1945
An attaché at the Soviet Embassy in Paris, from a confidential report

By chance, I happened to meet the well-known writer, Bunin. . . . He told me that, once and for all, he has decided to remain in Paris, despite his wretched living conditions. "I am dying from hunger," he said. He continues to write, rework, and publish things. . . .

Rumor has it that Bunin has turned sharply "to the left," i.e., he longs for the homeland and dreams secretly about an invitation to return home. He has stopped ranting and raving, comes off as an old man, but one with a lively mind. People also say . . . that he is now writing à la Artsybashev, but that his focus on sexual themes is far more daring. Bunin also says that his works are selling well in America. . . .

November 5, 1945
Ivan Bunin, from a letter to Mark Aldanov

God knows what awaits us, but I cannot tell you how touched I was by your words, "If only you would come [to America]. . . ."

November 9, 1945
Alexander Bakhrakh, from an article

Bunin said: "I have just finished rereading *War and Peace* for what has to be the fiftieth time. I read it lying down but I jumped up constantly from delight. Dear God, it is good . . . but there is something not quite right in *Ivan Ilych*. Here Ivan Ilych is lying down and thinks: 'I did not manage to do this,' 'I forgot to do that,' 'How repulsively I have lived my life.' . . . But the main thing is his horror before death itself, the horror of oblivion, the departure from this life. . . . The more basely one has lived life, the more terrible is the approach of its end." . . .

November 9, 1945
A reporter, from an article in Russian News

Those of us who have been with Bunin for so many years abroad, hail his new image . . . his anger at those who dared encroach upon . . . Russia, his faith in its final victory, and his brave behavior in the same circumstances that destroyed so many others. . . .

November 9, 1945
A reporter, from an interview with Ivan Bunin

It is very difficult to obtain an interview when the jubilarian refuses to be a jubilarian.

Bunin met us, saying: "Where you did get the idea that I am seventy-five years old? Take a good look at me. What kind of nonsense is this?"

"Excuse us," we said, "but it says in the *Encyclopedia Britannica. . . .*"

"That's just a stupid misprint. . . ."[1] . . .

And, truly, when we looked at I. A. Bunin—hale, hearty, and energetic—it began to seem that an annoying misprint had indeed crept into the *Britannica. . . .*

[We asked Bunin]: "Which of your works do you consider your very best?"

"My best works are the ones I wrote in the last few years, in emigration. My separation from Russia has not kept me from writing. Petrarch also wrote in exile . . . and Hugo, Heine, and Herzen[2] also created far from their native haunts. We writers carry our homeland within ourselves. . . ." . . .

"What are your plans for the future?"

"I regard the future with a very anxious frame of mind. Where can I take up writing here? I am interested in more urgent problems—how to heat my apartment, for example."

"And fame?"

"What can I do with fame here? Coal, wood—that is something entirely different. Fame is secondary."

November 11, 1945
Nikolai Teleshov, from a letter to Ivan Bunin

A book of yours is being published by the [Soviet] State Press. . . .

November 14, 1945
Ivan Bunin, from a letter to Mark Aldanov

There is no greater sorrow
than to remember happy times
in present misery.[3] . . .

---

[1]Bunin was indeed seventy-five years old.

[2]Hugo was exiled from France from 1851 to 1870; Heine from Germany from 1831 to 1856; and Herzen from Russia from 1847 to 1870.

[3]Bunin is citing from Dante's *Inferno*, 5:121–123.

Our apartment has already become devilishly cold, and I am already beginning to take sick. . . . I am borrowing money left and right . . . and we have had to pawn some small gold items, the last things that Vera and I have. It is disgusting! . . .

Mid-November 1945
Nikolai Teleshov, from a letter to Ivan Bunin
I am happy to know that you are alive and well. . . . [During the war] I heard rumors that you had refused categorically to cooperate with the fascists, and that you had been arrested by them and imprisoned in one of their torture chambers. All of this seemed true enough in those terrible years. I tried everything I could to find out something about you, but everyone kept saying that you had perished. Even Serafimovich kept assuring me that he knew without a doubt that you were no longer among the living. . . . I was also buried twice. . . .

Yes, dear friend, there are not many of us left around here. Almost no one. There is hardly any surprise in that. And those of us who are left are around eighty years old. . . .

November 23, 1945
The Soviet Ministry for External Affairs, from a confidential report
According to Ambassador Bogomolov, the writer Ivan Bunin is old and extremely unstable. (He drinks a great deal.) His political convictions are also erratic. One moment he wants to return to the USSR, but the next he babbles all kinds of anti-Soviet nonsense.

November 28, 1945
The Soviet Ministry for External Affairs, from a confidential report
Bunin is hysterical, and the members of our embassy will handle him carefully. . . .

Mid-December 1945
Alexander Bogomolov, from his diary
Bunin came to see me. He is seventy-five years old, but he appears to be hale and hearty. Our conversation was "enlightened" but did not touch upon any delicate questions.

When I told Bunin that it was time for him to look at his country from the inside, he said he would do so with pleasure. Our entire discussion passed in this vein, but without obligating anyone to do anything. . . .

At this point my impressions of Bunin are very superficial. He is an old man who is prone to all kinds of memories, habits, and triflings. He loves to drink, swears up a storm, and hangs around a "bohemia" of young writers. . . .

At times Bunin is somewhat posturing and coquettish . . . but he is an interesting individual. . . .

December 26, 1945
Ivan Bunin, from a letter to Marc Aldanov

I have received a telegram from Moscow . . . asking me to send an anthology of my latest stories "as soon as possible." . . . I asked [an officer at the Soviet embassy] where and to whom I should send these stories. . . . After about three weeks, there came an answer from Moscow, saying that people there wish to *publish* my stories . . . and some of my latest writings, to boot. . . . So I sent them my works, along with *The Liberation of Tolstoy* and *The Life of Arseniev*. I also sent them several of my latest pieces . . . things I am not entirely sure they would find interesting, since . . . I am for them a "historical" individual who is interesting only from an aesthetic point of view.

Almost at the very same time I received a letter from . . . the Russian embassy [in Paris], informing me that the Soviet ambassador would like to meet with me. A car came for me . . . and I met with the ambassador for about thirty minutes. We had an absolutely "social" and absolutely apolitical discussion, whereupon I took my leave . . . to face rumors that I had visited the embassy because I was intending to return to Russia. . . .

If I survive the winter, I swear that I will not spend another one in Paris for anything in the world.

Now that you have finally received a visa for France, how wildly happy I will be to embrace you, if I live that long! . . .

December 26, 1945
Mark Aldanov, from a letter to Ivan Bunin

Your story "The River Inn" will be coming out [in a special edition] in about ten days. We have printed 1,000 copies. . . . When it was published in *New Review*, everyone was enthralled by it, even your political enemies. . . .

Your description of the Volga and of the inn [in the story] is the summit of perfection. . . .

✳ 1946 ✳

Circa 1946
Sofya Pregel', from her memoirs

People have not commented sufficiently on how repulsed Bunin was by his illness. He looked upon his infirmity as something that was restricting and unnatural. He also found it insufferable that André Gide could wear a jacket . . . and go to the "Comédie Française," whereas he, Bunin, was in a housecoat and could barely make it to the dining room to receive guests. . . .

In fact, there were days when Ivan Alexeevich . . . spoke with visitors only through a closed door. No matter how much people protested or made clear their loyalty and love, he refused to show himself. "One cannot love me," Ivan Alexeevich would say. "For I am a repulsive old man. It is not me whom you pretend to love, but a Nobel laureate."

Sometimes, though, Bunin came out willingly and lay on the couch in the dining room. He resembled a plucked eagle, and his face showed the sickly shadows that heralded his end. "Go sit with him," Vera Nikolaevna would say [to me], in a voice that was full of love and without the slightest hint of sacrifice.

[Whenever I entered the room] Bunin came alive. In the vilest language he began cursing and swearing at some old writer for his mannerisms and passion for the dictionaries of Dal'.[4] As Bunin saw it, the writer was a poseur, and everything he wrote was a sham. Clearly, Bunin was treating the individual in an unjust way; but his attack on the writer was so full of indignation that I unwillingly let him have his way. The important thing was that Bunin go on living. Indeed, I could not imagine how a person could die such a slow death but also be consumed by such passionate hatred.

It was difficult, almost impossible to argue with Bunin. But Vera Nikolaevna was one of the few who could disagree with him openly. I remember how she spent evenings with him in his room, and how he talked with her about the past. Ivan Alexeevich was afraid to think of

---

[4]Pregel' is referring to Vladimir Dal''s four-volume work, *Explanatory Dictionary of the Living Russian Language* (*Tolkovyi slovar' zhivogo russkogo iazyka*), published between 1836 and 1866. To this day, Dal''s dictionary is unsurpassed for its inventory of Russian regional and dialectal expressions.

how Vera Nikolaevna would live without him. "Now don't go losing your head, Vera. Did you hear what I said? Don't go losing your head." . . . And she often went around, repeating what he had said. After Bunin died . . . she told me: "Yes it was difficult with him, but never boring." . . .

1946
Valentin Kataev, from his memoirs

Bunin had given up the two most precious things—Country and the Revolution—for the sorry porridge of the so-called freedom and independence which he had been seeking his entire life. I am sure of what I am saying if only because . . . in 1946 I received one of the best books that Bunin had ever written, *Lika*. I was greatly moved by the following passage:

"I often dropped in at the library. It was an old and extremely rich place. But how miserable it was, how unwanted it was by anyone! . . . I used to take out . . . all kinds of 'biographies of famous people,' always hoping to find some support for myself, to envy and compare myself with the people whose lives I read. . . . 'Famous people!' What countless numbers of poets, novelists, storytellers have lived on this earth, but how many of them have escaped death? Always those same eternal names! Homer, Horace, Virgil, Dante, Petrarch . . . Shakespeare, Byron, Shelley, Goethe . . . Racine, Molière. . . .

"Like a detective, I pursued first one passerby, then another, observing his back, his galoshes, trying to understand, to catch something within him, to get inside him. . . . To write! Yes, roofs, galoshes, backs—these are the things that one should write about, and not at all for the sake of 'fighting tyranny and oppression, of protecting the humiliated and injured, to render vivid types, and to draw broad pictures of society, of modern times, its moods and trends!' . . .

"Social contrasts! I thought caustically . . . as I passed by the dazzle and brilliance of the shop windows. . . . On Moskovskaya Street I stopped at a coachman's tea house, and amidst its conversations, its cramped and steamy warmth, I looked at the meaty, scarlet faces, at the red beards, at the rusty, peeling tray on which stood . . . two white teapots, with wet strings tying their tops to their handles. . . . Observations of folk? You are mistaken—[one needs] only observations of this tray, of this wet string! . . .

"Sitting in a sleigh . . . slipping and sliding from one pothole into another, I raise my head. The night, it seems, is moonlit; a pale face gleams whitely, flickering behind barely moving winter clouds. How high it is, how far it is from everything! The clouds move on, first exposing it, then covering it up again. But what does the moon care? It has nothing to do with such things! I crane my neck until it hurts, but I do not take my eyes from the moon, trying to understand what it is. Suddenly it emerges gleaming from behind the clouds. The white mask of a dead man? All radiant from within, but what kind of radiance exactly? Like that of a tallow candle? Yes, yes, that is it, like a tallow candle? That is how I will describe it somewhere!" . . .

[When Bunin was in Russia] he told me: "Describe a sparrow. Describe a girl!" But what was the result? I described a girl, but she was a "girl from a Communist party school," a heroine of the Revolution.

1946
Georgy Adamovich, from an article

If, by the will of God, Bunin had been born half a century earlier . . . he most likely would have been less dear to us than the contemporary, genuine Bunin we have now. But our love for him would have been . . . more peaceful. There would not have been the need to preserve and retain [something] of that Bunin . . . who is the "last" [of Russia's gentry writers]. . . . There also would not be that need to know that *Angst* that [when Bunin dies], something will be torn and lost forever. . . .

Bunin is dear to us because his work has an accessibility and fullness that his younger contemporaries have lost. . . . [In his writings] one feels a spiritual harmony . . . a higher structure and order. In Bunin everything is where it is supposed to be. The sun is the sun, love is love, people are people. By contrast, when one reads a young writer . . . one feels that he is being dragged through potholes and ruts . . . that he is hurriedly fumbling and wandering through life . . . and that the deeper he penetrates existence, the thicker the darkness. . . .

Bunin's pictures feature incomparable pictures of that Russian life which is gone and going. . . . As if recalling a magical line from *The Lay of the Host of Igor*, Bunin ends one of his stories sadly by saying: "Oh, Rus' still lives, but that Rus' is also on the wane." . . . But in his stories still lives Russia. . . .

January 5, 1946
Mark Aldanov, from a letter to Ivan Bunin

You devoted almost your entire letter to your visit [to the Russian embassy]. When, a long time ago, you wrote to me to say that you were thinking about returning [to Russia], I replied that nothing could diminish my love for you. But if you do go back, I think that you will be forced to write in the way other writers have to write there.

[If you actually do return to Russia] I "forgive" your sin in advance. . . . The older I get, the more indifferent and tolerant I become of politics. But do not tell me there is *no* politics when it comes to you. This is simply not so. Apart from your own feelings in the matter, and no matter what the extent or purpose of your call, your visit to the Russian embassy is being seen as a political act. I would be lying to you (and you, moreover, would not have believed me), if I had said that your visit there did not provoke irritation. While there are some people who approve of what you did . . . you must also take into account the larger group [who opposed your going]: conservative and aristocratic circles . . . and 95 percent of the clergy. . . . You are well aware of the storm that erupted when Maklakov visited the embassy; you had to know what you were doing when you went. . . .

Do you want to know my personal opinion? If you truly have decided to return to Russia, you were right to go [to the embassy] no matter what. . . . But if you have decided to stay [in the West], I do not understand why you went there.

I do not know if the Soviets will pay you for your books, but if you do get paid (which is highly likely), such arrangements could have been made without your visiting [Bogomolov and others]. After all, the Soviets got in touch with you . . . *before* you ever visited them. Assuming that you did not agree that your books be printed [in Russia]—I will leave aside the question of royalties—only dim-witted people can object [to their publication in the homeland]. True, the Soviets never asked your permission, but, thank God, you will be read there.

As you see, I am taking a practical view of things. What's done is done. Do not get overly angry at me (if you are angry at all). The furor you have caused will pass with time, and I will do everything I can to "mitigate" the results. . . . But for God's sake, decide *for yourself* once and for all: are you returning there or not? As far as I am concerned, all your subsequent actions depend on your decision.

January 23, 1946
Ivan Bunin, from a letter to Mark Aldanov

My visit [to the Soviet embassy] has taken on such significance that it has become simply absurd. I was invited, I *could not* refuse, I went without any objective in mind; and after an hour there, I returned home. That is all. . . . *I had no intention of going "home" {to Russia}, nor do I have one now.*

January 30, 1946
Ivan Bunin, from a letter to Nikolai Teleshov

I am writing both to the State Publishing House in Moscow and to you in the hope that you can personally speak to someone there and help me. . . . The edition that Moscow wants to publish is apparently an *anthology* of things that I have written throughout the course of my life. . . . I note (1) that there has been no input on my part (not to mention the fact that I did not agree to this publication in the first place); (2) that this anthology deprives me of the opportunity to reprint a collection of my works in Russian either in France or in some other country; and, (3) that Vera and I would lose the only source of money that we have in our old age, especially given my situation as an almost full-blown invalid. Dear one, I am going on my seventy-sixth year!

Furthermore, I protest fervently the fact that several of my books have already been published in Moscow (and in great quantity) without any royalties to me (for example, my translation of *The Song of Hiawatha*,[5] *Mitya's Love*—and, it seems, several other things) and I protest *even more vehemently* the publication of this new edition. . . . I am very upset because I am being treated as though I am not among the living (excuse the lack of modesty, but I am well known in the literary world of all cultured countries), and as though I am the personal property of Moscow. . . .

Finally, with equal passion, I request that you take pity on me and not publish this *anthology*. . . .

February 5, 1946
An attaché from the Soviet embassy in Paris, from a confidential report

Bunin is now an old man who is seriously ill and finds himself in difficult living conditions. I do not know if his complaints [about a Soviet edition of his works] are valid, but, in any case, a pleasant reply would calm him down and put an end to his grumbling. . . . Representatives from an emigré group in America are pressuring him to move there . . . but as far as I know, he has refused their invitation categorically and [says that] "he might even die in the Homeland." . . .

---

[5]It was Bunin's translation of *The Song of Hiawatha* ("*Pesn' o Gaiavate*"), together with his 1900 collection of poems, entitled *Leaf-Fall* (*Listopad*), that in 1900 earned him the first of his three Pushkin Prizes in Literature.

February 7, 1946
Mark Aldanov, from a letter to Ivan Bunin

I sympathize with your anger that the Soviet government is acting so badly. But I am also extremely glad that you are being published there in such a great number of copies. . . .

Incidentally, have you kept a copy of the film script that you and I wrote about Tolstoy's life à la [his story] *The Cossacks?* . . . Mine was taken away by the Gestapo along with my entire library, manuscripts, notebooks, and letters. Although our chances are nil and my ties to Hollywood are nonexistent, maybe we should give it a try? What if each of us would get a million dollars and buy a castle with the money? . . .

February 8, 1946
Vera Muromtseva-Bunina, from a letter to Maria Tseitlina

I do not know how to thank you for everything you have done for us. I would have perished a long time ago if it had not been for you. All our warm underclothing is from you. . . . There have been several times when you have genuinely rescued us. . . .

February 12, 1946
Ivan Bunin, from a letter to Mark Aldanov

I have reread Sirin's savage, repulsive story *The Gift,*[6] and I have been swearing like a sailor all along the way.

February 14, 1946
Ivan Bunin, from a letter to Mark Aldanov

What you want to pay me [for my work] is insulting. I will not take a kopeck from you! . . .

Also, the fact that the Soviet Publishing House will publish me in "large numbers" does not gladden me at all, since I am beside myself with grief. . . .

I did not save the film script.

March 26, 1946
The Soviet State Publishing House, from a telegram to Ivan Bunin

As you have requested, preparation for an edition of your works has been suspended. . . .

---

[6]Nabokov wrote *The Gift* (*Dar*) in 1937 and 1938.

March 27, 1946
Mark Aldanov, from a letter to Ivan Bunin

In vain are you perturbed by the publication of your works in Russia. Pushkin wrote to Bestuzhev: "I find it sad that I am being treated like a dead man, without any respect for my wishes or for my impoverished being." Assume that the Soviets will make a poor choice regarding which of your works they will publish. But it will be Bunin just the same, and, after many years of not knowing your writing, all of Russia will read you. No, if I were you, I would not be perturbed. . . .

April 1946
A Soviet reporter, from an article

A meeting of emigré writers . . . was like a strange and burdensome wake. . . . Old men kissed the hands of old women dressed in fashionable hats with bouquets of flowers in the brims. Very few young people were there. . . .

[At one such meeting] . . . a small and somewhat withered Bunin mounted the stage. He had the refined face of an aesthete. He wore a pince-nez, and his grey hair was neatly combed; but his eyes were tired and rimmed with dark circles. He was chewing his lips like an old man, and wiping his forehead in a tired and weary way.

With a sweeping gesture, [the announcer] introduced Bunin as "the jewel of Russian literature." Bunin shriveled up slightly. . . . He opened a book and began to read his old story, "Death."[7]

"In the name of the most merciful. Here is a story about the death of a prophet—peace be with him—so that doubters see the need to resign themselves to the Master. . . ."

He read in a somewhat irritated way, like a teacher who has too many examinations to grade, like someone who has read the same text many, many times.

Bunin slammed the book shut, rose, and walked off the stage, accompanied by applause. . . . [He later reappeared] . . . looking around with empty eyes and . . . as if he were angry at something. . . .

[At the end of the evening] when we approached Bunin, his face lit up when he learned that we were from the USSR. But his face immediately grew dark as he began to talk with forced liveliness:

"Well, how do you like Paris? Not a bad little city, huh? I have gotten used to it. . . . Do you know how long we have lived here?"

---

[7]Bunin wrote "The Death of a Prophet" ("*Smert' proroka*") at Capri in 1911.

Through the crowd came his wife, as grey as an old peahen.

"Yes, yes, since 1918. Now how many years is that? Twenty-eight. . . . Yes, twenty-eight years."[8]

Bunin kept repeating this number in a somewhat perplexed way, as if he realized for the first time how many years had passed since he had torn himself from the homeland. Somewhat distracted, he turned to his wife and said:

"You know where they are from? From Moscow. People fly there all the time. It is nothing for them to do so. After all, the old roads have been destroyed."

But as he talked, one could hear a muffled note of envy and sadness in his voice.

"Are you going to be here long?" Bunin asked.

"As soon as we finish things here, we will return home."

"And where are you staying now?"

"In a hotel."

"And they let you come and see us here?" Bunin's wife asked in genuine surprise.

Everyone laughed. . . .

The conversation turned to the difficult times of the war. Bunin told me that he had left Paris to live in the south. "I could not bear to see the Germans!" he said. . . .

Having learned that we had also stopped in Berlin, he was especially interested in knowing what the German capital looked like now. "Those scoundrels got exactly what they deserved!" he kept saying.

We asked Bunin if he was intending to return to the USSR.

"I am too old for that!" he said. "Of course, I should make a quick trip there. . . . But I really don't know." . . .

He said this in a way that was bilious and severe, since he was irritated and offended not only by his listeners but at his very self, his fate, and the fate of the entire emigration, who, to no purpose, wasted the best years of their lives in voluntary exile.

April 15, 1946
Ivan Bunin, from a letter to Mark Aldanov

I do not have a summer coat. Perhaps the "Tolstoy Foundation" has one to give me?

---

[8]Bunin is mistaken. He and his wife arrived in Paris in late March 1920.

April 22, 1946
Ivan Bunin, from a letter to Mark Aldanov

I would like to have a yellowish coat, a so-called waterproof one, but also one that is not rubberized but more silklike, *very light weight, with lining only in the shoulders.*

May 3, 1946
Vera Muromtseva-Bunina, from her diary

We have been in Paris for a year, but it seems that I have never experienced a more fruitless time. . . .

May 6, 1946
Mark Aldanov, from a letter to Ivan Bunin

Thank you also for your story "Galya Ganskaya."[9] It is a marvelous piece. [The editor], though, asks your permission to exclude three lines (about the kisses on the leg where the stocking ends).

I will not hide from you the fact that the publishers have received letters from readers protesting the "eroticism" . . . in your stories!!! One came from a scholar. . . . "How could you do such a thing?" he writes. "I have a wife" and so forth. We did not answer him. But the editor will not insist on changes. If you not wish to exclude these lines, he will leave them there. . . .

May 10, 1946
Ivan Bunin, from a letter to Mark Aldanov

[My story] "Galya" is no good without its "eroticism"; so it would be better if you did not print it at all. . . .

P.S. I have just received a proposal from England from the former director of Hogarth Press who, having founded his own publishing house, wants to publish *Dark Alleys*.[1] He is more daring [than you].

May 27, 1946
Vera Muromtseva-Bunina, from her diary

[The Soviets] have offered to fly Ian to Moscow for two weeks, and then back here on a return visa.

---

[9]Bunin wrote "Galya Ganskaya" on October 28, 1940.
[1]The project never materialized.

June 13, 1946
Umm-El-Banine Assadoulaeff, from her memoirs

Bunin lived a respectable life, in complete family harmony with his wife, a wonderful woman who has one great flaw: after forty years of marriage, she did not arouse in him the slightest love interest. But he needed it not only because he "loved to love" but also from the most elementary professional considerations: how could Bunin describe situations where lovers fell into the most improbable extremes—from murder to suicide—while he himself languished in a happy legal marriage with no adventures?

With exaggeration I can say that the heavens sent me to him because I possessed those qualities . . . that made me a favorite of his: I had the exotic aura of a Mohammedan woman from the Caucasus, a weakness shared by all the Russian writers of the north: Lermontov, Pushkin, and Tolstoy. Furthermore . . . I was a writer who occupied the lowest step of that staircase on which he stood at the top. Without a doubt Bunin imagined that we would ignite passion in each other, that we would inspire each other to write immortal lines, and that we would engage in such things under the gracious glance of his wife who had a golden heart and who thought of nothing other than to indulge and gratify him. . . .

When I entered Teffi's room, Bunin rose without difficulty from that chair that had been designated for honored guests. . . . The bags under his eyes hung so low that they seemed disproportionate for his thin face. He could do nothing about this unpleasant feature . . . but his head, which had a tendency to shake, Bunin held up like a sword. Such stonelike erectness was so artificial that it would have been better if he had been hunchbacked. Bunin's hands, which he nervously drummed on the arm of the chair, were covered with spots, with what the French gloomily call "cemetery flowers." But the hair on his head was thick and splendidly white. . . .

Bunin was grand in a majestic way, and his stance, whatever its faults, greatly supported the expression of his face. It was first haughty, then aggressive, then both haughty and aggressive. Indeed, the two expressions were so alike that it was difficult to tell them apart. Bunin wore his haughtiness like a Roman toga, to show the distance between a solitary genius and simple mortals. . . .

I liked Bunin's arrogance. Indeed, I even came to admire it, since he reminded me of my first love, Prince Andrei Bolkonsky, the cold and proud hero of *War and Peace*, for whom, as did many girls brought up on Tolstoy, I had nurtured an unfulfilled passion. . . . Ten minutes into his first conversation [with me], Bunin dropped that toga which he used to elevate himself in the eyes of others. He caught fire, his voice grew strong, he let loose with compliments with echoes of the good old days. He was especially taken with my Eastern features, my half-savage looks. . . . Within the half-hour he told me that I was that very "black rose" he had dreamed about his entire life. . . .

I was overwhelmed by the liveliness of this old man, his bile, his wit. He picked up on every word, every phrase, every expression of the face, every change in tone. His glance kept evaluating, measuring, and taking stock of things.

Because Bunin was so very attentive, he often mobilized my attention and forced me to live more quickly. In his company, one was both tempered and tyrannized. His medal had two sides: one either loved him or hated him. . . .

At first I was amused by Bunin's extreme reactions toward everything. The sense of moderation, so prized by the French, only evoked horror in him. . . . In life, Bunin surged and seethed; he loved and hated with equal force; he revered or despised with equal frenzy. In time I became very tired of these extremes, but I was never bored with him. . . .

[When we were together] Bunin drank in my compliments, and I drank in his flattery. We intoxicated each other. . . .

[Bunin said]: "Do you know what happiness is? People have tried to define it variously . . . but we can only have a presentiment of such an emotion. It is impossible to seize happiness, because when we think we have it in our hands, we look and see that such rapture is ruined by a toothache, nostalgia, or the death of a close one. . . .

"I have always waited for the letter that would bring me the miracle of happiness. Do not look me at so distrustfully! I am telling you the truth—[I want] the miracle of happiness. Yes, at my age! Every morning I rush to get the mail . . . and when I see handwriting that I do not recognize, my heart begins to pound. I tear open the envelope . . . but then I find there is nothing for me to be happy about. . . .

"Yes, my Nobel Prize brought me that kind of joy that makes the heart jump. But happiness is something that does not last, perhaps because our ephemeral existence poisons everything we have. . . . [People say] I was lucky to be awarded the prize! But I say that I deserved it more than any other writer on earth. Of all living writers today, I am the most important!" . . .

[When Bunin gave a public reading of his works] he stood as erect as an arrow and as imposing as a king. When he majestically entered the auditorium, he was greeted with loud applause. The snowy whiteness of his hair and the refined elegance of his manner testified to his inexpressible charm. When Bunin began to read . . . his voice reached all the corners of the room; it sounded like a horn, enchanting both his listeners and himself. On the wings of his worshipers, Bunin rose and reigned. . . . His entire being proclaimed: "It is I, Ivan Bunin." Indeed, it often seemed that Bunin invited his audience not to waste a moment but to delight in him more and more; and his listeners responded to his call eagerly. Every time he paused, the auditorium erupted into a storm of applause, acclaiming the well-known author, the great, the one and only Ivan Bunin. . . .

Bunin, though, did not abuse the admiration of his listeners. Unlike many others in his place, he did not prolong his reading. The way he spoke was impeccable: neither too fast nor too slow. His diction was excellent; he never became pompous. He read as he wrote, in the same restrained way. The evening always ended in triumphant ovations. A monarch answering the well-wishes of his subjects from his balcony could not have nodded to the mob with any more dignified majesty than Bunin. . . .

[When Vera Nikolaevna and I] first met, she was kind to me, complimenting me on my writing . . . smiling an enchanting smile at me with her lips and eyes. Despite her height, she was very comely, with strands of grey hair falling on a modest-looking dress. Tall, and as refined as her husband, she carried herself like a woman of society. (I quickly became convinced, though, that she could be quite self-willed when the need arose.) On that evening Vera Nikolaevna put herself at my service. Feelings of envy were alien to her; and in no way would she ever obstruct the many adventures of her husband. Who knows? Perhaps this magnanimity also had a dose of egoism? She was the only one to suffer the outbursts, caprice, and demands of her husband-tyrant; but, like a lightning rod, she often absorbed the fiery outbursts that her husband threw at others.

Most likely Vera Nikolaevna was flattered by all the attention given to her husband. She loved him so much that she wanted only his happiness. She was so very kind to him; she never got angry with him. . . . She loved him not as a woman but as a mother who spoiled her child. And what else was Bunin, if not an aging child, her child? . . .

Vera Nikolaevna was an intellectual. She had graduated from the science faculty of Moscow University; she knew several languages, she had translated Flaubert's *Éducation sentimentale*. She had a number of remarkable qualities which made her the ideal woman. Beautiful, modest, intelligent, and educated, she possessed an angelic, magnanimous character which allowed her to endure her husband's mercurial nature. Bunin had two major successes in life—a remarkable wife and the Nobel Prize. It is difficult to say which one served him better, but it is more than clear that Vera Nikolaevna served him longer. For forty years she renounced her self and endured her difficult husband. . . .

Bunin very much treasured and clung to his wife throughout his life. He loved her with all his heart. . . . Vera Nikolaevna herself wrote to her brother, Dmitri Muromtsev: "Ian has no one except me. No one could ever take my place. Such a thing he tells not only me but also our friends (when I am not around). . . . He tells me that if I would ever leave him, it would be a catastrophe for him. . . ."

[At the café] Bunin continued to flirt with me under the gracious gaze of his wife—his friend, sister, and mother. It was getting late, the café was closing, and Bunin became upset that none of his admirers intended to pay for the refreshments. One moment he was cheerful; now he had become gloomy. He was suffering not only because he had to pay the bill but also from the wounded pride of a great person whose worshipers had abandoned him at the very moment he needed them.

The waiter stood and waited. Bunin did the same—but in vain. The situation was becoming awkward. Finally, yielding to the inevitable, Bunin . . . paid for his wife and himself. He had forgotten all about me, despite the rules of gallantry and etiquette. . . . After all, it was Bunin who had insisted that I go with him to the café, and who had taken me by the hand so that I could not get away. Gasping from indignation, I was about to pay for myself when Vera Nikolaevna, pointing to my glass, said to the waiter: "Bring her another one, please." With a dissatisfied look, Bunin paid for it. . . .

Was Bunin tight with money? His most intolerant detractors said that he was. They insisted on his vile miserliness, his willingness to spare nothing for himself but to count every kopeck when it came to others. . . . Teffi . . . used to call Bunin "the devourer." . . . She told me that he often opened the food packages that his admirers had sent him . . . and devoured the largest and best parts of their contents. . . . One time, when both Bunin and his wife had fallen victim to food poisoning, an admirer brought vegetable soup . . . but Bunin ate the whole thing down to the last spoonful. . . . Another time a fan brought Bunin a very small chicken. . . . After Vera Nikolaevna had cooked it, she was called away by some emergency and was gone for an hour and a half. When she returned, she found only bones on the plate.

Summer 1946
Georgy Adamovich, from his memoirs

When Bunin first met Konstantin Simonov [in Paris], he treated the Soviet writer with a refined, slightly mannered politeness that was very much in keeping with the old regime. . . .

At first the atmosphere was tense. Bunin had "taken the bit between his teeth," as he was often wont to do. . . . He played dumb, asking Simonov inappropriate questions to which the Soviet writer answered shortly, curtly, like a soldier: "I don't know."

"Konstantin Mikhailovich, tell me please," Bunin asked, "there was this writer, Babel. . . . I've read a thing or two by him, and undoubtedly he is a talented individual. . . . But how come I have not heard anything about him in such a long time? Where is he now?"[2]

"I don't know."

"There's this other writer, Pilnyak. . . . To tell you the truth, I don't like him at all, but his name is also well known, and now you hear nothing about him. . . . What happened to him? Is he sick, perhaps?"[3]

"I don't know."

"Or Meyerhold. . . . That one thundered and roared; he even turned *Hamlet* inside out . . . but now no one remembers him. . . . Why?"[4]

"I don't know."

This went on for several minutes. Bunin kept bringing up one

---

[2]Isaac Babel was arrested on May 15, 1939, and died in prison two years later.

[3]Although Soviet sources claim that Boris Pilnyak died in 1941, evidence exists that the writer was shot shortly after his arrest in October 1937.

[4]The theatre director Vsevelod Meyerhold was arrested on June 20, 1939 on trumped-up charges that he had ties both to Japanese intelligence and to Trotskyist organizations, and that he and others had plotted to assassinate Stalin. After months of torture and interrogation, Meyerhold was executed on February 2, 1940.

Regarding his recasting of *Hamlet*, a Russian actress recalls a "mime"-étude of the mad Ophelia: "Ophelia was picking flowers by a pond and making them into a garland. From time to time she seemed to remember something, stopping what she was doing and pressing the flowers to her breast. She then began to pick more flowers . . . [seeing them] as real, living creatures. Next she moved around the blue oval of the carpet below the stage, giving the impression that the action was taking place around a small pond. . . .

"The étude was performed to music. Ophelia's repetitive movement—her circling around the pond—creating a heartrending sense of foreboding. At the same time . . . the heightened lyricism of Ophelia's emotional state contrasted with the mundane behavior of her nurse, who observed her closely but uncomprehendingly and who sometimes helped her by picking up a flower that Ophelia had thrown away. But then the nurse, sensing that something was wrong, began to express her horror and despair. At a loss as to what to do, she followed on Ophelia's heels, weeping as she realized the absurdity of her charge's behavior." See E. Braun, *Meyerhold: A Revolution in Theater* (Iowa City, 1995), 129.

name after another, people whose tragic fate was well known to everyone. Simonov sat there, pale, his head bend down. . . . Stunned by what Bunin was doing, Teffi kept looking at him and frowning. But she was a smart woman and quickly rescued the situation. She suddenly told an incredibly funny story. Bunin roared with laughter. He softened and kissed Teffi's hand. Someone had ordered a great variety of hors d'oeuvres . . . along with Swedish, Polish, and Russian vodka. Within the half-hour, Teffi entertained us with a guitar and the dinner ended in complete harmony.

I learned from Bunin that several days later he again met with Simonov in a café and had a heart-to-heart talk with him that lasted for two hours or more. The conversation made an excellent impression on Bunin. He especially esteemed his Soviet guest for his rare sense of tact. Most likely they talked not only about literature but also about politics. . . .

[During this meeting] Bunin said to Simonov: "It is an old Russian tradition that the first toast must be in honor of the guest. But you will forgive me if I make this toast to that people to whom we all belong. Let us drink to the great Russian people, the victorious Russian people. . . . And to the leadership of Comrade Stalin!"

June 14, 1946
The Soviet government, from a decree
The Government of the Soviet Union has decided to extend to everyone who does not have or has lost Soviet citizenship, the right to assume it once again and, in so doing, to become a fully franchised son of the Soviet Fatherland. . . . In the years of the Great Fatherland War, a large part of the Russian emigration expressed their unbreakable tie with the Soviet people who, on the fields of battle with Hitler's Germany, defended their homeland.

Circa mid-July 1946
A Soviet correspondent, from an article
In the summer of 1946 I spoke with Bunin in his apartment in Paris. The Presidium of the Supreme Soviet of the USSR had just published a decree granting citizenship to those emigrés living in France who had petitioned for [such a favor]. . . . Ivan Alexeevich . . . said: "The Soviet government has acted honorably in issuing this decree."

With sadness, Bunin said that the young Russians who had grown up in France were losing their national identity but . . . that the older generation still had an undying feeling of patriotism and of love for their native language. Delicately I asked Bunin about the war . . . but he quickly lost his peaceful demeanor.

Bunin said: "When we were in Grasse, I got hold of an issue of a German propaganda journal that was written in French. On the cover was a colored picture: a fascist patrol with machine guns and gas masks was sitting on top of one of the bell towers of the Kiev-Pechersk Monastery.[5] . . . Kiev, our greatest sacred place, the Mother of Russian cities; and, suddenly, Germans. . . ."

He swore profusely. When Bunin was greatly upset, he could let loose some powerful expressions.

"Germans. . . . What the hell were Germans doing there? No son-of-a-bitch . . . has the right to stick his nose in Russian affairs! I would not look at the journal anymore but tore the filthy thing into shreds and sent it to hell!"

Bunin's face convulsed into spasms; his hands shook. . . . He was so upset. He felt such anger, pain, grief, and spiritual anguish that I almost regretted bringing up the topic at all. Vera Nikolaevna was sitting next to him, stroking her husband's hand:

"You should not get so upset, Vanya," she said, "Calm yourself! You must forget the terrible things that have happened!" . . .

Ivan Alexeevich got hold of himself with difficulty. . . .

Bunin lived in a modest apartment on the fifth floor of a building on a small and quiet street: rue Jacques Offenbach. It was a genuine "Russian corner." . . . Whenever a visitor entered, he immediately sensed that he was in a Russian apartment, not a French one. . . . Whenever I rang the bell (under which was written "I. Bounine") . . . I was met by the mistress herself, Vera Nikolaevna, a very dear woman in a conventional black dress, with fluffy grey hair and a kind face that still preserved the traces of a rare beauty. Occasionally Ivan Alexeevich himself opened the door. He was a tall, thin, old man with a delicate face and eyes that were big, intelligent, and penetrating. He would pull together the sides of his warm blue robe; and, apologizing for the lack of order [in the apartment], he would invite me into the dining room, or, if he were working there on the table, into a small side room to the right of the corridor.

The room was quiet, sunny, and comfortable. In spring and sum-

[5]The Kiev-Pechersk Monastery, founded in 1051, is the oldest monastery in Russia. It had suffered greatly in World War II, with its treasures plundered and more than seventy monuments and buildings either damaged or destroyed. Restoration of the monastery, though, had begun as early as 1944.

mer, tulle curtains swayed gently against half-opened windows; trains rumbled monotonously nearby.

A small, comfortable study with one window also served as Bunin's bedroom. The furnishings were simple and modest in the extreme: a desk, a small table with a typewriter . . . several ordinary chairs, and a bed covered with a grey flannel blanket. In the corner was a row of suitcases . . . with hotel labels from many countries of the world. There was a wall mirror over the fireplace, and over it a marble shelf with many books. Photographs of relatives and friends hung on the walls. A picture of Chekhov with a personal inscription from the writer stood in a simple wooden frame. . . . There was also a gift from his mother: a small ancient icon with Old Russian letters in a copper frame.

The dining room had a big window, bright wallpaper, and, again, only the most essential furniture: a buffet, six chairs with soft seats and high backs, and a big round table. . . . Anyone who entered the place delighted in the purely Russian hospitality. . . .

The parquet floors were meticulously polished and shone in the slanting rays of the sun. No, this was not France but Russia: a typical room of a modest Russian intellectual. . . .

Although Bunin lived more than thirty years abroad . . . he lived and worked in Russian surroundings. . . . He remained Russian.

June 24, 1946
Vera Muromtseva-Bunina, from her diary
[The decree of the Supreme Soviet] has everyone in an uproar. Many families are split. Some want to go back, others want to stay here. Many wonder about military service.

June 28, 1946
A writer from Russian News, *from an interview with Ivan Bunin*
[Bunin said:] "Allow me to be brief, all the more so since there can be only one view of the Soviet decree [to grant citizenship to emigrés]. Of course, such a decision is a significant event in the life of the Russian emigration—not only in France but also in Yugoslavia and Bulgaria. One can only hope that the Soviet government will extend this magnanimous gesture to Russian emigrés in other countries."

June 28, 1946
A writer from Soviet Patriot, *from an interview with Ivan Bunin*
Vera Nikolaevna, Bunin's faithful companion, met me at the door

with a friendly smile. . . . There then entered Ivan Alexeevich, wearing a dark robe. His oval face was sad and severe, his eyes were attentive but tired and squinting. . . .

Joyously we drank to the Soviet decree. After all, the Soviet government acted wisely and nobly as regards us emigrés. Now each one will decide the question [of whether to return to Russia] for himself and his loved ones. . . .

I began to tell Bunin about the joy and excitement . . . of all those individuals who stood on the threshold of Soviet citizenship. . . . I also noted the emotion and tears in the eyes of our young men and women.

Bunin's face came alive. [He said:] "One cannot cut himself off from the Homeland without paying a price. I sometimes must visit emigré families. Several of the young ones are bored when they read *War and Peace* . . . and they do not understand Natasha Rostova. . . . They look upon her as I would someone from Greenland. To tell the truth, someone from Greenland would be closer and more comprehensible to me than the experiences of Natasha at her first ball or in the hunting scene would be to them. Of course, it is not the young ones who are at fault, nor is it always even the fault of their fathers. . . . But the young at least have a straight road to the Homeland."

We also talked about the trials and tribulations that Russian emigrés had suffered, and that after a quarter of century of wandering throughout the world, they would again step across their native border.

[Bunin replied:] "Yes, most likely many people will feel this way. . . . I myself recall how deeply moved I became when I went to Riga before the war. Latvia—why, it was almost like Russia itself. . . . People brought flowers, they made speeches, they even opened the tsar's rooms at the station."

[The writer:] "And that is how the Homeland will greet you, Ivan Alexeevich, with flowers and laurels. . . . Believe me when I say that it will not be otherwise."

June 30, 1946
Ivan Bunin, from a letter to the editor of Soviet Patriot

In the next issue of your newspaper, allow me to register my protest regarding your interview with me. . . . In the presence of witnesses, I firmly stated to . . . the author of the interview that I was giving him the right to publish only *one* single quote . . . my modest thought about the significance of the Soviet decree for the Russian emigration. *Soviet Patriot*, though, printed something entirely different: a description of my allegedly "mournful" and "agitated" face, and an entire group of enthusiastic phrases—things *I never even thought to utter*— as well as quotes that seriously distorted what I said in the brief and *personal* conversation I had with the interviewer. . . .

June 30, 1946
Vera Muromtseva-Bunina, from her diary
  [A friend] returned from a meeting . . . with [the Soviet ambassador] Bogomolov. . . . It seems that the people there got up and applauded about twenty times . . . and sent greetings to the Soviets.
  I find all this absurd, burdensome, and sad. Anyone here will be made to knuckle under!

July 1, 1946
Ivan Bunin, from a letter to Mark Aldanov
  I have never experienced more savage and base behavior than that of *Soviet Patriot*. But it is my fault that I had anything to do with . . . that super-shitty newspaper. Somehow I was not thinking. [The interviewer] was an old, close acquaintance of friends, a very sweet and shy individual. He also got caught in this shameful situation. The day before yesterday I was having dinner at friends'. [The interviewer] walked in, and in the presence of everyone there, told me that the editors of *Soviet Patriot* had so expanded and distorted the text of his interview that it was no longer recognizable. . . .
  Have you read his vile interview? [I supposedly said:] "The Soviet government acted *wisely and nobly* as regards *us emigrés*. . . ." The Soviet government no less! I would not even dream of ever saying such a thing. . . . I also never said a word about being torn from the homeland or the price that one has to pay for exile. . . .

July 1, 1946
Mark Aldanov, from a letter to Ivan Bunin
  I will remain an emigré. Politics arouses a deep revulsion in me; and when I read the newspapers, my depression grows worse. . . .

Early July 1946
Umm-El-Banine Assadoulaeff, from her memoirs
  [I asked Bunin:] "Why don't you admit that the Soviets promised you a harem in which every Soviet republic would hold a competition and choose a beauty [for you?]"
  [Bunin replied:] "Laugh on, laugh on, my dear. It is all the same to me whether I return to the USSR or not, for [such a return] would

not prevent me from being a famous writer . . . even if they covered me with gold. . . . But how could I forget my memories of the civil war? Do you know how many people who were dear to me perished [during that time]? The Reds hunted them down. . . . They robbed and shot them. . . . The civil war gave birth to a government that I hate, one that is tyrannical, godless." . . .

July 21, 1946
Konstantin Simonov, from his memoirs
      I met with Bunin five or six times in Paris in 1946.
      [At the meeting with the Soviet ambassador, explaining the new Soviet decree extending citizenship to emigrés], I remember that Bunin was sitting in the first row.[6] . . . He was an old man, but he still looked quite strong. He was somewhat thin, had gone completely grey, and was almost primly dressed. His grey hair, and the proud way he held his head and moved his hands and body, made for an impression that was sober-minded, elegant, sharp, and cruel. . . . He was very polite and restrained . . . but also quite cordial. . . .
      Bunin seemed to me to be a man of another time and epoch, an individual who would find it difficult to live in Russia and who could return home only after he had overcome a great many things in himself. . . . He impressed me as profoundly anti-democratic in everything he did. . . . [Bunin's antipathy to the Soviet Union] did not mean, though, that he could not empathize with us, Soviet compatriots . . . or that he could not love us . . . as Russians.
      But I was also certain that if he did return to the homeland, he would be irritated . . . by our current leaders . . . since he was a man who in no way could accept the changes in the Russia of the October Revolution. Indeed, his soul could not accept even the possibility of such changes . . . as a historical fact. . . . There were way too many things that Bunin could not understand, accept, and be comfortable with. . . .
      For instance, when I read his *Cursed Days* in Belgrade in 1944, I had a burdensome feeling, as if the ground was opening under my feet, and [as if] I were falling from the heights of great literature into a quagmire of petty spite, envy, and disgust, not to mention a blind, stubborn refusal to understand the simplest things. . . .
      When I came to Paris, I heard about Bunin's absolutely irre-

---

[6]Bunin, though, was not at the meeting at the Soviet embassy where, on June 30, 1946, and before an audience of several hundred onlookers, Bogomolov distributed the first Soviet passports to returning emigrés.

proachable behavior during the years of German occupation . . . that he had refused categorically to lift a finger for the enemy. . . . He told me: "Surely you understand that I was in a position that was different from that of other writers. By that time I had eaten through all the money from the Nobel Prize—only the gold medal remains—but the aura of being a laureate still shone over me and played an important role in the attitude of the Germans toward me. The Nobel Prize kept them in check, but it also enticed them to bring me into their orbit. I do not know if they had read my works or not, but everyone knew that I was a laureate and that I would be beneficial to the Germans if I collaborated with them in their work. Believing that I would be doomed to be the focus of far-reaching solicitations, I lived incognito in the south. . . ."

I regarded Bunin as a good writer and as an individual who had taken up an appropriate, patriotic position during the war. I respected him for his integrity, and this quality enabled me to overlook the severely unacceptable pages in his past. In a word, I wanted to know if Bunin would return home. . . .

Immediately before my meetings with Bunin, our ambassador told me that it would be a good idea if I could somehow prod Bunin into thinking about the possibility of returning [to Russia]. . . . Willingly I took this unofficial order to heart. . . . I told Bunin about everything that he might find interesting: the war, the people involved, what we endured—in a word, things that would bring us spiritually closer. . . .

I do not know if Bunin believed that I wanted to nudge him into returning to the homeland, or if he himself was thinking about such a thing. In any case, sometime in the middle of one dinner, apropos of nothing, Bunin suddenly began to talk about returning. I imagine that he was waiting for me to bring up the subject and that he had wanted to get the jump on me.

He said that he very much wanted to go [back to Russia], to visit and see the places that were familiar to him, but then he added:

"But it is too late [to return there], isn't it? I am already old. Of all my close friends there, only Teleshov is left, and I am afraid he will be dead by the time I get there. I also fear that I will be living in a void . . . and that it is too late to make friends at my age. Perhaps I would be better off to love you and Russia from afar? . . .

"To tell you the truth . . . I am very used to France . . . to the way of life here. . . . Indeed, France has become a second native land, and it would be hard to leave it. . . . For me to get a Soviet passport and then not to go—this is not the way I do things. After all, it is not a matter of documents but of feelings. . . .

"No, I will not return [to Russia]. . . . At my age it would be stupid for me to do so. . . . I am not Kuprin, I will not be 'carried off' like he was." (He said this in a very painstaking, irritated way.) . . .

Another time Bunin began talking about Merezhkovsky and Gippius, both of whom . . . he despised. He told me that sometime between the liberation of Paris and the end of the war, he happened to see Gippius walking toward him on a city street. Still quite far from her, Bunin crossed over to the other side so as not to greet her. But Gippius, seeing him, also crossed the street and met him head-on. Merezhkovsky had died only recently, and Gippius began to tell Bunin that [when Merezhkovsky was alive] everyone had been avoiding them, [that] people had turned their backs on Dmitry Sergeevich right before his death, [and that] no one noticed her, or they crossed over to the other side of the street so as not to talk to her.

"I answered her," Bunin said, "by saying that I also had no great wish to talk to her, and that she had no one else to blame for her predicament. I also told her that she and Dmitri Sergeevich had done very well when the Germans were here, but that now things were going poorly for them, while for me it was just the reverse. . . . After all, she and Merezhkovsky had served the Germans,[7] and before that, both of them had been in Mussolini's keeping—a fact I knew very well. . . . That is why I did not deem it necessary to conceal my contempt for them. . . ."

[Another time] Bunin suddenly began talking about Kataev, recalling that Kataev had visited him in Odessa. He then began talking about Kataev's prose with high regard. . . . "Yes," Bunin said, "at that time in Odessa it was difficult to imagine that he would turn out to be such a fine writer."[8]

August 11, 1946
Vera Muromtseva-Bunina, from her diary
    Simonov came by yesterday evening to invite us to a reading of

------

[7]Bunin's allegation here is false. Despite her hatred of bolshevism, Gippius never assisted the Germans and regarded Hitler as an "unskilled laborer" and a "flunky." As has been noted previously, though, Gippius and her husband were abandoned by friends and aquaintances when in 1939 the desperate Merezhkovsky delivered a radio speech supporting the Germans. See T. Pachmuss, *Zinaida Gippius: An Intellectual Profile* (Carbondale, Ill., 1971), 280, 283.

[8]See Marullo, *Ivan Bunin: Russian Requiem*, 287–290.

his works. . . . I liked his almost childlike sincerity. . . . He has written . . . a new story . . . about a professor who, having spent time abroad, returns to the homeland, to the Urals, but does not find his wife at home there. Waiting for her, he thinks and remembers things. He also thinks that everything in Russia is bad or worse than here [in the West]. Simonov thinks the censors will let it be published. After all, he is a member of the Supreme Soviet. . . .

Simonov's good fortune unnerves me. . . . For instance, when he told us that he has . . . secretaries and stenographers at his command, I thought about our writers here, old and young. Zaitsev does not have a typewriter; [another] does not have even the minimum for a normal life; and Ian is without the means to go somewhere to cure his bronchitis. . . .

Simonov, though, . . . is completely full of himself. He is a good man, though, so his conceit hardly angers or distresses me. Indeed, I am very happy that I spent an hour with him. Simonov is one of the most powerful defenders of the [Soviet] regime. The powers-to-be are pleased with him. He does not have to change . . . or to think about those who are calling the shots. He is having too good a time.

August 12, 1946
Umm-El-Banine Assadoulaeff, from her memoirs
[After Simonov gave a reading of his works in Paris], the crowd applauded him in a passionate and prolonged way.

Bunin screamed into my ear: "Now confess how magnanimous we Russians here in Paris can be! We may be poor emigrés, but we do not bear grudges and are happy for the success of our former enemies. How I recall the delight with which the Soviets once wanted to shoot us!"

"As if you were innocent sheep who never said an unkind word about any of them!" I cried out in his ear in reply. . . .

But Bunin was right. People were honoring Simonov, a representative of the regime that had humiliated them. They had seemingly forgotten the past. . . . Each side rejoiced and congratulated each other, but in the bottom of their hearts they were irreconcilable. Only an insignificant minority of emigrés had established some kind of ties with the Soviet Union. . . .

[Later in a café] I caught sight of Vera Nikolaevna who, it seemed, had been quietly sitting in the back row. She offered me her hand in a friendly way.

Shocked, I asked Bunin: "How could your wife be in the auditorium and you not say anything about it? Then you go and abandon her, allowing her to find her own place while you sit alone in the corner?"

Vera Nikolaevna agreed with what I was saying.

"This is what she herself wanted," Bunin explained to me in an absentminded way. "She did not want to make us feel awkward. Besides, she had a friend with her."

Make us feel awkward? How could this saintly woman make us feel awkward? But I could not cause a scene with Bunin over the way he treated his wife. So I kept silent, not knowing what to say.

August 15, 1946
Vera Muromtseva-Bunina, from her diary

The other day we had a genuine Muscovite dinner: vodka, herring, sprats, caviar, salmon, butter, white and black bread—all sent by airmail at Simonov's request. . . . Teffi was there and livened up the meal.

Simonov's wife[9] said that everything was worse here [in the West] than in Russia. She denied that people had been arrested before the war. . . . She also talked about Valya Kataev. He sometimes goes on a bender for three days in a row. Even when he is on the wagon, after he finishes a story or an article or a chapter of a book, he starts hitting the bottle again.

I think that Kataev responds to everything differently than others who seek oblivion. After all, he breathed in our culture for almost a quarter of a century. . . .

August 15, 1946
Umm-El-Banine Assadoulaeff, from her memoirs

[At dinner with the Simonovs and the Bunins] we conversed about literature, poetry, everything—except politics. But we were talking as though there was a dead man in the house and everyone was trying to forget that a corpse lay in the neighboring room. . . .

With a grand gesture, Simonov wished to pay for a taxi [for the Bunins]. . . . Angry, Bunin got up . . . and grabbed me by the hand. "Let's walk," he said. . . . Bunin's face became gloomy. He wanted to say something, but he became confused and hesitated. He then said quietly: "Come with me." I tore my hand from his . . . and repeated

[9]Simonov's wife, Larisa Alexeevna Zhadova, was an art historian who wrote on Malevich, Tatlin, and other Russian artists.

stubbornly, "No . . . no." His imperious manner had enraged me. Now both of us were furious.

On the street, Vera Nikolaevna came up to me and said confidentially:

"You know how Ian is. He is so jealous."

"He can go to the devil," I thought. But so as not to upset this woman whom I was coming to like more and more, I replied:

"It is nothing. He will get over it. After all, he is just a big kid."

With a happy nod of her head, she affirmed my words, her huge lucid eyes expressing tenderness:

"Yes, yes, a big kid," she said.

In the meantime, this big kid went back to the taxi . . . even his back expressed his anger. The luxurious limousine took off noiselessly.

August 16, 1946, and after
Umm-El-Banine Assadoulaeff, from her memoirs

Vera Nikolaevna opened the door for me. Her hair was less arranged than usual and fell in white strands about her neck. She grabbed hold of my hands fitfully, exclaiming:

"How glad I am to have you as a guest in my home. You know that yesterday Ian was angry, but I think he has forgotten about everything [with Simonov and the limousine]. He is the most forgiving person in the world."

She then added pleadingly: "Be a bit more affectionate with him. He deserves such treatment."

I felt like asking this remarkable woman: "He deserves such treatment? How does he deserve such treatment?" But she had evoked my admiration. I was struck by her kind soul, her complete lack of jealousy, and her devotion to a man who, in my opinion, did not deserve such loyalty. Comparing myself to her, I felt overwhelmed by shame for my shallow character, as well as for my inability to forgive others for their faults and to love people in an openhearted way. Having lost all restraint, I exclaimed:

"Vera Nikolaevna, you are a most remarkable woman!"

"Oh, what are you saying!" she cried out in a frightened way. "No, no, let me assure you . . . I . . ."

Not having finished her sentence, she led me, hastily and nervously, into a neighboring room where the *maître* was already sitting with Teffi and the Simonovs. How perennially erect, elegant, and impeccably dressed he seemed on that evening; it was as if he had been just washed, starched, pressed, and restored—a most chaste little boy of seventy years old, smelling of lavender. A tropical heat wave had turned Paris into a white-hot oven. Bunin was wearing a light white jacket over his shirt. Everything, including his hair, sparkled with whiteness. He looked magnificent. I said to him in an excited way:

"Ivan Alexeevich, you look splendid today!"

If he had been grumbling, he stopped right away. He gave me a devouring look and pressed my hand so hard that my fingers hurt. He then took me by the arm and led me to a table. The Simonovs were sitting on the left. Teffi, notwithstanding the respect due her age, he had seated in a most modest place on the pretext that she was an old friend. She easily forgave him for his lack of respect, preparing to focus her sharp glance on the old "little" boy whose behavior, in her view, was never beyond reproach. . . .

But Bunin paid attention only to me.

"This is classic Bunin," Teffi told me later. "The main thing in this world is his pleasure. We all were irritating him because he wanted only one thing—to be alone with you. That is why he spit on everyone else who was there."

Perhaps Teffi was exaggerating, but not by very much.

The table was set in the Russian style: [It conveyed:] "Made in Russia." It groaned from the weight of various vodkas and hors d'oeuvres. Sausages, various types of caviar, fresh sturgeon, anchovies, herring, marinated mushrooms, *pirozhki* with cabbage and meat, a luxurious *kulebyaka*,[1] and so forth. The solicitous Simonov even ordered bread and butter . . . and champagne. On that evening Bunin discovered in me a heretofore unknown virtue: I was lapping up the vodka like a trooper. As a result, he could forgive what he saw as my many vices: my quick temper, cynicism, mean streak, and even lack of respect for his writing.

"You really are something," he said to me with an air of respect.

The socialist vodka had a pleasant taste, but it was not very strong. Simonov kept insisting that it was, but Bunin—always the connoisseur—tested [its alcohol content] with a match.

"In tsarist times," he intoned, "vodka could take out an entire regiment of Hussars in a minute. It is not surprising that this Stakhanovite-made[2] vodka has no fragrance. This Stakhanov is a harmful type; he has appeared in order to keep people from living peacefully.

[1] *Kulebyaka* is a pie containing meat, fish, or vegetables.
[2] Bunin is referring to the Soviet miner Alexei Stakhanov, who, on the night of August 30, 1935, extracted 102 tons of coal in a six-hour shift. Three weeks later, Stakhanov set a new record by producing 227 tons of coal in a single shift.

You have substituted for the opium of religion the opium of labor. Do you really think that the more people work, the happier they will be?" . . .

[In the course of our conversation] I was surprised that Bunin and Teffi, who were usually so severe in their appraisals of France, were defending the country with all their might. In so doing they were heeding the principle: "I can complain [about France], but I will not let others do so." From the bottom of their souls, Bunin and Teffi apparently loved the land of their exile. Or did they want to show these "red" missionaries that a Marxist paradise could not measure up to a capitalist hell? Persistently the two praised the climate of freedom as well as the tolerance and acceptance of the local mores which they themselves enjoyed. They took every opportunity to embarrass and berate the land in which Stalin ruled not only external politics, military affairs, the economy, and the party but also literature and, more important, conscience. The night before, people were sober and restrained, but now the vodka had unleashed tongues and inclined everyone to extremes.

When Simonov's wife announced that French wine could not hold a candle to Soviet wine, the emigrés raised a howl in protest.

"One cannot seriously insist that *red* (Bunin emphasized the adjective) wines exceed the quality of French ones!"

Simonov rushed to defend his wife.

"You simply cannot imagine how much progress we [Soviets] have made in farming, especially wine producing."

Bunin nudged me with his knee under the table. His eyes glittering slyly, he shook his head and asked in a mocking way:

"Well, now tell me this, does the sun also rise on the special efforts of Stakhanov? Does it warm more powerfully than it did in tsarist times?"

He finally lost all sense of restraint. "Give me some of that bourgeois stuff," he said, pointing to the caviar. Or: "Soviet sausage is not worse than capitalist sausage." He called the vodka that he was drinking "Stakhanovka," and made up verse where he rhymed the word "vodka" with hunger, bitches, and strikes.[3] Simonov smiled politely. . . .

Not surprisingly, such accomplishments drew enthusiastic responses throughout the Donbas region and eventually the entire country. Stakhanov was seen as exemplar of the much vaunted "new Soviet man." His feats triggered the so-called Stakhanovite movement which embraced "outstanding workers" ("*otlichniki*") in coal mining and other fields of Soviet industry during the Second Five-Year Plan (1933–1938).

[3]That is, *golodovka, chertovka,* and *zabastovka.*

I have rarely been at a more lively dinner. Bunin and Teffi sparkled with wit, engaging in verbal fireworks and skirmishes, and exchanging caustic remarks. Spurred on by the vodka and acting like one possessed, Bunin surpassed himself. I could not stop admiring him; indeed, I had completely fallen in love with him. . . . [On that evening] Bunin appeared at least twenty years younger; he shone. . . .

[By contrast] Vera Nikolaevna kept serving us unobtrusively but attentively, noticing everything but eating in silence. Nothing in her wished to attract even the least bit of the attention that was focused on her famous husband. This was not a pose. No, Vera Nikolaevna's modesty was all the more touching because it was so genuine. Every time she glanced at me, she smiled; and, as if approving of me, she nodded her head. Why did she look favorably upon me? I think it was because of the way I conducted myself with her husband. Only one thing was important to her—that Bunin was happy. . . .

[Several days later] I asked Bunin if he would return to Moscow. "Well," he said with an important air, "this question is far more complex than you can imagine. The more I think about it, the more difficult it is for me to decide: to turn my back on my convictions, to surrender my freedom of thought, to sacrifice my freedom altogether—and all this for the sake of material well-being. . . ."

[I replied:] "Your convictions, though, did not prevent you from flirting with the Simonovs. After all, they are a mouthpiece for a regime that you consider the rebirth of hell. So where were your principles then?"

"I was curious to see what Soviet intellectuals looked like. I confess that I liked them. But I still do not go along with the fact that they cooperate with a country that persecutes the church and tramples on those values I hold dear. I have not surrendered my soul either to the devil or to the Bolsheviks. . . . Besides, if I would agree to return there, the powers-to-be would exploit my name to attract others there. . . . I would serve as an advertisement for them. I would also be forced to say things that I do not believe. . . ."

[Whenever I talked to Bunin] I could not tear my eyes from his hands, thin and covered with small brown spots. . . . They were like parchment; very soon, perhaps, they would become inert. Suddenly I was seized with pity for this old man who, with one foot in the grave, still tried to play the passionate lover so as to deceive himself and to forget the inevitable. . . .

August 30, 1946
Ivan Bunin, from an article

"Bunin-the-writer," [Ivan Tkhorzhevsky] says, "often confessed a persistent desire to stop the sun. He sees movement as intolerable; he is irritated by the wind of life. He wishes only calm and sun! He is an academician, a classical writer. . . ."

What kind of nonsense is this? Where and when in my writing did I "often confess" such an idiotic desire? Also, if I am "an academician and a classical writer," why did Tkhorzhevsky include me in a chapter of his work entitled "Artists-Impressionists"? Where did he get the idea "to link me with the *pochvennik*,[4] Goncharov, whose work recalls the stopped hours on a clock?" . . . Where also did he come up with these tirades, i.e., "Bunin accepted the style of Chekhov's 'In the Ravine'[5] with *all the passion* of his own temperament." . . . "Bunin's style is like a golden dryness." . . . "Bunin is little interested in people, since he believes himself to be a golden peacock in an impoverished chicken coop." . . . "Bunin was born and will die as a portrayer of landscapes who inserts himself into the picture. . . . Indeed, if one tears the landscape from a Bunin story . . . *nothing will remain*. . . ."

September 23, 1946
Vera Muromtseva-Bunina, from her diary

I have been teaching Russian . . . to students.

October 1, 1946
Ivan Bunin, from his diary

Today is the feast of the Protective Veil of the Virgin. It is also Vera's birthday.

I keep thinking about the monstrous day coming up in Nuremberg.[6] The horrible criminals deserve the gallows, but my soul does not

---

[4]Bunin is referring to the so-called *pochvenniki* or "men of the soil," a group of intellectuals in the 1860s and after who claimed that the educated classes of Russia had lost contact with the soil, and that they should strive to recover their roots, particularly, their ties to the folk. (Dostoevsky was a leading member of this group.) Unlike the Slavophiles who advocated a return to pre-Petrine culture, though, the *pochvenniki* hoped that their compatriots would seek a meld of Western and Russian Orthodox cultures as the guiding spirit for their land.

[5]Chekhov published "In the Ravine" ("*V ovrage*") in 1900.

[6]On October 1, 1946, after 216 grueling sessions, the judges at the war crimes trials at Nuremberg handed down verdicts for 22 defendants. Three were acquitted; 3 were incarcerated for life; 4 were sentenced to prison for terms ranging between 10 and 20 years; and 12 faced execution. In this last group, 10 were hanged on October 16, 1946. (Martin

accept that people can bring themselves to execute someone. I find it absolutely impossible to imagine that those who will soon be hanged like dogs can wait for that fatal hour, and that they can drink, eat, sleep, and go the bathroom during their last two nights on this earth. . . .

November 19, 1946
Ivan Bunin, from a letter to Nikolai Teleshov

It has been almost a year since I have heard from you! Write me! Are you alive and well? . . . Do you know anything about my nephews—Dmitri and Nikolai Pusheshnikov? Are they still alive? . . . Also, can you ask your Union of Writers to help me obtain at least some of my books that were printed in Moscow and republished in the twenties and thirties? . . .

November 28, 1946
Nikolai Roshchin, from a letter to Ivan Bunin

It is night. I cannot sleep because I am so excited. . . . I am going [to Russia] to the other shore. Of course, I am leaving behind all that is familiar and loved and dear, so much so that it breaks my heart. I do not regret the past; it is simply that I have chosen the better of two goods. But there are memories, memories. . . . You hold a place in so many of them, dear Ivan Alexeevich. . . . Good God, how many friends await you [in Russia], old ones and new ones. Russia holds out its hand to you, Ivan Alexeevich. . . .

Do you not want to leave the emigration, to "turn your back" on it? . . . In twenty-five years the wind will blow over the entire emigré field, and its very memory will vanish. . . .

The Revolution has sometimes stumbled, made mistakes, or taken drastic measures, but it has also led Russia to victory over age-old enemies. It has also brought about a material and spiritual well-being that has been unprecedented in the history of our country. . . . Dear Ivan Alexeevich . . . did you not also . . . in your "Tolstoy" period . . . profess what the Russian intelligentsia had dreamed about for a hundred and fifty years? Did your not mournful and splendid *Village* cry out [these same beliefs]? . . .

Do you really think, as do many others, that Soviet power is out to "deceive" the emigration, or that it is genuinely seeking its dissolu-

Bormann was tried and condemned to death *in absentia*; Hermann Göring committed suicide on the night before he was to be executed.)

tion? Would it not be obscene for a great government . . . to waste time on such a trifling and decaying group as [Russian emigrés], as if this group could decline any further? . . .

Dear, dear Ivan Alexeevich, who is pressing down on you . . . who is keeping you from going to the window, from opening it wide, from looking through it simply and straightforwardly, and from taking a deep breath of fresh air? . . .

Dearest Ivan Alexeevich, I am finishing this letter in Moscow. My most brightest, splendid, emigré dream has come true. I went to the Kremlin and burst into tears. . . .

November 30, 1946
Ivan Bunin, from a letter to Pyotr Bitsilli
We have been in Paris for a year and a half already. . . . We have been terribly hungry and cold; but I write and write. . . .

December 1946
An emigré critic, from an article
Bunin's story miniatures are so valuable . . . that one wants to put them under glass.

Early December 1946
Nikolai Roshchin, from his memoirs
[When I first returned to Russia] I was surprised to meet . . . young but well-known poets . . . who could recite Bunin's verse for hours on end. . . .

December 2, 1946
Vera Muromtseva-Bunina, from her diary
[A friend] has given an interview saying that, like other representatives of the Russian aristocracy . . . Ian is going to the USSR. Why does [this friend] lie so! I find it difficult to understand. . . .

December 25, 1946
Nikolai Teleshov, from a letter to Ivan Bunin
Your nephew, Dmitri Alexeevich, is alive and working as a lawyer.[7] . . .

You are completely wrong in your thinking about a Soviet edition of your works. . . . It would sell right away. So many people are waiting

---

[7]Bunin's other nephew, Nikolai, died in 1939.

for such an edition here that there would be only several copies for you and your friends abroad—ten at the most. . . .

You would also get a good royalty. Write to me or the State Publishing House . . . and allow this book to be published. . . . [Most likely] there will be a second edition in which you could exclude stories that you see as superfluous. . . . Leave well enough alone. . . .

December 30, 1946
Vera Muromtseva-Bunina, from her diary

Yesterday there was a breakfast to celebrate the publication of *Dark Alleys*. It was nice, simple . . . and even fun. Everyone was dancing toward the end . . . Teffi . . . Berberova. . . .

PART SIX

Pondering a Return Home
1947–1948

VERA MUROMTSEVA-BUNINA,
CA. 1940s

I n the thirty years since the founding of the Soviet state, Bolshevik leaders had surprised both "Russia Abroad" and the world in many ways. They had prevailed in revolution and civil war, modernized the homeland, and triumphed over Axis forces. In the immediate postwar era, though, such feats almost paled when compared to the cold (and sometimes hot) war with which the Bolsheviks engaged the West in their dream of "world communism."

In the first years of the uneasy peace, the denizens of "Russia Abroad" were host to still another momentous jolt from the Bolsheviks: the 1946 decree in which Stalin and company extended to Russian expatriates both the possibility of Soviet citizenship and, by implication, a return to the homeland.[1]

The Soviets had attempted to reconcile with the diaspora almost from the beginning of the emigration, but with limited success. In the 1930s they founded the Union of Return to the Homeland in France (*Soiuz vozrashcheniia na rodinu vo Frantsii*) to repatriate Russian emigrés whose knowledge and skills would be useful to the Bolshevik regime. Although the Union's "informational-literary bulletin," entitled "Our Union" ("*Nash soiuz*"), lauded the achievements of Soviet life over the poverty, unemployment, and alienation of the *emigrantshchina*, few emigrés heeded the "party" line. For one thing, they suspected— rightfully—that the Union was tied to Stalin's secret police. For another, they knew that individuals seeking repatriation had to pass searing tests of loyalty to the Soviet state. Some were told to serve the Republican cause in the Spanish Civil War; others were assigned to Soviet intelligence or ordered to assassinate key Soviet defectors in the West. The Union of Return, though, claimed that more than seven thousand Russian exiles had seen the light and that, as new Soviet

---

[1]In a sense, Russian emigrés in Europe should not have been surprised by the Soviet amnesty, since the Bolsheviks had issued previous edicts of reconciliation and return to expatriates in both Manchuria in November 1945 and in parts of China in January 1946.

citizens, they were "giving their strength and knowledge to the people, to their country, and to Soviet construction."[2]

The drafters of the 1946 decree showed similar perversity and intransigence. As reported in *Pravda* on July 8, 1945, the amnesty excepted individuals who had committed "counterrevolutionary crimes, banditry, and murder"—acts that the Soviets had routinely attributed to emigrés.[3] Also, the staff at the Soviet embassy in Paris did not welcome Russia's errant children with open arms. On October 31, 1945, the emigré newspaper *New Russian Word* noted that when hopeful exiles asked Soviet attachés about possible places of residence in the homeland, they were told that the USSR included Siberia as well as Moscow.[4]

Still, the 1946 decree caused a sensation throughout "Russia Abroad." With the possible exception of the 1941 Nazi invasion of the homeland, no other event in the three decades of exile caused so much division among the emigrés as the Soviet offer of reconciliation and return. Even as they evaluated their stance toward the homeland, they eyed each other suspiciously, watching for one or another to be the first to say or do what had been unthinkable only a few years before.

The reaction of the Union of Writers in Paris aptly illustrates the aura of disbelief and distrust that permeated much of postwar "Russia Abroad." Founded in 1921 with Bunin as its first president, the Union of Writers was crucial to the well-being of Russian exile *literati*. It provided its members with identity cards as well as letters of introduction or recommendation for entrance into foreign circles. Although it hardly possessed great resources, the Union raised money for the less fortunate in its ranks through charity balls, literary readings, and the like.

Politically the Union of Writers attempted to steer a middle course among rival factions. A cardinal rule among members was that individuals who were openly pro-fascist or pro-Soviet were denied admittance to the group. In the first twenty or so years of the Union's existence, this stipulation caused little difficulty. In the early 1920s, Alexei Tolstoy was expelled from the association for joining the

---

[2]As quoted in Johnston, 150. Although scholars judge this figure as somewhat high, they concede some emigré sentiment for return to the homeland. One Soviet source states that, by the end of the 1930s, some four hundred emigrés in Paris, together with an additional thousand exiles throughout France, wanted repatriation.

[3]See "Ob amnistii v sviazi s pobedoi nad gitlerovskoi Germaniei," *Pravda* (July 8, 1945), 1; Johnston, 179.

[4]"O sud'bakh russkoi emigratsii v Evrope," *Novoe russkoe slovo* (October 1, 1945), 2.

Bolsheviks. During the Occupation, emigré writers and journalists who published in Axis-driven Russian newspapers chose to withdraw from the Union and to form a group of their own.

The 1946 Soviet decree of amnesty, though, drove a wedge into the Union of Writers from which it never recovered. On June 14 members of the group voted by a majority of two to one to expel members who had accepted Soviet citizenship. In protest, 25 of the Union's 128 members, including Adamovich and Muromtseva-Bunina, withdrew from the group. Two weeks later, when Bunin also left the Union, many emigrés saw his departure as the final treachery in his purported "crossover" to the Bolsheviks. Berberova called Bunin's exit from the Union "a knife in the back"; Boris Zaitsev declared Bunin "dead"; and Maria Tseitlina ended a thirty-year friendship with the writer in a letter that circulated throughout "Russia Abroad."[5]

Still, many emigrés could not resist the lure of reconciliation and return. Soviet sources claim that at least in France eleven thousand Russian expatriates accepted the offer of Soviet citizenship (including Metropolitan Evlogy),[6] and that somewhere between two thousand and six thousand in this group actually left France for Russia.[7] Their reasons for doing so were not complex: they wished to end their drab existence under alien skies, to identify with a powerful, apparently forgiving motherland, and, most important, to make something useful of their lives before they were buried on native soil. Their hopes were cruelly deceived, however. Upon return to the homeland, many emigrés were seen as traitors and, together with deportees, forced repatriates, and prisoners of war, were sent to prison camps in Siberia. Ironically—and tragically—they had fallen victim to the very wretchedness and misery from which they had once escaped.

[5]Glad, 389.

[6]Supposedly the Soviets gifted the dying Evlogy with the first of these new Soviet passports. Such a story, if true, is the logical sequel to the metropolitan's decision to resubmit to the ecclesiastical jurisdiction of Moscow in the presence of Soviet Ambassador Bogomolov.

[7]Johnston, 180; Glad, 341.

$\ast$ I947 $\ast$

1947
An emigré critic, from an article
[With the publication of *Dark Alleys*], the attitude of the Russian reading public toward Bunin has entered a new spring.

1947
Marc Slonim, from an article
How remarkable . . . that Bunin, approaching the end of his seventies, can still, with such expressive force, talk about the charm of nature, the excitement of love, the onslaught of passion, and the eternal but illusory longing of humankind for the unattainable fullness of life.

1947
A representative from the Union of Soviet Citizens in France, from his memoirs
The resolution about the journals *The Star* and *Leningrad*, and the speeches by A. Zhdanov,[8] together with the sharp criticism of M.

[8]The "Resolution on the Journals *The Star* and *Leningrad*," promulgated on August 14, 1946, condemned both journals for publishing the works of the writers Mikhail Zoshchenko and Anna Akhmatova. The edict, together with two speeches by Andrei Zhdanov, established "official" policies on literature for the first fifteen years of the postwar era.
    For instance, the "Resolution" affirmed: "Our journals are a mighty instrument of the Soviet state to educate the Soviet people and particularly youth. They must therefore be controlled by the vital foundation of the Soviet order: its politics. The Soviet order cannot tolerate . . . youthful indifference . . . or a devil-may-care attitude . . . to Soviet politics.
    "The power of Soviet literature, the most advanced literature in the world, consists in the fact that it is has not and cannot have interests other than the interests of the people. Hence the task of Soviet literature is to aid the state . . . to rear a new generation that is vigorous and strong, that believes in the [Soviet] cause . . . and that overcomes all obstacles. . . .
    "Consequently, any preaching of ideological . . . or political neutrality, as well as of 'art for art's sake' is alien to Soviet literature and harmful to the interests of the Soviet people and of the Soviet state. Such preaching has no place in our journals."
    Zhdanov's speeches amplified such views. Sounding a warning to Russia's cultural

Zoshchenko[9] and A. Akhmatova,[1] caused exceptionally tragic repercussions in the literary circles of Russian emigrés in France. Many writers who were about to return to the Motherland, even those who had been standing on a patriotic platform, changed their minds [about Soviet Russia]. . . . Bunin also reacted negatively.

It was at this difficult time that the editor of *Soviet Patriot* demanded that I speak with Bunin . . . and find out about his plans to return to the homeland, and, first of all, about his attitude toward receiving a Soviet passport.

I went to Bunin's apartment [with one of his friends]. We entered Bunin's study, and through a crack in the door I heard [this friend asking Bunin]:

"Ivan Alexeevich, the secretary from the Union of Soviet Citizens in France is with me. Would you like to see him?"

"No!" . . .

[The friend], embarrassed, said to me:

"He does not want to see you. Perhaps this is a momentary whim, but I do not think so. . . ."

---

elite, Zhdanov castigated "the one-sided infatuation with historical themes"; "vacuous subjects of a purely diverting nature"; and "servility before contemporary bourgeois culture . . . which is in a state of chaos and corruption." Rather, Zhdanov insisted: "The Soviet people expect from Soviet writers genuine ideological argument and the spiritual nourishment that will aid in fulfilling the plans for the great social construction, and for the restoration and further development of our country's economy."

Zhdanov also insisted that Soviet writers focus on the future, not the past. He continued: "To show the new high qualities of the Soviet people, to show our people not only as they are today but also to give a glimpse of their tomorrow, to help illumine, with a searchlight, the road ahead—such is the task of every conscientious Soviet writer. . . . "

In the wake of such statements, the party discontinued the publication of *Leningrad* and appointed A. M. Egolin, acting director of the Central Committee's Agitation and Propaganda Department, as editor-in-chief of *The Star* (*Zvezda*). (The journal still exists to this day.) See H. Swayze, *Political Control of Literature in the USSR, 1946–1959* (Cambridge, Mass., 1962), 37, 39, 40.

[9]Zhdanov commented on Zoshchenko's 1945 story "The Adventures of a Monkey" ("*Prikliucheniia obez"iany*"): "If one reads the story carefully . . . one will see that Zoshchenko casts the monkey as the supreme judge of our social order who reads . . . a moral lesson to the Soviet people. . . . [He uses the animal to put forth] the vile, poisonous, and anti-Soviet sentiment that life is better in a zoo than in freedom, and that, among the Soviet people, one breathes more easily in a cage."

Although Zhdanov's reading of the story was both inaccurate and unjust, Zoshchenko was expelled from the Union of Writers. See E. Brown, *Russian Literature Since the Revolution* (London, 1969), 226–227.

[1]About the poetess, Zhdanov stated: "Akhmatova's poetry is pathetically limited. It is the verse of a half-crazy gentlewoman who tosses between the bedroom and the chapel. . . . Half nun and half harlot, or rather both nun and harlot, Akhmatova's harlotry is mingled with prayer." Like Zoshchenko, Akhmatova was also expelled from the Union of Writers. See Brown, 227.

This was my last visit to Bunin's apartment. . . . Soon our newspaper was closed, and I was ordered out of France. I returned to the Soviet Union.

January 1, 1947
Vera Muromtseva-Bunina, from her diary
We rang in the New Year in bed. We both had high temperatures, exhausting coughs, anemia, elevated heartbeats, and the main thing—weakness.

January 8, 1947
Ivan Bunin, from a letter to Nikolai Teleshov
I was *very* distressed to hear about my nephew Kolya's death. Would you ask his widow to write me and tell me how he spent his final years, what he died of, and what remains of his writings. . . . I also ask you to tell the State Publishing House in Moscow that they can publish whatever they want from my writings . . . as well as *The Liberation of Tolstoy*. . . .

January 16, 1947
Ivan Bunin, from a letter to Georgy Adamovich
Enclosed are some things from my [imaginary] anthology, entitled "Gems of World Literature":
(1) *He crawled high into the mountains and lay there.* . . . This is how Gorky begins his "Song about the Snake and the Falcon"[2] (in which the snake, not being a mortal reptile, somehow kills a falcon by biting into its heart, i.e., right through its feathers and bony chest). . . .
(2) Then there is this excerpt from Gorky's "Old Lady Izergil' "[3]: "Then Danko tore his flaming heart from his chest. . . . And it burned so brightly, like the sun, even brighter than the sun. And the entire forest grew silent, lit by this torch of great love for people. The darkness flew away from its light, and there, deep in the woods, its evil shade fell into the *rotting roar of the swamp*."

February 19, 1947
Vera Muromtseva-Bunina, from a letter to Maria Tseitlina
The only consolation is that Ian's heart is in good condition. . . . I hide our financial circumstances from him. . . . He has no appetite for

[2]More accurately, Gorky wrote "Song of the Falcon" ("*Pesnia o sokole*") in 1895.
[3]Gorky's "Old Woman Izergil' " ("*Starushka Izergil'* ") appeared in 1894.

anything, and I have to coax him to eat even the least little bit. And you know what that's like. . . .

I am very tired. From January 1st on, I have had to spend my nights with Ian. He coughs so much that I have to get up as often as three times a night and give him something warm to drink. The last three nights I have been sleeping in my ice-cold room, without getting undressed, so that if he should call I can run to him as quickly as possible. . . .

February 23, 1947
Ivan Bunin, from a letter to Mark Aldanov

Some American editor . . . wants to publish *Dark Alleys*, with an advance of two hundred dollars. What do you think about this? I think I will turn them down. Two hundred dollars will disappear in five minutes!

March 1, 1947
Ivan Bunin, from a letter to Nikolai Teleshov

What did they pay you in England for a translation of your *Reminiscences*[4] in English? . . .

A lack of paper is preventing my books from being published in many countries. And I'm being robbed left and right. I just found out that, without my knowledge, Holland has published no less than six of my books!

July 11, 1947
Gleb Struve, to the editors of Russian Life

In the June 19th edition of your newspaper, you printed an article . . . on Bunin's postwar visit to the USSR and his return from there. . . . As far as I know, Bunin has not visited the Soviet Union, nor does he intend to so do, although attempts have been made to "entice" him there. One can, from a moral-political view, reflect over several courses of action that I. A. Bunin took after the liberation of France, but cannot take a man to task for a crime that he did not commit.

---

[4]Teleshov's *A Writer Remembers* appeared in London in 1946.

Mid-July 1947
Ivan Bunin, from a letter to Andrei Sedykh

Who does Struve think he is? To "defend" me in such a half-hearted . . . and *ambiguous* way, the bloody bastard. . . .

August 9, 1947
Vera Muromtseva-Bunina, from her diary

Denikin has died. Ian was very upset. An entire epoch of life. I recall him at one reception . . . he had a black beard, and looked very elegant in his black uniform and smart-looking boots!

His last words were: "We will hear Moscow bell towers at Christmastime." He died in an American hospital.[5] . . .

August 18, 1947
Ivan Bunin, from a letter to Andrei Sedykh

Yes [my meeting with Bogomolov and my working for *Russian News*][6] were painful for me, but I did it out of need, need! But were such actions really so "amoral"? . . .

[The individual who charged that I had visited the Soviet Union] has written this:

"On July 11, 1947, *Russian Life* published a letter by Professor G. Struve, saying that I had uttered a falsehood as regards Bunin's visit to the Soviet Union and his *return* from there. I, of course, *do not know how accurate* Gleb Petrovich's information is, but I wrote about Bunin's trip based on the detailed letter of someone who is now living in Western Europe, and *whom I have a great deal of confidence in*. Perhaps, he, too, has made a mistake.

"Nonetheless, *the actions of Mr. Bunin* in recent times have given me the right to consider the facts of his trip as trustworthy. Even Gleb Petrovich *himself alludes to such a thing*. . . ."

I saw Gleb last fall in Paris . . . so how could he "doubt" as to whether I had gone to Soviet Russia or not? I do not know who is worse—Gleb or [the author of the article]. . . .

Bogomolov told me that if I would return to Russia, I would be a millionaire and have cars, dachas, and the like. *But I chose to remain {here*

---

[5]The seventy-five-year-old Denikin died in Ann Arbor, Michigan, on August 7, 1947.

[6]*Russian News (Russkie novosti)* was a pro-Soviet publication that appeared in Paris from 1945 to 1970. Although Bunin had published several of his works there, he refused to be a regular member of the staff, stating in a letter to its editor, Antonin Ladinsky, on August 8, 1945, that *Russian News* was a "sharply political" publication, and that he had "long ago lost all interest in politics." See T. Ladinskaia, "Pis'mo k A. P. Ladinskomu," in Shcherbina, 688.

in France} and to live out my truly last days in equally genuine poverty, and with all kinds of old-age sicknesses to boot. Who else would have done such a thing in my situation? Who?

Circa September 1947
A friend, from a letter to Alexander Baboreko

At that time Ivan Alexeevich was ill and lay in bed. He was slowly losing his strength; but his mind was sharp and clear. I usually looked over the new stories, novels, and anthologies of verse that were being sold in "House of Books." I was poor and could not buy anything ... but I caught sight of a book by Tvardovsky and asked if I could borrow it for a few days. . . . When I returned home, I gave it to Ivan Alexeevich.

"What's with you?" he asked. "Why are you so excited?"

"Read this, Ivan Alexeevich."

"It's probably nonsense," he said suspiciously, waving his hand.

He was tired of literary pomposity and tendentiousness; whenever he opened a book, he usually waved his hand.

"I'll take a look at it."

After ten minutes he called me. Having raised himself slightly, he exclaimed:

"This is really something! Genuine verse! . . . A poet! A genuine poet!"

Ivan Alexeevich was amazed, delighted, overjoyed. . . . He wanted to make notes and underline passages; but he could not, since I had to return the book.

"Tvardovsky has done a great job! It is most difficult . . . to write in a soldier's language. . . . This is a remarkable book; but our poets will not understand it, they will not feel it. . . . How can they? . . . After all, they have never heard how the people talk; they have never heard a soldier's speech. They have a tin ear. They do not know anything about Russian life, nor do they want to know anything about it. They are locked up in their own worlds, feeding on each other and themselves. . . ."

I took the book back to the store.[7]

---

[7]The book in question in Tvardovsky's *Vasily Tyorkin*, written between 1942 and 1945.

September 2, 1947
Ivan Bunin, from a letter to Mark Aldanov

I have been rereading my works. My *Village* is impressive. I was almost on the verge of hating it—I had not read the thing for a hundred years; but now I suddenly see that it is extremely cruel, forceful, and original.

Also, yesterday when I was rereading "Ignat," I came across this piece of absolute nonsense. Ten years ago I was correcting the proofs [for the story]; and, in a passage describing the icy night and the garden . . . I had crossed out the word "greenish" and wrote in "green." And to make sure that the printer saw it, I wrote *in the margins*: "Not 'greenish' but 'green'"! And so what did he do? He put the whole thing *into the text*. The result was so idiotic that last night I woke up three times from horror.

September 2, 1947
Vera Muromtseva-Bunina, from a letter to Maria Tseitlina

These past few months we have been living very quietly. We are taking a break from people. We almost never go anywhere, and very few people come and visit us.

September 7, 1947
Nikolai Teleshov, from a letter to Ivan Bunin

Everything [in Moscow] is so pretty, so wonderfully splendid and touching that I felt like writing to you so that you would feel, if only for a moment, what it means to live in the homeland. How sad that you did not take advantage of that time when you were so expected here, when your huge book was already typeset, when you could have been rich, well taken care of, and greatly honored.

September 15, 1947
Ivan Bunin, from a letter to Konstantin Paustovsky

I am writing to tell you of . . . the rare joy that I had in reading your story "The Tavern in Braginka."[8] If you omit the last phrase of your piece ("the end is in sight"), it belongs to the best stories of Russian literature.

---

[8]Paustovsky's "Tavern in Braginka" ("*Korchma na Braginke*") appeared in 1946.

September 15, 1947
Ivan Bunin, from a letter to Mark Aldanov

[Teleshov writes that if I return to Russia], I will be rich, have everything I want, and be held in high esteem. . . . I have been pulling my hair out for an entire hour now. But I immediately calmed down after I remembered what could be my lot at the hands of Zhdanov and Fadeev who . . . promise me riches and fame but who are both scoundrels.

September 25, 1947
Nikolai Teleshov, from a letter to Ivan Bunin

In his book,[9] Nemirovich-Danchenko wrote about your tragic end—that you had died from hunger. . . .

I now look at your portrait and marvel how you have turned into such an old fogey!! . . . But I am a bigger fogey than you. I would not recognize you if I met you on the street. Shaven (I am not used to any of this!), with grey whiskers, though a hat covers your head. . . . But there's nothing you can do about it, pal. . . . No beard, no hat will cover what is underneath. . . . And there is no reason to cover it. Old age has its own beauty, the culmination of a long life.

October 9, 1947
Vera Muromtseva-Bunina, from a letter to Maria Tseitlina

I gave my hat to Ian [for the winter].

November 8, 1947
Ivan Bunin, from a letter to Georgy Adamovich

[In one of your articles] you state that for Tolstoy in his last years, *The Brothers Karamazov* was his bedtime reading. Where did you get that from? I have before me a huge volume of Tolstoy's 1910 diaries, the very last ones he wrote, in which he says a thing or two about these "brothers." . . .

Take, for instance, Tolstoy's diary entry written on October 12, 1910. "I have read Dostoevsky's *The Brothers Karamazov*. What joking trifles he has in there: verbose, artificial, and not very funny." Also read his entry written on October 18, 1910. "I am reading Dostoevsky, and I am amazed by his slovenliness, artificiality, and fabrications."

It is quite possible that *The Brothers Karamazov* was one of the last

---

[9]Nemirovich-Danchenko's *From the Past* (*Iz proshlogo*), published in Moscow in 1936, says nothing about Bunin's demise.

books Tolstoy read. But what will a reader think after he reads what *you* wrote? Tolstoy's bedtime reading? How can you possibly say a thing like that?

December 20, 1947
Maria Tseitlina, from a letter to Ivan Bunin
  [You and those writers who have taken Soviet passports] have struck a great blow against the emigration. . . . And I must break off with you if only to lessen by the *least little bit* the hurt that you have caused me. . . . I will not be your judge. But the pain of our parting is so deep that it will be with me forever. I cannot stop loving you. You are, after all, my dear Ivan Alexeevich . . . [whom I love] as if you were my brother.

December 20, 1947
Boris Zaitsev, from a letter to Maria Tseitlina
  Bunin is among those who have left the Union! Naturally I find *such a thing* very distressing. . . . Bunin is unhappy and very ill as a seventy-seven-year-old man. . . . As far as I am concerned, he is no longer among the living, only his unhappy shadow remains. . . .

✳ 1948 ✳

Circa 1948
Nina Berberova, from her memoirs
  Bunin's destiny often disturbed him. . . . Some kind of beast ate at him from within, and his increasingly sharp judgments of his contemporaries, together with his even more malicious outbursts toward the end of his life—written and oral—bear witness to the fact that he could not forget [Modernist] "idiots and cretins"; that they had tortured him endlessly throughout his life; that in his old age they had become stronger than he; and that, having grown weak, he had sought to defend himself with vulgarity and crudeness. . . .
  I now think that the coarseness of Bunin's speech and behavior . . . was in part a smokescreen, a camouflage. Bunin feared individuals and the world no less than other people of his generation; so all his swagger . . . was in self-defense. He was coarse with his wife, a

dumb and very stupid woman (not moderately stupid, but exceptionally so). He was also crude with those he knew and those he did not,
and after being rude he liked to say something flattering or to make an
old-fashioned bow. . . .

The last time I visited [the Bunins' home in Paris] . . . I saw a
chamber pot, filled to the brim, right in the middle of the vestibule.
Evidently he was exhibiting it out of anger toward someone who had
not emptied it on time. He was sitting at the kitchen table with . . . a
well-to-do [Russian] individual, a proprietor of a huge hotel . . . [who]
had just been let out of prison, where he had served a sentence for col-
laborating with the Germans. He was either writing or had already
published a book about his childhood . . . and now both men were sitting and telling each other how splendidly they both wrote. . . .

When I saw the dirty kitchen and two slightly tipsy old men embracing and tearfully telling each other "You are a genius," "You are
our luminary," "You are the first," "I have to learn from you," I was so
dumbstruck that I could not regain my composure. . . .

Bunin said: "This [individual] is my only friend. He is a great
writer of the Russian land. From him all of you must learn how to
write."

I went through the vestibule (the chamber pot was no longer
there), down the stairs, and out onto the street. I never went to his
home again. . . .

January 1, 1948
Ivan Bunin, from a letter to Maria Tseitlina
[In your letter to me] you wrote something fantastic: "You offi-
cially left the Union with those who had taken Soviet passports." That
is simply absurd! . . .

Life in the Union used to be so quiet and calm. But then it became host to all kinds of quarrels and stormy sessions. . . . Generally
speaking, I have always had little to do with unions and all forms of
politics. And I will continue to do so especially now . . . if only because
I have long been so seriously ill that I can barely write to you. . . .

January 1, 1948
Vera Muromtseva-Bunina, from a letter to Maria Tseitlina
In my view, what the officials of the Union did was foolish. After
all, the people who took Soviet passports amounted to approximately
12 out of 138 members. . . .

January 2, 1948
Vera Muromtseva-Bunina, from her diary

I greeted this leap year in a very sad way. Ian was greatly agitated. Maria Tseitlina's letter has destroyed his equilibrium. . . .

January 10, 1948
Ivan Bunin, from a letter to Alexander Bakhrakh

Oh this Prishvin! He writes: the forest "listened open-mouthed"! Such junk could make you puke!

January 10, 1948
Vera Muromtseva-Bunina, from her diary

I have received a letter from Teffi who writes: "Does Tseitlina understand what you lost when you refused to return to the Soviet Union? What you flung back into the faces of the Sovietchiks? Millions of rubles, fame, all the comforts of life? They would have named a square after you; they would have even put a statue in the middle of it. They would also have honored you with a metro stop . . . given you a car, servants, and a dacha in the Crimea. Just think! A writer-academician, winner of the Nobel Prize. It would have been a shot heard around the world. . . . And you flung it all back in their face. I do not know anyone else who could have done such a thing. Even I could not have done it. . . .

Tseitlina has upset me terribly. We should get a papal bull and pronounce anathema against her. . . ."

January 12, 1948
Ivan Bunin, from a letter to Nadezhda Teffi

I kiss even the blanket on which your hand rests. . . . That is how much I both love and pity you. . . .

January 13, 1948
Boris Zaitsev, from a letter to Ivan Bunin

I do not want talk about your departure from the Union of Writers. . . . I only say that *I do not understand why you did what you did* (your inner reasons). . . . My *general* impression is that you were supporting the Soviets and their sympathizers. I will not hide how difficult such a thing was for me. . . .

January 15, 1948
Ivan Bunin, from a letter to Boris Zaitsev

I did not quit the Union to support "the Soviets and their sympathizers." . . .

January 26, 1948
Boris Zaitsev, from a letter to Ivan Bunin

I repeat that your departure [from the Union] is being seen as sympathy for the Soviets—and [that such a view] issues forth not only from "our circle." It is enough to hear what emigrés are saying about you in churches, stores, and conversations. . . . Indeed, news of your action has spread quickly . . . including to Russians in New York. . . .

I do not want any more explanations from you. . . . Besides, it is too late to talk. I learned about your actions from a *Soviet newspaper* . . . [though many emigrés] have long looked askance at you for your contacts with Bogomolov and your participation in *Russian News*. . . .

I [and others] should also warn you that your leaving the Union . . . might affect your financial situation . . . as people might boycott you in America. I hope that this will not be the case. . . .

January 29, 1948
Ivan Bunin, from a letter to Boris Zaitsev

What truly has *infuriated* me is the letter that [a friend] wrote to me, informing me that many in Paris think that because of Maria Tseitlina and her intercession with "everyone" in America, I have been privy to gifts and rivers of gold, and that now . . . I will be done for! Greater nonsense than this is impossible to imagine!

February 2, 1948
Ivan Bunin, from a letter to Nadezhda Teffi

Do not surrender to depression and indifference to life. Indeed, in itself, "not to surrender" means a great deal. . . .

February 2, 1948
Maria Tseitlina, from a letter to Vera Muromtseva-Bunina

I am very distressed that there has occurred between us a misunderstanding that was completely unexpected for me. . . . I very much regret what I did, and I most sincerely ask that you forgive me. . . . Although I am not trying to justify myself, I was greatly upset [when I heard that you and Bunin had left the Union of Writers]. . . .

February 9, 1948
Ivan Bunin, from a letter to Mark Aldanov

Maria Tseitlina addressed her letter to Vera Nikolaevna alone. . . .
As she sees it, the "nature" of my "deed" still stands. . . .

March 12, 1948
Nina Berberova, from a letter to Maria Tseitlina

For all of us and our work here, [Bunin's leaving the Union of
Writers] was a "knife in the back" in the fullest sense of the word.
Zaitsev said straight out that "for me, Ivan is dead." . . .

I keep asking myself why did Bunin leave. Can it really be that
they [the pro-Soviets] have such power over him? Or that he still
dreams of being published in Moscow? Or his dotage? Or his bitterness toward everyone and everything? . . . I understand nothing. . . .

March 25, 1948
Ivan Bunin, from a letter to the editors of the Soviet journal October

As regards the absolutely absurd fabrications in Yury Zhukov's article "In the West After the War," that appeared in the tenth issue of
October last year,[1] I wish to set the record straight. I am not "puny or
wizened" but thin, above average in height, with broad shoulders and
build. I stand firm and erect. As one Soviet POW told me: "You still
cut quite a figure, old man!"

Moreover, only a complete fool would say that I have the "refined
face of an aesthete." I do not chew my lips or wear a pince-nez. I put on
glasses only when I am looking out into the distance. Also, my voice is
not "squeaky" but so sonorous that when I give a public reading in an
auditorium filled with a thousand people, I can be heard in the farthest
corners of the room.

Furthermore, at the literary evening sponsored by the Society for
Russian-Jewish Intelligentsia, I did not read with "irritation in my
voice" but firmly, even imperiously, as befits a story written partially in
the tone of the Koran. . . . [I also object to Zhukov's portrait of me] as
a bilious . . . old codger . . . and a feeble, saintly half-idiot who mutters
in a confused sort of way. . . .

[1]See the excerpt in this book, "April 1946 and after."

March 27, 1948
Vera Muromtseva-Bunina, from her diary

Today the newspapers reported . . . that Mochulsky died on March 21st, and Berdyaev on March 23rd.[2]

April 2, 1948
Mark Aldanov, from a letter to Ivan Bunin

Yesterday I ran into a good friend of mine . . . who asked me in an irritated way: "Is it true that Bunin has turned Bolshevik?" I quickly told him the truth. He got angry, pulled out his checkbook, and handed me a check for five hundred dollars, requesting that I give it to Ivan Alexeevich "as a gift, as a token of my deep affection for him. . . ."

June 2, 1948
Ivan Bunin, from a letter to Mark Aldanov

If I were rich, I would immediately fly off somewhere to the Sahara . . . or to Egypt. To die in the warm, dry air would be a hundred times better than to do so in the cold and dampness here in Paris. Yes, and also to be buried there, in some sandy cave would be quite unlike finding one's resting place in a Parisian grave. There would be no worms, no decay! I even dreamt of such a grave as early as 1907 . . . when I first visited Egypt. . . .

I have just read [Alexei] Tolstoy's *Nikita*.[3] It is splendidly written. . . .

The other day I managed to see Teffi. . . . She is beyond pity. . . . Day after day she lies all alone in a cold, dark room. . . .

June 9, 1948
Ivan Bunin, from a letter to Mark Aldanov

I have just been informed that the American journal *Story* has published a translation of my story "Calling Cards."[4] . . . As I need every kopeck I can get, can your "Literary Foundation"[5] force *Story* to pay me for the translation?

---

[2]Mochulsky died in Cambo (now Cambo-les-Bains) in southwestern France, roughly four hundred miles southwest of Paris. Berdyaev died in Clamart, France, roughly twenty minutes from the French capital.

[3]Tolstoy wrote *Nikita's Childhood* (*Detstvo Nikity*) in 1920.

[4]*Story* was published in New York from 1931 to 2000. Bunin's "Calling Cards" ("*Vizitnye kartochki*"), which he wrote on October 5, 1940, appeared in the spring 1948 issue of *Story.*

[5]The "Literary Foundation" ("*Literaturnyi Fond*") was established in 1918 in New York to assist needy Russian writers, artists, and others throughout the world.

July 1, 1948
Ivan Bunin, from a letter to Mark Aldanov
Yesterday I saw friends . . . who attended the gathering *"In honor of Ivan Bunin."* . . . Of course, it was all very sweet nonsense . . . arranged by the head of the French section of the P.E.N. Club. . . .

August 6, 1948
Boris Zaitsev, from a letter to Ivan Bunin
I have just learned of your illness. . . . God grant you energy and health; God also grant that you write yet still another very good story. This I wish with all my heart. . . .

August 7, 1948
Ivan Bunin, from a letter to Mark Aldanov
It seems that there will be no war [between Russia and the West]. England and America will swallow everything, for they are enduring all kinds of slaps from Moscow, and they will continue to do so. . . .

October 1948
Ivan Bunin, from an interview
Here I am on the verge of death and I sit here annoyed and thinking: How many interesting things lay ahead—congresses, strikes, and wars—but I will die and know nothing about them, since [at the cemetery] at Sainte-Geneviève-des-Bois, everything is peaceful and quiet, without radios, not to mention that my neighbors there will not be very talkative. . . .

November 5, 1948
Mark Aldanov, from a letter to Ivan Bunin
The gathering in your honor in Paris has netted you more than two thousands francs! I congratulate you. Such an accomplishment, of course, is a world record which, until now, no one in the emigration has managed to attain. . . .

November 10, 1948
From "A Small Feuilleton. To the Great One, His Very Self"
The Great One was sitting at the table and drinking tea. Yes, the most ordinary tea, the kind that all mortals drink. But if this Zeus had been sipping nectar, his face could not have been more majestic. He was wearing a robe. His belly "was all decked out in pearls; he was all in gold." . . .

At the end of the table, at a most respectful distance, sat the interviewer. . . . He still could not get over the shock called forth by the recent somersault with which the Great One had crossed over to the [Soviet] camp, at which, for the past thirty years, he had hurled thunder and lightning.

"I have been astounded only one time in my life," the Great One told me. "I once was looking at a star hovering over the ocean; and I could not understand how the world could hold two such heavenly luminaries: this star and myself. . . . I found such an occurrence to be so painful that I asked the Creator: 'The universe can hold up this star, but were You not the least bit afraid to raise me so high over the world?' . . .

"But how it could not be so?" the interviewer prattled on. "After all, I recall one of your poems:

'Like a flaming star,
Like a chalice filled with earthly sorrows
And heavenly tears unfurled. . . .
Why, O Lord, have you raised
My being so very high over your blessed world?'

"Those lines are from another poet, but the thought is mine, no matter how modest and grateful it might sound. But just the same, I will come down [from my heights] and talk to you. . . . You can also publish several of my invitations [to speak], as well as pictures of my baptismal dress and feeding bottle. But alas, my diapers have been lost for all time." . . .

The interviewer: "You have been fated to meet so many famous people. . . ."

"Well, let's just say that I didn't see anything great about them, though there were one or two that deserved my attention. But now I will say something that everyone should remember for all time. This day marks the millennium of [the beginning of] my ancient gentry clan . . . something I have written about many times and in several languages, to boot. . . . [To mark this occasion] I have received [congratulations] from the honored academies of France and other countries. . . . Such recognition is hardly surprising, though. After all, without me there would be no Pushkin or Leo Tolstoy. They are my direct ancestors—insignificant writers, to be sure, but deserving of mention. . . .

"Incidentally, I rarely meet with people these days. Indeed, I find it repulsive to do so, if only because I have grown fond of my loneliness. More and more often, I stroll down the dark alleys of my garden. . . ."

November 24, 1948
V. Lazarevsky, from an article in Russian Thought
My recent piece, "A Small Feuilleton. To the Great One, His Very Self" . . . has greatly distressed Russian literary circles in Paris. . . . Indeed, people have accused me of a "lack of respect for a great Russian writer."

[But the facts are these:] This great Russian writer has taken every opportunity to blacken the name of his fellow writers. . . . He has also contributed to a pseudo-emigré newspaper . . . with open Soviet leanings. . . .

People tell me that "everyone knows that the 'great one' has not changed his anti-Soviet views" . . . and that "one should take into account his age and social position." . . . As I see it, though, such claims only intensify the guilt of his actions. . . .

Further, I should not be the one to be censured for "overthrowing an authority," since it is the "great one" himself, who, in the eyes of the emigré masses, has destroyed the credibility of Russian literature and enlightenment. Indeed, he has facilitated the destructive work of the Soviets . . . who, in their demagoguery, have thrown all culture overboard. . . . [Let us not forget that] it was the "great one" who left the Union of Russian Writers and Journalists . . . at the very moment when the Soviets were waging a campaign against this organization. . . .

I assert not only that I am correct in my opinion of the "great one," but also that most everyday Russian emigrés share my views, i.e., I. A. Bunin, having lost his ways in the dark alleys [of life], is no longer the pride of the Russian emigration; rather, he now exemplifies the moral renunciation, if not desertion, of its elite. . . .

Circa December 31, 1948
Nikolai Roshchin, from a letter to Ivan Bunin
Young poets [in Russia] recite your poetry with delight and by heart for long periods of time . . . There are no prose writers who can compare to you. . . . Your name is so very greatly respected. . . .

K. G. Paustovsky prizes your postcard [to him] as if it were a relic. . . . Teleshov passed on your praise of "Tyorkin" to Tvardovsky . . . who blushed like a high school kid.

PART SEVEN

Bidding Farewell

1949–1953

BUNIN, 1948

If Bunin was the "hero" of "Russia Abroad," Vera Muromtseva-Bunina was its "heroine." She seemed like a nineteenth-century Russian heroine come to life—from a naive maiden filled with ideas of adventure and romance, she became a stately, even regal woman who, representing the best of her country, captivated most of all the emigrés.

At each stage of her life, Vera Muromtseva-Bunina was an intriguing mix of both old and new. Having grown up in a prestigious Muscovite family with ties to education, politics, and law, she knew the privileges of power and caste as well as her role as a woman in society. She studied languages, played the piano, and, with her statuesque beauty, caught the eyes of men who could give her comfort and security. Even as a young woman, though, Muromtseva charted her own course through life. In 1907 she announced to her father that she intended to accompany the thirty-year-old Ivan Bunin to the Holy Land. "I have changed my life radically," the twenty-six-year-old Vera noted in her diary, "from a settled person to a nomad."[1] Little did she know how prophetic her words would be.

As an emigré, Muromtseva-Bunina pursued the same binary path. On one hand, she was the consummate *hausfrau*. She was Bunin's wife-sister-mother who delighted whenever her husband gifted her with his wisdom or presence, and who endured whenever he ignored her or, worse, abused her in both public and private. It was Muromtseva's chosen fate to live for the happiness and peace of her husband and others, with little time, friends, or money to call her own. Memoirists recall with both astonishment and annoyance how she fulfilled Bunin's slightest expectations and wishes; how she denied herself to ensure that he had the best food and clothing; and how she remained in the background as Bunin took bows, flirted with the ladies, or took credit for the little peace and happiness in their lives.

[1]See M. Grin, *Ustami Buninykh. Dnevniki*, vol. 1 (Frankfurt/Main, 1977), 55.

Particularly in the latter years of their relationship, though, Muromtseva-Bunina struggled to be her own woman. She sought increasing solitude to reflect upon her life. She returned to her religious faith, obsessed with her weaknesses and failings but grateful for what God had given her. She even boasted how she had surpassed her husband in wisdom, spirituality, and strength, and how she went forward in life while Bunin remained static or regressed.

However "constrained" or "liberated" her existence, Muromtseva-Bunina fulfilled her role with dignity and grace. Intuitively she understood the importance of Bunin and his work to both "Russia Abroad" and the world. Equally instinctively, she served as a buffer between Bunin and the many storms—political, social, and aesthetic—that thundered about him. In war, revolution, and exile, amidst poverty, hunger, and fatigue, she saw to it that Bunin had the support and surroundings to nurture his craft, to preserve the memory of his homeland, and to keep faith, hope, and charity alive for the millions of fellow emigrés who looked to him as their leader.

Other writers of Bunin's generation searched for "Sophia" in mysticism and cults, in hallucinations and dreams, and in alcohol and drugs. Bunin had a unique stroke of good fortune: his "eternal feminine" was alive, genuine, and always at his side.

✳ 1949 ✳

Early in 1949 several friends in Paris wrote to tell me that although the food situation there had gotten better, people were still half starving, that the Bunins were very much in need, and that emigré writers living in the city had received a "ration" from some "literary group" which consisted of dry milk, eggs, and tasteless "wadded-up cheese"—the height of insult and stupidity.

So I immediately headed for one of the central food stores in Moscow, and there I spent an entire thousand rubles on all kinds of truly "mouthwatering" things, including the type of cured filet of salmon that Bunin could only lust after during his entire exile—it was not made in France—and when he did remember it, would say that he "would give his right arm" to have some.

I rejoiced when I thought of my package arriving there, since I recalled one of Bunin's humorous letters from Grasse saying what an "indomitable sinful glutton he was."

But alas, a month later, my package was returned along with a short dry note in which the person to whom it had been addressed wrote something to the effect that "Moscow victuals went against his grain."

The swamp mosquitoes [of the Russian emigration] had again done their job: twenty-five years of a kind, chaste, and sometimes tender friendship had come to an absurd and evil end. But despite the grief that Bunin's letter had caused me, I chose not to answer it.

January 4, 1949
Vladimir Nabokov, from a letter to Edmund Wilson

The "decline" of Russian literature in the years between 1905 and 1917 is a Soviet invention. . . . Bunin and others wrote their best things in those days.

March 11, 1949
Ivan Bunin, from a letter to Nadezhda Teffi

I am convinced of my complete lack of talent. . . . In my head I hear a voice saying, "You are finished, Ivan Alexeevich!"

March 28, 1949
Ivan Bunin, from a letter to Nadezhda Teffi

I often write nonsense to other people . . . but I dare not, I cannot with you. . . . I have taken up . . . sitting in the sun next to the house. . . . But then you go and write: "I hate . . . old men who sit in the sun. . . ." Imagine what I go through being precisely that old man "in the sun!" . . .

Thank you also . . . for worrying about my Inquisition-like torments. Thank God, I am no longer suffering! I just waved everything away with my hand, grabbed hold of the first nonsense that came into my head, sat down for two evenings in a row, and from nine to one, hurriedly wrote about twelve pages. (I had neither strength nor spirit for more.) Then I got under the bedcovers just like Sonya Marmeladova[2] did with her shawl, complete with "trembling shoulders." . . .

But I do not want to be Sonya Marmeladova. After all, I am still in my youth, in the days and years of the most abject poverty, selling God-knows-what to the literary market.

April 1949
Ivan Bunin, from a letter to Andrei Sedykh

Here is something that should surprise you. I am beginning to think . . . about [coming to] America! I am serious! Do you think we could live *not far* from New York but in a *different climate*? After all, in no way can one live in New York itself.

---

[2]Sonya Marmeladova is a character in Dostoevsky's *Crime and Punishment* (*Prestuplenie i nakazanie*), written in 1866.

April 1949
A critic, from the journal The Explicator

At first glance, *The Gentleman from San Francisco* . . . appears to be charged with socialist (or more pointedly, communist) import. Something like this is implied by Brooks, Purser, and Warren (*An Approach to Literature*, 1946, p. 24), when they declare: "In the story . . . there is the idea of a struggle between those who have economic power and those who do not."

One could, indeed, find evidence which on the surface suggests that the story intends to hasten the barricades and the Coming Revolution against capitalism. . . .

The Gentleman appears laden with communist social significance. . . . [The hero] is anonymous throughout, thus representing not an individual so much as a type, a group, the class of bloated capitalists; the luxury liner on which he travels is a bright tight world of ease and sybaritic comfort, supported by the perilous and incessant labor of sailors and stokers, the common workers; the constant feeding by the wealthy passengers symbolizes their wastefulness, grossness, and arrogance; the storm that batters at the vessel is the elemental forces of revolution and human indignation raging to break in upon the smug and rapacious world of the capitalist—and so on throughout the story.

Unfortunate for this theory are three counter-positions. . . . *The Gentleman from San Francisco* was conceived before World War I, before the Communist Revolution. . . . Bunin was and is a violent anti-Communist; the last thing in the world he wished to do was abet a doctrine which he execrates and which has brought him anguish, exile, and poverty. . . . He is also a traditionalist Russian writer of the spiritual generation of Dostoevsky and Tolstoy. . . .

The Gentleman from San Francisco is thus not a restricted story of socialist propaganda. It is an unrestricted revelation of the spiritual rot infecting the whole world. In locale and intent it is not parochial but universal. It is a study of fatness, insensitivity, and solipsism pervading a whole society regardless of class lines. Its center is not the Revolution; it is the Condition of Man.

May 5, 1949
Ivan Bunin, from a letter to an editor

I know that you and your journal use [the new orthography]. *That is precisely why* I am asking that you make printing blocks for my signature . . . to show that I write in the old orthography, for the new one is absolutely insufferable for any cultured Russian individual. I some-

times put up with it, but I also take every opportunity to avoid it altogether. I find it offensive to see the name "Alexander Sergeevich
Pushkin" written in the new style rather than the old way which is sacred to Russian literature. No one asked Pushkin's permission to write
his name differently. . . . It is a repulsive thing to see.

May 8, 1949
Vera Muromtseva-Bunina, from a letter to Tatyana Loginova-Muravieva

I have made a firm decision—to be "invisible" for six days and to
spend at least some of this time with friends. Otherwise I will never
get away from the dishes; and I do not have that much more time to
live life with a sound mind and a firm memory. . . . For the past two
years I have lived like a crazy woman. . . .

Today . . . I took a walk by the sea. It was wonderful. . . . How I
felt like going to an island and lying under a pine tree and listening to
the rustling of the waves. But I have never been able to do such a
thing! . . .

June 21, 1949
Ivan Bunin, from a letter to Andrei Sedykh

A century and a half ago, God gave to Russia a great happiness.
But it was not fated for our country to preserve such good fortune.
With its connivance, there was cut short, at a certain terrible hour, the
worthy life of the One, Who personified the very best of His country.
And what happened to this country, Pushkin's Russia, and again with
its connivance, is known throughout the entire world.

That is why we would be liars and hypocrites, and . . . these days,
unworthy to pronounce His immortal name, if our hearts did not carry
a great sorrow for both Him and His land.

> Flaunt your power and beauty, o city of Peter!
> Stand firm, like your country, Russia![3]

Remembering Him, how can one keep silent not only that there
is now no city of Peter, but also that Russia is tottering even to its most
sacred foundations? Only one thing is sure: our firm faith that the Russia that gave birth to Pushkin can neither perish nor betray its eternal
roots, and that the gates of hell cannot truly prevail against it.

[3]Bunin is again quoting from Pushkin's "The Bronze Horseman."

July 17, 1949
Ivan Bunin, from a letter to Mark Aldanov

In the cemetery by Novodevichy Monastery in Moscow . . . there is a monument to *someone*—without a name but with the remarkable inscription . . . "Here lies a man." I feel like writing the same thing (about myself). But apparently God will not let me. I do not have the strength to do so.

August 3, 1949
Mark Aldanov, from a letter to Ivan Bunin

You *must* write. . . . Only then will you feel better. I understand why you feel the way you do. Ever since I turned fifty . . . I also have been thinking about death. Derzhavin has a poem that is both stupid and charming:

> And death awaits like a guest.
> Pensive, it curls its moustache. . . .

Not long ago a doctor told me: "People do not die from emphysema, or asthma, or hemorrhoids. . . ." The reason why people die is because for them the joys of life become less and less. . . . So one should take advantage of all the joys that are still around.

September 12, 1949
Vera Muromtseva-Bunina, from a letter to Tatyana Loginova-Muravieva

I have fallen ill (!)—my fourth vertebra has become calcified. . . . Because of it, I am in constant pain. . . . In a word, it is really fun to have. I am forbidden to do anything. . . .

Ian and I have been receiving guests here on the first and third Thursday of every month. . . . Sometimes we have more than twenty people. . . . I am doing everything I can so that Ian can be with people a bit. . . . But I simply do not have the strength for the life that I had last year. . . .

October 2, 1949
Ivan Bunin, from his diary

There was so much [in my life] that was burdensome and offensive, so many things I tolerated. But there was also much that was happy and splendid—things I seemingly did not value. How many things did I miss or let slip from my life—and so very dully and stupidly at that! Oh, if I could only bring them back! But there is nothing ahead for me now. I'm a cripple, and death is almost at the door.

October 24, 1949
Ivan Bunin, from a letter to Princess Sofya Volkonskaya

Dear, sweet, most wonderful Sofochka. I was so very, very touched by your birthday card. . . . If I were young, I would fall in love with you like I *once* fell in love a long, long time ago. . . . On your behalf I would set sail to fight with Non-Believers to the Holy Land; and on the way there I would be taken captive by pirates who, for seven years, would make me their slave. But I would escape from them and come to your castle on foot. My face would be wrinkled and almost black; I would be grey and thin as a skeleton. I would fall on my knees and ask for your hand; but you would order that I be beaten for my boldness and thrown into an underground dungeon filled with toads and spiders and owls. And I would die there, singing your praises on a lute or even without one.

November 12, 1949
Vera Muromtseva-Bunina, from her diary

Kerensky was here for about an hour and a half. . . . He has gotten grey, quiet, and less nervous. . . . But he laughed when Ian told him about his visit to Bogomolov.

November 16–17, 1949
Ivan Bunin, from a letter to Mark Aldanov

Galina Nikolaevna [Kuznetsova] has left for America.[4] . . .

Late 1949
A French writer, from his memoirs

[When I went to give Bunin the money that some French writers had collected for him] I was chagrined. The furnishings of his apartment were the most wretched [I have ever seen]. But there was also a crowd of people there . . . eating and drinking any way they could. I thought to myself: "With so many guests, the money won't hold out for long, and there is no way I am going to take up a second collection for him."

---

[4]Kuznetsova had been living in Germany since 1945, but in 1949 she immigrated to America and eventually worked for Voice of America. In 1955 Kuznetsova joined the staff of the Russian Press Department of the United Nations and a year later became an American citizen. She also contributed frequently to Russian newspapers and journals.

Late 1949
Ivan Bunin, from an interview

When Bunin was asked how he managed to spend "almost a million francs" [from the Nobel Prize], he was genuinely surprised.

"Has a Russian intellectual ever been able to hold onto money? Alas, I am the same way!"

Late 1949
Ivan Bunin, from a letter to Andrei Sedykh

I congratulate you for your praise of my poetry! My verse is extremely brilliant. What rhythms, how natural the language! No one has yet to write like I do! Merci! Merci!

✳ 1950 ✳

Circa 1950
Mark Aldanov, from his memoirs

Bunin said: "You talk to me about the grave, and my hands grow cold from fear. But I beg you: do not try to comfort me, for such comfort lacks courage. I also ask that you do not call attention to my body, for it will rot. . . . But I also often say to myself: the hour of death is not as terrible as we think. For without it, the world and the human race could not exist."

Circa 1950
Alexander Bakhrakh, from his memoirs

For the most part, Bunin spent the last years of his life . . . reworking almost all of his old pieces. . . . Metaphorically speaking, he squeezed them out until they were bone-dry. For the umpteenth time, he took out everything he thought was superfluous, trite, insufficiently clear, or extremely lyrical. . . .

January 1, 1950
Vera Muromtseva-Bunina, from her diary

We did not "greet" the new year. I attended . . . prayer services instead.

354 IVAN BUNIN: THE TWILIGHT OF EMIGRÉ RUSSIA

January 17, 1950
Ivan Bunin, from a letter to Mark Aldanov

Maurois and, it seems, Mauriac are organizing something for my "jubilee," though, as they say in Provence, it is too late "to sew up some pants for someone who lacks an ass!" . . .

Did Blok die, as people always write these days, from "a lack of air, of freedom under the Bolsheviks?" Nonsense! . . . They should all fuck themselves. . . .

Circa February 1950
Ivan Bunin, from a letter to Mark Aldanov

"Is my Lyudmilla asleep or not?" . . . "See the majestic moon. . . ."[5] It was Zhukovsky-Bunin, not Pushkin, who first gave us a new literary language. . . .

You have probably read Gorky's 1906 pamphlet about France. Its loutish baseness and stupidity, its piglike boldness and conceit are without equal in world literature.[6] . . .

March 20, 1950
Ivan Bunin, from a letter to Mark Aldanov

I have just received Gide's *Journal (1942–1949)*. Half of it focuses on his terrible existence in Tunisia.[7] I lost my mind reading the page and a half of his notes for August 3, 1942, when he was already 73 years old: a detailed account of the two nights he spent with some

[5]Bunin is quoting from Zhukovsky's famous ballad *Lyudmilla*, written in 1808.

[6]Bunin is referring to Gorky's sketch *Fair France (Prekrasnaia Frantsiia)*, in which he criticized French bankers for granting loans to the tsarist government which faced financial ruin because of the Russo-Japanese War. In characteristic fashion, Gorky raged: "Fair France! Your best children know you no longer. . . . You are a woman, kept by bankers. . . . You, the Mother of Liberty, you, Joan of Arc, have allowed beasts to crush humankind yet again.

"O great France, once the guide of civilization, do you not realize the vileness of your act? In your love of money, you have kept an entire country from taking the road to freedom and culture. . . . With the aid of your gold, the blood of the Russian people will once more be shed. . . .

"So then may this blood suffuse the flabby cheeks of your lying face with the red of eternal shame. Accept my spit of blood and gall into your eyes!" See K. Alexander, *Maxim Gorky and His Russia* (New York, 1968), 387; and H. Troyat, *Gorky* (New York, 1989), 103.

[7]Most likely Bunin is referring to Gide's description of the incessant Allied bombing of Tunis in mid-December 1942. "Three times I went over to the window to watch the strangely illuminated sky," Gide wrote on December 14. "A huge fire . . . lasted until almost dawn: an Italian munitions ship, it is thought. Such destruction awakens all that is darkest and most primitive in us, a savage, elemental state of existence, at once irrepressible and unacceptable." See A. Sheridan, *André Gide: A Life in the Present* (Cambridge, Mass., 1999), 555–556.

youth who was roughly fifteen years old and in such mutual, ineffable delight that it seemed to Gide that he was also a young man! How could he not only write this down but publish it and not be ashamed of what he did![8] . . .

March 30, 1950
Ivan Bunin, from a letter to Mark Aldanov
How Moscow so lacks humor! . . . In front of me is a "Soviet post-card" . . . with a picture of geese in a pond and the inscription—"Geese at the Karl Liebknecht collective farm." Just imagine the peasants there trying to say such a famous name. . . .

May 1, 1950
Vera Muromtseva-Bunina, from her diary
Ian is in a rage because he is not supposed to have salt. He sprinkled an entire spoon of salt in his soup today. I told him that he was not supposed to have it, and he hit the roof. Now he will not eat anything. . . .

May 31, 1950
Vera Muromtseva-Bunina, from her diary
Ian said: "I did not think that dying would be so difficult."

---

[8]Of his experiences with the young man, Gide wrote in his *Journal* that there were "two nights of pleasure such as I did not think that I would be able to experience at my age." Gide continued: "Both nights were marvelous, but the second was more surprising than the first. F. [probably an employee at the hotel where Gide was staying] came to my room at curfew. . . . He told me that he was fifteen, but he looked younger. His body was even more beautiful than his face. I noticed him on my first day here, but he seemed to be so wild that I hardly dared to speak to him. The boy brought to pleasure a sort of joyful lyricism and an amused frenzy which probably had about as much to do with his inexperienced surprise as it did his sensuality.

"Since he took as much initiative as I did, there was no question of compliance on his part. He seemed to care so little about my age that I came to forget myself. Indeed, I do not recall ever experiencing pleasure so fully or strongly. The boy left me in the early hours of the morning, and then only because I had asked him to leave me so that I could get some sleep. The first night, he had come at my invitation. The second night, four days later, the boy came of his own accord. A third night, some days later, he again knocked at my door. . . . How I regret that I did not let him in, but [my refusal] was probably from a fear that I might not rediscover such perfect joy [as previously] and thus spoil, by superimposition, my memories [of my earlier encounters with him]. . . . Many people, when still young, have no need of youth and beauty in their partners to attain with them—and thanks to them—the height of ecstasy to which their own youth and beauty invite us." See Sheridan, 553.

June 12, 1950
Pearl Buck, from a letter to Andrei Sedykh

A celebration is being planned next October to observe the eightieth birthday of the great writer Ivan Bunin. . . . Bunin is in desperate straits and is very ill. He could very easily improve his condition if he would accept the invitation to go back to Soviet Russia where his royalties have accumulated for thirty years. But he does not want to go back. As André Gide has said, Bunin has "chosen misery" to keep his freedom. . . .

July 17, 1950
Mark Aldanov, from a letter to Ivan Bunin

Your *Life of Arseniev* is such a masterpiece! I am rereading it for the fourth or fifth time! . . . Even peasants and beggars lived better in Russia than they do now. . . .

September 24, 1950
Ivan Bunin, from a letter to a friend

Over the course of the last year, I have had four bouts of pneumonia. . . . Then I began having spasms of the colon and discharging not urine but this *fiery* stream. . . . Fortunately it ended with . . . an hourlong operation that was so painful that even the Cheka could not have imagined what I went through. An enlarged prostate had entered the colon, and no doubt I would have died if the doctor . . . had not cut the thing into pieces and extracted them—an entire 56 fragments in all. . . .

The flesh is becoming exhausted, but the spirit is still destined to triumph!

October 16, 1950
François Mauriac, from a letter to Ivan Bunin

On the occasion of your eightieth birthday . . . I wish to express to you the delight which your works call forth in me, as well as my empathy for the severe fate which has been your lot. . . .

Circa October 23, 1950
Alexander Bakhrakh, from his memoirs

[For Bunin's eightieth birthday] . . . his friends decided to collect some money so that he could have a telephone in his apartment, something he constantly kept asking to have. . . . At that time such a request was not easy to fill. . . . New telephones were very expensive . . .

and people often had to wait years [for one]. . . . But Bunin got one in
record time . . . and used it constantly to call doctors and nurses. . . .

October 23, 1950
Vera Muromtseva-Bunina, from her memoirs
The celebration for Bunin's birthday was a modest event and took
place in our home. Ivan Alexeevich sat in a chair, dressed in a blue
robe—a birthday gift from one of our friends. There were, of course,
friends, acquaintances, and representatives of various emigré institutions in Paris . . . about twenty people in all. . . .

October 23, 1950
A memoirist, from a letter
[At the party for Bunin's eightieth birthday] the first thing that
visitors saw was a huge poster saying that the doctor had forbidden all
applause.

October 24, 1950
André Gide, from a letter to Ivan Bunin in Le Figaro
We are almost the same age, but in the honors that have been be-
stowed on you, you have surpassed me by fifteen years. . . . But also
being a Nobel Laureate[9] . . . may I, in the name of all France, today
congratulate you on the eighty-first year of your life, and take you into
brotherly embrace?
I feel that I must do so because it was precisely France that you
chose as the haven for your prolonged exile. You, a Russian citizen,
found among us a refuge from a revolution that you could not accept,
from countrymen to whom you still are not reconciled. As a result, you
had recourse to my profound empathy, a feeling that not only unites us
but that also includes my delight over your writing, which had made
me a fan of yours long before . . . our paths finally crossed. . . .
[When I met you at Grasse] I sensed an atmosphere that was
somewhat bohemian and strained, but also one that was deeply
human . . . and that smelled of . . . Russian literature. . . .
Your influence is truly beyond words. When I looked out from
the windows of your villa in Grasse, I saw not the Russian steppe, with
its fog, snow . . . and white birch trees, but the landscape of southern
France. But your inner world . . . has triumphed over the external one.
For you, it is the true reality.

[9]Gide received the Nobel Prize in Literature in 1947.

When I visited you . . . I kept hearing things that were truthful and assured, and nothing that was forced, false, or contrived. It would be impossible for me to imagine an ethics and an etiquette, a literary heaven and a literary hell that were more removed from my own ideas than yours. But your positions were unwavering and firm. That is what is most important . . . that great artists are great, each in their own way.

When I listened to your stories, I forgot about everything. . . . I do not know any other writer whose external world is so closely tied to another, whose sensations are more exact and indispensable, and whose world is more genuine and also . . . more unexpected than yours.

With equal assuredness you describe well-being on one hand, and on the other, poverty and wretchedness, but all the time respecting the most unfortunate people in the world. . . . It also seems . . . that [in your works] the artistic canvas is being torn to pieces, and that the most pervasive hopelessness is staring back at you. And it is precisely in this [darkness] that we are especially unlike each other! . . .

France can be proud that it has offered you refuge.

October 24, 1950
A reviewer, from an article in Le Monde
Eighty years. . . . Not many Russian writers reach and cross over to that age. But Ivan Bunin, still full of creative energy, is following in the steps of Leo Tolstoy. His extensive career is divided into two parts: 50 years in Russia, 30 in France. Fortunately, his exile has not interfered with the development of his gifts. . . .

October 26, 1950
Ivan Bunin, from a letter to Mark Aldanov
I am tormented by the "holiday" of my old age.

October 30, 1950
Ivan Bunin, from a letter to Mark Aldanov
Gide's letter is splendid. . . .

November 5, 1950
Ivan Bunin, from a letter to Mark Aldanov
I reread Dostoevsky's *Bobok*.[1] There has never been a more foul,

---

[1] Dostoevsky wrote *Bobok* in 1873.

base, and stupid thing in all of world literature. You remember it, of course: a conversation of dead people.

December 2, 1950
Nadezhda Teffi, from a letter to her daughter
Bunin . . . is as wicked as I. Everyone else is a fool.

December 5–6, 1950
Ivan Bunin, from a letter to Mark Aldanov
[When I die] I want my face to be covered immediately and for all time, so that no one will see its deathly horror and chaos. I do not want anyone to read the Psalter over me, or put that inexpressibly vile *venchik*[2] on my forehead. I also do not want people to pile earth on my grave, but to make a simple wood coffin. . . .

December 10–11, 1950
Ivan Bunin, from a letter to Mark Aldanov
My death is at hand, it is *unavoidable*—so why should I wail and stamp my feet? I await my execution with a type of dullness—or should I say wisdom—before my unalterable fate. But if I had to sit and wait in a stockade for someone to drag me at dawn to meet the axe, then, even if I were bound by ropes, I would let out such a howl, I would so twist and turn, I would act so demonically possessed, that even the executioner's hair would stand up on end!

December 25, 1950
Vera Muromtseva-Bunina, from her diary
Aldanov [and a friend] came by for Christmas Eve. . . . It was not a happy time. I think Ian shocked everyone by appearing so disabled. . . .

[This friend] supposedly spent more than two years in a Soviet prison in Prague. He says that many Russians, even those from the secret police, have a great deal of humanity. What a fairy tale. . . .

December 30, 1950
Ivan Bunin, from a letter to Nadezhda Teffi
My eighties are going to waste! . . .

---

[2]A *venchik* is a paper or silk band that is placed on the forehead of a dead person to symbolize the "crown of righteousness" noted by Saint Paul in Timothy 4:8.

✳   1951   ✳

1951
Ivan Bunin, from his "Literary Testament"
    After I die, someone might think to publish my letters, diaries, and notebooks. . . . I earnestly implore this individual *not* to publish them. . . . I always wrote these letters . . . extremely carelessly, and often not in a completely sincere manner. . . . Many of them are simply not interesting. But this individual can use several selections and excerpts . . . as *biographical material*. (If only a bright and exacting individual could be found to do such a thing!) . . .

1951
Ivan Bunin, from a letter to Mark Aldanov
    I have just received a letter and a telegram from the International P.E.N. Club. The telegram says: "The 23rd Congress of the P.E.N. Club . . . extends its very best to Ivan Bunin, a courageous man, a great writer, and a generous heart." And the letter: "Most honorable and dear Colleague: We wish to thank you most warmly for accepting the title of our first Honorary Member."[3]

January 25, 1951
Ivan Bunin, from a letter to Mark Aldanov
    I really do not want to die. . . .

January 28, 1951
Ivan Bunin, from a letter to Fyodor Stepun
    I am dying little by little . . .

February 9, 1951
Ivan Bunin, from a letter to Mark Aldanov
    What is Pearl Buck like? She has not lifted a finger to help me! . . .

---

[3]More specifically, Bunin was named the first honorary member of the P.E.N. Center for Writers in Exile, which had been formed in London and was ratified by the XXIII International Congress of the P.E.N. in Lausanne in June 1951.

March 10, 1951
Ivan Bunin, from a letter to Fyodor Stepun

What a pity that you wrote [in your review of *Dark Alleys*] that I am preoccupied with how women entice men. . . . How can you say such a thing! I have written about only one-thousandth of what men of all tribes and peoples everywhere have "discerned" about women from nine to ninety (right down to feminine *fashions*). Look for yourself at how avidly men "look at" women, especially when one puts her leg out on the step of a tram! Is this only depravity, or something a thousand times different, almost shocking?

March 26, 1951
Ivan Bunin, from a letter to Fyodor Stepun

John Chrysostom supposedly said: "My sleepless nights are like a vast sea!" And now each and every night of mine is also an "endless sea." I do not sleep and gasp for breath. I sometimes go from my bed to my desk, write down a thing or two . . . and then back to my bed—to read something but more often, to think . . . is this what lying in the grave is like?!

I have become monstrously thin. I look like something I saw in a . . . museum in Cairo—the mummy of Ramses;[4] and I am so weak that after just two or three steps around the room . . . it seems like I am flying across the floor because my heart is beating and my head is spinning so soundly. . . . Two months ago the window was open for about ten minutes; I was lying down, all wrapped up in bed. I took a gulp of fresh air—and came down with pleurisy!

"And when King David reached a ripe old age . . . he could not stay warm, no matter how many clothes he wore . . . and a young maiden was placed in bed alongside him to give him warmth, but he did not know her. . . ."[5]

This is my situation exactly. . . . But young maidens are so rare these days! And it is just as well that there are none around: I would not be able to do anything with them anyway . . . even though I, to my great shame, wrote the supposedly obscene *Dark Alleys*!

March 26, 1951
Mark Aldanov, from a letter to Ivan Bunin

Yesterday's evening in your honor [in New York] was splendid.

---

[4]See Bunin's story "Scarabs" ("*Skarabei*"), written on May 10, 1924.
[5]Bunin is citing from First Book of Kings, 1:1–4.

The auditorium of 470 seats was filled to overflowing. The mood was exactly what we wanted. *Everyone* talked about you in the most glowing tones. . . .

April 22, 1951
Vera Muromtseva-Bunina, from her diary
    Tomorrow it will be 44 years that Ian and I entered upon the same path.

May 25, 1951
Ivan Bunin, from a letter to Mark Aldanov
    You can imagine what my life would be like if I did not receive help [from patrons and friends]. . . . Perhaps it would not be all that difficult for you to get me a *pension for life*. . . . After all, I do not have much longer *to live*. . . .

June 10, 1951
Ivan Bunin, from a letter to Mark Aldanov
    A friend brought me a repulsive book by Nabokov. The cover had a tsarist crown over his name. In it there is some savage nonsense about me—that I supposedly dragged him into a restaurant to have a "heart-to-heart" talk with him.[6] That sounds just like something I would do! Then the buffoon wrote that he gave me quite a drubbing and that I envy him terribly. . . .

June 22, 1951
Ivan Bunin, from a letter to Fyodor Stepun
    I was so very flattered when you wrote . . . that you gave a public reading of my works that lasted for "an entire three hours" . . . and that you were well received by the German students in the audience. French students are not like that. They look at everything from top to bottom and despise *everything* that is not French!

June 29–30, 1951
Ivan Bunin, from a letter to Mark Aldanov
    I have been making all too frequent use of the "white poppy,"[7]

---

    [6]Bunin is citing from Nabokov's *Conclusive Evidence*, published in New York in 1951. Also see Marullo, *From the Other Shores*, 301–302.
    [7]The "white poppy" is one of several varieties of the flower used in the manufacture of opium.

and am beginning to fear for my intellectual faculties. I think I am getting stupid and will write something even dumber. . . .

July 10, 1951
Ivan Bunin, from a letter to Georgy Adamovich
How should one write in the new orthography? How should one pronounce it? . . . Whom is this Russian writing destined to please? Stalin? The "De-Pe"—those motherfuckers who see themselves as belonging to a most talented people? . . . *Not a single* people has allowed such baseness in its language!

July 29, 1951
Ivan Bunin, from a letter to Galina Kuznetsova
Where are you, all the intelligent and beautiful women of my life? Have you returned home? Today Vera recalled how we all met in that July twenty-five years ago . . . and then went to visit to the Zaitsevs . . . in a splendid wild forest . . . not far from a deserted, half-ruined abbey. . . . Your dear Ivan Alexeevich.

August 1, 1951
Ivan Bunin, from a letter to Mark Aldanov
I am sending you a copy of the absolutely idiotic letter that I received from [Chekhov Publishers] in which the people there propose to publish a wretched little anthology [of my works], beginning with "Late Hour," a story which I very much esteem, but also to be followed by edifying *fragments* from my collection *God's Tree.*
I do not care if they do such a thing with Pushkin . . . but I will not agree to this with my own writing. . . . Should I tell them that I am talking to [other people] about publishing my works? . . . Apparently all my hopes for an edition of my writings and for a means of subsistence have fallen by the wayside! . . . I will continue dying like an animal, saving myself [from starvation] only with gifts from New York.

August 16, 1951
Vera Muromtseva-Bunina, from her diary
[An acquaintance] is again spreading slander about Ian, saying that Ian "is negotiating with the Soviets about publishing a complete edition of his works." Actually, it is just the reverse—he has done everything he could so that his writing will not be published with the Bolsheviks in Russia.

September 9, 1951
Ivan Bunin, from a letter to Chekhov Publishers

I received your letter, informing me that "Chekhov Publishers" will publish three of my books only if I agree to publish them in the so-called "new" orthography. *In no way can I agree to such a thing.* Would Chekhov himself agree to such conditions? I knew Chekhov well, and I can assure you that he would not.

I reproduce word for word, and in *your* orthography what you wrote to me:

"The Board of Trustees, at a meeting in late August, passed a resolution that *all books* published by 'Chekhov Press' will be in the new orthography, and that *no exceptions will be made.* The reasons for this decision are considerable. A study has shown that New York does not have typesetters who know the old alphabet. Furthermore, the new orthography will cut down on the *volume* (!) of books by almost one-quarter. . . . Finally, today's readers, especially the younger generation, do not know the old way of writing."

I counter:

It cannot be that New York does not have a single typesetter who could set up my books in the *old* orthography. After all, it was only four years ago that *New Review* published my story "The Huntsman"[8] in the *old* orthography. Where did this typesetter disappear to? Could it be that he died and that there was no one to take his place? . . .

You also say that the "De-Pe," especially the younger generation there, does not know the old orthography. What does that mean— "they do not know"? . . . This simply cannot be. After all, how can the "De-Pe" not know the old orthography when young people in Russia read hundreds of books that were printed before the Revolution . . . including my own? . . .

Is it perhaps the case that "Chekhov Publishers" is refusing to publish emigré writers? . . .

Of course, the fact that I am *forced* not to publish with "Chekhov Publishers" will be a financial catastrophe for me. But there is nothing I can do. I *will live out my last days*, enduring *my poverty* in a staunch and steadfast way.

---

[8]Bunin wrote "The Huntsman" ("*Lovchii*") in 1946.

September 9, 1951
Vera Muromtseva-Bunina, from her diary
G. Fedotov has died suddenly. . . . He was a talented individual. An entire epoch is gone. . . .

September 19, 1951
Ivan Bunin, from a letter to Mark Aldanov
[The editor] of "Chekhov Publishers" writes: "We are greatly distressed to inform you that [as regards orthography] we cannot make an exception in your case. We regret that we will not be able to publish your works. . . . We are, however, willing to reopen negotiations at any time . . . should you wish to reconsider your decision." . . .

I am in such terrible material and financial shape that I do not know what to do. . . . I will write to the publishers and tell them that *I will think about it*. . . .

October 14, 1951
Ivan Bunin, from his diary
Dear Lord, give me many more years and my health!

Circa November 1951
Alexander Bakhrakh, from his memoirs
I remember that right before Bunin's train left for the south of France, Adamovich and I stopped in at his compartment. Bunin was extremely tired . . . silent and helpless; but then he suddenly came to life and exclaimed with fervor: "If I live and God gives me the strength, I will hurl Dostoevsky from his pedestal!"

December 1951
Andrei Sedykh, from his memoirs
The last time I saw Bunin . . . he could no longer leave his bed. . . . His illness had changed him greatly. . . . Vera Nikolaevna, herself old, haggard, and with a look of perpetual fear in her eyes . . . told me in a confused sort of way:

"Ian is doing poorly. He does not leave his bed and receives no one. But he will, of course, be happy to see you. . . ."

We went into the dining room and sat at a table covered with oil-cloth. She went on and on, complaining about her old age, her ill health. From time to time, behind the glass door to the neighboring room, one could hear Ivan Alexeevich coughing. His cough was dry, anguished, and seemed to tear through his chest.

Finally she led me into Bunin's room. The place was semi-dark, stuffy . . . and smelling of medicine, strong Turkish tobacco, and a sick old man's body. A single light burned in the room. In the corner, on a low iron bed, half-sat Bunin covered with a soldier's blanket.

At first I was frightened—he was so very terrible to behold. Somehow he had become dried-up and small. His cheeks were sunken and covered with grey bristle. . . . But on this tortured face, etched with deep wrinkles, I saw huge eyes looking attentively at me. Apparently he wanted to see what kind of impression he was making. . . . I was so stunned by what I was seeing that I could not make my face assume that "hale and hearty" expression that people should have when they visit someone who is seriously ill. Mercilessly, I stood for several seconds before I took a step forward to embrace him. But Ivan Alexeevich stopped me:

"My dear boy, I no longer kiss anyone or greet them by taking their hand. . . . I am afraid that people will immediately get what I have. Yes, I can infect you too; this fever just does not quit."

I gradually became calm and looked around. The Bunins' apartment . . . was old and not particularly distinguished by its cleanliness. . . . Repairs had not been made from time immemorial. I was suddenly repulsed by the absolute desolation of the place. I asked Bunin if he still smoked; and he answered that he did, but French, not American cigarettes. He added that someone had brought him some Turkish tobacco. . . .

It soon became apparent that our conversation tired him, and that this was the first time [in our relationship] that he not once smiled, or imitated someone, or joked at someone's expense. Indeed, he was in no condition to do such things! Just the same, though, I quickly became convinced that for all his worsening physical weakness, his almost complete helplessness, his mind was still in splendid condition, and his thoughts were fresh, sharp, and wicked. . . .

Bunin was angry at the entire world. He was angry at his old age, his illness, his poverty. In his view, everyone was out to insult him; he was surrounded by enemies. I was struck by one phrase which he suddenly uttered without any connection to what had preceded it:

"Soon I will die," he said, having lowered his voice almost to a whisper. "You will see. Vera Nikolaevna will write *The Life of Arseniev* anew."

At first it seemed to me that he was joking. But no. Bunin was not joking. He was looking at me in a frightened way, not taking his fixed eyes off of me. As always happens in moments of spiritual duress, and as if answering his own personal thoughts, he repeated:

"Yes, she will . . . she will."

I only understood what he was talking about much later, when after his death, she published her book, *The Life of Bunin*.[9]

December 2, 1951
Vera Muromtseva-Bunina, from her diary

Ian said: "One hears this all the time . . . 'You fell as a sacrifice to.' . . . I could never understand a similar saying: 'the selfless love for the folk.' Who are these people who so loved the folk? Several generations lived by such false feelings. And just who are the folk?"

✳ 1952 ✳

Circa 1952
Zinaida Shakovskaya, from her memoirs

The last time I saw Bunin . . . he kept excusing himself for the "terrible way he looked." . . . "Who do you think I look like?" he said. "Like Voltaire," I replied, "only more noble." "I don't look like Voltaire at all," he shot back indignantly, "but like Suvorov." Of course, he looked like Suvorov in those years when he often said: "Long have I chased after glory, but now my soul is at peace at the throne of the Almighty." . . .

It once happened that I could no longer endure how Ivan Alexeevich attacked Vera Nikolaevna. Being with them, I said: "I cannot listen to how you talk to your wife. I am taking her out for some coffee. . . ."

When we were in the café, Vera Nikolaevna had her usual smile on her plain face. She told me: "You should not be offended on my account, Zinochka. After all, I am strong, stronger than Ian. He fears everything . . . especially sickness and death. But I am afraid of nothing. . . . In vain do you fear for me."

[9]Muromtseva-Bunina published *The Life of Bunin: 1870–1906* (*Zhizn' Bunina. 1870–1906*) in Paris in 1958.

January 1, 1952
Vera Muromtseva-Bunina, from her diary
   We greeted the New Year without wine. Ian made the sign of the cross over himself.

January 11, 1952
Mark Aldanov, from a letter to Ivan Bunin
   [We must face] a bitter truth—we have no other printing channels other than "Chekhov Publishers." What happens if they are not around for long?

February 1, 1952
Vera Muromtseva-Bunina, from her diary
   This morning Ian cried that he no longer has the time to do what he wants to do. He then asked me to take care of myself. "If you die," he said, "I will kill myself. I cannot live without you." I cried when I heard this.

March 19, 1952
Mark Aldanov, from a letter to Ivan Bunin
   Didn't "Chekhov Publishers" do a nice job of *The Life of Arseniev*? I find it very pleasant to read it. . . . The typos in it are few.[1] . . .

June 17, 1952
Ivan Bunin, from a letter to Galina Kuznetsova
   My dear, sweet one. . . . Thank you for your wonderful letter! You brought to mind the roses and lizards of Grasse. . . . Write, write me again (but simply . . . without any Rilke-isms). I would be *very* happy to hear from you!

June 21, 1952
Ivan Bunin, from a letter to Mark Aldanov
   It never occurred to me to offer my *Cursed Days* [to the publishers]. [A friend] once told me that it was the one book that had something to say about the Bolsheviks. . . .

---

[1] The book was published in the "new" orthography.

June 30, 1952
Mark Aldanov, from a letter to Ivan Bunin

Today I received news . . . that cheered me up greatly. "Chekhov Publishers" has decided to publish a second large edition of *Arseniev*! That means that the work is not a success but a triumph!

July 7, 1952
Ivan Bunin, from a letter to Mark Aldanov

I fear for Vera terribly. . . . Her face is swollen with bags under her eyes. Sometimes when I look at her, I cannot hold back the tears. . . .

May "Chekhov Publishers" be cursed to the -nth generation. . . . The people there are publishing an anthology of Russian poetry, and what they chose of my verse to print had me howling throughout the entire house from anger and indignation. . . . Half the stuff they want to publish was written about seventy years ago and is unbelievably wretched! So you have yet one more proof as to what hands this press has fallen into! A very criminal affair!

August 3, 1952
Vera Muromtseva-Bunina, from her diary

I am living as though in a nightmare. . . .

October 7, 1952
Ivan Bunin, from a letter to the editor of New Russian Word

Yesterday at 5 p.m., Nadezhda Alexandrovna Teffi passed away after three days of terrible suffering from angina pectoris. . . .

October 9, 1952
Ivan Bunin, from a letter to Mark Aldanov

It never occurred to me that Teffi would die so soon. . . . [The last letter] I received from her was pitiful and written in a large and very uneven scrawl; but just the same she was far from death. . . .

Circa mid-November 1952
Ivan Bunin, from a letter to Galina Kuznetsova

I keep thinking about Teffi. . . . What is with her now! Where has it all gone—her life, her talent, her emotions, intelligence, and wit? And soon *all of mine* will be gone too. . . .

* 1953 *

Circa 1953
Vera Muromtseva-Bunina, from a letter to Alexander Baboreko
　　Bunin was bedridden for the last year of his life. . . . But his head was always clear.

Circa 1953
Ivan Bunin, from a letter to Mark Aldanov
　　What I am living for now? What is life in the highest sense of the word? This is very difficult for me to say. Most of all, it seems that I am living with thoughts and feelings about something that is painfully inert . . . seemingly monstrously false, tormenting, impossible, but also devilishly immutable. I am living with the thoughts and emotions of someone who is greeted by people in early morning and told: "Take courage, for your hour has come."

January 1, 1953
Vera Muromtseva-Bunina, from her diary
　　Ian and I "greeted" the New Year. He had a sip of wine, and I, a glass.

January 8, 1953
Mark Aldanov, from a letter to Ivan Bunin
　　I have nine volumes of the Petropolis edition of your work. . . . I do not know how many times I have read all nine of them. . . .

January 23, 1953
Vera Muromtseva-Bunina, from her diary
　　Ian would not let me out of his sight until 3 a.m. He is afraid to be alone.

January 27, 1953
Ivan Bunin, from his diary
　　It is amazing! I keep thinking about the past and most often . . . about things that were lost, happy, not appreciated, or had slipped through my hands. [I also think] not only about deeds that were stupid, even insane and irreparable, but also about actions that hurt or insulted others because of my weakness, lack of character, or short-

sightedness. I also keep recalling that people did not take revenge for my insults and hurts; that I forgave way too many things; and that I did not become bitter even to this very day. But just the same, the grave will swallow everything, everything!

February 2, 1953
Ivan Bunin, from a letter to a friend

As an adolescent, I was honest to the point of stupidity. . . . But then something incomprehensible happened to me. When I was about eight years old, I, suddenly and for no reason at all, started telling the most passionate, pointless, and even idiotic falsehoods. For example, I often ran out . . . into the house, screaming at the top of my lungs that the threshing barn . . . was on fire; or that a mad wolf had . . . run through the kitchen . . . all the time believing passionately in what I had said. This went on for about a year or so, but then stopped as suddenly as it had started.

But [my wish to tell falsehoods] returned . . . in the "lie" which is artistic literature. . . .

Hitler was a genius when he said that people believe a big lie much more easily than they do a small one. . . . In my stories I lie just as Hitler did. . . . How should one lie? Just like Hitler! . . .

With the years, my ability to "lie" has grown so convincingly that not only my readers but also the critics believed and continue to believe that all my stories happened to me in real life. . . .

March 10, 1953
Ivan Bunin, from a letter to Mark Aldanov

Stalin, that pig, that beast, that sucker of human blood, has finally died. But will be it any better with those other animals, Malenkov and Beria? Most likely . . . they will attempt to deceive the public with some improvements and indulgences. . . .

April 20, 1953
Ivan Bunin, from a letter to Mark Aldanov

I do not know if Teleshov will again invite me to Moscow, but no matter how many times I am invited there, and even if the city is host to the fullest freedom in all respects . . . I would *never* go to a place where, on Red Square, two vile corpses lay in aspic.[2] . . .

---

[2]A reference to the embalmed bodies of Lenin and Stalin in the mausoleum in Red Square in Moscow.

April 23, 1953
Vera Muromtseva-Bunina, from her diary

Ian and I have been together for 46 years. We drank [to our time together].

April 23, 1953
Ivan Bunin, from a letter to Georgy Adamovich

Have you read my recent works? Can you not praise them in print? I very much need your help, otherwise they will not sell and I will die from hunger and leave you nothing as an inheritance. . . .

May 14, 1953
Vera Muromtseva-Bunina, from her diary

I am in complete despair. Ian distresses me. "I am dying," he says. He sleeps all the time. He is beginning not to notice many things.

October 9, 1953
Boris Zaitsev, from a letter to Ivan Bunin

No doubt you are very surprised to receive this letter. I myself am surprised that I am writing it. . . .

I have long wanted simply to send you my very best wishes. That moment has come . . . to say that between us, there has been a *huge* misunderstanding. Anyone can make mistakes . . . but one thing I know *for sure*: I have never done you any wrong (although you think that I did). . . .

But taking the blame for our rift, and with a completely open heart, I simply want to wish you . . . all that is good—health, happiness, and peace. Yesterday [in church] . . . the priest read the following words from Saint Paul: "Righteousness, peace, and joy in the Holy Spirit."[3] These are what are important; all the rest—discord, "enmity," Ivan Ivanych and Ivan Nikiforovich[4]—*are but trifles*.

November 3, 1953
Vera Muromtseva-Bunina, from a letter to Tatyana Loginova-Muravieva

The Prince [Bunin] . . . is apathetic and weak, and has completely lost his appetite. He will not let me out of his sight, even to leave the room. He takes his medicine with "big tears" in his eyes.

In a word, it has been one merry affair. . . .

[3]Zaitsev is quoting from Paul's letter to the Romans 14:17.
[4]Zaitsev is referring to Gogol's 1833 story, "How the Two Ivans Quarrelled" ("*Povest' o tom, kak possorilsia Ivan Ivanovich s Ivanom Nikiforovichem*").

November 5, 1953
Mark Aldanov, from his memoirs

Three days before his death, Bunin and I talked until midnight. . . . In my *final* conversation with him, the topic turned to literature. "I have always thought that our greatest poet was Pushkin," Bunin said, "but, no, it was Lermontov." . . .

He spoke with difficulty, in a very quiet, barely audible voice. . . . He kept repeating: "The oak leaf has been torn from its native branch; it flies off to the steppe, chased by a cruel wind. . . ."[5]

November 6, 1953
Andrei Sedykh, from his memoirs

Just before his death, seemingly on the very night before [his passing], Ivan Alexeevich told his wife: "My soul is separating from my body."

November 7, 1953
Alexander Bakhrakh, from his memoirs

When I entered Bunin's room, the blinds were drawn and it was half dark. A heady, sickly smell wafted from the pile of medicine bottles and boxes that were heaped on his night table. Bunin was lying down. His eyes were half closed. . . . Since I had seen him last, he had become thin, depressed, and exhausted. His handsome face was covered with bristle and was almost ashen-colored. . . .

Bunin opened his eyelids, turned, and coughed. Then, with markedly increasing agitation, he began talking about the senselessness of death, that it was something he could neither understand nor accept. He did not understand how such a thing could be happening to him, that he was now a man but then he would be no more. He himself said that he could imagine everything, understand everything, feel everything, except "nonexistence." . . .

Throughout my acquaintance with him, Bunin loved to repeat a key saying from Marcus Aurelius: "Our highest purpose—is to prepare for death," but it was clear that he was not prepared for it.

I remembered that during one of our daily "exchange of opinions" in Grasse, Bunin had categorically denied the possibility of life after death, insisting that such a concept would contradict any higher logic. [He believed] that after our "minute"-long existence on this planet (which he called both "repulsive" and "splendid"), there would stretch

[5]Bunin is citing from Lermontov's "Tree-Leaf" ("*Listok*"), written in 1841.

forward myriads and aeons of years, which had not existed before birth and which now embraced an incomprehensible, undecipherable existence. Once there is a beginning, Bunin said, there has to be an end. . . .

A volume of [Leo] Tolstoy lay on his bed. When I asked him what he was reading, it seemed to cheer him up a bit. He replied that he wanted to read *Resurrection*[6] one more time. But he also said that he found it difficult to read, that it was hard for him to concentrate, and that it was especially burdensome for him to hold a book in his hands. In almost angry tones, he added: "Ah, Tolstoy was such a great man, such a splendid writer in all respects. . . . But even now I cannot understand why *Resurrection* has so many unnecessary, unartistic pages. . . ."

Bunin uttered these words . . . with seemingly deep inner suffering. . . . At that moment it seemed that to reproach Tolstoy gave him physical pain. . . . He again closed his eyes, turned to the wall, and asked to be left alone for a while. I went out into the next room while he continued to mutter, saying something to himself in an undertone: "How could Tolstoy do it, how could he do it?" . . .

This was the last time I would ever hear an exclamation from his lips. I left soon thereafter.

November 7, 1953
Vera Muromtseva-Bunina, as told to Andrei Sedykh

It was ten o'clock and we were alone. Ian asked me to read him some letters by Chekhov. I read one or two. . . . Then he said: "I am tired. That's enough for now."

"Do you want me to lie down with you?" I asked. "Yes," he said.

I went out to get undressed and threw on a light robe. He began ringing for me.

"What is taking you so long?"

"I have to wash my face and take care of a thing or two in the kitchen."

It was midnight when I . . . got into his narrow bed. His hands were cold. I began to warm them up, and we quickly fell asleep. Suddenly I felt that the he had raised himself up slightly. I asked him what was the matter. He answered: "I am gasping for breath. I do not have a pulse. Give me some medicine."

I got up and counted twenty drops.

[6]Tolstoy's *Resurrection* (*Voskresenie*) appeared in 1899.

"Did you sleep?" I asked.

"A little bit," he answered. "I had a dream . . . but I am fine now. I want to stretch my legs."

I went to help him. He was sitting on the bed. Within the minute I saw that he had lowered his head onto his arm. His eyes were closed, his mouth open. I said to him: "Grab hold of my neck and raise yourself up a bit. I will help you to lie down."

But he remained silent and inert. . . . At that moment he departed from me.

November 7, 1953
Vera Muromtseva-Bunina, as told to Valentin Kataev

"It was here on this couch that Ivan Alexeevich died." Vera Nikolaevna went over to a sagging mattress on legs, covered with an ancient carpet. At its head was a small table with an ancient folding icon in blackened silver, which Bunin took with him wherever he went. On the wall hung several other icons in gilded mountings, as well as baptismal crucifixes and even, so it seemed, cut-glass Easter eggs. Such things, though, only accentuated the shabby appearance of the couch on which Bunin had died.

"How did it happen?" I asked.

"Ivan Alexeevich had been extremely healthy. He was hardly ever ill. The doctors used to say that he had the chest of a blacksmith. He suffered from only one disease in his entire life, and you know what that was," Vera Nikolaevna said, addressing me with a half-smile as if I were "one of the family" and for whom there was no need to be shy. "Hemorrhoids. But people do not die of that," she smiled sadly.

"Ivan Alexeevich died simply of old age. He was eighty-three. Toward the end of his life he had become very weak. He had to be carried to the bathroom. I did not want to leave him alone at night, so I slept with him on this couch. So as not to disturb him, I would roll myself up in a ball at his feet and lie very still.

"On November 7th—the very day that you celebrate the anniversary of your Revolution—he went to bed in the evening and slept nearly the entire night quite peacefully. But all of a sudden, sometime between two and three in the morning, he jumped up as if had received an electric shock, and, having pushed me, sat up in bed with an expression of such indescribable horror on his face that a chill went up my spine. I knew that this was the end.

"The light from the Passy streetlamps was very dim, but it seemed to me that what was left of his grey-white hair was actually standing on end over his thin, bald head. He tried to say something, or perhaps even to shout. His entire gaunt body began to tremble, and suddenly his mouth fell open in a strange way. His lower jaw dropped like this. . . ."

And, as if in a trance, Vera Nikolaevna imitated Bunin's death agony. Her mouth fell open strangely, her lower jaw dropped. In front of me, I suddenly saw the face of Bunin as it must have been in the last moment of his life, the crazed white eyes of Ivan the Terrible, the skull covered with cold sweat, and the black cavern of his gaping mouth with its sagging jaw.

"Then he fell back on the bed, dead. I tied up his jaw with a napkin and laid out his body while it was still warm. I crossed his withered arms on his chest, closed his eyes, pressed my thumbs on his eyelids, and did not call anyone until morning.

"I spent the rest of the night, our last night together, lying as usual at his feet as they grew cold, on the torn sheet under the threadbare blanket. I remembered the agonizingly difficult life that we had lived together, our former love, our wanderings.

"While I lay alone with him there, I cried and cried until I could cry no more. Since then I have lost the ability to cry. My eyes are dry forever. I have no more tears."

November 8, 1953
Bunin's doctor, from his memoirs

When I arrived [at the Bunins' home], Bunin was no longer among the living. As he had requested, Vera Nikolaevna had covered his face with a handkerchief, since he did not want anyone to see it after he died. For me, though, she withdrew the cloth slightly; and for the last time I saw that handsome face which had suddenly become so peaceful and remote. It was as if Bunin had seen something, and that he had solved the riddle of death which had tormented him throughout his life.

I helped put Bunin's body in order and carry him into the other room. Around the neck of the deceased, Vera Nikolaevna had tied a scarf. "I know," she said, "that he would have liked such a thing, since it was given to him by . . ." and she named a woman's name. . . .

Circa November 12, 1953
Vera Muromtseva-Bunina, from a letter to Tatyana Loginova-Muravieva

Everyone with whom I have come into contact in this difficult time has showed me such love and concern that I will remember them with gratitude for as long as I live. Generally speaking, the atmosphere of these past five days has been unusually light. Do not be surprised when I say that . . . everything has been filled with a singularly sad love. I felt that everyone was grieving, but not from pity and empathy for me alone. I was so deeply touched by the love that everyone bore for Ian as both an individual and a writer, as well as by the genuine simplicity with which they conducted themselves. . . . Despite my sadness, my soul will always cherish the feeling of unspeakable joy that people brought to me [in my hour of need]. . . .

November 23, 1953
Vera Muromtseva-Bunina, from a letter to Tatyana Loginova-Muravieva
I find it difficult to get used to the thought that Ian is no longer among the living. Because I cannot cry, my loss is all the more difficult and burdensome. I have grown thin; and mornings I feel completely vanquished. . . . But I have to live on if only to bring order to Ian's things and to preserve his memory. . . .

I live in the study where Ian himself lived and died. His pictures are on the desk, the fireplace, and the walls . . . but I never tire of looking at them. . . .

December 14, 1953
Vera Muromtseva-Bunina, from a letter to Natalya Kodryanskaya
He is no longer here. Never again will I hear him call out "Vera!" But I have to live . . . most of all, to keep his memory alive.

✳ CODA ✳

December 7, 1953
Mark Aldanov, from a letter to Vera Muromtseva-Bunina
I keep rereading Ivan Alexeevich's books, and his (and your) letters to me. . . . After I do, I usually . . . take a strong swig of cognac to calm my nerves.

1954
Konstantin Fedin, from a speech delivered to the Second All-Union Congress of Soviet Writers
Ivan Bunin lacked the strength to return home. . . . But we

should not exclude him from the history of Russian literature. Russian readers have as much right to his fiction as they do to Kuprin's.

February 28, 1954
Vera Muromtseva-Bunina, from a letter to Natalya Kodryanskaya
If you only knew how boring it is for me without Ivan Alexeevich. For the entire forty-seven years of our life together, we were never bored. . . . But now everything has grown dull. . . . My mind understands his passing, but my heart does not.

April 23, 1954
Vera Muromtseva-Bunina, from a letter to Tatyana Loginova-Muravieva
Two weeks ago there was a literary evening to honor the Prince [Bunin]. Everyone was pleased with the way it turned out, but I found it difficult to be there, even though the atmosphere in the auditorium was extremely friendly. . . .

November 17, 1954
Vera Muromtseva-Bunina, from a letter to Natalya Kodryanskaya
On November 7 there was a memorial service for Ivan Alexeevich. . . . About forty people were present. On the following day, eleven of us went to his grave. There were twelve vases of heather; someone had also brought a large spray of yellow chrysanthemums. . . . It was all a fitting tribute to Ivan Alexeevich. . . .

1956
Konstantin Paustovsky, from an article
A remarkable Russian writer—a writer of classical strength and simplicity—has died in France: Ivan Bunin.

He has died under a foreign sky in needless and bitter exile, which he himself created, and in unbearable longing for Russia and its people.

Who knows how much suffering from this separation this outwardly calm and restrained individual carried alone within himself.

We will not judge Bunin; it is not worth recalling his fatal mistake. That is not important now.

What is important is that he is ours, that we have returned him to our people, to our Russian literature, and that from now on he will occupy a high place in it, a place that is his by right.

At the first literary evening to honor Bunin [in Russia],[7] I was

---

[7]In October 1956 the literary community in Moscow publicly celebrated what would have been Bunin's eighty-sixth birthday.

asked to give the introduction [to the event]. To prepare for it, I opened one of Bunin's books at random—and that was the end of the lecture! I became so engrossed in reading him that I almost did not have time to jot down a few remarks about Bunin on paper.

I had forgotten about everything. Such was the force of Bunin's talent, Bunin's words, the force of his merciless, splendid, and impeccable mastery.

He was so severe because he put aesthetic truth above everything else.

How often and profoundly do we err in our assessments of writers as the result of an undying need to attach labels to them. Chekhov was called a "pessimist" and a "singer of twilights" throughout his life. Bunin was typed as a "cold master" and a "dispassionate Parnassian."

How pitiful all these labels seem when one reads Bunin's books and discovers . . . a huge human heart subsisting on the black grief of the Russian village, its lonely and bitter fate. . . .

[Whenever I read Bunin] I feel as though an icy razor has slashed my heart. . . .

Yes, Bunin is severe, almost merciless. But he also writes about love with great force. . . . Bunin associates love with all the beauty and complexities of the world . . . with nights, days, the boundless noise of the ocean, books, and thoughts—in a word, with everything that surrounds him. . . .

March 1956
Nikolai Roshchin, from an article
  [Since Bunin's death] there have been literary gatherings [to honor his memory] in Russia, literary journals in Moscow have published his stories, and scholars are preparing a multi-volumed edition of his works.[8] But I am sorry about one thing—how happy Bunin would have been . . . if he could have seen how carefully, how with such loving exactingness all the previous editions of his works are being studied—both here and abroad—and how attentively all of his later corrections are being taken into account!

And what great happiness this "last classic of Russian literature" would have had, had he had the urge to return to his native shores, about which he had created so many inspiring, so many splendid images in the icy murk of a foreign land.

---

[8]Almost as herald to the so-called Thaw (the easing of cultural restrictions in the wake of Khrushchev's 1956 denunciation of Stalin), the editors of the liberal journal *New World* (*Novyi Mir*) printed selections by Bunin in the June 1955 issue. A year later a five-volume collection of Bunin's works, the first since the Revolution, was published.

Easter 1956
Vera Muromtseva-Bunina, from a letter to Tatyana Loginova-Muravieva

This is the third Easter that I have been without Ian. We had 46 Easters together. Not long ago I saw him in a dream. I was so happy, but then, when I woke up, I realized that he was not there and felt a cruel sadness.

January 17, 1957
Vera Muromtseva-Bunina, from a letter to the Soviet embassy in Paris

It is necessary that I call your attention to the following:

I have been receiving a pension of 800 rubles a month . . . [as per] a contract with the representatives of the Soviet embassy in France . . . in which I agreed gradually to surrender the archive of Ivan Alexeevich Bunin [to the homeland].[9] . . .

This year the cost of living here in France has increased considerably; and so the money that I am receiving [from Russia] is covering only the most necessary expenses. During this time, also, my health has so deteriorated that I must visit doctors frequently, particularly for the osteoporosis that came about from my poor nutrition in the years of the last war. I also have cataracts in both eyes and need an operation. Further, since I do not have health insurance, I often have to go without expensive medicine and medical services.

Additionally, I have debts from the many illnesses of Ivan Alexeevich which I still have not been able to pay.

Finally, my apartment is in a wretched condition because I do not have money for expensive repairs which my landlord demands be done.

In light of the massive printings of several editions of my late husband's works [in Russia], I make bold to ask the Soviet government for a one-time gift [to assist me in my financial affairs]. . . .

January 22, 1957
An attaché from the Soviet embassy in Paris, to the Ministry of Foreign Affairs of the USSR

Considering the huge printings of Bunin's works [in the Soviet Union] . . . the embassy supports the request of Vera Nikolaevna Bunina [for additional financial assistance from the Soviet government].[1] . . .

---

[9]Concerning her husband's archives, Muromtseva-Bunina was first approached by the Soviets in December 1955.
[1]In late 1955 the Soviet government had already given to Muromtseva-Bunina 1.5 million francs in royalties for a two-volume edition of her husband's works.

November 17, 1957
Vera Muromtseva-Bunina, from a letter to Natalya Kodryanskaya

The letters I have been receiving from Russian literary scholars are filled with nothing but praise for Ivan Alexeevich. One writes: "I know many people of varying ages and walks of life who, with reverence and ecstasy, talk about the incomparable works of Ivan Alexeevich. No matter whom I write to . . . be they in Moscow or the provinces . . . everyone talks about his books with delight . . . a delight that is *special* to him alone, that is unlike a love for, say, Chekhov or Tolstoy . . . but that enters the soul as a flickering light and brings on eternal, universal life."

Another scholar, telling me that he knows Bunin's stories almost by heart, asks me to tell him something about Ian, since everything about him is a "treasure." . . .

In a word, I have never received such attention from strangers in emigration. . . .

May 22, 1958
The Soviet Union of Writers, from a letter to Vera Muromtseva-Bunina

The members of the commission of the Soviet Union of Writers [to preserve] the literary heritage of I. A. Bunin wish to express their gratitude to V. N. Bunina for preserving and presenting us with the personal archive of I. A. Bunin.[2]

October 10, 1958
Vera Muromtseva-Bunina, from a letter to Tatyana Loginova-Muravieva

On the 30th I visited the cemetery and sat by Ian's grave. It was an ineffably charming autumn evening, and the trees were still green. . . .

I celebrated my name day by accident. On the morning of October 1st, the concierge brought me some roses, two tortes, and a huge pretzel. I got on the phone and called everyone I could to help me eat them. Whoever was healthy came—and polished off everything. My liver did not notice what I was eating.

---

[2]In the West, Bunin's archives are housed at the Bakhmeteff Archive at Columbia University, and at the University of Leeds, England. In Russia most of Bunin's materials are located at the Russian State Library, the Russian State Literary Museum, the Gorky Institute of World Literature, and the Russian State Archive of Literature and Art in Moscow; at the Saltykov-Shchedrin Public Library in Saint Petersburg; and at the Turgenev State Museum in Oryol.

January 30, 1959
Vera Muromtseva-Bunina, from a letter to a Soviet critic
You are correct when you say that Ivan Alexeevich underestimated the value of many of his works. He never allowed his works to be read in his presence—they always sounded poor to him. For that reason, of course, he kept reworking his pieces, most often shortening them. . . . He was never satisfied with what he had written.

Even right before his death, he said that he "had not done everything he could have done."

March 8, 1959
Vera Muromtseva-Bunina, from a letter to a Soviet critic
Perhaps, one has to live in Russia, in its very center, to understand Bunin's creativity in a true and genuine way. . . .

June 8, 1959
Vera Muromtseva-Bunina, from a letter to a Soviet critic
I lived for 46, even 47 years in close contact with an artistic individual, and I have come to the conclusion that creativity is a mystery. There is no way to explain it. But such creativity is affected more by the events of life than by one or another idea. . . .

Stories from *Dark Alleys* came into being because we wanted to leave the world of war and to enter one where blood did not flow and life was not being snuffed out. We were all engaged with its writing to help us to bear the unbearable. . . .

Circa 1960
Valentin Kataev, from his memoirs
I learned to see the world from . . . both Bunin and Mayakovsky. But the two were different.

Bunin thought, and apparently was profoundly convinced, that he was completely independent, a pure artist. . . . He wanted to be completely free of any obligations to the society in which he had lived, to his homeland. He believed that, as an emigré, he had achieved his goal. Abroad it seemed to him that he was completely free to write anything that came into his head, without submitting to state censorship or to the judgment of the group.

The French state, Parisian society, and the Catholic church did not care about Bunin. He wrote whatever he wanted to write, unhampered by any moral circumstances or even, sometimes, by considerations of simple decency. As a portrayer [of life], he grew [as an artist] and, by the end of his time here on earth, achieved the highest degree of plastic perfection. But the absence of any moral pressure from the outside meant that Bunin the artist had lost a focus for his abilities, his spiritual energies. He could not grapple with the "thousand-headed hydra of empiricism" of which Goethe had spoken; and this moral pressure swallowed him up, or, more accurately, tore him to pieces, like a deep-water fish which, having grown accustomed to the constant pressure of tens, hundreds, perhaps, thousands of pressures, suddenly finds itself on the surface, experiencing almost no pressure at all.

For Bunin, artistic creation had ceased being a struggle and had become simply the habit of portraying, a gymnastics of the imagination.

Bunin once told me it was possible to express everything in words, but there was a barrier which even the greatest poet could not overcome. There would always be something that "no words could express," and one had to be reconciled to such a fact. Perhaps this was true. But Bunin set this barrier, this hurdle, for himself too early.

At one time it seemed to me that his portraits of the most profound subtleties of our world, of nature, had reached complete and final perfection. In this respect, of course, Bunin surpassed Polonsky and Fet, but, although he himself was not aware of it, he in some respects fell short of Innokenty Annensky and, later, of Pasternak and Mandelshtam in their later periods. . . .

All these thoughts flashed through my mind as [my wife and I], having rung the bell, stood at Bunin's door. A moment later it clicked open and revealed a neglected Moscow entrance hall that was not at all Parisian but very much [Russian] old regime. In front of me was Vera Nikolaevna. She was now a very old, tall, ungainly, and badly dressed lady, a kindly, helpless, and much decayed gentlewoman who wore big, patched shoes but who had retained something of the manners of an old-time Muscovite student from a liberal family. Her once delicate, light-flaxen hair had long since thinned and was now white as snow, but it was still tied back in a sparse little bun. But her rather pointed, lean nose with its azure vein around her once beautiful eyes, and her unwrinkled forehead, still reminded me in some way of a Greek goddess. She was probably in her nineties.[3]

Joyfully and sadly, through tears, she scrutinized us, and I actually felt a sense of kinship in her tired, transparently white, bloodless, and kindly face.

[3]Vera Muromtseva-Bunina was approximately eighty years old at this time.

"So at last we meet again, Valya," she said, moving her slightly shaking hand from side to side. "Yes, Ivan Alexeevich and I imagined your wife to be exactly as she is, but we could not picture what your children would look like. To Ivan Alexeevich, that somehow seemed altogether incredible—Valya Kataev's children! All we knew was that you had a boy and a girl."

"And not long ago a granddaughter," I said, not without a boastful touch.

"Good Lord, Good Lord!" Vera Nikolaevna exclaimed, clasping and unclasping her old-looking hands. "You know, Valya, it has been forty years since we last saw each other. Forty years! We did not even have time to say goodbye."

"I was sick with typhus."

"We knew that. Ivan Alexeevich wanted to visit you in the hospital. . . . But you know Ivan Alexeevich. . . . He was so afraid of infection. . . . He was sure that you would not live, but I had faith. . . . I prayed for you and believed. . . . Again and again. . . . And seeing you like this, alive and . . . But let's not talk about it. . . . It's all so incredible, incredible. . . ." . . .

"So you are Valya's wife!" Vera Nikolaevna turned to my wife and kissed her on her tear-stained cheek. "Ivan Alexeevich loved Valya and always spoke about him. He knew all about him, read everything he had written, and took great pride in his success. You see, Ivan Alexeevich was your husband's literary godfather. . . ."

I looked at Vera Nikolaevna with the same fixed attention with which the young Bunin had once looked at the moon, wishing to describe it as exactly as possible. What did she look like? A tallow candle? . . . No . . . the whiteness that dominated Vera Nikolaevna's entire appearance was that of a white mouse with pinkish eyes.

She took us into the dining room, and again I was overwhelmed by the neglect, the blackness of the unpolished parquet floor, the horrible, pre-Revolutionary Russian sideboard with its top burned through in several places, and the dinner table covered with a Russian oilcloth that was also pre-Revolutionary and rusty brown, frayed at the edges, and marked by round glass stains. I was also struck by a badly burned kettle standing on a wire gas ring, various sizes of Russian Kuznetsov and French Limoges cups, and among them, a plate of meringues—the only attractive thing on the table.

"Your favorites," she said, noticing the pleasure with which I looked at the meringues.

"How did you know that I like meringues?"

"I remember," she replied sadly. "One day you said that when you got rich, you would buy meringues with whipped cream . . . every day."

"Did I really say that?"

"Yes, you did. Ian roared with laughter when he heard you say such a thing—'How little he needs to be happy,' he remarked. Don't you remember how you once ate almost all the meringues when you went to tea at Natasha N.'s, and how her high-society *maman* was on the verge of never letting you into the house again?"

"You even remember that!"

"I remember everything," she said sadly, moving her shaking head from side to side. . . .

"Here is the Ivan Alexeevich that you knew," she said, taking us into a small room where, on the dark, flimsy wallpaper of one wall, there was a kind of iconostasis[4]—photographs of Bunin at various periods of his life, and among them, the Bunin that I knew, the best known pre-Revolutionary photograph of him: Iv. Bunin, Academician, at the zenith of his fame, and with features that I would remember all my life—his haughty face, his dandyish, pointed beard, and his farsighted eyes that looked as though they would burst into tears.

There was also a photograph of another Bunin, one I did not know—a young man with a nobleman's military cap and a black sheepskin cloak about his shoulders, and also [one of] Bunin in his later years, without any moustache or beard, with a face that was clean-shaven, muscular, and aged, but with the same sharp glance, perhaps even more arrogant and inflexible, one that seemed to say, "No, there can be no return to the past!"—but also with the same narrow, goatlike cheeks, with which one could easily recognize the former Bunin.

"Just imagine," Vera Nikolaevna said, observing the expression on my face as I examined Bunin's photograph. "One fine day he came back from the barber's without his moustache and beard. I simply gasped! At first I could not stand it. There was something actorlike, foreign, naked about it, but then I got used to it. But tell me, why did he have to do such a thing?"

I had seen the photograph of the clean-shaven Bunin many times before and had become accustomed to his new face. For me the old and the new Bunin seemed to have fused into a single whole that differed very little from my usual conception of him. He was still the same

---

[4]In the Eastern church, the iconostasis is a wall-like screen of icons of Christ, the Mother of God, and the saints, which separates the sacristy from the rest of the church.

man, artist, poet, teacher, great portrayer of nature, the one who, while
he was still quite young, had written:

> Now a drop, like the top of a nail, has fallen
> And hundreds of needles furrow still ponds
> As the sparkling downpour begins its surge. . . .

One day, as though wishing to make a final and decisive break
with the past, Bunin [again] shaved off his beard and moustache, fear-
lessly exposing his aged and energetic mouth. It was with this new
look, together with a tailcoat and a starched shirtfront covering his
broad chest, that he received from the hands of the king of Sweden the
diploma of a Nobel Prize–winner, a gold medal, and a small briefcase
of yellow embossed leather that was specifically decorated *à la russe*, a
style that Bunin, incidentally, detested.

Vera Nikolaevna also showed us a yellowed French newspaper
with a full-length picture on the front page of "Jean Bounine," winner
of the "Prix Nobel," in the same tailcoat with his bare, Catholic chin
jutting out. In all this, there was something endlessly bitter . . . even
cruelly absurd. . . .

January 7, 1960
Vera Muromtseva-Bunina, from a letter to a Soviet critic
I could listen to Ivan Alexeevich's stories without end, but there
is no one here to read them aloud. I myself often reread his works . . .
especially at night when I cannot sleep . . . and right after I finish, I
drowse off right away. . . .

January 11, 1960
Vera Muromtseva-Bunina, from a letter to a Soviet critic
Oh, old age is no joy! Everything has become so difficult. I get so
tired of everything, and I do not have money even for a taxi. . . .

I live like a complete hermit. I visit friends more and more rarely
now, and I do not go to concerts, theatres, or the movies. . . .

But it is good that I can still converse with my memory. It is my
most favorite thing to do.

April 2, 1960
Vera Muromtseva-Bunina, from a letter to a Soviet critic
[I remember that] Ian and I were once on an Italian ship that was

sailing to Odessa. How truly wonderful it was! Since there were few passengers on aboard, we became friends with all the sailors, drinking and singing with them. Ivan Alexeevich, who, when he was on a ship, was always so unusually happy and full of *joie de vivre*, kept doing the tarantella, which he had learned during his visits to Capri. How he could mimic the Italians! Generally speaking, he was talented with anything that involved the body. He could have been a ballet dancer. . . .

October 12, 1960
Vera Muromtseva-Bunina, from a letter to Tatyana Loginova-Muravieva
For the past two weeks I have been answering people who sent me cards for my name day. There is no end in sight. . . .

October 24, 1960
Vera Muromtseva-Bunina, from a letter to a Soviet critic
Were you at the literary gathering in Moscow [that celebrated what would have been Bunin's ninetieth birthday] on October 22nd? Please tell me all about it, for not a single newspaper in Paris took note of it. . . .

[On that day] I [and several friends] went to the cemetery to attend a memorial service for Bunin, and to visit almost all the graves of our departed friends. . . .

Of all the "friends" who saw me that day, I recall only a group of poets, along with several letters that people had sent me. . . .

I am always inwardly depressed in October. Seven years have passed since the time [of Bunin's death], but it all seems so recent. But life goes on, and everyone is busy with his or her own things. . . .

November 19, 1960
Vera Muromtseva-Bunina, from a letter to a Soviet writer
I look at pictures of your little home with envy. We do not have things like that here.

You are correct: All of you [in Russia] find it as difficult to imagine our life and ways as we do endlessly imagining yours. . . .

Many of our people here have visited your country, and I now find it pleasant . . . to hear what they have to say [about it].

Most of all, I miss "our" nature. We have nothing like it here. How I would like to lay in a meadow or a forest and quietly watch the sky, "our" clouds.

January 9, 1961
Vera Muromtseva-Bunina, from a letter to Tatyana Loginova-Muravieva
 I spent the holidays in a quiet way, seeing one or two people.

January 14, 1961
Vera Muromtseva-Bunina, from a letter to a Soviet critic
 How nice that you can now visit your family home, your own natural surroundings. We have been deprived of such things and espe-
cially suffer for this loss. . . .
 I am very surprised that [Bunin's first wife] Anna Nikolaevna
[Tsakni] refused to talk to you about Bunin. It must be her "feminine
outrage."[5] After all, from the letters I have, it is very clear that Ivan
Alexeevich did not leave her, but that she was the one who did not
want to live with him. It is true, though, that when Ian and I were already living together, she came to be on very good terms with him.
Perhaps she is angry that he did not leave me for her?

January 19, 1961
Vera Muromtseva-Bunina, from a letter to a Soviet critic
 I have always been surprised why at one time, people attacked
Ivan Alexeevich for *The Village*. After all, Tolstoy's *The Power of Dark-
ness*[6] is a much more terrible thing.

February 3, 1961
Vera Muromtseva-Bunina, from a letter to a Soviet writer
 So far the New Year has treated us kindly. We have lost only one
friend. . . .
 I greeted the New Year in loneliness. I had dinner, drank a little
bit of spirits, ate some candy, and wished all my friends and acquaintances a happy new year. Then I went to bed, read a little from Lev
Nikolaevich Tolstoy, and quickly fell asleep. . . .
 There once existed the [Russian] village. . . . What a wealth of
melodies the peasants kept alive, things no city dweller would understand! Such folkways and organic emotions are found nowhere else in
the world; they have been the seedbed for all our creativity. . . . How
much was there in our village life, how wise were its peasants!

---

[5]Tsakni was eighty-two years old at this time.
[6]Tolstoy wrote *The Power of Darkness* (*Vlast' t'my*) in 1886.

March 3, 1961
Vera Muromtseva-Bunina, from a letter to Tatyana Loginova-Muravieva

Today I put on my grey suit. The trees are all in bloom. The sky is cloudless and blue. . . . I write letters and "converse with my memory," but not as much as I should. I have way too many things to do . . . but I do not have the energy to do them. I only feel like "conversing." . . .

April 4, 1961
Vera Muromtseva-Bunina, from a letter to Tatyana Loginova-Muravieva

I am sitting in a café . . . waiting for the Easter vigil to begin and not knowing what to do with myself until that time. . . .

I wanted to visit the Struves, but they were not at home. . . . I called [a friend], but she was playing cards. . . . I called [another friend], but no one answered the phone. So here I am sitting and looking at the passersby. . . .

I keep writing letters and my "Conversation with Memory," but not as much as I should. I have all kinds of trifling and household things to deal with, and I do not have the strength to keep up with them. . . .

P.S. There are so few of us left!

April 7–14, 1961
From various obituaries for Vera Muromtseva-Bunina

One could have said many things to Vera Nikolaevna Bunina. If I were not afraid of grandstanding, I, as a "writer of Russian literature," would tell her . . . about her insatiable and inexhaustible concern for people, about her simplicity and kindness, about her modesty, and about the world that issued forth from her way of looking at things. . . .

Who in Russian Paris will forget Vera Nikolaevna, who will not feel that without her, Russian Paris is already not the same as it was previously? What has Russian Paris lost? Why does it look so empty, so deserted?

More important for the future, though, is what Vera Nikolaevna was for her husband. Not all major and even great Russian writers—do we have to name names?—had the good fortune to find in marriage a friend who was not only loving but also so completely loyal, so ready to sacrifice herself, to defer in everything, yet always to remain a living person who did not become a silent shadow. Now is not the time to recall in print what Bunin said about his wife. But at the same time I can also attest to the fact that for Vera Nikolaevna's staunch devotion to her husband, Bunin was forever grateful and that he esteemed her beyond all measure.

In everyday life the departed Ivan Alexeevich was not an easy individual, something he himself, of course, often acknowledged. But the more deeply he felt things, the more indebted he was to his wife. I think that if in his presence, someone had insulted or offended Vera Nikolaevna, his passionate nature would have made him kill the individual—because Bunin would have seen him not only as an enemy but also as a slanderer and as a moral monster who could not distinguish between good and evil, light and darkness. . . .

[If I were to tell] all the stories about Bunin's life, the splendid, simple, and pure image of Vera Nikolaevna would rise to its full height. In the years of her widowhood, when her life was filled only with memories of her husband . . . one could clearly see her rare spiritual gifts. Today in Russia people read Bunin with a passion; and it seems that they love him very much. I would very much like to see that in these days, those far-off, endless numbers of Russian readers would say a kind and sincere word for a woman who has done more than they most likely can imagine. . . .

When Ivan Alexeevich and his wife . . . appeared . . . at [pre-Revolutionary] gatherings . . . in Moscow, everyone in the hall whispered approvingly: "What a beauty she is!" And truly, Vera Nikolaevna, wearing an emerald velvet or a light grey dress, was stunning. She had Raphael-like eyes and profile and a Titian-like figure. She was a classic beauty from the paintings of the Italian masters. This charming woman has remained in my memory as a graceful flourish of then "young" Moscow.

Here, abroad, Vera Nikolaevna gave us Russians a stirring example of gentleness and patience. She endured everything without complaint: the far from easy character of Ivan Alexeevich, the long months of starvation in Grasse during the years of occupation, and many other things which would be too painful to talk of here. She always remained collected and serene, even though the heart of this genuinely Russian woman bore scar upon scar.

May she rest in peace!

April 26, 1961
Leonid Zurov, from a letter to Alexander Baboreko
Vera Nikolaevna took sick on March 21. . . . She was conscious until the last hour of her life. On the morning of her death on April 3, she spoke freely, seeking advice from the doctor as to whether she

should go to Geneva, Switzerland. After 12 noon, though, her speech became labored. At 3:30 p.m., I folded her arms. . . . Ivan Alexeevich's deathbed was also her own. An unfinished manuscript of her reminiscences lay on his desk. . . .

At the Russian cemetery of Sainte-Geneviève-des-Bois in Paris, Bunin's burial vault was opened and I saw his coffin. A place alongside it had been saved for her. . . . [Her doctor] later told me that she did not want to live anymore, that she wanted to die, and that she had lost the will to live probably because life had destroyed her.

Late April 1961
Valentin Kataev, from his memoirs

[When I heard that] Vera Nikolaevna had died, I imagined Passy . . . the little street [where she lived], and the temporarily deserted flat, squalid and neglected, with its stagnant smells of dirty bed linen, its unwashed windows through which one could see the lights of Paris at night. [I also called to mind] its bathroom where darned underclothes hung on a line, the yellow water that still lay trapped at the bottom of the peeling bathtub, the thick black water pipes and the cast-iron tank that oozed rusty drops of cold water, the wooden seat that stood in a damp corner like a yoke, and the tiled floor that was slightly slimy. Through the open door of the kitchen, one could see a gas stove with unwashed saucepans, covered with yellowed sheets of *Figaro*, while in the corner, tied up with string, stood a pile of copies of *Dark Alleys.* . . .

[Outside of Paris] my wife and I . . . visited . . . a cemetery with an open gate.

"Perhaps, madame and monsieur would like to see a Russian emigré cemetery? It has a curious little church built in the ancient Novgorod style, and done from sketches by the late Russian artist Alexander Benois. If you wish, you can also see the grave of Bunin, winner of the *Prix Nobel*, whom I believe you knew. . . ."

The cemetery keeper, a carelessly dressed Russian gentleman with a rather ironical expression on his worn but still fully presentable face . . . led us down a straight little path, past Orthodox crosses and towering tombs, and stopped beside a grey granite cross. It was not the usual cross but a kind of military one carved in stone, perhaps even a Cross of Saint George, but also rather squat, dark, and heavy.

"Here is your Bunin. Take a good look," the keeper said. "As for the cross, the experts claim that it is a copy of some old Russian or Pskovian or Byzantine monument from olden times which was found in some excavation or other. . . . But as for Bunin's grave, you can see that it is not too much in the shadows and that it is surrounded by some rather good company." With a hospitable sweep of his arm, the man pointed to neighboring graves, on whose tombstones one could read some very illustrious Russian names that are now long since forgotten in the homeland.

"They bring [Russians] here . . . from all over the world," the keeper continued, "from Britain, Switzerland, even from America. . . . Soon there will not be a single vacant plot left. We have already started putting two people in one grave—so long as they are of the same family, of course. For instance, not long ago, we had to bury Vera Niko-laevna in the same grave as Ivan Alexeevich Bunin—at his feet. So now, at last, they are together again, both lying under the same cross."

With a commanding air, he, with his foot, pushed aside a few broken crocks, withered flowers, funeral ribbons that had not yet faded, and the wire frame of a small, typically French ring-shaped wreath. . . .

"The remains of her funeral," he remarked fastidiously. "They still have not cleared away the rubbish. Oh dear! I am really going to let the watchman have it!" he said, looking up anxiously at the sky. From behind the light-blue fir trees, the clusters of flowering chestnuts . . . and the blue dome and white walls of a splendid, ancient Russian church, darkish storm clouds had gathered unnoticed, heavily diluted with greyish white. Suddenly a streak of light shot up like the flame of a powder fuse and flashed over our heads with a dry snap of a lit firecracker. Faint rumbles of dry April thunder came tumbling down, like a small mountain landslide. . . .

The light-blue downpour hovered over the spiraling cemetery roses, over the yellow-red fingers of the begonias, and over the stone cross with the gold-inscribed names of Bunin and of Vera Nikolaevna lying faithfully at his feet. . . . I could not help remembering Ivan Alexeevich's lines:

"Cold wafted over the naked graves. . . . Among dry, dead leaves you glowed. . . . My pure young soul forever joined forever with your fragrance. . . . Moistly fresh, but sharp and cold."

"But where is Ivan Alexeevich's favorite ashtray?" I asked during my last visit to Vera Nikolaevna. "You remember, the one that was always on the round polished table . . . [at the house in Odessa]? Has it survived?"

"You remember such a thing?" Vera Nikolaevna asked, her aged, pale, bloodless face becoming slightly animated.

"I will never forget it," I replied.

She stood for a moment and looked straight into my eyes with profound and gentle sorrow. She then went into another room and returned, carrying in her large arthritic hands the ashtray I found so agonizingly familiar and dear.

"This one?" she asked.

I did not answer, for I could not take my eyes off that thin brass cup, with its Eastern ornament, which now seemed to me much smaller than before, as though it had shrunk with age. It had not been polished for a long time, and it no longer gleamed with fire. Rather, it had turned completely black, like the icon lamp that Bunin had once found in the hills of Sicily. . . .

He had written: "And you, my heart, do not forget. . . . With fire and fragrance filled. . . . Burn, too, until blackness charred . . . until death and darkness met."

Or better still:

"Play with a cat's head in your mouth, play until your aorta bursts. There were three devils, and you're the fourth—the last, loveliest flower cursed!"

INDEX OF PROMINENT INDIVIDUALS
MENTIONED IN THE TEXT

BIBLIOGRAPHY

SELECTED TRANSLATIONS OF BUNIN'S WORKS

Robert Bowie, *Ivan Bunin: In a Far Distant Land: Selected Stories* (Tenafly, N.J., 1983).

John Cournos, *Grammar of Love and Other Stories* (Westport, Conn., 1977).

Bernard Guerney, *The Elagin Affair and Other Stories* (New York, 1969); *The Gentleman from San Francisco and Other Stories by Ivan Bunin* (New York, 1964).

Richard Hare, *Dark Avenues and Other Stories by Ivan Bunin* (London, 1984).

Graham Hettlinger, *Sunstroke: Selected Stories of Ivan Bunin* (Chicago, 2002).

Thomas G. Marullo, *Cursed Days: A Diary of Revolution* (Chicago, 1998, and London, 2000).

Thomas G. Marullo, *The Liberation of Tolstoy: A Tale of Two Writers* (Evanston, Ill., 2001).

William Ranson, *The Gentleman from San Francisco and Other Stories* (London, 1975).

David Richards and Sophie Lund, *The Gentleman from San Francisco and Other Stories* (London, 1993).

Mark Scott, *Wolves and Other Stories* (Santa Barbara, Calif., 1980).

Olga Shartse, *Ivan Bunin: Shadowed Paths* (Moscow, 195- and 1979); *Light Breathing and Other Stories* (Moscow, 1988).

Andrew Wachtel *et al.*, *The Life of Arseniev: Youth* (Evanston, Ill., 1994).

CRITICAL WORKS

On Bunin:
Julian Connolly, *Ivan Bunin* (Boston, 1982).
Serge Kryzytski, *The Works of Ivan Bunin* (The Hague, 1961).

Thomas G. Marullo, *If You See the Buddha: Studies in the Fiction of Ivan Bunin* (Evanston, Ill., 1998).

Thomas G. Marullo, *Ivan Bunin: Russian Requiem, 1885–1920: A Portrait from Letters, Diaries, and Fiction* (Chicago, 1993).

Thomas G. Marullo, *Ivan Bunin: From the Other Shore, 1920–1933: A Portrait of Letters, Diaries, and Fiction* (Chicago, 1995).

ON THE RUSSIAN EMIGRATION

W. Chapin Huntington, *The Homesick Million: Russia-out-of-Russia* (Boston, 1933).

John, Glad, *Russia Abroad: Writers, History, Politics* (Tenafly, N.J., 1999).

Robert Johnston, *"New Mecca, New Babylon": Paris and the Russian Exiles, 1920–1945* (Montreal, 1988).

Marc Raeff, *Russia Abroad: A Cultural History of the Russian Emigration, 1919–1939* (Oxford, 1990).

SOURCE NOTES

[1934]

Circa 1934. V. Zenzinov, "Ivan Alekseevich Bunin," *Novyi zhurnal*, No. 3 (1942), 299–303.

Circa 1934 and later. Z. Shakovskaia, "O Bunine," *Vozrozhdenie*, No. 143 (1963), 71–72; "Otrazheniia," *Nashe nasledie*, No. 1 (1990), 92–93.

1934. A. Belyi, *Mezhdu dvukh revoliutsii* (Moscow, 1934), 217.

1934. Umm-El-Banine Assadoulaeff, "Poslednii poedinok Ivana Bunina," *Vremia i my*, No. 40 (April 1979), 31.

January 1934. A. Lavren'tev, "O tvorchestve I. A. Bunina," *Vrata*, No. 1 (1934), 178–182.

January 19, 1934. M. Gor'kii, "Po povodu odnoi diskussii," *Sobranie sochinenii v tridtsati tomakh*, vol. 27 (Moscow, 19530, 138.

February 1934. A. Bakshy, "Nobel Prize," *American Mercury*, No. 31 (February 1934), 223.

February 8, 1934. G. Struve, "Iz perepiski s I. A. Buninym," *Annali*, vol. 11 (1968), 24.

February 15, 1934. M. Grin, "Pis'ma B. K. Zaitseva k I. A. i V. N. Buninym," *Novyi zhurnal*, No. 149 (1982), 132–133.

February 25, 1934. A. Nazaroff, "Ivan Bunin, Artist in Prose," *New York Times Book Review* (February 25, 1934), 2.

February 26, 1934. M. Grin, "Pis'ma M. A. Aldanova k I. A. i V. I. Buninym," *Novyi zhurnal*, vol. 80 (1965), 285.

March 10, 1934. V. Lavrov, *Kholodnaia osen'. Ivan Bunin v emigratsii (1920–1953)* (Moscow, 1989), 234–236.

March 10, 1934. Grin, "Pis'ma B. K. Zaitseva," 133.

March 15, 1934, Struve, 25.

April 1934. A. Kaun, "Ivan Bunin," *Books Abroad* (April 1934), 143–146.

April 23, 1934. M. Grin, *Ustami Buninykh*, vol. 3 (Frankfurt, 1982), 8–9.

April 27, 1934. A. Baboreko, "I. A. Bunin o L. N. Tolstom," *Problemy realizma*, vol. 6 (Vologda, 1979), 178.

May 5, 1934. M. Grin, "Pis'ma M. A. Aldanova," vol. 80, 285.

May 6, 1934. Grin, *Ustami*, 9.

May 7, 1934. S. Kotkov, "Novoe o Bunine," *Uchenye zapiski Kabordino-Balkarskogo nauchno-issledovatel'skogo instituta*, vol. 24 (1967), 227.

May 29, 1934. Struve, 26.

June 8, 1934. Grin, *Ustami*, 10.

June 11, 1934. A. Baboreko, "V. N. Muromtseva-Bunina," *Pod'em*, No. 3 (1974), 115–116.

June 12, 1934. A. Baboreko, "Pis'ma I. A. Bunina N. D. Teleshovu (1941–1947)," *Istoricheskii arkhiv*, No. 2 (1962), 156.

June 14, 1934. Grin, 10.

June 22, 1934. Struve, 28.

Summer 1934. M. Grin, "Iz dnevnikov I. A. Bunina," *Novyi zhurnal*, No. 111 (1973), 135–136; *Ustami*, 7.

July 23, 1934. Grin, *Ustami*, 11.

August 5, 1934. *Ibid.*, 11.

August 17, 1934. Grin, "Pis'ma B. K. Zaitseva," 136.

August 18, 1934. Kotkov, 227.

September 1, 1934. S. Skitalets, "Predsmertnaia agoniia emigrantskoi khudozhestvennoi literatury, *Pravda* (September 1, 1934), 1.

September 17, 1934. A. Zweers, "Pis'ma I. A. Bunina k B. K. i V.A B. Zaitsevym, *Novyi zhurnal*, No. 134 (1979), 180.

October 3, 1934. Grin, *Ustami*, 12.

October 6, 1934. A. Kaun, "Bunin: Grammar of Love," *Literary World* (October 6, 1934), 7.

October 11, 1934. G. Blagasova, "I. A. Bunin i M. A. Sholokhov," *Pod'em*, No. 1 (1979), 122.

October 26, 1934. S. Voitsekhovskii, "Pod russkim stiagom," *Novoe russkoe slovo* (March 27, 1973), 3.

October 28, 1934. Grin, "Pis'ma B. K. Zaitseva," 137.

November 1, 1934. V. Zenzinov, "Zapisi. Besedy s I. A. Buninym," *Novyi zhurnal*, No. 81 (1965), 275.

November 3, 1934. Baboreko, "V. N. Muromtseva-Bunina," 116.

November 5, 1934. A. Baboreko, "Pis'ma I. A. Bunina N. D. Teleshovu," 156.

November 9, 1934. Grin, *Ustami*, 12.

[1935]

1935–1939. T. Loginova-Muravieva, "Zhivoe proshloe. Vospominaniia ob I. A. i V. N. Buninykh," in V. Shcherbina et al., eds., *Literaturnoe nasledstvo. Kniga vtoraia* (Moscow, 1973), 301–302, 305–308.

Circa 1935. R. Davies and E. Haber, "Perepiska Teffi s I. A. i V. N. Buninymi, 1920–1939," *Diaspora I. Novye materialy* (Paris, 2001), 198.

1935. N. Roshchin, "Vospominaniia o Bunine i Kuprine," *Voprosy literatury*, No. 6 (1981), 160.

1935. E. Peshkova, "Ivan Alexeevich Bunin," in Shcherbina et al., 249.

January 5, 1935. Grin, "Pis'ma M. A. Aldanova," vol. 81, 115–116.

January 20, 1935. *Ibid.*, 116.

February 3, 1935. A. Nazaroff, "Masterly Stories by Ivan Bunin," *New York Times Book Review* (February 3, 1935), 2.

February 5, 1935. Baboreko, "V. N. Muromtseva-Bunina," 116.

February 14, 1935. Grin, 116.

May 16, 1935. *Arkhiv A. M. Gor'kogo. M. Gor'kii i sovetskaia pechat'*, vol. 10, bk. 2 (Moscow, 1965), 416.

June 2, 1935. M. Tsvetaeva, *Neizdannye pis'ma* (Paris, 1972), 492–493.

June 15, 1935. L. Kotliar, "Zhizn' i tvorchestvo I. Bunina posle velikoi oktiabr'skoi revoliutsii," *Uchenye zapiski Kabordino-Balkarskogo nauchno-issledovatel'skogo instituta*, No. 32 (1966), 204.

June 22, 1935. Grin, "Pis'ma M. A. Aldanova," vol. 80, 285–286.

June 26, 1935. A. Zweers, "Pis'ma I. A. Bunina k N. A. Teffi," *Novyi zhurnal*, No. 117 (1974), 147.

July 3, 1935. Grin, "Pis'ma B. K. Zaitseva," 138–139.

July 6, 1935. Grin, *Ustami*, 15.

July 7, 1935. Grin, "Pis'ma M. A. Aldanova," 286.

July 25, 1935. Grin, *Ustami*, 15.

August 15, 1935. Grin, "Iz dnevnikov I. A. Bunina," 136.

September 1, 1935. Grin, "Pis'ma B. K. Zaitseva," 140–142.

September 19, 1935. Baboreko, "Pis'ma I. A. Bunina N. D. Teleshovu," 156.

December 28, 1935. M. Tsvetaeva, *Pis'ma k A. Teskovoi* (Prague, 1959), 131.

[1936]

1936. As quoted in Kotkov, 227.

February 2, 1936. C. Boyd, *Vladimir Nabokov: The Russian Years* (Princeton, 1990), 423.

March 30, 1936. Grin, 142.

April 16, 1936. Zweers, "Pis'ma I. A. Bunina k B. K. i V.A B. Zaitsevym," 182.

April 23, 1936. Grin, "Iz dnevnikov I. A. Bunina," 136.

April 26, 1936. *Ibid.*, 136–137.

April 26, 1936. Grin, *Ustami*, 17.

May 8, 1936. Grin, "Iz dnevnikov I. A. Bunina," 137.

May 9, 1936. Grin, *Ustami*, 18.

May 10, 1936. Grin, "Iz dnevnikov I. A. Bunina," 137.

May 15, 1936. M. Shrayer, "Bunin i Nabokov: Poetika sopernichestva," *I. A. Bunin i russkaia literatura XX veka* (Moscow, 1995), 50–51.

May 16, 1936. Meshcherskii, 155.

Late May 1936. T. Loginova-Muravieva, *Pis'ma Buninykh khudozhnitse T. Loginovoi-Murav'evoi (1936–1961)* (Paris, 1982), 19.

May 28, 1936. Grin, *Ustami*, 19.

June 6, 1936. I. Bunin, "Bosonozhka," *Illiustrirovannaia Rossia* (June 6, 1936), 2.

June 7, 1936. Grin, 19–20.

June 14, 1936. *Ibid.*

July 1936. Shakovskaya, "Otrazheniia," 93; Shrayer, 52.

August 16, 1936. Grin, 20.

September 17, 1936. Grin, 21.

September 21, 1936. *Ibid.*

October 26, 1936. Tsvetaeva, *Neizdannye pis'ma*, 505.

November 1, 1936. I. Bunin, "Pis'mo v redaktsiiu. Zlokliucheniia I. A. Bunina v Germanii. Pis'mo v redaktsiiu," *Poslednie novosti* (November 1, 1936), 1–2; Grin, 21–22.

November 5, 1936. Kotkov, 230.

November 8, 1936. A. Kriukova, ed., *A. N. Tolstoi. Materialy i issledovaniia* (Moscow, 1985), 190; Iu. Krestinskii, "Pis'mo A. N. Tolstogo o Bunine," in Shcherbina, 392.

November 27, 1936. I. Bunin, "Pis'mo" *Poslenie novosti* (November 27, 1936), 2.

December 1, 1936. Grin, "Iz dnevnikov I. A. Bunina," 138.

[1937]

January 1, 1937. Grin, *Ustami,* 22.

January 23, 1937. *Ibid.*, 23.

January 30, 1937. *Ibid.*

February 1, 1937. *Ibid.*

February 4, 1937. *Ibid.*

February 6, 1937. I. Bunin, "Pushkinskie torzhestva," *Illiustrirovannaia Rossiia* (February 6, 1937), 34.

February 11, 1937. Tsvetaeva, 508.

March 31, 1937. Grin, 24.

July 24, 1937. M. Roshchin, *Ivan Bunin* (Moscow, 2000), 304.

Late August 1937. Lavrov, 242.

August 31, 1937. A. Baboreko, *I. A. Bunin. Materialy dlia biografii* (Moscow, 1983), 288.

August 31, 1937. A. Afinogenov, *Dnevniki i zapisnye knizhki* (Moscow, 1960), 405–406.

November 28, 1937. *Ibid.*, 459–460.

December 7, 1937. Shrayer, 53.

[1938]

1938. Loginova-Muravieva, "Zhivoe proshloe," 309.

1938. E. Malozemoff, *Ivan Bunin, as a Writer of Prose*, Unpublished Ph.D. dissertation (University of California, Berkeley, 1938), 271.

Circa April 25, 1938. Lavrov, 241–242.

April 30, 1938. Grin, "Iz dnevnikov I. A. Bunina," 138.

May 9, 1938. V. Shmidt, "Vstrechi v Tartu," in Shcherbina, 337.

Circa May 9, 1938. Shumakov, *Poslednee svidanie*, 202.

July 5, 1938. A. Baboreko, "Pis'ma k M. V. Karamzinoi, 1937–1940," in Shcherbina, *Kniga pervaia*, 669.

July 28, 1938. Zweers, 185.

August 25, 1938. Grin, *Ustami*, 25–26.

September 17, 1938. Baboreko, 673.

September 27, 1938. Grin, "Pis'ma B. K. Zaitseva," 145–146.

October 18, 1938. *Ibid.*, 146.

November 12, 1938. *Ibid.*, 147–148.

[1939]

Before 1939. Shakovskaia, "O Bunine," 72–73; "Otrazheniia," 93.

Before 1939. S. Pregel', "Iz vospominanii o Bunine," in Shcherbina, *Kniga vtoraia*, 353, 355.

Circa 1939. N. Berberova, *Kursiv moi*, vol. 1 (New York, 1983), 297–298.

1939. B. Mikhailovskii, *Russkaia literatura XX veka. S devianostykh godov XIX veka do 1917 g.* (Moscow, 1939), 58–64.

January 1, 1939. Grin, *Ustami*, 27.
January 14, 1939. *Ibid.*
March 5, 1939. *Ibid.*, 28.
March 9, 1939. *Ibid.*, 28–29.
March 15, 1939. *Ibid.*, 29.
March 29, 1939. Baboreko, 680.
June 17, 1939. Grin, "Pis'ma M. A. Aldanova," 286–287.
June 20, 1939. M. Grin, "Pis'ma B. K. Zaitseva k I. A. i V. N. Buninym," *Novyi zhurnal*, No. 150 (1983), 202–203.
July 30, 1939. Grin, "Pis'ma B. K. Zaitseva," 205.
August 2, 1939. Grin, *Ustami*, 30–31.
August 10, 1939. *Ibid.*, 31.
August 17, 1939. *Ibid.*
August 28, 1939. Baboreko, 684.
August 31, 1939. *Ibid.*, 32.
September 3, 1939. V. Antonov, "I. A. Bunin vo Frantsii v gody voiny," *Inostrannaia literatura*, No. 9 (1956), 250.
September 3, 1939. Grin, 32.
September 4, 1939. *Ibid.*
September 6, 1939. *Ibid.*
September 7, 1939. *Ibid.*, 32–33.
September 8, 1939. *Ibid.*, 33.
September 12, 1939. *Ibid.*
September 18, 1939. *Ibid.*, 34.
September 22, 1939. *Ibid.*
September 26, 1939. *Ibid.*, 34–35.
October 1939 and later. Loginova-Muravieva, 309–313.
October 2, 1939. Grin, "Pis'ma B. K. Zaitseva," 205–206.
October 17, 1939. Grin, *Ustami*, 35.
October 20, 1939. A. Zweers, "Pis'ma I. A. Bunina k B. K. Zaitsevu," *Novyi zhurual*, No. 136 (1979), 130.
October 20, 1939. Grin, 35.
November 2, 1939. Zweers, 130.
November 2, 1939. Grin, "Pis'ma B. K. Zaitseva," 206–208.
November 10, 1939. *Ibid.*, 209.
November 11, 1939. *Ibid.*, 210.
November 16, 1939. Grin, *Ustami*, 35.
November 21, 1939. Kotov, 230–231.
December 1939. N. Berberova, *Kursiv moi*, vol. 2 (New York, 1983), 452–455.
December 3, 1939. Grin, 35.
December 9, 1939. Grin, "Pis'ma B. K. Zaitseva," 211.

December 29, 1939. *Ibid.*, 212.
After 1939. Pregel', 353, 356.

[1940]

Circa 1940. A. Bakhrakh, *Bunin v khalate. Po pamiati, po zapisiam* (Bayville, N.J., 1979), 26–27.
1940. Loginova-Muravieva, 314–315.
January 5, 1940. Grin, *Ustami*, 37.
January 21, 1940. T. Loginova-Muravieva, *Pis'ma Buninykh Khudozhnitse T. Loginovoi-Murav'evoi (1936–1961)* (Paris, 1982), 27.
February 27, 1940. Grin, "Pis'ma B. K. Zaitseva," 215.
April 3, 1940. Grin, "Iz dnevnikov I. A. Bunina," 141.
April 4, 1940. Grin, *Ustami*, 41.
April 4, 1940. Baboreko, 686–687.
April 16, 1940. Grin, "Pis'ma B. K. Zaitseva," 217.
April 17, 1940. Grin, *Ustami*, 44.
April 21, 1940. Grin, "Iz dnevnikov I. A. Bunina," 143–144.
April 27, 1940. Grin, "Pis'ma M. A. Aldanova," vol. 81, 116.
May 7, 1940. Grin, "Iz dnevnikov I. A. Bunina," 146.
May 7, 1940. Lavrov, 314.
May 9–10, 1940. Grin, 147–148.
Mid-May 1940. *Ibid.*, 148.
May 19, 1940. Z. Gippius, *Dnevniki*, vol. 2 (Moscow, 1999), 501.
May 22, 1940. Grin, 148.
Late May 1940–1945. G. Adamovich, "Bunin. Vospominaniia," *Novyi zhurnal*, No. 105 (1971), 127–130.
June 1, 1940. Grin, 147.
June 2, 1940. *Ibid.*, 149.
June 4, 1940. Grin, "Pis'ma B. K. Zaitseva," 217–218.
June 8, 1940. Grin, "Iz dnevnikov I. A. Bunina," 149.
June 9, 1940. *Ibid.*
June 10, 1940. M. Grin, "Iz dnevnikov I. A. Bunin," *Novyi zhurnal*, No. 112 (1973), 224; "Iz dnevnikov I. A. Bunina," No. 111, 148–149.
June 10–15, 1940. Grin, "Iz dnevnikov I. A. Bunina," No. 111, 148–149.

June 16, 1940. *Ibid.*, 149.
June 17, 1940. *Ibid.*
July 5, 1940. Zweers, 133.
July 14, 1940. Loginova-Muravieva, 29.
July 22, 1940. Grin, "Pis'ma B. K. Zaitseva," 218–219.
July 23, 1940. Grin, "Iz dnevnikov I. A. Bunina," 148.
July 30, 1940. "Iz dnevnikov I. A. Bunina," No. 112, 209.
August 9, 1940. Grin, *Ustami*, 57.
August 10, 1940. Grin, "Iz dnevnikov I. A. Bunina," 209–210.
August 11, 1940. Loginova-Muravieva, 31, 32.
August 17, 1940. Grin, 210–211.
August 19, 1920. *Ibid.*, 211.
August 20, 1940. *Ibid.*, 212.
August 21, 1940. *Ibid*, 212–213.
August 22, 1940. *Ibid.*, 213.
August 23, 1940. Grin, "Pis'ma M. Aldanova," 116.
August 24, 1940. Grin, "Iz dnevnikov I. A. Bunina," 214.
August 25, 1940. *Ibid.*, 214–215.
August 29, 1940. *Ibid.*, 215–216.
September 5, 1940. N. Vinokur, "Novoe o Buninykh," *Minuvshee. Istoricheskii al'manakh* (Moscow, 1992), 289.
September 6, 1940. Grin, 217–218.
September 7, 1940. *Ibid.*, 218–219.
September 13, 1940. *Ibid.*
September 13, 1940. Grin, "Pis'ma M. A. Aldanova," 117.
September 25, 1940. Vinokur, 292.
Circa October 1940. Bakhrakh, 15–20.
October 14, 1940. Grin, "Iz dnevnikov I. A. Bunina," 220–221.
October 17, 1940. Grin, Ustami, 70–71.
October 18, 1940. Grin, "Iz dnevnikov I. A. Bunina," 221.
October 23, 1940. Grin, 221–222.
October 23, 1940. Grin, *Ustami*, 72.
October 23, 1940. A. Baboreko, "Bunin v nachale voiny, 1939–1941," *Individual'nost' pisatelia i literaturno-obschchestvennyi protsess* (Voronezh, 1978), 116.
October 30, 1940. Grin, "Iz dnevnikov I. A. Bunina," 222.
November 14, 1940. *Ibid.*
December 1, 1940. Lavrov, 266–267.

December 15, 1940. Vinokur, 293–295.
December 25, 1940. Grin, "Iz dnevnikov I. A. Bunina," 226.
December 27, 1940. Grin, "Pis'ma M. Aldanova," 117–118.

[1941]

Circa 1941. Bakhrakh, 58–62.
January 1, 1941. Grin, "Iz dnevnikov i zapisei I. A. Bunina," *Novyi zhurnal*, No. 113 (1973), 131.
January 16, 1941. Lavrov, 265–266.
January 29, 1941. Vinokur, 298.
January 29, 1941. Loginova-Muravieva, 33–37.
January 30, 1941. Grin, 133, 134.
February 1, 1941. *Ibid.*, 134.
February 3, 1941. *Ibid.*, 134–135.
February 12, 1941. Grin, *Ustami*, 83.
February 23, 1941. Grin, "Iz dnevnikov i zapisei I. A. Bunina," 136.
March 6, 1941. *Ibid.*, 137–138.
March 8, 1941. *Ibid.*
March 8, 1941. A. Zweers, "Perepiska I. A. Bunina s M. A. Aldanovym," *Novyi zhurnal*, No. 150 (1983), 160.
March 8, 1941. *Ibid.*, 160–161.
March 9, 1941. Grin, 138–139.
March 12, 1941. *Ibid.*, 139–140.
March 20, 1941. Zweers, 161.
March 21, 1941. Grin, "Pis'ma M. A. Aldanova," 118.
March 25, 1941. Grin, *Ustami*, 90.
April 6, 1941. V. Sukhomlin, "Vstrechi s Buninym," *Otchizna* (1966), 14.
April 11, 1941. Grin, "Iz dnevnikov i zapisei I. A. Bunina," 141.
April 11, 1941. R. Fedoulova, "Lettres d'Ivan Bunin à Mark Aldanov I (1941–1947)," *Cahiers du monde russe et soviétique*, No. 4 (1981), 473.
April 12, 1941. Grin, 141–142.
April 13, 1941. Sukhomlin, 14.
April 15, 1941. Zweers, 161–162.
April 16, 1941. *Ibid.*, 162.
April 19, 1941. Vinokur, 298–299.
April 20, 1941. Grin, "Iz dnevnikov i zapisei I. A. Bunina," 142.
April 27, 1941. *Ibid.*
April 27, 1941. Vinokur, 299–300.

May 2, 1941. Grin, 142–143.

May 2, 1941. Kriukova, 191.

May 6, 1941. A. Baboreko, "I. A. Bunin o L. N. Tolstom," *Problemy realizma*, vol. 6 (Vologda, 1979), 175.

May 8, 1941. Bakhrakh, 152.

May 16, 1941. Grin, 143.

May 16, 1941. Grin, *Ustami*, 94.

May 17, 1941. Grin, "Iz dnevnikov i zapisei I. A. Bunina," 144.

May 25, 1941. *Ibid.*

June 15, 1941. Baboreko, "Bunin v nachale voiny," 120.

June 16, 1941. Grin, 145.

June 18, 1941. Kriukova, 191; Lavrov, 271.

June 21, 1941. Grin, 145–146.

June 22, 1941. *Ibid.*, 146.

June 23, 1941. M. Grin, "Iz dnevnikov i zapisei I. A. Bunina," *Novyi zhurnal*, No. 114 (1974), 126.

June 24, 1941. *Ibid.*

June 25, 1941. Grin, *Ustami*, 98.

June 27, 1941. *Ibid.*

June 30, 1941. Grin, "Iz dnevnikov i zapisei I. A. Bunina," 127.

June 30, 1941. Baboreko, "Bunin v nachale voiny," 122–123; *I. A. Bunin*, 297–298.

June 30, 1941. Grin, 128.

Circa July 1941. V. Lavrov, "Tragediia russkogo intelligenta, ili neizvestnye pis'ma I. A. Bunina," *Russkii arkhiv*, No. 3 (1993), 126.

July 1, 1941. Grin, 128.

July 2, 1941. *Ibid.*, 129.

July 3, 1941. *Ibid.*

July 4, 1941. Baboreko, *I. A. Bunin*, 299.

July 6, 1941. Grin, 130–131.

July 9, 1941. Grin, *Ustami*, 103.

July 10, 1941. *Ibid.*, 104.

July 13, 1941. Grin, "Iz dnevnikov i zapisei I. A. Bunina," 131.

July 14, 1941. Grin, 131–132.

July 17, 1941. *Ibid.*, 132.

July 24, 1941. *Ibid.*

August 2, 1941. *Ibid.*

August 2, 1941. Zweers, 166.

August 3, 1941. Grin, 132–133.

August 6, 1941. *Ibid.*, 133.

August 7, 1941. *Ibid.*

August 11, 1941. Grin, *Ustami*, 106.

August 12, 1941. Grin, "Iz dnevnikov i zapisei I. A. Bunina," 133–134.

August 17, 1941. *Ibid.*, 135.

August 22, 1941. *Ibid.*, 134–135.

August 24, 1941. *Ibid.*, 135.

August 24, 1941. Berberova, 436–437.

August 28, 1941. Grin, 135.

August 28, 1941. A. Gide, *The Journals*, vol. 4 (New York, 1951), 83.

August 29, 1941. Grin, 135.

August 30, 1941. *Ibid.*, 135.

August 30, 1941. Grin, *Ustami*, 109–110.

Early September 1941. Loginova-Muravieva, "Zhivoe proshloe," 315–316.

September 5, 1941. Grin, 136.

September 7, 1941. *Ibid.*

September 14, 1941. *Ibid.*, 136–137.

September 16, 1941. Baboreko, "I. A. Bunin o L. N. Tolstom," 178.

September 19, 1941. Grin, 137.

September 22, 1941. *Ibid.*

September 23, 1941. Berberova, 437–438.

September 28, 1941. Grin, *Ustami*, 113.

October 9, 1941. Grin, "Iz dnevnikov i zapisei I. A. Bunina," 139.

October 17, 1941. *Ibid.*

October 17, 1941. *Ibid.*, 139–140.

October 18, 1941. *Ibid.*, 140.

October 19, 1941. Loginova-Muravieva, "Pis'ma," 43–44.

October 23, 1941. Grin, 140.

October 23, 1941. *Ibid.*, 140–141.

October 24, 1941. *Ibid.*, 140.

October 29, 1941. *Ibid.*, 141.

Late Fall 1941. Bakhrakh, 5.

November 1941. Bakhrakh, 111.

November 11, 1941. M. Grin, "Iz dnevnikov I. A. Bunina," *Novyi zhurnal*, No. 115 (1971), 140.

November 23, 1941. Loginova-Muravieva, 45–46.

November 25, 1941. Grin, 141.

December 5, 1941. *Ibid.*, 142.

December 7, 1941. *Ibid.*

December 8, 1941. *Ibid.*

December 10, 1941. *Ibid.*

December 13, 1941. *Ibid.*, 142–143.

December 14, 1941. *Ibid.*, 143.

December 23, 1941. *Ibid.*

December 24, 1941. *Ibid.*, 144.

December 28, 1941. *Ibid.*

December 30, 1941. *Ibid.*

December 31, 1941. *Ibid.*, 144–145.

[1942]

Circa 1942. A. Bakhrakh, "Bunin i 'Okhota na Kavkaze'," *Po pamiati, po zapisiam. Literaturnye portrety* (Paris, 1980), 16–17. Also see *Bunin v khalate*, 29–31, 35, 39, 57–58, 60–61, 65, 67–69, 85, 96–97, 113, 115, 153; "Po pamiati, po zapiskam (II) . . .," 282–283, 286, 288.

January 1, 1942. Grin, 145.

January 1, 1942. *Ibid.*

January 22, 1942. Loginova-Muravieva, 48–49.

February 19, 1942. Grin, "Iz dnevnikov I. A. Bunina," 147.

February 26, 1942. *Ibid.*

February 28, 1942. Grin, *Ustami,* 128.

Spring 1942. H. Iswolsky, "Twenty-five Years of Russian Emigré Literature," *Russian Review*, vol. 1 (No. 2, 1942), 63–66.

March 31, 1942. Grin, "Iz dnevnikov I. A. Bunina," 149.

April 4, 1942. *Ibid.*

April 12, 1942. *Ibid.*, 150–151.

April 26, 1942. A. Sedykh, "Zavtrak s Buninym," *Novoe russkoe slovo* (April 26, 1942), 8.

May 1942. P. Viacheslavov, "Literaturnoe zaveshchanie I. A. Bunina," *Moskva*, No. 4 (1962), 222.

May 2, 1942. Grin, *Ustami*, 135.

May 6, 1942. Grin, "Iz dnevnikov I. A. Bunina," 152.

May 23, 1942. *Ibid.*, 153.

May 26, 1942. *Ibid.*

May 26, 1942. Grin, "Pis'ma M. A. Aldanova," 119.

June 1942. Loginova-Muravieva, "Zhivoe proshloe," 319.

June 3, 1942. Grin, "Iz dnevnikov I. A. Bunina," 153–154.

July 1, 1942. *Ibid.*, 154.

July 14, 1942. *Ibid.*

July 18, 1942. *Ibid.*

July 19, 1942. *Ibid.*, 154–155.

July 28, 1942. Zweers, 168.

Mid-August 1942. A. Baboreko, "Poslednie gody I. A. Bunina (Novye materialy)," *Voprosy literatury*, No. 3 (1965), 253–254.

August 23, 1942. Grin, *Ustami*, 139.

September 3, 1942. M. Grin, "Iz dnevnikov I. A. Bunina," *Novyi zhurnal*, No. 116 (1974), 162.

September 16, 1942. *Ibid.*, 162–163.

September 18, 1942. *Ibid.*, 163.

September 22, 1942. *Ibid.*, 164.

September 23, 1942. *Ibid.*

September 24, 1942. *Ibid.*, 165.

October 1, 1942. *Ibid.*

October 14, 1942. *Ibid.*

October 23, 1942. *Ibid.*

October 27, 1942. *Ibid.*

November 12, 1942. Grin, 166; Baboreko, *I. A. Bunin*, 304.

Mid-November 1942 and after. T. Geller, "Istoriia dvukh pisem I. A. Bunina k G. T. Shemetillo (1944)," *Russkaia literatura*, No. 4 (1990), 225.

November 25, 1942. Grin, 166.

December 25, 1942. *Ibid.*, 166–167.

December 27, 1942. *Ibid.*, 167.

December 31, 1942. *Ibid.*

[1943]

Circa 1943. A. Bakhrakh, "Iz razgovorov c Buninym," *Neva*, No. 8 (1993), 301; "Po pamiati, po zapisiam. Razgovory s Buninym," *Novyi zhurnal*, No. 131 (1978), 119; *Bunin v khalate*, 73–79, 81–86, 88–94, 97–111, 147.

1943. B. Guerney, *A Treasury of Russian Literature* (Philadelphia, 1943), 904–905.

1943. O. Mikhailov, "Prolog," *Literatura russkogo zarubezh'ia* (Moscow, 1993), 80.

1943. N. Teleshov, *Zapiski pisatelia* (Moscow, 1943), 89–90.

January 1, 1943. Grin, "Iz dnevnikov I. A. Bunina," 167.

January 3, 1943. Grin, *Ustami*, 146.

January 27, 1943. Loginova-Muravieva, "Pis'ma," 59–60.

February 1, 1943. Grin, "Iz dnevnikov I. A. Bunina," 167–168.

February 2, 1943. *Ibid.*, 168.

February 8, 1943. *Ibid.*

February 17, 1943. *Ibid.*

February 24, 1943. *Ibid.*

Circa March 1943. N. Roshchin, "Moi Bunin," *Voprosy literatury*, No. 6 (1981), 175.

March 12, 1943. *Ibid.*, 175–176.

March 16, 1943. Loginova-Muravieva, "Zhivoe proshloe," 320.

March 28, 1943. Grin, 168.

March 29, 1943. Grin, *Ustami*, 147.

April 2, 1943. Grin, "Iz dnevnikov I. A. Bunina," 168.

April 10, 1943. *Ibid.*

April 11, 1943. *Ibid.*

April 14, 1943. *Ibid.*

April 14, 1943. Berberova, vol. 1, 301.

Circa April 18, 1943. Grin, "Pis'ma B. K. Zaitseva," 220–221.

April 25, 1943. Zweers, "Pis'ma I. Bunina k N. A. Teffi," 148.

May 2, 1943. Grin, *Ustami*, 149.

May 2, 1943. Loginova-Muravieva, 320.

May 4, 1943. Grin, *Ustami*, 149.

May 7, 1943. *Ibid.*, 150.

May 10, 1943. A. Baboreko, "Zlatoe drevo zhizni," *Al'manakh bibliofila*, No. 12 (1982), 67.

May 17, 1943. A. Baboreko, "Pis'ma I. A. Bunina," *Literaturnyi Smolensk. Al'manakh*, No. 15 (Smolensk, 1956), 324–325.

May 23, 1943. P. Struve, "Perepiska I. A. Bunina i P. B. Struve (1920–1943), *Zapiski russkoi akademicheskoi gruppy v SSHA*, vol. 2 (New York, 1968), 104.

May 26, 1943. Grin, "Iz dnevnikov I. A. Bunina," 168.

June 1943. B. Zaitsev, "Povest' o Vere," *Russkaia mysl'* (January 21, 1967), 3.

July 17, 1943. Grin, *Ustami*, 151.

July 25, 1943. Grin, "Iz dnevnikov I. A. Bunina," 170.

August 2, 1943. Zweers, "Pis'ma I. A. Bunina k B. K. Zaitsevu," 137.

August 4, 1943. Grin, 171.

August 9, 1943. Zweers, "Pis'ma I. Bunina k N. A. Teffi," 148–149.

August 22, 1943. Grin, 171.

August 22, 1943. *Ibid.*

August 27, 1943. M. Grin, "Pis'ma B. K. Zaitseva I. I V. Buninym," *Novyi zhurnal*, No. 146 (1982), 115–116.

September 2, 1943. Grin, *Ustami*, 154.

September 3, 1943. Grin, "Iz dnevnikov I. A. Bunina," 171.

September 7, 1943. *Ibid.*, 171–172.

September 8, 1943. *Ibid.*, 172.

September 8, 1943. Grin, *Ustami*, 154.

September 9, 1943. Grin, "Iz dnevnikov I. A. Bunina," 172.

September 12, 1943. Zweers, "Pis'ma I. A. Bunina k B. K. Zaitsevu," 138.

September 17, 1943. Grin, *Ustami*, 155–156.

September 24, 1943. *Ibid.*, 155.

September 25, 1943. Grin, "Iz dnevnikov I. A. Bunina," 172.

September 25, 1943. Grin, "Pis'ma B. K. Zaitseva," 117–118.

October 8, 1943. Zweers, 137.

October 23, 1943. Grin, "Iz dnevnikov I. A. Bunina," 172.

October 29, 1943. *Ibid.*, 173.

November 1, 1943. *Ibid.*

November 6, 1943. *Ibid.*

November 6, 1943. Grin, *Ustami*, 158.

November 8, 1943. Zweers, 139.

November 9, 1943. A. Zweers, "Pis'ma I. A. Bunina k B. K. Zaitsevu," *Novyi zhurnal*, No. 137 (1979), 124.

November 10, 1943. Grin, "Pis'ma B. K. Zaitseva," 119–121.

November 11, 1943. Grin, "Iz dnevnikov I. A. Bunina," 173.

November 11, 1943. Zweers, 125.

November 15, 1943. *Ibid.*, 126.

November 19, 1943. Zweers, 126–127.

November 21, 1943. Grin, "Pis'ma B. K. Zaitseva," 127.

November 28, 1943. Grin, 122–123.

Late November 1943. Bakhrakh, "Po pamiati, po zapiskam (II) . . . ," *Mosty*, 283.

Circa December 1943 and after. Antonov, 251–252. Also see Baboreko, "Pis'ma I. A. Bunina N. D. Teleshovu," 157; "Poslednie gody I. A. Bunina," 253.

Circa December 1943 and after. Geller, 225–226.

December 3, 1943. Zweers, 127–129.

December 3, 1943. Grin, 124–125.

December 10, 1943. Grin, "Iz dnevnikov I. A. Bunina," 173.

December 18, 1943. *Ibid.*

December 30, 1943. Grin, "Pis'ma B. K. Zaitseva," 126.

[1944]

Circa 1944. Baboreko, "I. A. Bunin o L. N. Tolstom," 176.

January 1, 1944. Grin, "Iz dnevnikov I. A. Bunina," 174.

January 2, 1944. *Ibid.*

January 3, 1944. Grin, *Ustami*, 159–160.

January 6, 1944. *Ibid.*, 160.

January 7, 1944. Grin, "Iz dnevnikov I. A. Bunina," 174.

January 8, 1944. *Ibid.*

January 17, 1944. *Ibid.*, 175.

January 18, 1944. Zweers, 130.

January 19, 1944. Grin, 175.

January 20, 1944. *Ibid.*

January 22, 1944. Grin, "Pis'ma B. K. Zaitseva," 127.

January 31, 1944. Grin, *Ustami*, 162.

Circa early February 1944. Zweers, 131.

February 2, 1944. A. Baboreko, "Bunin v gody voiny (1943–1944)," *Daugava*, No. 10 (1980), 122.

February 8, 1944. Grin, "Iz dnevnikov I. A. Bunina," 175.

February 12, 1944. Grin, "Pis'ma B. K. Zaitseva," 127.

February 15, 1944. Grin, "Iz dnevnikov I. A. Bunina," 176.

February 19, 1944. Grin, 163.

February 23, 1944. Baboreko, "Neizvestnye pis'ma Bunina," 135.

February 25, 1944. Grin, "Pis'ma B. K. Zaitseva," 130.

March 1, 1944. Geller, 224.

March 4, 1944. Grin, *Ustami*, 164.

March 6, 1944. Zweers, 133.

March 9, 1944. Grin, "Pis'ma B. K. Zaitseva," 131.

March 12, 1944. Loginova-Muravieva, "Pis'ma," 65.

March 27, 1944. Grin, 131.

March 30, 1944. Zweers, 134.

April 27, 1944. Loginova-Muravieva, 67.

May 2, 1944. *Ibid.*, 69–70.

May 4, 1944. Grin, 133.

May 8, 1944. Grin, "Iz dnevnikov I. A. Bunina," 176.

May 10, 1944. Berberova, 302.

May 19, 1944. Zweers, "Pis'ma I. Bunina k N. A. Teffi," 151–152.

May 20, 1944. Grin, "Pis'ma B. K. Zaitseva," 134–135.

May 21, 1944. *Ibid.*, 135.

May 25, 1944. Zweers, "Pis'ma I. A. Bunina k B. K. Zaitsevu," 136–137.

May 30, 1944. Loginova-Muravieva, 76.

June 8, 1944. *Ibid.*, 77.

June 19, 1944. Grin, 135–137.

June 21, 1944. Grin, "Iz dnevnikov I. A. Bunina," 176–177.

June 22, 1944. *Ibid.*, 177.

June 27, 1944. Grin, *Ustami*, 166.

June 28, 1944. Grin, "Iz dnevnikov I. A. Bunina," 177.

July 1, 1944. *Ibid.*

July 11, 1944. Zweers, 138–139.

July 14, 1944. *Ibid.*, 139.

July 15, 1944. Grin, "Pis'ma B. K. Zaitseva," 137–138.

July 22, 1944. Grin, "Iz dnevnikov I. A. Bunina," 178.

July 23, 1944. *Ibid.*

July 25, 1944. Loginova-Muravieva, 78–79.

July 25, 1944. Grin, "Pis'ma B. K. Zaitseva," 138–139.

Early August 1944. Zaitsev, 4–5.

August 1, 1944. Grin, "Iz dnevnikov I. A. Bunina," 178.

August 3, 1944. *Ibid.*

August 5, 1944. Zweers, 140.

August 12, 1944. Grin, "Iz dnevnikov I. A. Bunina," 178.

August 15, 1944. *Ibid.*, 179.

August 15, 1944. Bakhrakh, 155.

August 18, 1944. Grin, 179.

August 24, 1944. Baboreko, *I. A. Bunin. Materialy*, 306.

August 24, 1944. Grin, *Ustami*, 169–170.

August 24, 1944. Bakhrakh, 155.

August 25, 1944. Grin, "Iz dnevnikov I. A. Bunina," 179.

August 27, 1944. Grin, *Ustami*, 170.

August 29, 1944. *Ibid.*, 170–171.
August 31, 1944. Grin, "Iz dnevnikov I. A. Bunina," 180.
September 9, 1944. Grin, *Ustami*, 172.
September 21, 1944. Zweers, 140–141.
September 23, 1944. Grin, 172.
October 13, 1944. *Ibid.*, 173.
October 22, 1944. Grin, "Iz dnevnikov I. A. Bunina," 180.
October 26, 1944. A. Zweers, "Pis'ma I. A. Bunina k B. Zaitsevu," *Novyi zhurnal*, No. 138 (1980), 155–156.
October 28, 1944. Grin, "Pis'ma B. K. Zaisteva," 139–140.
October 29, 1944. Grin, *Ustami*, 173.
November 4, 1944. Zweers, 156–157.
November 8, 1944. M. Grin, "Pis'ma B. K. Zeitseva k I. A. i V. N. Buninym," *Novyi zhurnal*, No. 140 (1980), 157–158.
November 11, 1944. Roshchin, 160, 162.
November 17, 1944. Grin, 158–159.
November 23, 1944. Zweers, 160.
November 27, 1944. Grin, 159–160.
December 1, 1944. Grin, "Iz dnevnikov I. A. Bunina," 180–181.
December 2, 1944. Zweers, 161–162.
December 8, 1944. Roshchin, 162.
December 18, 1944. *Ibid.*, 163.
December 19, 1944. Fedoulova, 476–477.
December 27, 1944. Bakhrakh, "Po pamiati, po zapiskam (II) . . . ," 292.
December 28, 1944. Grin, "Pis'ma B. K. Zaitseva," 163–164.
December 30, 1944. Zweers, 163.

[1945]

Circa 1945. Baboreko, "Poslednie gody I. A. Bunina," 253–254; *I. A. Bunin*, 307.
1945–1946. T. A. Ladinskaia, "Pis'mo k A. P. Ladinskomu," in Shcherbina, *Kniga pervaia*, 689.
January 1, 1945. Loginova-Muravieva, "Zhivoe proshloe," 322.
January 14, 1945. Grin, "Pis'ma B. K. Zaitseva," 164–166.
January 17, 1945. Zweers, "Perepiska I. A. Bunina," 170.
January 21, 1945. Zweers, "Pis'ma I. A. Bunina k B. K. Zaitsevu," 164.
Early February 1945. Zweers, 164–165.

February 4, 1945. Grin, 166–167.
February 10, 1945. Lavrov, 326–327.
February 12, 1945. Berberova, 296, 297.
February 23, 1945. Grin, "Iz dnevnikov I. A. Bunina," 182.
February 24, 1945. *Ibid.*
February 25, 1945. *Ibid.*
February 26, 1945. *Ibid.*
February 26, 1945. Zweers, 168.
Spring 1945. Struve, "Iz perepsiki," 29–30.
March 2, 1945. Loginova-Muravieva, "Pis'ma," 101.
March 5, 1945. Grin, "Pis'ma B. K. Zaitseva," 169–170.
March 6, 1945. Lavrov, 328–329.
March 9, 1945. *Ibid.*, 330.
March 10, 1945. V. Vishnevskii, "Iz dnevnikov voennykh let (1941–1945)," *Stat'i, dnevniki, pis'ma* (Moscow, 1961), 486.
March 21, 1945. Zweers, "Pis'ma I. A. Bunina k N. A. Teffi," 152.
March 23, 1945. Zweers, "Perepiska I. A. Bunina," 171.
March 27, 1945. Zweers, "Pis'ma I. A. Bunina k B. K. Zaitsevu," 168.
April 7, 1945. Grin, *Ustami*, 177.
April 8, 1945. Grin, "Pis'ma B. K. Zaitseva," 172–173.
April 15, 1945. Grin, "Iz dnevnikov I. A. Bunina," 183.
Early May 1945. Zweers, "Perepiska I. A. Bunina," 171.
May 2, 1945. M. Roshchin, 305–306.
After May 1945. Khmara, 4.
May 28, 1945. Zweers, 172–173.
May 30, 1945. Grin, "Pis'ma M. A. Aldanova," 120–122, 136.
Circa June 1945. I. Bunin, *Povesti, rasskazy, vospominaniia* (Moscow, 1961), 623–624; N. Roshchin, "Pis'ma," 2; "Moi Bunin," 174.
June 12, 1945. Fedoulova, 479–480.
June 29, 1945. Zweers, 173.
July 5, 1945. Loginova-Muravieva, 105.
July 25, 1945. Vinokur, 303.
July 31, 1945. *Ibid.*
August 8, 1945. Berberova, vol. 2, 515.
August 14–15, 1945. Grin, *Ustami*, 178.
August 16, 1945. Zweers, 174–175.
August 17, 1945. *Ibid.*, 174, 176.

August 27, 1945. Grin, "Pis'ma M. Aldanova," 122, 134.

September 4, 1945. Zweers, 180–181.

September 8, 1945. Khmara, 4.

September 9, 1945. Grin, *Ustami*, 178–180.

October 1, 1945. Zweers, 181.

October 11, 1945. *Ibid.*, 182–183.

October 11, 1945. A. Dubovikov, "Perepiska s N. D. Teleshovym, 1897–1947," in Shcherbina, 624; L. Zurov, "Pis'ma N. D. Teleshova k I. A. Buninu," *Novyi zhurnal*, vol. 85 (1966), 132.

October 13–November 1, 1945. Vinokur, 305–307.

October 24, 1945. Zweers, 185.

October 24, 1945. *Ibid.*, 184.

October 25, 1945. Grin, 180.

October 31, 1945. Roshchin, 308.

November 5, 1945. Zweers, 186.

November 9, 1945. A. Bakhrakh, "Chetyre goda s Buninym," *Russkie novosti* (November 9, 1945), 5.

November 9, 1945. "I. A. Bunin. K ego 75-letiiu," *Russkie novosti* (November 9, 1945), 1.

November 9, 1945. B. Brodskii, "U I. A. Bunina," *Russkie novosti* (November 9, 1945), 5.

November 11, 1945. Dubovikov, 625; Zurov, 132.

November 14, 1945. Zweers, 186–187.

Mid-November 1945. Baboreko, "Pis'ma I. A. Bunina N. D. Teleshovu," 160–161; Zurov, 132–134.

November 23, 1945. Roshchin, 309.

November 28, 1945. *Ibid.*, 309.

Mid-December 1945. *Ibid.*, 309–310.

December 26, 1945. Zweers, 189–190.

December 26, 1945. Grin, "Pis'ma M. Aldanova," 137.

[1946]

Circa 1946. Pregel', 352–353.

1946. V. Kataev, *Trava zabven'ia* (Moscow, 1969), 325–326.

1946. G. Adamovich, "Bunin," *Russkii sbornik* (Paris, 1946), 5–7.

January 5, 1946. A. Zweers, "Perepiska I. A. Bunina s M. A. Aldanovym," *Novyi zhurnal*, No. 152 (1983), 154–155.

January 23, 1946. Zweers, 155.

January 30, 1946. Baboreko, "Pis'ma I. A. Bunina N. D. Teleshovu," 162–163; and Zurov, 135–137.

February 5, 1946. Roshchin, 310.

February 7, 1946. Grin, "Pis'ma M. Aldanova," 124, 137.

February 8, 1946. Baboreko, "Zlatoe drevo zhizni," 70, 72–73; Vinokur, 309–310.

February 12, 1946. Shrayer, 53.

February 14, 1946. Zweers, 158.

March 26, 1946. Zurov, 138.

March 27, 1946. Grin, 124.

April 1946 and after. Iu. Zhukov, "Na zapade posle voiny," *Ok'tiabr'*, vol. 10 (1947), 128–131.

April 15, 1946. Zweers, 164.

April 22, 1946. *Ibid.*

May 3, 1946. Grin, *Ustami*, 181.

May 6, 1946. Grin, "Pis'ma M. Aldanova," 124–125, 137.

May 10, 1946. Zweers, 165–166.

May 27, 1946. Grin, *Ustami*, 181.

June 13, 1946. Umm-El-Banine Assadoulaeff, "Poslednii poednikok," 8–11, 17–18, 27–31, 42–43.

Summer 1946. Adamovich, "Bunin. Vospominaniia," 131–132; Lavrov, 342.

June 14, 1946. Lavrov, 339.

Circa mid-July 1946. Antonov, 255.

June 24, 1946. Grin, 181.

June 28, 1946. Lavrov, 339.

June 28, 1946. Zweers, 167–168.

June 30, 1946. *Ibid.*, 168.

June 30, 1946. Grin, 182.

July 1, 1946. Zweers, 168–169.

July 1, 1946. Grin, "Pis'ma M. Aldanova," 125.

Early July 1946. Umm-El-Banine Assadoulaeff, 35–36.

July 21, 1946. K. Simonov, "Iz zapisei o Bunine," *Sobranie sochineii v shesti tomakh*, vol. 6 (Moscow, 1970), 740–747; Lavrov, 340, 342–343.

August 11, 1946. Grin, *Ustami*, 182–183.

August 12, 1946. Umm-El-Banine Assadoulaeff, "V Parizhe posle voiny," *Slovo*, No. 10 (1990), 74.

August 15, 1946. Grin, 183.

August 15, 1946. Umm-El-Banine As-sadoulaeff, 74.

August 16, 1946 and after. Umm-El-Banine Assadoulaeff, "Poslednii poedi-nok Ivana Bunina," *Vremia i my*, No. 41 (May 1979), 16–17, 21; "V Parizhe posle voiny," 75.

August 30, 1946. I. Bunin, "Panorama," *Russkie novosti* (August 30, 1946), 4.

September 23, 1946. Grin, 183.

October 1, 1946. Grin, "Iz dnevnikov I. A. Bunina," 183.

November 19, 1946. Baboreko, "Pis'ma I. A. Bunina N. D. Teleshovu," 163–164; Zurov, 138.

November 28, 1946. M. Roshchin, 163–164.

November 30, 1946. A. Meshcherskii, "Neizvestnye pis'ma I. Bunina," *Russkaia literatura*, No. 4 (1961), 153–156.

December 1946. V. Aleksandrova, "I. A. Bunin," *Novyi zhurnal*, vol. 12 (1946), 168–178.

Early December 1946. N. Roshchin, "Pis'ma kanadskim druz'iam," 2; "Moi Bunin," 175–176.

December 2, 1946. Grin, *Ustami*, 184.

December 25, 1946. Dubovikov, 630; Zurov, 135.

December 30, 1946. Grin, 184–185.

[1947]

1947. V. Aleksandrova, "Ivan Bunin. Tem-nye allei," *Novyi zhurnal*, vol. 15 (1947), 295.

1947. M. Slonim, "Literaturnye zametki," *Novosel'e*, Nos. 31–32 (1947), 96.

1947. Geller, 226.

January 1, 1947. Grin, *Ustami*, 185.

January 8, 1947. Baboreko, "Pis'ma I. A. Bunina N. D. Teleshovu," 164.

January 16, 1947. A. Zweers, "Pis'ma I. A. Bunina k G. V. Adamovichu," *Novyi zhurnal*, No. 110 (1973), 161.

February 19, 1947. A. Baboreko, "Zlatoe drevo zhizni," 74–75;Vinokur, 313.

February 23, 1947. Zweers, "Perepiska I. A. Bunina," 171–172.

March 1, 1947. Baboreko, "Pis'ma I. A. Bunina N. D. Teleshovu," 164–165.

July 11, 1947. A. Sedykh, "I. A. Bunin," *Dalekie, blizkie* (New York, 1962), 216.

Mid-July 1947. *Ibid.*

August 9, 1947. Grin, 185.

August 18, 1947. D. Bethea, "1944–1953: Ivan Bunin and the Time of Troubles in Russian Emigré Literature," *Slavic Review*, vol. 43 (Spring 1984), 16; Struve, 215–217.

August 31, 1947. Zweers, 184.

Circa September 1947. Baboreko, "Pis'ma I. A. Bunina N. D. Teleshovu," 158–159.

September 2, 1947. Zweers, 184–186.

September 2, 1947. A. Baboreko, "Perepiska Bunina," *Literaturnaia Rossiia* (September 2, 1977), 22.

September 7, 1947. Dubovikov, 636; Zurov, 138.

September 15, 1947. As quoted in V. Afansas'ev, *I.A. Bunin. Ocherk tvorchestva* (Moscow, 1966), 375; Zweers, 188.

September 15, 1947. A. Baboreko, "Osen-niaia kliukva," *Novyi mir*, No. 1 (1990), 267.

September 25, 1947. Dubovikov, 638; Zurov, 140.

October 9, 1947. Vinokur, 325.

November 8, 1947. Baboreko, "I. A. Bunin o L. N. Tolstom," 165–178; Zweers, "Pis'ma I. A. Bunina, k G. V. Adamovichu," 168.

December 20, 1947. A. Dubovibov, "Vykhod Bunina iz parizhskogo soiuza pisatelei," in Shcherbina, *Kniga vtoraia*, 402.

December 20, 1947. Baboreko, "Zlatoe drevo zhizni," 82.

[1948]

Circa 1948. Berberova, vol. 1, 293–296, 313.

January 1, 1948. Dubovikov, 402–404.

January 1, 1948. *Ibid.*, 405.

January 2, 1948. Grin, *Ustami*, 186.

January 10, 1948. Bakhrakh, "Po pamiati, po zapiskam (II) . . .", 294.

January 10, 1948. Grin, 186–187.

January 12, 1948. A. Baboreko, "Bunin i Teffi. Neizvestnye pis'ma," *Literaturnaia Rossiia* (April 6, 1979), 16.

January 13, 1948. Grin, "Pis'ma B. K. Zaitseva, 174; Lavrov, 356.

January 15, 1948. Zweers, "Pis'ma I. Bunina k B. Zaitsevu," 173.

January 26, 1948. Grin, 175–177.

January 29, 1948. Zweers, 174.

February 2, 1948. Baboreko, 16–17.

February 2, 1948. Zweers, "Perepiska I. A. Bunina," 137.

February 9, 1948. *Ibid.*, 135.

March 12, 1948. Bethea, 14.

March 25, 1948. D. Sannikov, "Vopreki nelepym vymyslam.... Pis'mo I. A. Bunina v redaktsiiiu 'Oktiabria'," *Novyi mir*, vol. 6 (June 1991), 240–241.

March 27, 1948. Grin, *Ustami*, 188.

April 2, 1948. Grin, "Pis'ma M. Aldanova," 128.

June 2, 1948. Zweers, 143.

June 9, 1948. *Ibid.*, 143–144.

July 1, 1948. *Ibid.*, 147–148.

August 6, 1948. Grin, "Pis'ma B. K. Zaitseva," 179.

August 7, 1948. Zweers, 148–149.

October 1948. Bakhrakh, *Bunin v khalate*, 166.

November 5, 1948. Grin, "Pis'ma M. Aldanova," 128.

November 10, 1948. "Malen'kii fel'eton. 'Emy, velikomu,'" *Russkaia mysl'* (November 10, 1948), 4.

November 24, 1948. V. Lazarevskii, "Ne na zlobu dnia. 'Buria negodovaniia,'" *Russkaia mysl'* (November 24, 1948), 2.

Circa December 31, 1948. Roshchin, 167.

[1949]

Early 1949. Roshchin, 165, 176.

January 4, 1949. S. Karlinsky, ed., *The Nabokov-Wilson Letters* (New York, 1979), 220.

March 11, 1949. Baboreko, "Bunin i Teffi," 19.

March 28, 1949. Zweers, "Pis'ma I. A. Bunina k N. A. Teffi," 154–155.

April 1949. Sedykh, 231.

April 1949. W. Jacobs, "Bunin's 'The Gentleman from San Francisco,'" *The Explicator*, No. 6 (1948), item 42.

May 5, 1949. I. Bunin, "Okaiannye dni," *Literaturnoe obozrenie*, No. 6 (1989), 110.

May 8, 1949. Loginova-Muravieva, 120–121.

June 21, 1949. Sedykh, 220.

July 17, 1949. Zweers, 153.

August 3, 1949. *Ibid.*, 155.

September 12, 1949. Loginova-Muravieva, 122.

October 2, 1949. Grin, "Iz dnevnikov I. A. Bunina," 183.

October 24, 1949. S. Ostrovskaia, "Pis'ma I. A. Bunina k Kniazhne Sof'e Petrovne Volkonskoi," *I. A. Bunin i Russkaia Literatura XX veka*, 243–244.

November 12, 1949. Grin, *Ustami*, 194.

November 16–17, 1949. Zweers, 157.

Late 1949. Lavrov, 236.

Late 1949. *Ibid.*

Late 1949. Sedykh, 233.

[1950]

Circa 1950. M. Aldanov, "O Bunine," *Novyi zhurnal*, vol. 35 (1953), 130, 133, 134.

Circa 1950. Bakhrakh, 280.

January 1, 1950. Grin, 194.

January 17, 1950. R. Fedoulova, "Lettres d'Ivan Bunin à Mark Aldanov (1948–1953)," *Cahiers du monde russe et soviétique*, vol. 23, Nos. 3–4 (1982), 475.

Circa February 1950. Fedoulova, 476.

March 20, 1950. Zweers, "Perepiska I. A. Bunina," 163.

March 30, 1950. *Ibid.*, 165.

May 1, 1950. Grin, *Ustami*, 196.

May 31, 1950. *Ibid.*, 197.

June 12, 1950. S. Kryzytski, *The Works of Ivan Bunin* (The Hague, 1971), 271.

July 17, 1950. Grin, "Pis'ma M. A. Aldanova," 142.

September 24, 1950. Lavrov, "Tragediia," 128–129.

October 16, 1950. Zweers, 167.

Circa October 23, 1950. Bakhrakh, *Bunin v khalate*, 159.

October 23, 1950. Lavrov, 129.

October 23, 1950. Baboreko, *I. A. Bunin*, 312.

October 24, 1950. A. Gide, "Pour les 80 ans d'un réfractaire," *Figaro* (October 24, 1950), 4.

October 24, 1950. A. Pierre, "Ivan Bounine à quatre-vingts ans," *Le Monde* (October 24, 1950), 6.

October 26, 1950. Zweers, 167.

October 30, 1950. *Ibid.*, 168.

November 5, 1950. Fedoulova, 477.

December 2, 1950. Trubilova, 203.

December 5–6, 1950. A. Zweers, "Perepiska I. A. Bunina s M. A. Aldanovym," *Novyi zhurnal*, No. 154 (1984), 98.

December 10–11, 1950. *Ibid.*, 99–100.

December 25, 1950. Grin, *Ustami*, 201.

December 30, 1950. Baboreko, "Iz perepiski Bunina s Teffi," 132.

[1951]

1951. Struve, "Perepiska I. A. Bunina," 106–107.

1951. Fedoulova, 488.

January 25, 1951. Zweers, 101.

January 28, 1951. A. Zweers, "Pis'ma I. A. Bunina k F. A. Stepunu," *Novyi zhurnal*, No. 118 (1975), 120.

February 9, 1951. Zweers, "Perepiska I. A. Bunina," 101–102.

March 10, 1951. Zweers, "Pis'ma I. A. Bunina k F. A. Stepunu," 121.

March 26, 1951. *Ibid.*, 121–123.

March 26, 1951. "Perepiska I. A. Bunina," 103.

April 22, 1951. Grin, *Ustami*, 202.

May 25, 1951. Zweers, "Perepiska I. A. Bunina," 106–107.

June 10, 1951. A. Zweers, "Perepiska I. A. Bunina s M. A. Aldanovym," *Novyi zhurnal*, No. 155 (1984), 131–132.

June 22, 1951. Zweers, "Pis'ma I. A. Bunina k F. A. Stepunu," 123–124.

June 29–30, 1951. Zweers, "Perepiska I. A. Bunina," 133–134.

July 10, 1951. Zweers, "Pis'ma I. A. Bunina k G. V. Adamovichu," 173–174.

July 16, 1951. Zweers, "Perepiska I. A. Bunina," 135.

July 29, 1951. Kuznetsova, 188.

August 1, 1951. Zweers, "Perepiska I. A. Bunina," 135.

August 16, 1951. Grin, *Ustami*, 202–203.

September 9, 1951. Fedoulova, 487.

September 9, 1951. Grin, 203.

September 19, 1951. Fedoulova, 487.

October 14, 1951. Grin, *Ustami*, 203.

Circa November 1951. Bakhrakh, 91.

December 1951. Sedykh, 238–240.

December 2, 1951. Grin, 204.

[1952]

Circa 1952. Shakovskaia, "O Bunine," 75, and "Otrazheniia," 95–96.

January 1, 1952. Grin, 204.

January 11, 1952. A. Zweers, "Perepiska I. A. Bunina s M. A. Aldanovym," *Novyi zhurnal*, No. 156 (1984), 143.

February 1, 1952. Grin, 204–205.

March 19, 1952. Zweers, 146–147.

June 17, 1952. Kuznetsova, 188.

June 21, 1952. Zweers, 149–150.

June 30, 1952. *Ibid.*, 150.

July 7, 1952. *Ibid.*, 150–151.

August 3, 1952. Grin, 205.

October 7, 1952. A. Rannit, "Pis'ma I. A. Bunina i M. E. Veinbaumu," *Novyi zhurnal*, vol. 133 (1978), 184–185.

October 9, 1952. Zweers, 151–152.

Circa mid-November 1952. Kuznetsova, 190.

[1953]

Circa 1953. Baboreko, "Poslednie gody I. A. Bunina," 254.

Circa 1953. M. Aldanov, "Predislovie," in I. Bunin, *O Chekhove* (New York, 1955), 20.

January 1, 1953. Grin, 206.

January 8, 1953. Zweers, 154.

January 23, 1953. Grin, 207.

January 27, 1953. *Ibid.*

February 2, 1953. M. Grin, "Bunin o sebe i svoem tvorchestve," *Novyi zhurnal*, No. 107 (1972), 166–168.

March 10, 1953. N. Ivanova-Gladil'shikova, "'Okaiannye dni,' ili Bunin bez kupiur," *Literaturnaia gazeta* (August 25, 1993), 6.

April 23, 1953. Grin, *Ustami*, 207.

April 23, 1953. Zweers, "Pis'ma I. A. Bunina k G. V. Adamovichu," 174.

May 14, 1953. Grin, 208.

October 9, 1953. Grin, "Pis'ma B. K. Zaitseva," 180–181.

November 3, 1953. Loginova-Muravieva, "Zhivoe proshloe," 328.

November 5, 1953. Aldanov, 134.

November 6, 1953. Sedykh, 244.

November 7, 1953. Bakhrakh, 160–163.

November 7, 1953. Sedykh, 244.

November 7, 1953. Kataev, 333–335.

November 8, 1953. V. Zernov, "Vospominaniia vracha," in Shcherbina, 360.

Circa November 12, 1953. Loginova-Muravieva, 328.

November 23, 1953. *Ibid.*

December 14, 1953. Kodryanskaya, 349.

[Coda]

December 7, 1953. Grin, "Pis'ma M. A. Aldanova," 144.

1954. K. Fedin, "Rech' na vtorom vsesoiuznom s"ezde sovetskikh pisatelei," *Pisatel', isskustvo, vremia* (Moscow, 1973), 584.

February 28, 1954. Kodryanskaya, 350.

November 17, 1954. *Ibid.*

December 17, 1954. *Ibid.*

1956. K. Paustovskii, "Ivan Bunin," *Sobranie sochinenii v shesti tomakh*, vol. 5 (Moscow, 1958), 618–620.

March 1956. Roshchin, 177.

Easter 1956. Loginova-Muravieva, "Pis'ma," 133.

January 17, 1957. M. Roshchin, 314–315.

January 22, 1957. *Ibid.*, 316.

November 17, 1957. Kodryanskaya, 350.

May 22, 1958. Roshchin, 320.

October 10, 1958. Loginova-Muravieva, 134.

January 30, 1959. N. Smirnov, "Pis'ma V. N. Buninoi," *Novyi mir*, No. 3 (1969), 211.

March 8, 1959. Lavrov, 304; Smirnov, 214.

Circa 1960. Kataev, 327–333.

January 7, 1960. Smirnov, 222–223.

January 11, 1960. *Ibid.*, 224.

April 2, 1960. *Ibid.*, 225.

October 12, 1960. Loginova-Muravieva, 135.

October 24, 1960. Smirnov, 227.

November 19, 1960. N. Sokolov-Mikitov, "Davnie vstrechi," *Zvezda*, No. 11 (1964), 176.

January 9, 1961. Loginova-Muravieva, 135.

January 14, 1961. Smirnov, 228.

January 19, 1961. *Ibid.*, 229.

February 3, 1961. Sokolov-Mikitov, 177.

March 3, 1961. Loginova-Muravieva, "Zhivoe proshloe," 329.

April 4, 1961. Loginova-Muravieva, "Pis'ma," 136.

April 7–14, 1961. *Russkaia mysl'* (April 8, 1961); *Russkie novosti* (April 14, 1961); as quoted in Loginova-Muravieva, "Pis'ma," 139–141.

April 26, 1961. Baboreko, "V. N. Muromtseva-Bunina," 117.

Late April 1961. Kataev, 338–343.

INDEX

A NOTE ON THE AUTHOR

This is the concluding volume of Thomas Gaiton Marullo's re-creation of the life of Ivan Bunin. Mr. Marullo is professor of Russian and Russian literature at the University of Notre Dame. Born in Brooklyn, New York, he received a bachelor's degree from the College of the Holy Cross, and M.A. and Ph.D. degrees from Cornell University. He has held fellowships from the Lilly Endowment and the National Endowment for the Humanities. He has also written *If You See the Buddha* and translated and edited Bunin's *Cursed Days* and *The Liberation of Tolstoy*.